A Quarter Century of Pension Reform in Latin America and the Caribbean:

Lessons Learned and Next Steps

Carolin A. Crabbe

Editor

Inter-American Development Bank
2005

Produced by the IDB Sustainable Development Department

To order this book, contact:
IDB Bookstore
Tel: 1-877-PUBS IDB / (202) 623-1753
Fax: (202) 623-1709
E-mail: idb-books@iadb.org
www.iadb.org/iadbstore

**Cataloging-in-Publication provided by the
Inter-American Development Bank
Felipe Herrera Library**

A quarter century of pension reform in Latin America and the Caribbean: lessons learned and next steps / Carolin A. Crabbe, editor.

p. cm.
Includes bibliographical references.
1597820202

1. Pensions—Latin America. 2. Pensions—Latin America—Finance. 3. Pensions—Caribbean Area. 4. Pensions—Caribbean Area—Finance. I. Crabbe, Carolin. II. Inter-American Development Bank. Sustainable Development Dept.

658.3253 C338 —dc22

ISBN:1-59782-020-2

CONTENTS

ACKNOWLEDGEMENTS

During this decade, the Inter-American Development Bank has sponsored a series of pension reform forums intended to bring together the pension industry, policymakers and regulators to discuss progress made, identify issues that still need to be addressed and to share experiences in dealing with the complexities of the reforms. The last forum held in Washington, D.C. in December 2004, brought together an impressive group of experts with diverging views on the reforms. They were in general agreement on the need to continue to assess the reforms in order to fine tune and consolidate them as they mature. The experts also agreed that understanding the successes and failures of the reforms would provide parameters for second-generation efforts as well as lessons for countries contemplating similar reorganizations.

The chapters of this book evolve from the experiences and lessons that were debated at the 2004 forum. The authors, experts in their fields, have provided important insights into the problematic. The participation of the authors in developing these chapters and sharing their experiences are gratefully acknowledged.

In developing the forum and the book I would like to particularly acknowledge the outstanding support and suggestions of Juan Giral. His many years of experience in social security matters and in Latin America and, above all, his humor have added much to all stages of the production and quality of this book. In addition, the forum and the book greatly benefited from the assistance of Martha María Gutiérrez who helped with logistics, programs, editing and research in the production. Pietro Masci encouraged the development of the forum and preparation of the book at every step of the way and without this support, these tasks could not have been done.

I would also like to thank my colleagues in the IDB who reviewed various chapters at an early stage. Particularly valuable were the suggestions of William Armstrong, Hunt Howell, Guillermo Collich and Héctor Salazar.

FOREWORD

The structural reform of the pension systems in Latin America and the Caribbean during the decade of the 1990s and early 2000s entailed creating privately managed and invested pension pillars with defined contributions and undefined benefits. These deep reforms shifted the responsibility and burden from the public to the private sector and changed the way old age security is viewed.

The focus of this book is on the experiences and lessons learned from the sweeping reforms in the region. While in many cases it is still too early to assess the success of the reforms, it is not too early to examine some of the barriers and difficulties encountered and to propose viable solutions to them. This is important since much of the literature is focused on determining whether or not the reforms were successful. The methodology of this book goes beyond this in two ways. First, it assesses why the reforms succeeded or failed and clearly identifies conditions that contributed or impeded them and possible solutions, with a view toward providing options to countries that have not yet undertaken first-generation reforms. Second, it suggests the next steps required to consolidate and deepen existing pension reforms.

The book's main objective is to provide a road map for policymakers in the region and other parts of the world as they contemplate either first- or second-generation reforms. It is especially useful to countries that have not yet reformed their social security systems, to provide guidance on undertaking the first generation of reforms. In this context, the book provides an invaluable new tool.

Clearly, there is an urgent need to better understand the successes and failures of the first generation of reforms, to provide parameters for second-generation reforms, and to assemble the lessons learned for the benefit of countries that have not yet begun their reforms. The book is especially timely since so many countries in the region are faced with a worsening demographic equation in which the ageing population is growing more rapidly than the labor force. Indeed, because of these demographic changes countries such as the United States are contemplating this type of structural reform anew and are studying the Latin American experience.

Antonio Vives
Manager a.i.
Sustainable Development Department

SECTION ONE

Overview

Lessons Learned from Pension Reform in Latin America and the Caribbean

Carolin A. Crabbe and Juan Giral*

The Motivation for Reform

The reform of pension systems in Latin America and the Caribbean has been among the most profound and extensive of any region. The structural reform of pension systems during the 1990s and early 2000s entailed creating privately managed and invested pension pillars with defined contributions. While three countries reformed only their social security systems (Brazil, Paraguay, and Venezuela), ten countries undertook far-reaching structural reforms that shifted the responsibility and burden from the public sector and changed the way old age security was viewed (Box 1.1).[1] In the twenty-first century, this type of structural reform is being con-

Box 1.1.	Year of Structural Pension Reforms
Year[a]	Country
1981	Chile
1993	Peru[b]
1994	Colombia[b]
1994	Argentina
1996	Uruguay
1997	Bolivia
1997	Mexico
1998	El Salvador
2001	Costa Rica
2003	Dominican Republic

[a] Year in which reforms began. Legislation preceded the reforms by several years in some cases.
[b] Included parametric reforms.

* Carolin A. Crabbe is a financial specialist and Juan Giral is a consultant in pension reform at the Inter-American Development Bank.
[1] Nicaragua explored structural reform of its pension system, but has not undertaken them to date.

templated anew and countries such as the United States are studying the Latin American experience.

This chapter assesses some of the lessons learned from the structural reforms. It is divided into five sections. The first describes the motivation for the reforms and how the macroeconomic and financial situation, coupled with aging populations, made the reforms imperative. The second section discusses the factors that influenced the design of reforms. Because financial and fiscal considerations were so urgent at the time of design, low-income groups and women were not considered. Today this poses a serious concern in many countries, as some of these groups lack pension coverage. While most countries considered labor markets, demographics, and geography and took steps to develop consensus among key groups, none undertook a thorough diagnostic with an appropriate actuarial model. The third section describes how most countries failed to adequately assess and strengthen the capabilities of existing institutions to administer the reform, but in general did well in creating new institutions to regulate and supervise the new pension system. The fourth section analyzes some of the reasons why all countries underestimated the fiscal costs of the reform, while one country still came out well because it set in place a well-balanced fiscal reform program in conjunction with the pension reform. The last section assesses coverage under the reformed system, explains why contributions may be declining, and discusses the impact of administrative costs and commissions. It examines the effect of pension reforms on the region's capital markets, and argues for the need to liberalize investment options and work toward reinstating confidence in the system.

Macroeconomic Influence on the Reform Environment

What motivated these reforms? At the top of the list for most countries was concern over growing financial costs and fiscal deficits. The 1980s were a tumultuous period, with low growth throughout the region. Gross domestic product grew 1.7 percent on average, compared with 3 percent in the United States and 7.4 percent in East Asia. The high indebtedness of most countries dictated the agenda that policymakers were forced to follow, concentrating resources on debt restructuring and repayment, debt-for-equity swaps, and stabilization and structural adjustment programs. Important investment in social services, education, and infrastructure was deferred throughout the 1980s. The period has come to be known as the "Lost Decade" for the region because it not only lost GDP growth but experienced a decline in the standard of living.

Chile was the first country in the region to reform its pension system, launching the initiative in 1981. The timing of Chile's reform is particularly significant. It followed a period of growth from 1965 to 1980 that was lower than most countries in the region (Table 1.1). Chile was also recovering from the disastrous experience of its aborted experiment in socialization under the Allende administration. Nonetheless, Chile's military government undertook an ambitious and far-reaching program to restore economic stability and institute fiscal discipline. It included the privatization of public corporations, banks, and the social security system, as well as the introduction of free market principles in the provision of health, education, and other social services. Pension reform was an integral part of Chile's reform package.

Other countries in the region did not reform their pension systems until fully a decade later. By the 1990s, countries had begun to recover from the negative developments of the Lost Decade and growth resumed at modest rates. That is not to say that the 1990s was an easy

Table 1.1	Gross Domestic Product Growth by Country and Region (average percentage for the period)			
Country	1965–80	1980–90	1990–99	1999–2003
Argentina	3.5	−0.7	4.9	−2.1
Bolivia	4.5	−0.2	4.2	2.2
Brazil	9.0	2.7	2.8	2.5[a]
Chile	1.9	4.2	7.2	3.3
Costa Rica	6.2	3.0	4.1	3.0
Colombia	5.6	3.6	3.3	2.5
Dominican Republic	7.3	2.7	5.7	2.0
Ecuador	8.7	2.1	2.2	3.7
El Salvador	4.3	0.2	4.9	3.6
Guatemala	0.8	0.8	4.2	2.6
Honduras	5.0	2.7	3.2	2.1
Jamaica	1.3	2.0	0.1	1.2
Mexico	6.5	1.1	2.7	2.1
Peru	3.9	0.5	4.2	2.6[a]
Uruguay	2.4	0.4	3.7	−3.6[a]
Venezuela	3.7	1.1	1.7	−2.4
Latin America and Caribbean	6.0	1.7	3.4	1.4
United States	2.7	3.0	3.4	2.0
Europe and Central Asia	—	2.4	−2.7	0.2
East Asia and Pacific	—	8.0	7.4	7.2
South Asia	—	5.7	5.7	5.5

— Not available.
Note: a. 1999–2002.

decade,[2] for after so many years of debt restructuring and swaps, the large debt overhang continuing into the 1990s restricted expenditures in health, education, and social programs, making it difficult to regain previous living standards.

Policymakers had begun to reassess the results of past economic policies, the inefficiencies of the public sector, misguided exchange rates that reduced competitiveness and encouraged capital flight, the fiasco of import substitution policies, and the impact that rampant inflation and high real interest rates had on savings and investment. Because they still had to deal with the debt overhang, governments were especially focused on divesting themselves of unprofitable State programs and creating opportunities for greater private sector participation.

The reform packages that emerged from this reassessment were far-reaching. The Inter-American Development Bank's Economic and Social Progress Report for 1991 even dubbed the 1990s "a Decade of Hope." The reforms included liberalization of interest rates and trade and massive privatizations, as governments strove to rid themselves of costly State-owned enterprises and banks. This included energy, telecommunications, airlines, other State-run companies and inefficient State banks that were restructured or closed. Finally, governments looked at inefficient social security systems that drained public funds and undertook deep structural reforms of these systems.

The Social Security Equation

In the last two decades of the twentieth century, the region's social security programs faced serious difficulties. Social security expenses had grown with inflation in the 1980s as wages were adjusted upward. Administrative expenses ranged between 11 and 32 percent of total social security spending, as compared with 2 to 4 percent in developed countries (IDB 1991). Revenues to the social security system had declined because of unemployment, the drop in real wages, and widespread tax evasion.

Most of the social security systems were pay-as-you-go (PAYG), financing benefits to retirees from current contributions by workers. These types of systems are operationally viable when worker contributions are adequate to cover retiree pensions. However, the demographics of the

---

[2] Although the macroeconomic environment improved in the 1990s, the financial systems were adversely affected by the Tequila (1994–96), East Asia (1997), and the Russia crises (1998).

region shifted, from high birth and mortality rates to low birth and mortality rates, because of improved health conditions and lower infant and child mortality. Population growth in the region peaked in 1965 at a rate of about 2.8 percent a year, and the rate of growth of the working age population peaked around 1980 and has been declining ever since (IDB 2004). The reformers were concerned that the balance of the social security equation was shifting as the aged population grew faster than the labor force.

In addition to the PAYG social security systems, numerous private and quasi-public social security systems (*cajas de previsión*) provided retirement benefits for service or sector workers. These systems also financed benefits from current contributions and were under financial stress. Governments in many cases were coming under increasing political pressure from workers and unions that participated in these private social security systems to help bail them out.

Policymakers were also concerned about inefficiencies and inequalities inherent in the benefits in the social security systems. For instance, the administration of the systems relied on antiquated practices that facilitated fraud. In many cases, benefits were excessive and permitted early retirement at age 40, and loopholes made it possible for individuals and even entire groups of citizens to abuse the system. Brazil is a case in point, where certain groups of workers received special entitlements or privileges because of their bargaining power. These entitlements included being able to retire at an earlier age than other Brazilians and receiving higher benefits (Chapter 6). Concerns about inefficiencies and inequalities, coupled with concerns about ensuring old age security and reducing costs, provided powerful motivation for the reform of pension systems.

Design Considerations

Selection of the Reform Model

Among the countries that undertook structural reforms, there were two common denominators in selecting a reform model. The first was concern and desire to resolve the many problems, including the financial debility associated with social security based on the PAYG systems (Arenas de Mesa and Marcel 1991). The second was the Chilean model itself, which had been in place for a decade and had a good track record. The growth of assets invested by the privately managed pillar was attractive to reformers who were looking for a solution to their fiscal deficits.

It was only natural that in the planning stages of the reforms in the region, the Chilean reform was the one most discussed by other reformers and policymakers and emulated by such countries as Argentina, Bolivia, Mexico, and Peru. Furthermore, as other countries in the region began to undertake their reforms, Chilean pension experts were retained as advisors.

Some countries opted to phase out their social security systems altogether as Chile had done, while others chose models that incorporated certain features of the Chile model. The reforms basically followed one of three structures. The first was substitution of the social security PAYG with individual funded retirement schemes: Chile (1981), Bolivia (1997), El Salvador (1998), and the Dominican Republic (2003–05). The second was a parallel system where one must choose either the invested retirement system or the PAYG: Peru (1993) and Colombia (1994). The third was a mixed system where both models exist and complement each other: Argentina (1994), Uruguay (1996), Mexico (1997), and Costa Rica (2001).

Mexico phased out the PAYG for private sector workers and replaced it with a privately managed and invested pillar, but retained the plethora of other retirement systems it had, including the PAYG for public sector workers. In most countries in the region, it was difficult to adjust or reform the existing social security systems because of political commitments and promises that had been made regarding the benefit structure and contribution level. Brazil was an exception; it initiated a series of reforms in 1995 and launched a parametric reform of its social security system in 2003.

Interestingly, at the time of the reforms, many countries—notably Argentina, Bolivia, Chile, Costa Rica, Peru, and Uruguay—already had a public noncontributory social safety net for the elderly and disabled that served as a pension. This safety net was intended for those who could not participate or qualify in either a PAYG or private pension system because of very low earnings or other factors. For the most part, it was disregarded or did not receive consideration in designing the structural reforms. In the final analysis, this safety net for the elderly and disabled became quite vital in many countries, as discussed later.

Country Characteristics

The experience with pension reforms underscores the need to adequately reflect local conditions in the design of the systems, specifically market potential, labor market composition and informality, and gender and poverty. While most countries in the region are generally considered to be Spanish-speaking and homogenous, the reality is that there is considerable variation in demographics, level of economic activity, and the potential labor and financial market for the funded pillar. Language and literacy rates are also important, as can be seen in Table 1.2. In Bolivia, in addition to Spanish, Aymara constitutes a major language group spoken among the indigenous population. Geography is also of great consequence because it affects the reliability and collection of actuarial data, as well as the facility with which pension reforms can be communicated and consensus for them developed.

Assessment of Market Potential

A major consideration in designing a pension reform is the assessment of the potential market for the funded pillar. Factors that are particularly important include small population and territory, an aging population because of low birth and death rates and emigration of the young, and dependency on a few sources of income or lines of export production that are subject to sharp fluctuations in terms of trade. Small econo-

Table 1.2 Country Characteristics							
	Argentina	Bolivia	Chile	Colombia	Costa Rica	Mexico	Peru
Population (millions, 2003)	38	9	16	45	4	102	27
Population density per sq. km.	14	8	21	43	78	54	21
Labor force (millions, 2002)	11	3	7	20	2	42	11
Female workers (% of labor force)	34	38	35	40	33	34	32
GNP per capita ($, 2003)	3,650	890	4,390	1,810	4,280	6,230	2,150
Overall deficit (% of GDP, 2001)	3.3	6.7	0.4	4.7	1.6	1.3	1.8
Social expenditures (% of total fiscal expenditures)	63.6	51.2	71.3	45.2	59.6	48.1	—
Language	Spanish	Aymara/Sp	Spanish	Spanish	Spanish	Spanish	Spanish
Topography	Mostly flat	Rugged	Rugged	Rugged	Rugged	Mixed	Rugged

— Not available.
Note: Data are for 1999, unless otherwise indicated.
Source: World Bank, *World Development Report,* 2001/2002 and 2003/2004; *World Development Indicators,* 2005.

9

mies and the size of contributions may move inversely with pension fund management costs, making those costs too high. Large markets are also required for insurance products that count on spreading risk over a sizeable population. A small market and pool of potential participants can make insurance for death, disability, or survivors' pensions extremely costly. In many large countries such as Mexico, the government provides this type of insurance.

Market size was a major consideration in the design of the reforms in Bolivia, which has a relatively small population and a total labor force of about 3 million (Table 1.2). This meant that there would likely be a lower level of contributions than might be attractive to professional fund managers. In light of this consideration, the reformers took several pivotal decisions. First, to enhance returns on fund management, Bolivia eliminated the need for marketing costs. This was accomplished by accepting the bids of only two fund managers, allowing the country to be divided between them, thus creating a virtual monopoly. The elimination of marketing costs benefited the participants in the form of reduced fees.

Second, to provide the fund with initial liquidity, the government transferred shares or assets from the capitalization of State-owned enterprises in 1995. These assets were the basis for an annuity called the *Bonosol* to be paid to all Bolivian citizens when they reached retirement age (65), provided they were 21 years old in 1992 (Box 1.2). Recently, with the merger of the banking side of Bolivia's two pension fund administrators, Bolivia effectively has had only one fund manager.[3] In 2002 Bolivia had plans to add another pension fund manager to the system, but a bidding process resulted in a very low level of interest among fund managers. The reason was the small size of the market.

The lessons from the reforms in the region demonstrate that the size of the economy is essential to determine

> **Box 1.2. The *Bonosol***
>
> Bolivia's 1996 Pension Reform Law terminated the old social security system that covered about a quarter (22 percent) of the population. It created a new system where pension contributions would be invested and the assets managed by private fund managers. The year before the Pension Reform Law was enacted, Bolivia also created an annuity for Bolivian citizens, the *Bono Solidario* (*Bonosol*). The *Bonosol* was comprised of shares from the sale of State-owned companies that were capitalized/privatized. The *Bonosol* was to be paid to all Bolivians who qualified. Its main purpose was to benefit the poor and the rural population.

---

[3] The two funds were originally Banco Bilbao Vizcaya (BBV) and Argentaria, now merged into BBVA.

if a funded pillar would be viable, both in terms of contributions and of investment options within the country. In small markets, a funded pillar might still be viable, as demonstrated by Bolivia. As noted above, the Bolivian reformers considered and dealt with this factor by allowing a two-fund monopoly that has effectively reduced marketing costs and made the system affordable in terms of the level of commissions.

Composition of Labor and Informality

Another important country-specific consideration in the design of pension reforms has been the composition of the labor force. The level of formality, informality, urban, rural, seasonal, and family workers and the structure of the labor force in terms of employment or unemployment is important in determining the percentage of the labor force able to participate and contribute to a pension plan. In particular, Argentina, Bolivia, and Mexico had large informal markets at the time of the reforms, implying that the number of workers making contributions would automatically be lower than expected. In retrospect, in these cases, incentives to encourage and attract labor into the formal economy would have made the reforms more complete.

The informal sector in Argentina, which is largely comprised of small companies and microentrepreneurs, has become prominent since the 1994 reforms, and increased significantly after the economic crisis of 2001–02. A recent study estimated that about a quarter of all economic activity in Argentina is performed in the informal economy, while some government agencies estimate that the informal economy is larger and growing. A 2003 estimate placed informality in Argentina at about 70 percent of all economic activity, although more recent figures for 2004 indicate a significant decline as the economy is recovering (Ministerio de Trabajo 2004; Fundación Mediterránea 2004). Not surprisingly, contributions to the pension system in Argentina have been declining, an aspect discussed later on in this chapter.

The experience in the region underscores the need to consider the composition of the labor force, especially where there is rampant informality, as in Argentina. If informality is large and growing, contributions will be much lower than anticipated, possibly threatening pension fund viability and definitely reducing coverage of the population. Informality is clearly an important area of focus for policymakers and a key consideration in designing first- and second-generation pension reforms.

Gender and Poverty Concerns

In designing pension systems, very little attention was given to poverty and gender. The World Bank has undertaken simulations comparing internal rates of return before and after the reform in the region and concluded that in two countries—Chile and Argentina—the reforms increased the returns to poorer workers of both sexes vis-à-vis better-off workers (Gill, Packard, and Yermo 2005). However, the same study concludes that in every other country that undertook structural reforms, women earned lower internal rates of return than men.

Gill, Packard, and Yermo (2005) also conclude, based on their analysis, that women in Colombia and Chile received a higher internal rate of return relative to men. Further, poorer women in Argentina, Chile, and Mexico received a higher pension benefit under the reformed pension system because of a better targeted first pillar, according to James, Cox-Edwards, and Wong (2003).

Most countries have a guaranteed minimum pension that requires a certain number of years and contributions. It is often difficult for women to qualify for a minimum pension because they drop out of the workforce to raise children and thus lack sufficient years to qualify. Furthermore, when they return to the workforce, they often receive lower salaries; thus they might not meet the level of contributions required. In Chile, the contributions of 45 percent of women in the funded pillar do not reach the level of the minimum government guaranteed pension (Chapter 3). In these cases, the government tops up the difference between the invested contributions and the minimum pension.

It is not surprising that women have lower pensions than their male colleagues because they stay in the labor market fewer years, retire earlier, and live longer (see Chapter 7; Arenas de Mesa and Gana Cornejo 2003). These factors are not taken into account in annuity projections, according to Mesa-Lago (see Chapter 2). The life expectancy of women is four to five years longer than men, so the annuity they receive is spread over a longer period. This may lead to a pension level that cannot sustain them.

In the special case of Argentina, as a result of the economic crisis of 2001, the income gap and related increase in inequality grew disproportionately. By 2001, over a third of Argentina's population over 65 years old did not have a pension or other source of income and relied on the old age noncontributory social safety net. At the end of 2004, about half of Argentines were ranked below the poverty line as a result of widespread unemployment and the drop in real incomes (World Bank 2003c). In these circumstances, the social safety net became indispensable.

Clearly, the first-generation reforms focused narrowly on those able to contribute, and not on the very poor. With hindsight, it probably would not have been possible to consider reform of the social safety net systems simultaneously because of the macroeconomic environment and financial factors driving the reforms. As part of the agenda for second-generation reforms, countries without adequate mechanisms to provide for the poor should address this and analyze the funding and level established for the safety net (Holzman and Stiglitz 2001; ILO 2002, 2003). Also, it is clear that the impact of pension reform on gender is gaining importance and is likely to receive more attention as the percentage of women participating in the labor force increases.

Reliability and Adequacy of the Data

Another aspect that was problematic for some of the reformers in the region pertained to the quality and adequacy of the data on which the pension reform designs were based. The Bolivian reformers were concerned about the reliability of the data in 1996. Demographically, Bolivia has a comparatively small population with a high percentage of indigenous peoples. Some of these peoples have avoided participating in demographic surveys, census, and polling registries because of custom and culture. Moreover, Bolivia's topography is challenging and has kept some parts of the country relatively isolated, hindering reliable data on births and deaths. The combination of cultural and geographic conditions has made the development of reliable databases and the collection of good data a daunting task.

The reformers made the best assessment that they could based on the data, but it became apparent that the estimate of future retirees was short of the mark. This considerably increased expenditures and—coupled with other factors—widened the fiscal gap, so that it had reached troubling proportions by 2002. Moreover, the same data were used to determine the adult population eligible to receive shares in former State-owned companies, the *Bonosol*. Almost seven years after the reform, Bolivia has still not been able to determine which citizens are eligible to receive the *Bonosol*, underscoring the consequence of good quality data.

Projection Capability and the Actuarial Model

All the countries that undertook structural reform of their pension systems completed assessments or diagnostics of costs, benefits, and results.

However, none of them used a high-quality actuarial model capable of accurately predicting the impact when small changes in costs or benefits are introduced. This turned out to be a significant flaw and led to considerable disparity between actual and anticipated results in some countries.

In particular, Argentina and Bolivia introduced many changes to the reforms as originally proposed. The lack of an actuarial model made it virtually impossible to predict the impact of what may have seemed to be minor changes made during and after the implementation of the reform. In the case of Bolivia, the base pension was raised during implementation, increasing costs dangerously. Several groups not originally included in the reforms were added, such as the military (which had its own pension system). So many changes were introduced to the original proposal that the initial estimates of costs and benefits were no longer valid. Argentina slightly decreased the level of contribution in 2001 to stimulate the economy's growth and reduce unemployment. This change disproportionately increased the fiscal deficit. In both cases, costs skyrocketed, increasing transition costs and the fiscal deficit rather than reducing it.

In retrospect, several measures could have been undertaken during the planning stages that would have improved the systems. The first would be to undertake a thorough diagnostic of the existing retirement system. This diagnostic would need to reflect existing commitments to the citizenry; assets, if any; the quality of the pension administration and institutions in place; and the timeliness and quality of the record keeping of institutions responsible for tracking worker's contributions and years of employment. The second would be to gather sound data and conduct a solid actuarial evaluation. Both measures could well be revisited in the future, particularly in Bolivia, where this has posed a stumbling block.

A good actuarial model with sufficient variables to permit fine-tuning as the new system is rolled out could have made all of the difference in the implementation of the reforms and the end result. Often, when politicians are faced with hard facts, they can be deterred from enacting measures that can be shown to have catastrophic effects a priori.

Developing Consensus for the Reform

Another lesson from the structural reforms undertaken in the region is that political consensus is a necessary condition for reform. To garner support, the reformers needed to enlist key sectors of society before enacting the reform. This included identifying opposition groups such as labor unions, and discussing the reforms with them to win their support. Political legitimacy has proven to be essential for the consolidation of the reform, irrespective of political changes. The approaches used for developing consensus have varied in the region.[4]

For instance, in Chile, the military government in power supported the reform fully and paved the way for the highly disciplined reform package that encompassed many aspects, including fiscal measures and the transfer of education and health liabilities to the municipalities (Collins and Lear 1995). In both Argentina and Mexico, one political party dominated the political arena and was backed by a powerful alliance of labor unions. Nevertheless, in Argentina, while the administration strongly supported the reform, other groups did not, such as the independent labor movement and some of the provincial governments. In Bolivia, the executive branch managed to win support for the reform from two of the three political parties.

The business community in all countries viewed the reforms and the addition of a privately managed funded pillar as advantageous. In general, they expected an expansion of the capital market, which would provide broader financing opportunities; and a significant opening of profitable business opportunities for bankers, insurance companies, and future pension fund managers—activities that are closely interrelated. Chile made the reforms attractive to companies by eliminating the employers' contribution. Passing the cost on to the worker offset the loss in employer contribution. At the same time, to diminish worker dissatisfaction, wages were raised.

Furthermore, the media can have an important role in the reform process. IDB studies of four countries—Argentina, Bolivia, Chile, and Mexico—indicate that the media can heighten the awareness of the workers and explain the potential benefits and shortcomings of the proposed reform (Domeniconi, Perrotto, and Bertin 2004; Salinas 2004; Bustamante 2004; Alonso y Caloca 2004). In particular, Chile, and later Uruguay, made extensive use of the media and established an understanding among a broad group of workers of the pension reforms. In Argentina, supporters of reform relied on forging alliances to create political pacts rather than undertaking an intensive media campaign. In Mexico, the strength of the single party PRI and its relationships with the

---

[4] Long-term support from the population requires transparency. Argentina and Bolivia are examples of countries where lack of transparency resulted in loss of trust among the citizenry. The risks were not fully explained and discussed.

labor union, the Confederación General de Trabajadores (CGT), served this purpose.

Institutional Structure for Reform: Some Prerequisites for Success

Prior to the pension reforms, the social security systems throughout the region consisted of numerous institutions. These included institutions that administered the government PAYG and occupational or sector-specific pension systems called *cajas de previsión* (*cajas*). The *cajas* were created to cover the retirement needs of specific groups of workers and professionals. At the time, Argentina had over 135 *cajas* (Fundación Mediterránea 2003; Ministerio de Trabajo 2004), Bolivia had 22 (Salinas 2004), and Chile had 32 (Bustamante 2004). In Peru, private *cajas* covered fishermen, public servants, miners, newsmen, and pilots; in Brazil, they covered university professors, judges, and members of congress; in Costa Rica, they covered teachers and the judiciary; and in Uruguay, they covered the military, banking employees, police, and notaries. Furthermore, Argentina and Mexico had complex federal and provincial systems, and in Mexico, separate public PAYG systems existed for federal and state workers (Alonso y Caloca 2004).

Both the PAYG and *cajas* increased benefits over time, placing a heavy burden on contributors. Many were under-funded and financially unsustainable. Although many of the *cajas* had begun with partial capitalization or investment, ultimately they became nominally PAYG. In Chile, the *cajas* had accumulated large nominal assets, but inflation had dwindled their real value. In Argentina, in 1980, the government arbitrarily reduced the value of public bonds that were held by the *cajas* to 0.5 percent of GDP (Domeniconi, Bruno, and Perrotto 2004). Governments in the region were concerned with the financial position of many of the *cajas* and they were apprehensive that they might be faced with not just the contingent liability of the PAYG systems, which was supposed to be included in the budgeting, but also that of the *cajas*, which was not.

Administrative Institution Building for Pension Reform

Most countries in the region did not perform a diagnostic of the institutional capability of the social security institutions, with a view toward their functions and responsibilities before the reform and the new ones they would be assigned. Most of the institutions had been responsible for maintaining the contributions and employment records of their participants, including dates of service, disability, leave, and discontinuation in service.

At the time of the reforms, most of the institutions administering the PAYG and the *cajas* were under-funded and ill-equipped. They lacked up-to-date business infrastructure, such as computers and well-designed computer programs to track workers' employment history and contributions. The PAYG institutions were experiencing difficulty in maintaining up-to-date records within their own systems. They were even less prepared to assume their expanded role of collecting, processing, and consolidating the records of the numerous *cajas*, which often had different systems of recordation. Consolidating the various *cajas* under a single institution, usually the government PAYG, magnified these problems.

For the most part, the social security institutions continued to maintain records and make pension payments to pre-reform retirees and the members of *cajas* absorbed by the public system. They also took on responsibility for recording the recognition bonds (*bonos de reconocimiento*) issued to acknowledge workers' contributions to the system prior to the reforms. Moreover, in countries that established the concept of guaranteed minimum pension, the institutions also administered the payments to gross up pensions when contributions were insufficient to reach the guaranteed minimum level. They also managed the old age noncontributory pensions (social safety net) provided to those over 65 who had insufficient income to contribute to social security. Some governments provided some support to these institutions to fulfill their expanded role. In addition, in Argentina, Bolivia, and Uruguay, the Inter-American Development Bank and the World Bank made loans to strengthen the institutional capabilities (World Bank 1998). An evaluation of why they did not function at a higher level of efficiency would be important for future reforms.

Chile is a case in point. Its Servicio de Seguro Social was expected to manage records of retirees under the prior system as it was gradually phased out. It also managed payments for the old age, noncontributory pension (social safety net), and workers retiring under the private invested pillar who did not accumulate sufficient contributions to reach the minimum guaranteed pension (see Chapter 3). Additionally, the Servicio de Seguro Social was responsible for managing recognition bonds.

Bolivia's Dirección Nacional de Pensiones was also responsible for managing the records and contributions of workers under the old social security system, along with the numerous *cajas* that were consolidated under the reforms, as well as the *Bonosol*. As a consequence of this overload of responsibilities, coupled with widespread fraud associated with the pension reform transition, the Dirección Nacional de Pensiones still has not been able to ascertain clear records of all retirees and contributors to the pension system (before and after the reforms). As a result, there are still discrepancies over who was eligible to retire in 1997 under the pre-reform system and who was eligible for the *Bonosol*.

In Argentina, the existing national social security administration (Administración Nacional de Seguridad Social, ANSES) continued to maintain records for all retirees, as well as those for the new privately managed pension system. Moreover, while Argentina's reforms were initially to have embraced only those under the old social security system, they were expanded to include eleven public provincial *cajas*, a dozen municipal *cajas* for public bank employees and the police, and 65 *cajas* for professionals (Rapp and Merlinsky 2000). ANSES had the responsibility of verifying employment and contribution records of contributors to the private funds and *cajas* to determine their eligibility to receive a pension payment. ANSES was not adequately prepared to process pensions quickly under the PAYG system, so the additional burden of the private pension funds stretched its already inadequate resources. Verifying records for the private pension contributors took up to a year, during which time no pension was being paid. The time delay has recently been reduced to about six months by streamlining some of the procedures.

By contrast, Mexico did not consolidate the various social security institutions. Mexico chose to reform only the PAYG system of private sector workers under the Instituto Mexicano de Seguro Social (IMSS). The pension systems for federal and state government workers and the various armed services continued to be administered by other existing institutions (Alonso y Caloca 2004). Thus, it did not have the expanded role and added responsibilities that characterized institutions in countries that consolidated many pension systems into one.

Nonetheless, the new Mexican private pension system had some difficulties with record keeping, including discrepancies between members and contributors. These discrepancies have not yet been adequately explained. Among the reasons cited were definitional problems. Accounts are considered active if workers earn three times the minimum wage (many workers contribute, but with earnings below this level) and if workers have contributed at least twice a month over a 12-month period. Moreover, IMSS turned over registration to the pension funds that use a numbering system for accounts (especially when workers change jobs) that do not match the system previously used by the IMSS.

Regulatory and Supervisory Institution Building and the Framework for the Funded Pillar

The introduction of a funded private pillar, the transfer of revenues from the public to the private sector, and the investment of these resources by private fund managers required a significant effort in institution building. Strict regulation and supervision of the pension fund managers (Administradoras de Fondos de Pensiones, or AFPs; and Administradoras de Fondos de Jubilaciones y Pensiones, or AFJPs) was an essential requirement of the reforms to ensure high-quality performance by pension administrators and maximum protection of retirement savings for old age security.

Institution building for the regulatory structure also required a careful diagnostic, taking into consideration the constraints arising from the level of development of financial institutions, insurance companies, and capital markets. It also required consideration of the effectiveness of supervisory institutions and their legal powers to monitor the newly created pension funds. Other aspects, such as harmonization of regulations among financial services and having appropriate procedures in place to intervene and liquidate failing institutions, were also important because of the interrelationships between pension funds and the insurance annuity business.

Thus, in the ten countries that created private pension fund pillars, about a year before the pension reform became effective, regulatory authorities were approved and authorized to supervise and regulate the new pension system (Table 1.3).

By the end of 2004, these ten regulators supervised 65 pension funds with assets totaling over $147 billion. The quality of this supervision and

Table 1.3	Overview of Pension Fund Regulators		
Country	Legislation	Year	Internet http://www.
Argentina	Ley 24241	1993	safjp.gov.ar
Bolivia	Ley 1732	1996	spvs.gov.bo
Chile	Decreto Ley 3500	1980	safp.cl
Colombia	Ley 100	1993	superbancaria.gov.co
Costa Rica	Ley 7983	2000	supen.fi.cr
Dominican Republic	Ley 87-01	2001	sipen.gov.do
El Salvador	Decreto 927	1997	spensiones.gob.sv
Mexico	Ley SAR	1996	consar.gob.mx
Peru	Decreto Ley 25897	1992	sbs.gob.pe
Uruguay	Ley 16713	1995	bcu.gub.uy

Source: AIOS 2004.

regulation affects the well-being of 65 million workers and retirees who belong to these pension funds (AIOS 2004).

In general, the pension reforms established a new system of regulatory oversight, which, coupled with reforms in other financial services, has heightened the transparency and sophistication of regulation and supervision in the region. The systems of regulatory oversight are still being fine-tuned and harmonized with other regulations, guidelines, and laws. In Argentina and Mexico, the regulation has become increasingly sophisticated, moving toward risk-based supervision and identification of potential risks before they become problematic.

Pension regulation and supervision have also had an impact on other financial services, such as the insurance industry. For instance, the annuity business in the region has developed fairly recently with the support of the pension framework. In Argentina, because of the difference between a pension annuity and a regular annuity, special regulations have been issued to protect the underlying assets of the annuity. The regulations prevent insurance companies from pledging the equity capital backing its annuities to other areas of its insurance business.

An assessment of existing institutions and their strengths and weaknesses, along with a plan for improving them based on their new responsibilities, would have made the reform transition period easier. This was apparent in Argentina with ANSES, in Mexico with the IMSS, and in Bolivia with the Dirección Nacional de Pensiones, which all experienced difficulties with their expanded roles. Only Chile and its Servicio de Seguro Social planned well for this institutional transition. The supervisory and regulatory frameworks established in all four countries have evolved over time and been extensively fine-tuned as the reform has rolled out. Overall, the institutional arrangements for supervision and regulation of the new pension fund industry have made financial services more transparent. While there have been some difficulties, the framework is working well.

Fiscal Discipline and Sustainability

An important underlying principle of the reforms was the expectation that fiscal costs of the PAYG system would be lowered, enabling countries to begin to invest in their social and physical infrastructure, which had deteriorated during the 1980s. All countries had developed projections of fiscal costs and established scenarios for the break-even point, where the deficit would begin to shrink because of the reforms.

Unfortunately, no country estimated these costs well and many did not stick to their original plan. Thus in the end, costs were not lowered as anticipated.

Transitional Fiscal Costs and Contingent Liabilities

The primary factors that needed to be considered were the fiscal costs associated with the reform. These could be divided into two categories: the costs associated with the social security system, whether it was terminated or allowed to operate in parallel with the newly created private pillar; and the costs generated by the reform itself with the addition of the private pillar. In determining these costs, the reformers did not consider several factors. With respect to the costs of the existing social security system, the following costs should have been reflected:

• The reduction in contributions under the PAYG system, whether or not it was terminated
• The need to finance deficits generated by special pension systems that remained outside the reform (military and other professional groups)
• The costs of reinforcing the staff and budget of existing institutions as their responsibilities were increased.

The fiscal costs associated with the addition of the private pillar also needed to be taken into account and covered, including:

• The costs of establishing the legal framework to regulate the new system and the creation of new institutions
• The loss of contributions from the workers who would switch to the private pillar
• The recognition bonds issued to workers moving to the private pillar in recognition of past contributions to the PAYG
• The costs associated with the government commitment to top off the pension of participants in the private pillar when it did not reach the guaranteed minimum level.

Moreover, during implementation of the reforms, various unforeseen or unaccounted costs arose. Most of these could have been controlled, but many governments gave in to political pressures and made changes to the reform model that increased fiscal costs rather than reduced them. These changes included:

- Changing parameters while the reforms were being implemented: increasing the level of the minimum pension, reducing the level of contributions, adding other benefits
- Including groups of workers in the reformed system that had their own pension program and were not foreseen as part of the reformed system
- Failing to exercise strict control over eligible participants and thus encouraging fraud, such as falsification of birth records to qualify for a pension.

In the case of Chile, the portion of the fiscal deficit associated with the reform increased from 3.8 percent to 5.8 percent from 1981 to 2003, as seen in Table 1.4. The Chilean reformers underestimated the fiscal effects of the reform by excluding from their calculations the minimum government guaranteed pension (Garantía Estatal de Pensión Mínima, GEPM) owed to contributors of the private system. Arenas de Mesa (see Chapter 3) confirms that about half the low-income workers participating in the private pillar did not have sufficient earnings and contributions to reach the level of the guaranteed minimum pension. In these cases, the government tops up the pension so that it attains the level of the minimum pension. The reformers also ignored the fiscal liability arising from the noncontributory old age pensions. This was a social security-related cost that should have been included in the cost of the reform.

In contrast to Chile, Argentina made numerous changes to the reform model, which undermined its original fiscal projections. From 1994 to 2001, more participants than anticipated switched from the social security system managed by ANSES to the newly created private pillar. In 2001, this situation was further exacerbated when the government

Table 1.4	Chile's Pension System Deficit (percent of GDP)						
Year	Operational deficit	Recognition bonds	Non-contributory	Minimum pensions	Civil deficit	Military deficit	Total deficit
1981	3.6	0.0	0.2	0.00	3.8	—	3.8
1982	6.0	0.1	0.3	0.00	6.4	—	6.4
1985	6.0	2.0	0.5	0.00	6.7	—	6.7
1990	3.3	0.5	0.3	0.01	4.1	1.2	5.3
1995	2.8	0.7	0.2	0.02	3.8	1.1	4.9
2003	2.9	1.1	0.4	0.06	4.5	1.3	5.8

Source: Chapter 3, Arenas de Mesa (2004).
Note: — Not available

reduced the employer's contribution to the pension systems from 16 percent to an average 8 percent (Domeniconi, et al. 2004). This measure was taken in the face of growing unemployment resulting from the economic crisis, as an incentive to encourage companies to retain their employees. The impact of these two factors was that contributions were reduced and revenues dropped by about 45 percent. At the same time, contributions to the system were dropping because both unemployment and informality were growing. Moreover, the government established a single tax for low-income, self-employed workers (*monotributistas*), thus reducing its tax base. Previously, the government had counted on the revenues from two separate taxes for these workers: a tax on earnings, and a social security contribution. As a consequence, Argentina's pension-related deficit increased from 1.1 percent of GDP in 1994 to 2.1 percent in 2003 (Table 1.5).

When Bolivia drafted its pension legislation (*Ley de Pensiones* No. 1732) in 1996, it anticipated that the discounted value of all future payments from 1997 to 2060 would total $2.3 billion, and that the long-run savings to the Treasury of transitioning to the new pension system would be about $1 billion. Instead, the fiscal deficit increased. By 2002, over three-quarters of the fiscal deficit was explained by the transition costs of the pension system, and the deficit had reached 8.9 percent of GDP.

Most of the cost may be explained by the fact that the number of pensioners turned out to be far greater than anticipated. There were a variety of reasons for this. First, the inadequate quality of official records and the database made it difficult to establish who was eligible and who was not. As a consequence, between 1997 and 2001, many were able to alter birth records to qualify for early retirement, while others were granted pensions although they had not made the required number of contributions. Second, while some of the social security funds, such as the *cajas*, were not originally included in the reform, they were added to it later. Third, a

Table 1.5	Pension and Fiscal Deficits *(percent of GDP)*				
Deficit	Argentina	Bolivia	Chile	Mexico	Peru
Pension deficit	1994 = −1.1	1997 = −2.5	1981 = −3.8	1996 = −0.2	1994 = −3.0
	2003 = −2.1	2002 = −5.0	2003 = −5.8	2003 = −1.1	2003 = −2.7
Fiscal deficit	1994 = −0.7	1997 = −3.3	1981 = +2.6	1996 = 0.0	1994 = −3.0
	2003 = −6.3	2002 = −8.9	2000 = −0.1	2003 = −1.1	2001 = −1.8

Source: Bustamante (2004); Salinas (2004); Domeniconi, Bruno, and Perrotto (2004); Alonso y Caloca (2004); IMF (2004c).

cut-off date for admitting new benefit claimants under the old social security system was never established and enforced. Thus many years after the reform, retirees were still being admitted to the old system.

Moreover, the rules of the reform were not enforced. For instance, pension payments were made to retirees who had taken other jobs although the law required that they could not receive a pension until fully retired. Pension payments were also made to deceased persons, and laws preventing this were not enforced. Finally, the base pension level was raised to above the minimum wage once the reforms were underway, which added another cost to the original fiscal projections.

Mexico apparently did a better job at estimating the fiscal costs of the reform. It projected a small addition to the fiscal deficit from the reform of 0.5 to 0.6 percent of GDP for 1998 to 2003. In actuality, the deficit increased to 1.1 percent of GDP, slightly higher than projected, but still a reasonable level. Peru's social security programs had a deficit the year the reform was launched (1992) of about 3 percent of GDP. The deficit has remained close to that level, measuring 2.7 percent in 2003.

The relationship between pension and fiscal deficits is summarized in Table 1.5. The table confirms that Chile planned well for the rising costs of the transition to the reformed system, while in Bolivia, the transition has contributed significantly to the rapid increase of the fiscal deficit. Peru has shown some improvement and Mexico registered a slight increase above the projections. The apparent slight improvement of the fiscal deficit in Argentina is more difficult to assess in view of the 2001–02 collapse of the economy.

The fact that the pension reform failed to attain one of its primary objectives—to reduce government expenditures—has been used by opponents as evidence that the reform failed. The reform has had a far-reaching impact in many countries such as Bolivia, but the expected fiscal impact has been disappointing. This reflects the fact that the original reform model in many countries failed to account for all the costs it generated. Additionally, in some cases the model was not adhered to and numerous changes were made to it without an adequate analysis of the fiscal implications.

Offsetting Fiscal Costs Through Revenue and Expenditure Reforms

An important lesson emerging from the region's experience with the reform of pension systems is that it may not lower the fiscal deficit as intended. As discussed, the reform must be accompanied by discipline to resist changes that would increase costs, rather than lower them. Pension reform by itself without other elements of fiscal discipline will not have the intended positive impact on reducing the fiscal gap.

In this regard, Chile is an excellent example of a country that took an integrated approach to pension reform. The reform was undertaken in consonance with a much broader reform package that included fiscal reforms to offset the imbalance generated by the loss of contributions to the public pillar and other costs. This plan included reducing expenditures by transferring some responsibilities for covering social expenditures to the municipalities (Collins and Lear 1995). It overhauled the tax system, introducing a value added tax at a rate of 35 percent to raise revenues to finance the reduction of the public debt and the social security reform. It also passed a series of measures supporting fiscal discipline, including a prohibition against central bank financing of the government.

Finally, Chile enjoyed the benefit of a fiscal surplus of 5 percent of GDP generated by a non-privatized public corporation: the copper company (Compañía del Cobre, CODELCO). However, that is not to say that Chile had an easier time than the other countries. From 1981 to 1986, copper prices dropped significantly. Public revenues also declined between 1982 and 1983 as the private sector experienced a crisis. The financial sector required huge transfers to banks because of this systemic crisis. However, by 1989 copper prices had recovered, CODELCO transfers to the fiscal accounts reached $1.5 billion, compared to the average of $537 million from 1982 to 1987, and the fiscal position stabilized. The combination of these factors resulted in a highly disciplined fiscal transition.

Argentina also had an additional source of revenues from the sale and privatization of public enterprises. However, the fiscal side of the reform was not well managed, as it attempted to promote other goals, such as attracting workers from the informal sector to the pension system and using the contribution rates as a countercyclical unemployment policy measure. These and other contravening measures previously cited offset the beneficial effects that this additional source of revenue might have had.

The Role of Fiscal Incentives

Countries in the region did not introduce income tax incentives as a way to encourage contributions at the time of the reforms. Income tax incentives could have had a positive impact designed to attract informal workers to the pension system. Brazil has had some success in introducing income tax incentives to reduce informality and encourage contributions to the pension system. In January 1997, a new system for tax and fees payments was introduced for smaller businesses.[5] The system (Sistema Integrado de Pagamento de Impostos e Contribuições das Microempresas e das Empresas de Pequeno Porte, SIMPLES) consolidated all taxes into a single monthly tax with a tax rate of 3 to 5 percent of sales. This single tax is imposed on all small businesses and covers the employer contribution to social security. Since many workers are not reported as part of the payroll, this single tax is more effective in insuring that the employer contribution is made for all employees (IDB 1998). Chile has also begun to introduce a preferential tax treatment of retirement savings, but not for the private pension funds (Gill, Packard, and Yermo 2005).

The United States did not tax social security benefits for decades after it launched its social security system in the 1930s. However, beginning in 1984, it taxed benefits at a rate of 45 percent if a retiree had other income above a certain threshold. After 1996, the rate increased to 85 percent. In effect savings are taxed twice: first when the income is earned and saved, and again when the benefits are paid to retirees. However, most countries in the region are far from being able to do this because their tax structures and enforcement is weak.

> **Box 1.3   A Tax Incentives Model**
>
> The United States has introduced several instruments to promote retirement savings, such as individual retirement accounts (IRAs) for individuals and 401k plans for employees of corporations. The IRAs incentive to the individual is that, upon retirement, taxes would be paid at a lower marginal tax rate. However, this does not avoid the double taxation of wages. The 401k plans are an important source of retirement savings. However, they have come under scrutiny because many corporations, including car manufacturers, airlines, oil companies, and technology firms, have under-funded or terminated their plans. The costs to the government have been significant; it must make up some of the benefits through the Pension Benefit Guarantee Corporation, which insures the participant's benefits. Moreover, the effectiveness of the 401k plan has been reduced as shifts in the labor market have occurred and increasing numbers of employees no longer stay with the same company for their entire working lives.

Financial Considerations

The Capital Market Effect

One of the benefits expected from the reform of the pension systems in all countries was a growth in capital markets. It was widely held that creating large institutional investors such as the private pension funds

---

[5] Large corporations follow the standard, more complex tax system.

would result in an enlarging of market liquidity, which could reduce dependency on foreign capital. It would create broader demand for equities and debt instruments, especially bonds, and stimulate savings and investment. Downstream, as institutional investors began to purchase domestic securities from local companies, this would have a positive catalytic impact on other domestic and individual investors. Indeed, this was a major contributing factor to the reformers' ability to develop consensus and secure the support of the financial and business sectors.

Pension funds have undoubtedly become an important force in financial markets since the reforms. In each country, the pension fund industry represents the largest domestic institutional investor. It is also the largest purchaser of sovereign debt and has enabled many governments to operate with large fiscal deficits. As can be seen in Table 1.6, pension funds assets have grown in all countries since the reforms, and especially in Chile from 1981 to 2004, and in Mexico between 1997 and 2004. Further, in the case of Chile, pension fund assets represent almost 70 percent of GDP. In the case of Argentina, there has been somewhat of a decline in the assets under management since 2001, reflecting the economic crisis in that year and the government's asymmetric policy measures, which affected pension portfolios (see discussion below).

While private pension fund assets have grown, the expected catalytic effect on capital markets has been less than hoped for. Selected indicators of capital markets development are shown in Table 1.7. Stock market

Table 1.6	Pension Fund Assets Under Management Since the Reforms (US$ millions)							
Country	1981	1995	1997	2001	2002	2003	2004	Percentage of GDP, 2003
Argentina	n.a.	2,497	8,827	20,786	11,409	16,139	18,306	14.10
Bolivia	n.a.	n.a.	98	936	1,144	1,493	1,716	18.40
Chile	300	25,143	30,525	35,460	43,432	49,690	60,799	68.60
Colombia	n.a.	n.a.	n.a.	n.a.	n.a.	7,322	11,069	9.40
Costa Rica	n.a.	n.a.	n.a.	n.a.	n.a.	305	476	1.70
Dominican Republic	n.a.	n.a.	n.a.	n.a.	n.a.	240	488	1.50
El Salvador	n.a.	n.a.	n.a.	n.a.	n.a.	1,572	2,148	10.90
Mexico	n.a.	n.a.	615	27,146	31,748	35,748	42,524	5.70
Peru	n.a.	n.a.	n.a.	n.a.	n.a.	6,311	7,820	10.30
Uruguay	n.a.	n.a.	n.a.	n.a.	n.a.	1,272	1,678	11.40

Note: n.a. Not applicable (years before the reform).
Source: World Bank 2005; AIOS Statistical Bulletin No. 12, December 2004.

Table 1.7	Size of Capital Markets, Selected Indicators							
	Stock market capitalization (percent of GDP)		Market liquidity (value traded as percent of GDP)		Listed companies (number)		Turnover ratio (value of shares traded as percent of market capitalization)	
	1990	2003	1990	2003	1990	2004	1990	2004
Latin America & Caribbean	7.7	33.2	2.1	6.0	1,748	1,648	29.8	22.0
East Asia & Pacific	16.4	53.5	6.6	32.8	774	3,582	118.1	103.5
World	48.0	89.7	28.5	83.4	25,424	50,038	57.2	72.4
United Kingdom	85.8	134.4	28.2	119.8	1,701	2,311	33.4	100.6
United States	53.2	130.3	30.4	142.0	6,599	5,295	53.4	122.8

Source: World Bank, World Development Indicators, 2005, and IMF, 2004.

capitalization, which measures the overall size of the market, has remained relatively small throughout the region. While the region's market capitalization in 2003 represented about a third of GDP, it has not kept pace with other regions of the world such as Asia, where it represents over 50 percent of GDP, or the United States and the United Kingdom, where it exceeds GDP. Market liquidity, which measures the value traded as a percentage of GDP, is even less impressive in the region. It has stagnated, whereas in other regions it has grown impressively. Market liquidity reflects the ability to buy and sell easily. It complements market capitalization, as it shows whether market size is matched by trading.

Another indicator of market development is the number of companies listed on the domestic exchanges. As seen in Table 1.7, there has been a decline in the region as a whole. One final indicator of the capital markets is the turnover ratio, which measures both market liquidity and transaction costs. The turnover ratio is related to the size of the market, whereas the liquidity ratio (value traded as a percent of GDP) is related to the size of the economy. A small liquid market will have a high turnover ratio but a low value traded ratio. As can be seen, the region is not liquid and its turnover is low.

The data in Table 1.8 are even more revealing. Market capitalization has grown since the reforms, but liquidity and turnover remain low. Liquidity is essential to growth, as it enhances the allocation of capital. The number of listed companies has increased in Bolivia, Chile, Colombia, and El Salvador, but has declined in other countries. To some extent, pension funds are unable to play a large role in market capitalization because

Table 1.8	Size of Capital Markets in Seven Countries								
	Market capitalization (percent of GDP)		($ millions)		Listed domestic companies (number)		Market liquidity (value traded as percent of GDP)		Turnover ratio (value of shares traded as percent of market capitalization)
	1990	2003	1990	2004	1990	2004	1990	2003	1990	2004
Argentina	2.3	30.0	3,270	46,432	179	104	0.6	3.8	33.6	17.8
Bolivia	—	16.3	—	1,282	—	32	—	0.0	—	0.2
Chile	44.9	119.2	13,600	117,065	215	239	2.6	9.0	6.3	12.1
Colombia	3.5	18.1	1,420	25,223	80	114	0.2	0.5	5.6	7.7
El Salvador	—	22.1	—	3,286	—	34	—	0.1	—	0.3
Mexico	12.4	19.6	32,700	171,940	199	152	4.6	3.8	44.0	29.4
Peru	3.1	26.5	812	20,115	294	194	0.4	1.3	19.3	6.3

— Not available.

Source: World Bank, World Development Indicators 2005; Standard and Poor's, Emerging Market Fact Book, 2004.

there are limits placed on the level that they might invest in equities and certain types of debt. In the region as a whole, pension funds may invest only about 9 percent in equities. The pension funds' investment guidelines are more liberal with respect to investment in the instruments of financial institutions and especially government debt, which on average comprises about half (51 percent) of the portfolios in the region. As seen in Figure 1.1, this amount is even higher in Argentina, Bolivia, and Mexico.

The previous analysis of the limited impact of the pension fund industry on capital markets development in the region does not reflect any defect in the system per se. However, it does reflect several essential elements that make equity investments attractive to private investors and pension funds. These include:

- Macroeconomic stability
- Good corporate governance
- Transparency of systems, such as those associated with accounting and auditing
- Well-functioning legal systems, particularly in enforcement of contract law.

It also reflects the effects of globalization, as large corporations in most countries have tended to list and to issue ADRs (American Depository

Rights) on the New York or European exchanges, rather than in their domestic markets.

In most countries in the region, with the exception of Chile and to a lesser extent Mexico, corporate governance is weak. Transparent guidelines on corporate governance are extremely important to investors and help insure that a company will be well managed by professionals, a sine qua non for making an investment in a company's shares. These guidelines better insure transparency through controls, including accounting and auditing standards and disclosure; an independent board with clearly defined roles, including management oversight; and protection for shareholders.

Another aspect that affects the growth of markets and investor choices is the structure and enforcement of the legal system, especially as it pertains to contract law. The legal structure in Spanish- and Portuguese-speaking countries in the region is based on a civil law structure. In most instances, this makes it difficult to enforce contracts in the event of defaults and disputes. Mexico has recently revised its legislation to make enforcement more straightforward, especially of mortgage loans. This measure has been followed by the first mortgage-backed security, a standard instrument for markets where contract enforcement issues are less of a concern. Chile has also made changes to its laws. It will be revealing to see how these changes affect capital markets and pension portfolios over the next few years.

The pension industry, its administrators, and regulators could play an important role in promoting good corporate governance, transparency, and changes in the legal framework to permit contract enforcement. By taking the role of advocate, the pension industry could be a catalyst to provoke policymakers and companies to change.

Investment Liberalization and Maintaining Financial Integrity

A key constraint to the growth of the pension fund industry is the parameter that governments set that restricts investment in equities and foreign securities, but encourages or even requires heavy investment in sovereign debt in some countries. As a consequence, pension funds are one of the largest purchasers of government debt in the region (Figure 1.1). There are consequences associated with this large exposure to sovereign debt.

Table 1.9 presents the proportion of investment by category in countries that undertook structural reforms. Pension funds in Chile and Peru have a fairly balanced investment profile, but others are heavily

Figure 1.1. Distribution of Portfolio Investment in Five Countries

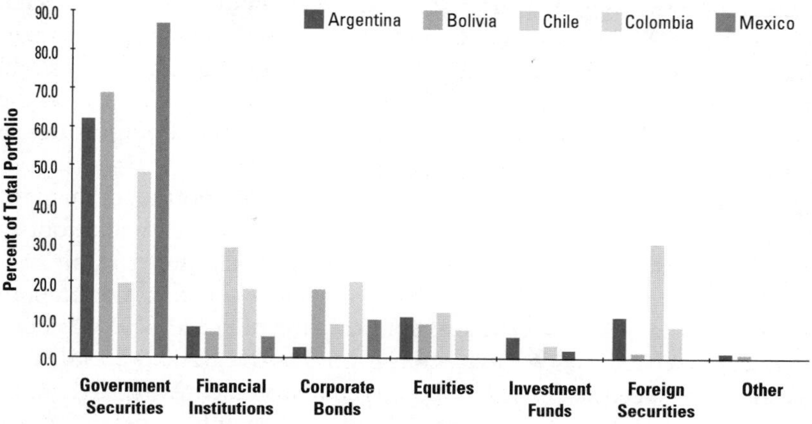

Source: AIOS (2004).

invested in government securities. This policy has had a negative impact on pension portfolios in several countries. The most serious has been in Argentina, where about three-quarters of the assets were invested in government securities. During the economic crisis of 2001, the government undertook a number of asymmetric policy measures as it struggled to meet huge debt payments, including converting debt instruments,

Table 1.9	Investment of Pension Fund Portfolios, 2004 (percent)						
	Government securities	Financial institutions	Corporate bonds	Equities	Investment funds	Foreign securities	Other
Argentina	62.0	6.6	2.0	12.7	4.8	10.3	1.7
Bolivia	67.5	5.6	16.9	7.5	0.0	1.5	1.1
Chile	18.7	28.5	7.1	15.7	3.1	26.8	0.2
Colombia	48.5	16.6	19.6	6.2	2.2	6.7	0.1
Costa Rica	73.1	14.2	7.9	0.1	1.5	0.0	3.2
Dom. Rep.	32.5	61.8	0.7	3.8	0.0	0.0	1.3
El Salvador	83.5	10.5	5.8	0.2	0.0	0.0	0.0
Mexico	85.5	4.3	10.1	0.0	0.0	0.0	0.0
Peru	24.2	11.4	11.5	37.7	1.4	10.2	3.4
Uruguay	57.9	36.9	4.2	—	—	—	1.0

— Not available.
Source: AIOS 2004.

altering interest rates, and eventually defaulting on its debt. The peso devaluation and changes to the terms of government debt instruments has raised concerns over the real value of the pension portfolios. This has led to questions of how to protect portfolios in the future and how to engender confidence among the people in their pension systems. The second part of the equation, restoring confidence and assuring citizens that the government will act responsibly, encompasses a plethora of measures in areas other than pension reform.

Another effect of the requirement that such a large portion of the portfolios be held in government securities has been the crowding out of financing of the private sector through bonds and equities. Moreover, while the returns on government debt are relatively robust, the preponderance in the pension portfolios represents too high a level of sovereign risk, as evidenced by the situation in Argentina (IMF, 2004a). In discussions on the need to liberalize the investment guidelines, governments have been unwilling to relinquish this easy source of funding.

The liberalization of investment guidelines, providing more investment choices to pension funds—thereby diversifying risks and achieving better-balanced portfolios—is an important consideration for the viability of the systems. Two issues will need to be addressed. First, what incentive can be offered to governments in the region to lure them away from the easy temptation to issue debt that will be purchased by the pension funds and which can be used to finance the deficit? Policymakers will need to find ways to create incentives that can accompany pension reform and that will encourage government to exercise fiscal discipline.

The second issue concerns the degree to which investment guidelines may be liberalized, given the special responsibility of the pension and insurance administrators to future retirees and the adequacy of risk-based analysis—particularly in view of the need to match long-term pension payments with a long-term stream of investment returns. This issue is receiving considerable attention (IMF, 2004b and Chapter 7). The success of the reforms in the long term will be linked to the portfolio diversification and liberalization of investment guidelines to reduce exposure to sovereign risk.

Commissions System and Administrative Costs

In general, the commission structure in the region is not cost based and is quite high (Table 1.10). The administrative costs include account and assets' management expenses representing the largest part of the commissions.

Table 1.10	Commissions and Pension Contributions, 2004 (as a percent of salary)					
Country	Total commissions (1)	Disability and death insurance (2)	Net commissions (3) = (1) − (2)	Pension contribution (4)	Total commissions/ Pension contribution Gross (5) = (1)/ (4) + (1)	Net (6) = (1)/ (4)
Argentina	2.5	1.4	1.1	4.4	36	56
Bolivia	2.2	1.7	0.5	10.0	18	22
Chile	2.3	0.7	1.5	10.0	18	23
Colombia	3.0	1.5	1.5	10.0	23	30
Costa Rica	Commission is a percent of gross return and capped at 8%			4.2	n.a	n.a
Dom. Rep.	2.0	1.0	0.5	5.5	26	36
El Salvador	3.0	1.2	1.7	10.0	23	30
Mexico	4.0	2.5	1.5	7.0	36	57
Peru	3.1	0.9	2.2	8.0	28	38
Uruguay	2.8	0.9	1.9	12.1	19	23

n. a. = Not applicable.
Source: AIOS (2004).

Additional commissions can be charged in some countries. In Argentina if a worker fails to contribute, death and disability insurance premiums are taken out of the accumulated balance of his individual account. Bolivia exacts an additional administrative commission of 0.0229 percent, in line with limits established by the pension law. Colombia charges a commission for switching from one fund to another. The net commission for the Dominican Republic does not include 0.1 percent charged by the pension regulator, nor 0.4 percent contribution to the social solidarity fund (AIOS 2004). Uruguay charges an additional custodial commission of 0.002 percent of the balance of the individual account for account management.

Bolivia, Chile, and Uruguay have lower commissions with respect to pension contributions, at about 23 percent. Between 10 and 12 percent of the salary goes to their pensions and the commissions and fees are about 2 percent of the salary. In Argentina, Costa Rica, the Dominican Republic, and Mexico, only between 4.2 and 5.5 percent of the salary goes to pension investment. In Argentina, the contribution rate was about 9 percent of salary but was halved in December 2001 with the economic crisis to help people continue to make their payments. In five countries, the total salary deduction for a pension contribution is between 10 and 12 percent. The commission rates have been slow to come down to a more reasonable level. For the average middle-class worker, this level is probably feasible. However, for lower-income

Table 1.11	Administrative Expenditures of the Pension Funds ($ millions)					
			Marketing			
	Administration	**Promotion**	**Sales and commissions**	**Total marketing**	**Other**	**Total**
Argentina	129.2	28.6	115.3	143.8	5.4	278.4
Bolivia	4.0	0.1	—	0.2	0.4	4.5
Chile	167.0	6.4	54.4	60.8	8.8	236.5
Colombia	172.1	11.8	3.3	15.0	19.3	206.4
Costa Rica	—	—	—	—	—	21.2
Dominican Republic	4.2	—	2.6	2.6	2.5	9.4
El Salvador	24.4	—	4.0	4.0	—	28.4
México	331.9	30.2	22.3	52.1	216.0	600.0
Peru	51.1	—	—	32.9	—	84.0
Uruguay	4.4	1.2	1.2	2.4	2.9	9.7
Total	888.2	78.2	203.1	313.8	255.2	1,478.5

— Not available.
Source: AIOS (2004).

groups where there is no excess disposable income, the upper rates are too high.

Nonetheless, the end result is that over half the workers' contributions go to pay commissions and fees in Argentina and Mexico and 30 to 38 percent in Colombia, the Dominican Republic, and Peru. To achieve a benefit amount commensurate with the contribution before the commissions, the rate of return on the individual portfolios would need to be higher (one-third higher, in the case of Argentina) to make up for the up-front deduction of the commission from the workers' contribution.[6]

Moreover, as a result, the number of people who do not qualify for a minimum pension based on a certain level of contribution is significant. In Chile, only half the members of the private funds would qualify for the minimum pension, while in Argentina, about 60 percent would qualify.

In Bolivia, removing the need for competition and marketing significantly reduced the commissions. On the other hand, Argentina has 12 pension funds and large marketing costs, as seen in Table 1.11. Between 1995 and 1999, it had a sales force that grew to about 30,000 persons. The average marketing cost at that time was about $200 per member,

---

[6] The total value of an annual contribution a, earning a rate of interest r, for n years is equal to: $S = a (1 + r)^n$. The individual pension is the sum of the number of annual contributions over n years.

which was underwritten by the up-front commission of one-third of every pension contribution. This left only two-thirds of each contribution that could be invested.

There is also debate in the region over the level and size of the administrative costs of the pension system. The industry earns $1.5 billion in commissions per year. Most of the administrative cost consists of expenditures for administering the funds and promotion and sales commissions. A comparison of administrative expenditures among similar funds has not been undertaken. Thus a determination of whether the administrative expenditures are too high cannot be made. What is clear is that a significant part of workers' contributions go to pay this cost.

The assessment of the experiences in the region suggests that the level of contributions in some cases is too high, particularly for the poor, leaving many workers and their families without old age coverage. High contributions rates are also a disincentive for workers to save for their retirement and participate in the pension system. The high level of the commissions is not linked to performance results of the pension fund managers. In fact, the high level of commissions reduces the potential invested by contributing workers, to the detriment of their old age security.[7] Reductions in the commission structure could enhance the system, make it more attractive to save, and possibly increase pension coverage.

Declining Contributions and Shortfalls in Coverage

In addition to the positive capital markets effect and the closing of the fiscal gap, the reforms were expected to generate increased savings for retirement and insure that a larger proportion of the population would be covered by the pension system. In theory, providing individual retirement accounts for each worker would increase coverage by providing an incentive to contribute to a stable funded pillar. The fact that private pension fund managers would manage the individual retirement accounts would further engender a savings culture.

The experience with the coverage rates both before and after the reform is not entirely encouraging. While the coverage of the privately funded pillars of workers who participate and are registered has increased, as seen in Table 1.12, their contributions to the pension system have not. Only 11 percent of workers registered in the pension system in Bolivia contribute. In Argentina and Mexico, between 21 and 30 percent of

---

[7] This affects adversely the retirees' annuities options. For a full discussion on annuities' markets and benefits, see Palacios and Rofman (2001).

Table 1.12	Coverage Before and After the Reform (percent of workforce)		
Country and year of reform	Coverage before reform	Coverage as of Dec. 2004	
		Participants	Contributors
Argentina (1994)	50	58	21
Bolivia (1997)	12	25	11
Chile (1981)	64	111[a]	56
Colombia (1994)	32	28	11
Costa Rica (2001)	53	72	49
Dominican Republic (2003)	30	32	16
El Salvador (1998)	26	41	17
Mexico (1997)	37	77	30
Peru (1993)	31	29	12
Uruguay (1996)	73	43	22

a. The level of participation in Chile is skewed because it includes inactive members who have dropped out of the labor force.
Source: AIOS (2004); Mesa-Lago (2004).

workers contribute. In Chile, 56 percent of workers who belong to the plan contribute to it. While this is the highest contribution rate in the region, it is by no means satisfactory and means that many workers will not receive an adequate pension.

A more detailed analysis is presented in Table 1.13, which provides the number of workers participating and contributing in the private pension pillar since the reforms. In Chile, both members and contributors have

Table 1.13	Members and Contributors from First Year of the Reform to End 2004 (number of persons)					
Country	1982	1986	1995	1998	2003	2004
Chile						
Members	1,440,000	2,591,484	4,899,115	—	6,883,566	7,046,146
Contributors	1,060,000	1,774,057	2,432,456	2,560,158	3,377,029	3,619,606
Argentina						
Members	n.a.	n.a.	7,069,503	9,164,725	11,810,732	9,711,577
Contributors	n.a.	n.a.	4,347,104	4,858,165	4,462,441	3,619,606
Bolivia						
Members	n.a.	n.a.	n.a.	760,959	809,179	854,989
Contributors	n.a.	n.a.	n.a.	450,000	360,045	365,285
Mexico						
Members IMSS	n.a.	n.a.	n.a.	11,188,114	30,400,000	32,321,677
Contributors	n.a.	n.a.	n.a.	7,709,610	12,327,534	12,573,110

n.a. Not applicable (years before the reform).
— Not available.
Sources: Bustamante (2004); Salinas (2004); Alonso y Caloca (2004).

increased steadily since 1982. However, while the number of members has increased fivefold, those who contribute has increased only three and a half times. In Mexico, participants have increased since the reform in 1998 almost threefold, and the number of contributors increased by only one and a half times. In Bolivia, the number of members has increased by only 12 percent since the reform and the contributors have declined by 10 percent. In Argentina, the participants have increased by 37 percent since 1995 but the contributors have declined by 17 percent. In the case of Chile, Mexico, and to a lesser extent Argentina, progress has been made in attracting members and increasing the number of those contributing but with a wide gap between those joining the system and those contributing to it. Moreover, the low growth in membership and contributions undermines expectations on coverage.

It is worth highlighting that the region has had a history of macroeconomic instability, rampant inflation, and inappropriate policies that have left its citizenry skeptical. Under this scenario, there is widespread mistrust of government in general, lack of confidence in financial institutions, and in particular skepticism about contributing to individual accounts. Moreover, the employment situation has also affected the coverage rates, particularly in Argentina, where informality is now estimated at 70 percent. These factors combine to make a powerful counterweight to the goal of increasing contributions and savings.

Bolivia and Argentina are not likely to increase coverage in the short term, given recent developments in both countries and a general lack of confidence. In the first instance, a public sector obligation, the *Bonosol,* was transferred to the private pension accounts. In the second, government paper, which the pension funds were forced to purchase, was arbitrarily converted to pesos, the interest rate was lowered, and the asset value of retirement savings was severely undermined. Restoring confidence and trust will imply a variety of interactions, from fiscal discipline to tax incentives. This is an area that has been studied very little and that will challenge policymakers over the next decade.

This mistrust is pervasive, the *Global Financial Well-being Study* confirms, in its annual survey of 12 countries, including Chile and Mexico, as well as the United States and some European countries. It concludes, "a majority in every country don't believe they can trust the government to help them save for retirement, and are also not convinced they will receive the benefits they are entitled to from their employers' retirement or pension funds" (Chapter 12, p. 377). The survey found an overall profound and deep-seated pessimism about living out a financially secure retirement. These are sentiments that are being raised around the world.

How policymakers deal with this problem will undoubtedly impact pension security and coverage in the future.

References

Alonso y Caloca, Salvador Gerardo. 2004. Los sistemas de pensiones en México: Breve estudio monográfico. Paper presented at workshop, Pension Reform, Inter-American Development Bank, December 8, Washington, D.C.

Arenas de Mesa, Alberto and Pamela Gana Cornejo. 2003. Protección social, pensiones y género en Chile. In *Protección social, pensiones y género en Argentina, Brasil y Chile,* eds. Fabio M. Betranou and Alberto Arenas de Mesa. Santiago: International Labour Organization.

Arenas de Mesa, Alberto and Mario Marcel. 1991. Reformas a la seguridad social en Chile. *Serie de Monografías No.5.* Inter-American Development Bank.

Asociación Internacional de Organismos de Supervisión de Fondos de Pensiones (AIOS). 2004. *Statisical Bulletin No.12* (December). Buenos Aires, Argentina.

Bronton, P. D. and P. Masci. 2005. *Workable Pension Systems: Reform in the English-speaking Caribbean.* Washington, D.C.: Inter-American Development Bank.

Bustamante Jeraldo, Julio. 2004. El sistema de pensiones en Chile. Paper presented at workshop, Pension Reform, Inter-American Development Bank, December 8, Washington, D.C.

Collins, Joseph and John Lear. 1995. *Chile's Free-Market Miracle: A Second Look.* Oakland, Calif.: Institute for Food and Development Policy.

Domeniconi, Hector, Julia Domeniconi, Bruno Domeniconi, Andrea Perrotto and Hugo Bertin. 2004. El sistema de pensiones en Argentina. Paper presented at workshop, Pension Reform, Inter-American Development Bank, December 8, Washington, D.C.

Fundación Mediterránea, Instituto de Estudios sobre la Realidad Argentina y Latinoamericana (IERAL). 2003. *Revista Jubilaciones y Pensiones.* September/November, No.76, Buenos Aires, Argentina.

Gill, Indermit, Truman Packard, and Juan Yermo. 2005. *Keeping the Promise of Social Security in Latin America.* Stanford, CA: Stanford University Press.

Holzman, Robert and Joseph Stiglitz, eds. 2001. *New Ideas About Old Age Security: Towards Sustainable Pension Systems in the 21st Century.* Washington, D.C.: The World Bank.

Inter-American Development Bank (IDB). 1991. *Economic and Social Progress Report (IPES)*. *Social Security*. Washington, D.C.: Inter-American Development Bank.

————. 1998. PR-2316. Brazil August 1998. Propuesta de Préstamo al Banco Nacional de Desarrollo Económico (BNDES) for a Multisectoral Sectoral Program. pp. 20–21.

————. 2004. *Economic and Social Progress Report* (IPES). *Good Jobs Wanted*. Washington, D.C.: Inter-American Development Bank.

International Labour Organization (ILO). 2002. *Pensiones no contribuciones y asistenciales: Argentina, Brasil, Chile, Costa Rica, Uruguay*. eds. Fabio Berstranov, C. Solorio, and W. Van Ginnekan. Santiago: International Labour Organization.

————. 2003. 2003 Labour Overview: Latin America and the Caribbean. Lima: International Labour Organization.

International Monetary Fund (IMF). 2004a. Argentina Second Review Under the Stand-by Arrangement and Request for Modification or Waiver of Performance Criteria (March 12). Washington, D.C.: International Monetary Fund.

————. 2004b. Global Financial Stability Report, Markets and Issues. September. Washington, D.C.: International Monetary Fund.

————. 2004c. *International Financial Yearbook*. Washington, D.C.: The International Monetary Fund.

James, Estelle, Alejandra Cox-Edwards, and Rebeca Wong. 2003. The Gender Impact of Reform: A Cross-Country Analysis. World Bank Policy Research Working Paper No. 3074. Washington, D.C.

Mesa-Lago, Carmelo. 2004. *Las reformas de pensiones en America Latina y su impacto en los principios de la seguridad social*. Santiago: Economic Commission for Latin America and the Caribbean.

Ministerio de Trabajo, Empleo y Seguridad Social de Argentina. 2004. Dirección General de Estudios y Formulación de Políticas de Empleo. Buenos Aires.

Palacios, Robert and Rafael Rofman. 2001. Annuity Markets and Benefit Design in Multipillar Pension Schemes: Experiences and Lessons from Four Latin American Countries. Social Protection Discussion Paper Series No. 0107. The World Bank, Washington, D.C.

Principal Financial Group. 2004. *Global Financial Well-Being Study*. Des Moines: Principal Financial Services, Inc.

Rapp, Jorge García and Eduardo Merlinsky. 2000. *Argentina, el sistema previsional: situación actual y perspectivas*. Washington, D.C.: Inter-American Development Bank.

Salinas, Helga. 2004. La reforma de las pensiones en un grupo de países latinoamericanos seleccionado: estudio comparativo, Bolivia. Paper presented at workshop, Pension Reform, Inter-American Development Bank, December 8, Washington, D.C.

Standard and Poor's. 2004a. *Emerging Market Fact Book,* 2004. New York, NY.: Standard & Poor's.

The World Bank. 1998. Implementation Completion Report, Argentina: Provincial Pension Reform Adjustment Loan (PPRL), Loan No. 4116-AR. Washington, D.C.

_____. 2002, 2003a, 2004, 2005. *World Development Report.* New York, N.Y.: Oxford University Press.

_____. 2003b, 2005. *World Development Indicators.* Washington, D.C.: The World Bank.

_____. 2003c. Argentina's Challenge: Growth, Social Inclusion and Governance. Policy Notes. Washington, D.C.

SECTION TWO

Structural Reform Dilemmas

Evaluation of a Quarter Century of Structural Pension Reforms in Latin America

Carmelo Mesa-Lago*

By mid-2004, twelve Latin American countries had implemented or approved structural reforms that fully or partially privatized their social security systems. No other region in the world, including Central and Eastern Europe, has undertaken such a profound and wide-ranging transformation (Müller 2002). Latin America's experience has influenced reforms in other regions of the world and affected the agenda of international and regional financial organizations such as the World Bank, the International Monetary Fund (IMF), and the Inter-American Development Bank (IDB). Moreover, the reforms present a challenge to international and regional organizations that specialize in social security, such as the International Labour Organization (ILO), the International Social Security Association (ISSA), the Inter-American Social Security Conference (CISS), and the Ibero-American Social Security Organization (OISS).

This chapter describes and compares three different models that have evolved in the region, as well as the characteristics of the reforms. Using data available from nine countries (and occasionally, information from

---

* Carmelo Mesa-Lago is Distinguished Professor Emeritus of Economics at the University of Pittsburgh. He has written widely on social security and pension issues and has been instrumental in advancing discussion on this important topic. This chapter is an updated summary of Mesa-Lago (2004).

all twelve), it analyzes the challenges facing reformers and proposes policies to resolve some of them. These challenges include coverage of the labor force, collection of contributions, competition among pension fund managers, administrative costs, capital accumulation and the impact on national savings, the fiscal cost of the transition, development of the capital markets and portfolio diversification, real return on the investment, the amount of the pension, gender equity, and solidarity.

While some countries adapted the reforms to their financial, economic, social, political, and social security requirements, others simply copied what was thought of as a "universal model." Unfortunately, far from being universal, this model cannot function in the absence of certain essential basic conditions. Those countries that have not yet embarked on the process of reforming their social security system should study carefully the experience of the 12 countries described here, including their failures as well as their successes, before deciding to go forward with structural or parametric reforms. Countries opting for undertaking structural reforms should select a general model and adapt it to their requirements.

Key Concepts and Description of the Reforms

Public vs. Private Pension Systems

Public and private pension systems are defined according to four fundamental characteristics: contributions, benefits, administration, and financial structure. Public pension systems are characterized by undefined contributions and defined benefits, and are administered by the government or social insurance system. The financial structure for the pay-as-you-go (PAYG) system has no reserve. Retirees are paid from current worker contributions, whereas the *capitalización parcial colectiva* (partial collective capitalization, or CPC) has a partial reserve. By contrast, private pension systems are characterized by defined contributions and undefined benefits and are administered by private fund managers (Mesa-Lago 2004). The financial structure is fully funded (FF) or contains a reserve.

Structural vs. Parametric Reforms

Structural reforms fundamentally transform the public system, replacing it in whole or part with a private one. Nonstructural or parametric reforms attempt to provide long-term financial strengthening to a public system by increasing the retirement age and/or contributions, or by tightening the calculation formula (for more on reform policies, see Madrid 2003; Mesa-Lago and Müller 2004).

Structural reforms undertaken by the 12 Latin American countries reviewed here were based on one of three models: substitutive, parallel, or mixed. Table 2.1 lists each country and the type of reform model that it followed, as well as the starting date for the new system and its basic characteristics (contributions, benefits, finance structure, and adminis-

| Table 2.1 | Pension Reform Models and Characteristics in Latin America, 2004 |

Model, Country, and Starting Date of Reform	System	Contribution	Benefit	Regime	Financial Administration
Structural Reforms					
Substitutive model Chile: May 1981 Bolivia: May 1997 Mexico: Sept. 1997 El Salvador: May 1998 Dominican Rep.: 2003–06 Nicaragua: (2004, pending)	Private	Defined	Not defined	FF	Private
Parallel model Peru: June 1993 Colombia: April 1994	Public or private	Not defined Defined	Defined Not defined	PAYG[a] FF	Public Private[a]
Mixed model Argentina: July 1994 Uruguay: April 1996 Costa Rica: May 2001 Ecuador: (2004, pending)	Public or private	Not defined Defined	Defined Not defined	PAYG FF	Public Public & Private
Parametric Reforms or Unreformed					
Brazil[b] Guatemala Haiti Honduras Panama Paraguay Venezuela[b]	Public	Not defined	Defined[c]	PAYG or FF	Public

PAYG = pay-as-you-go
FF = fully funded
[a] Partial collective capitalization (CPC) in Colombia and Costa Rica.
[b] Parametric reforms recently introduced or in progress.
[c] Defined contribution in part of the private sector program in Brazil (notional accounts).
Source: Legislation of the 12 countries.

tration). The lower half of Table 2.1 lists the seven countries that still have public social security systems and describes the basic characteristics of their systems.

Six countries followed the substitutive model: Chile (which pioneered it in 1981), Bolivia and Mexico (1997), El Salvador (1998), the Dominican Republic (which implemented it gradually between 2003 and 2005), and Nicaragua (planned to begin in 2004 but suspended because of extremely high transition costs). This model requires closing down the public system (that is, no new members are permitted to join) and replacing it with a private system. Worldwide, 22 countries have enacted structural pension system reforms, and only one outside of Latin America has introduced a replacement model (Mesa-Lago and Hohnerlein 2002).

Two countries, Peru (1993) and Colombia (1994), opted for the parallel model. Under this alternative, the public system is modified rather than closed down, a new private system is created, and the two compete with each other. The characteristics of the public and private systems remain as described previously according to contributions, benefits, financial structure, and administration, except that Colombia has a CPC system with a partial reserve instead of PAYG. Outside of Latin America, no country has followed this model, possibly because of its complexity.

Argentina (1994), Uruguay (1996), Costa Rica (2001), and Ecuador have instituted a mixed model.[1] The public system under this model remains in operation and provides a basic pension (pillar one). In addition, a private system is instituted to provide a complementary pension (pillar two). Both the public and private pillar are characterized as described above in terms of contributions, benefits, and financial structure. However, the administration is mixed (public and private). This is the most widespread model worldwide and is in place in at least 12 countries in Western and Eastern Europe (Mesa Lago and Hohnerlein 2002; Müller 2002).

The seven countries listed in the lower half of Table 2.1 preserved their public social security systems. Brazil introduced parametric reforms in 1998–99 (which include a structured financial regime of notional accounts within the general regime for private workers). The parametric reform of the regime for public employees is currently awaiting congressional approval (Schwarzer 2004). While Venezuela initially approved a structural reform (substitutive model), the current government abolished

---

[1] As of June 2004, the mixed model had not been implemented in Ecuador, pending an appeal before the court.

46

it and enacted a parametric reform in 2002 (LOSSS 2002). In Panama, workers, employers, and the government agreed to implement a parametric reform with the help of the International Labour Organization in 1998, but the government postponed its implementation. This exacerbated the actuarial imbalance and generated a deficit for the first time (Mesa-Lago 2003). Structural and parametric reforms have been considered in Guatemala, Honduras, and Paraguay.

The Structural Pension Reforms

Benefits from the Structural Reforms

Structural reforms have resulted in many benefits and improvements. In Bolivia, Chile, Costa Rica, El Salvador, and Peru, structural reforms permitted the consolidation of disparate systems, making pension portability possible.[2] However, the segmentation of pension systems persists in Argentina, Colombia, and Mexico. The reforms have also led to more equal treatment by promoting uniformity of access requirements and standards for pension calculation in most systems (with the exception of the armed forces in all countries except Costa Rica). Reforms have also strengthened long-term financial sustainability by introducing eligibility requirements (such as retirement age) that are more closely linked to life expectancy at retirement. Another benefit of structural reforms is the establishment of a much closer relationship between contributions and pensions, as well as the potential for middle- and high-income persons to save for their old age and thus increase their retirement income. Reformed pensions systems in all countries maintain government guarantees to continue to pay pensions to retirees. In addition, they recognize pre-reform contributions to the public system and, in most countries, establish a minimum private pension. Reforms have also led to the elimination of the public monopoly and the introduction of competition.[3] A substantial accumulation of capital in the pension fund has also been a positive result of reform (although this has been offset by the transition costs, which have increased the fiscal burden). The reforms have also produced increased efficiency in key areas such as record keeping, maintaining individual accounts, providing periodic information to plan

---

[2] Pension portability permits workers who change employment to carry their pension contributions from one pension system to another.

[3] Competition has yet to yield the anticipated results.

participants, and processing pensions in a timely manner. Under the reformed system in Chile, plan participants now enjoy the freedom of selecting an investment fund. Finally, reform has resulted in the creation of technical regulatory and supervisory agencies that are relatively independent (although this varies from country to country).

The importance of the private sector once the public sector's monopoly was eliminated and private pension management was introduced varies considerably from country to country because of the variety of reform models introduced. At the end of 2002, 100 percent of those affiliated in Bolivia, Mexico (IMSS only),[4] and Costa Rica had joined the private system (or the private pillar, in a mixed system). The comparable figure was between 91 and 98 percent in Chile, El Salvador, and Peru and 80 percent in Argentina (Table 2.2).

Changes in participation from one system to the other depend not only on the good features of the private system, but also on four other factors. One factor is the degree of freedom that workers have to remain in the public system or to move to the private or mixed system. In some countries, the person's age and income also play a role. Another factor is the legal measures and incentives provided by the government to encourage the shift to the private system. Advertising also plays a role. A third factor is the rate of return of the public system compared with the investment yield (return on capital) of the private one. The fourth factor is how long the reform has been in place. The law in Bolivia, Costa Rica, and Mexico requires all participants to change to the new system, affording them no freedom to choose. In addition, in the six countries with the substitutive model, as well as in Costa Rica[5] and Ecuador (mixed model), new workers entering the labor force are required to join the private system. With the passage of time, as new entrants join the mixed system and older workers in the public system retire, the percentage of workers in the private system will increase. The majority of young workers in the Dominican Republic, El Salvador, and Nicaragua were required to switch to the private system. As a result, they have very high participation rates (91 percent in El Salvador).

Chile and Peru created strong incentives to switch because the amount of the contribution to the private system was less than that required to

---

[4] In Mexico, where there are several pension systems, only the IMSS that covers workers in the private sector was reformed.

[5] Costa Rica is a unique case because the law mandates that all insured persons (at the time of the reform and in the future) must be members of the mixed system. Thus everyone is in the public (the first pillar and the most important one) and also in the private systems (the second pillar, which provides for a complementary pension).

Table 2. 2	Distribution of Workers in the Public, Private or Mixed System, 2002				
Model/ country	Both systems (million)	Public system		Private system	
		(million)	% of total	(million)	% of total
Substitutive					
Chile	6.9	0.17	2.0	6.71	98
Bolivia	0.8	0.00	0.0	0.76	100
Mexico	29.4	0.00	0.0	29.42	100
El Salvador	1.1	0.09	9.0	0.99	91
Parallel					
Peru	3.1[a]	0.14[a]	4.0	2.99	96
Colombia	10.5	5.74[b]	55.0	4.72	45
Mixed					
Argentina	11.3[c, d]	2.21	20.0	9.11	80
Uruguay	1.2	0.60[d, e]	49.0	0.62	51
Costa Rica [d, e]	1.2	1.18	100.0	1.18	100
Total	65.5[f]	10.15	15.2	56.49	84.8

[a] Author's estimates.
[b] January 2003.
[c] Includes undecided.
[d] All the insured in the second pillar (private system) are also in the first pillar (public system).
[e] There are no figures for affiliates in the public system; the active contributors are shown and the number of affiliates should be larger.
[f] Costa Rica is counted only once.
Sources: AIOS 2002; ANSES 2002; BCU 2002; CONSAR 2002, 2003; SAFJP 2003; SAFP 2003; SBC 2003; SBS 2003; SPa 2002, 2003; SPb 2002; SPVS 2002, 2003; SSS 2002.

remain in the public system. Moreover, once workers have moved to the private system, they are not allowed to return to the public system. In Argentina, those entering the labor market are free to choose between the public and mixed systems. However, undecided workers are assigned to the mixed system, and those switching from the public to the mixed system cannot go back to the public system (as a result, 80 percent of workers are in the mixed system).[6] Advertising has also played a crucial role in encouraging people to switch because the private system has promised higher pensions and lower administrative costs than the public system, as well as protection from government intervention (Mesa-Lago 2004). Unlike the other seven countries, Colombia's public system (parallel model) has retained 55 percent of workers, while Uruguay (mixed model) retains 49 percent as a result of the strengthening of the public system. Uruguayan law gave workers over 40 a period of time to de-

---

[6] Following the economic crisis of 2001–02 and the subsequent deterioration of the pension funds, debate in Argentina has arisen about maintaining the mixed system or allowing workers affiliated to it to return to the public system.

cide which system they wanted to join: the reformed public system or the mixed system. Most preferred the former. Moreover, only workers above a specified level of income may join the mixed system in Uruguay. In Colombia, workers have the option of changing systems every five years.[7]

Challenges Facing the Structural Reforms

Despite the improvements described above, the reforms failed to produce the significant benefits that they were expected to generate.[8] This section analyzes eleven challenges to structural reforms based on legal information from the twelve countries, as well as statistics from nine countries. In addition, this section provides policy recommendations to overcome these challenges and identifies areas requiring further study (for more details, see Mesa-Lago 2004).

Drop in Labor Force Coverage

Before the structural reforms, Latin America's public systems were classified into three groups, based on when the pension system was introduced and the degree of labor force coverage. The pioneers—Argentina, Chile, Costa Rica, and Uruguay—are those countries where coverage fluctuated between 63 and 81 percent of the labor force in 1980.[9] Colombia, Ecuador, Mexico, and Peru are in-between; coverage in these countries ranges from 26 to 42 percent. Bolivia, the Dominican Republic, El Salvador, and Nicaragua are considered latecomers, with coverage ranging between 12 and 20 percent (Mesa-Lago and Bertranou 1998). Generally, a private system offers two types of participatory incentives for affiliation that do not exist or have deteriorated in a public system: ownership of an individual account, and equivalence between contributions and the amount of the pension. It is also assumed that labor force coverage will increase because of these incentives.

Table 2.3 shows the percentage of the labor force covered by public and private systems. It excludes some groups that have separate plans,

---

[7] Initially, workers were allowed to change every three years. A 2002 law extended the period to five years, but with no changes ten years before retirement (LRP 2002).

[8] There is worldwide debate about the expected effects of the structural reforms of pensions (see Orszag and Stiglitz 2001; Barr 2002; Mesa-Lago 2002, 2004).

[9] Costa Rica belongs to the second group if classified according to the date the system was established, but to the first group according to labor force coverage and development of the system.

Table 2.3.	Labor Force Coverage, Before Reform and in 2002 *(percent of labor force, except as indicated)*				
Model/ Country	Coverage before reform		Coverage in 2002		Poverty rate
	year before reform	% contributors	Participants	Contributors	%[a]
Substitutive					
Chile	1980	64	111	58	21
Bolivia	1996	12	23	11	61
Mexico	1997	37	72	30	41
El Salvador	1996	26	40	19	50
Dominican Republic	2000	30	—	—	30
Nicaragua	2002	16	—	16	68
Parallel					
Peru	1993	31	28	11	48
Colombia	1993	32	59	24	55
Mixed					
Argentina	1994	50	69	24[c]	25
Uruguay	1997	73	77[d]	60[d]	10
Costa Rica	2000	53	65[e]	48[e]	21
Ecuador	2002	21	—	21	61
Average[b]		38	63	27	42

—Not available.
[a] Percentage of the total population in 2000, and of the urban population in Ecuador and Uruguay.
[b] Covered population weighted by the author; poverty rates for the region from ECLAC.
[c] Excludes portion of active contributors in the public system.
[d] Figures for 2000 for the public system.
[e] As of June 2003.
Source: Mesa-Lago (2004).

such as the armed forces (in all countries except Costa Rica), government employees (civil servants in most Argentine provinces), and other small groups. The center columns of Table 2.3 present two estimates of coverage in 2002 based on participants (that is, all workers who are registered in the system), and the active contributors or those who contributed in the last month. Coverage of participants is approximately twice that of those actually contributing.

The value for Chile indicates that 111 percent of the labor force contributing to the pension system is under coverage. However, this is obviously overestimated. Furthermore, this figure excludes an additional 26 percent of the labor force, which is covered through the armed forces system, and 23 percent, which is not covered. Including the armed forces would push the figure to 137 percent. Based on active contributors, however, coverage in Chile is only 58 percent.

Estimates of coverage based on active contributors before the reforms and in 2002 (after the reforms were in place) show that coverage decreased in every country. The weighted average of coverage in the countries fell from 63 percent before the reforms to 27 percent by 2002 (Table 2.3). However, this overestimates coverage before the reforms in most of the countries because it is not based on data for the last month to determine if the participant was an active contributor, as was done for 2002. Nevertheless, two standardized statistical series for Chile based on active contributors indicate that coverage declined from 79 percent in 1973 to 62 percent in 1975 and 58 percent in 2002 (Arenas de Mesa and Hernández Sánchez 2001; SAFP 2002). A similar series for Argentina shows a drop from 35 percent in 1994 to 26 percent in 2002 (Hujo 2004). The numbers indicate that coverage fell by half based on active contributors, and by a third in Argentina because of the severe crisis in 2001–02. This highlights the importance of developing better statistics on pension coverage to accurately determine who is covered, as well as the characteristics of those with no coverage, in order to design mechanisms for inclusion. The most serious challenge facing private and public pension systems is how to stop the decline in coverage in the formal labor market and expand coverage in the informal market.

In the last 25 years, there has been a significant increase in the size of the informal labor force in Latin America. This increase was exacerbated by labor flexibilization resulting from globalization and increased international competition. The informal sector increased from 42 percent of urban employment in 1990 to 47 percent in 2001. This was the result of declining formal employment and increasing self-employment, microenterprise, and domestic service employment (ILO 2002b). A growing trend in the region is that self-employed workers make up most of the informal sector. Their coverage by the pension systems is much lower than that of formal sector employees. The percentage of independent workers in the labor force is lower in the countries that fall into the pioneer group and higher in the countries identified as intermediate or latecomers. Because the number of self-employed workers is so much higher in these two groups, it is more difficult to include them in the pension systems. Furthermore, Argentina and Uruguay are the only countries where legislation mandates coverage for self-employed workers. In all others countries, such coverage is voluntary.[10] Mandated coverage would not necessarily solve the problem in most countries (especially in

---

[10] Laws to be implemented in Colombia, Costa Rica, the Dominican Republic, and Ecuador make coverage of self-employed workers mandatory.

the intermediate and latecomer countries) because a high percentage of independent workers have low-incomes, unstable employment and no employer contributions. Moreover, there are formidable obstacles to register them, collect contributions and oversee compliance. Other groups that are difficult to include are self-employed small farmers, domestic servants, laborers without contracts, and unpaid family members (Mesa-Lago 2004).

Another challenge for pension reform is protecting low-income workers by providing assistance through noncontributory pensions. In 2000, 42 percent of the region's population lived below the poverty line—and the trend is rising. In Argentina, Chile, Costa Rica, and Uruguay, the government assists those who are not covered by a pension plan through a noncontributory pension. These four countries have the broadest coverage and the lowest poverty rates in the region (ranging between 10 and 25 percent of the population; see Table 2.3). However, the pensions are not guaranteed to all the needy because they are dependent on available tax revenues. As a result, most of these countries have a waiting list. The number of people receiving noncontributory pensions as a percentage of the total population between 2000 and 2001 was very small (ranging from 0.9 percent in Argentina to 2.3 percent in Chile), but the impact of these pensions in reducing poverty and indigence was considerable (Bertranou, Solorio, and van Ginneken 2002). Argentina's 2001–02 crisis reversed these improvements. It is estimated that poverty increased to 50 percent of the population and 22 percent of pensioners as a result (MTESS 2003).

The eight countries that do not currently provide special assistance through noncontributory pensions have low coverage (which is difficult to extend) and high poverty rates (ranging between 30 and 68 percent of the population). For instance, Bolivia's reform created a social assistance program (*Bonosol*) that would provide an annuity to citizens over the age of 65. It was financed by dividends from privatized companies, but it paid benefits for only a few months in 1997. It was later replaced by the *Bolivida,* which provided an annuity at the end of 2000. The *Bonosol* was reintroduced in 2002 and granted 420,000 benefits in 2003 (Mesa-Lago 2004). Although the pension reform laws in Costa Rica (2001), Ecuador (2001), and Colombia (2002) require the establishment by mid-2004 of a type of minimum pension, acting as a social safety net, they had not been implemented at the time of writing this chapter, and information was lacking about the effectiveness of this protection. Legislation in the Dominican Republic introduces a subsidized, noncontributory pension for those who are indigent, disabled, single mothers, or unemployed without income. Its implementation was planned for 2004 but has been postpone (LPT 2000; LDSS 2001; LSS 2001; LRP 2002). The World Bank now strongly supports a first pillar to help prevent poverty, managed by a public PAYG system that complements and does not distort or replace the private system (Gill, Packard, and Yermo 2005).

Regardless of the type or model, pension reforms should give priority to extending coverage to independent and other workers who are difficult to include. Social security systems must be adjusted to changes in the labor market, including developing new ways to incorporate informal workers. Because it is essential that priority be given to preventing poverty, countries should study how to provide minimum pensions for the elderly and poor, which would cost only a fraction of GDP.

Decline in Contributions

Most structural reforms have eliminated or reduced employer contributions and increased worker contributions. Argentina, Costa Rica, Ecuador, and Mexico did not legally change worker and employer contributions, but Argentina cut employer contributions by half through exemptions and bonuses; worker contributions were also reduced by half in 2001, although they began to increase in 2003. Costa Rica reassigned existing contributions to other programs. Ecuador raised contributions for workers with incomes over a certain amount, and Mexico increased the State's contribution based on payrolls. Bolivia, Chile, and Peru eliminated employer contributions, while Bolivia, Colombia, the Dominican Republic, El Salvador, Nicaragua, and Peru increased worker contributions. Uruguay slightly reduced employer contributions and proportionally increased that of the worker. The only countries to have increased employer contributions are Colombia, the Dominican Republic, and Nicaragua. In most countries, the elimination or reduction of employer contributions, to a large extent, has resulted in increased fiscal costs or worker contributions, or both (LPT 2000; LSAP 2000; LDSS 2001; LSS 2001; Mesa-Lago 2004).

It has been argued that ownership of the individual account and the equivalence principle of the private system (the relationship between contribution density and future pensions) will also stimulate prompt payment of contributions, given that the larger the contribution (and the return on the individual account), the larger the accumulated fund, and thus the pension (see the critique by Uthoff 2002). However, mandatory increases in worker contributions could create disincentives to participate. Based on the percentage of participants who were active contributors between 1998 and 2003, Table 2.4 suggests that disincentives have been stronger than the anticipated incentives. The lower the percentage in the table, the higher the rate of noncompliance in making contributions. With one exception, the trend toward noncompliance is evident in all countries. In 2003, compliance ranged from 33 percent in Argentina (the lowest because of the crisis) to 74 percent in Costa Rica (the highest, but this could be due to the way the contribution period is defined). The weighted average of participants in the nine countries that were active contributors decreased from 58 to 42 percent between 1998 and 2003; that is, 58 percent of participants did not actively contribute in 2003. In Chile, compliance declined steadily from 76 percent in 1983 to 49 percent in 2003. (SAFP 1983, 2003; Hujo 2004).

This shows that the incentives to increase contributions that were expected from the reform have not worked. Instead, total contributions have declined. It is clear that additional research into the causes of declining contributions is needed in order to design appropriate remedies. Also, policymakers must carefully evaluate the impact of eliminating or reducing employer contributions. Doing so may increase the finan-

Table 2.4	Percentage of Active Contributors to the Private Systems, 1998 to 2003[a]					
Model/Country	1998	1999	2000	2001	2002	2003
Substitutive						
Chile	52.8	53.4	50.9	53.7	51.0	49.1
Bolivia[b]	—	—	—	47.0	46.9	44.5
Mexico	63.4	60.2	57.9	44.7	41.7	40.6
El Salvador	67.2	63.7	55.2	53.2	47.6	45.0
Parallel						
Peru	45.6	45.7	41.7	41.2	39.4	39.2
Colombia	51.8	50.7	49.4	48.7	47.6	47.7
Mixed						
Argentina	48.9	44.3	39.1	29.0	33.2	33.5
Uruguay	67.4	58.7	53.9	53.2	45.1	52.7
Costa Rica[c]	n.a.	n.a.	n.a.	—	—	74.2
Average[d]	57.9	55.5	51.0	43.5	42.1	41.8

—Not available.

n.a. = not applicable.

[a] Participants who contributed in the last month (December), except Mexico in the last two months in 1998–2000; the year 2003 refers to June.

[b] Until 2001 a contributor was considered any participant who had made at least one contribution since the start of the system

[c] The system began in May 2001, and until 2002 a contributor was considered any participant who had made at least one contribution in the last year.

[d] Author's estimated average using the total participants and total contributors.

Sources: AIOS 1999 to 2003, except Colombia, which is SBC 1999 to 2003.

cial burden on participants (or the fiscal cost) and have adverse effects. However, it should be borne in mind that the public systems have also faced declining contributions. To a large extent, this has resulted from the growing share of the labor force that moved from the formal to the informal sector, as well as more flexible labor arrangements, the emergence of subcontracted employment, employment without a contract, and part-time work. Noncompliance increases to the extent that participants shift from covered formal employment to employment without coverage.

In addition, there is strong evidence that evasion of contributions and delinquency by employers have reached significant levels in some countries. For example, employer delinquency in Chile increased six-fold between 1990 and 2002, reaching $526 million, or 1 percent of the total value of the pension funds in 2004. Of this amount, 43 percent was uncollectible because employer companies had become bankrupt (Mesa-Lago 2004).

More effective measures are needed to reduce employer evasion and delinquency, including making it a crime, imposing severe penalties against violators, strengthening inspections, using electronic means for prompt detection of delinquent employers, and creating special courts that have jurisdiction over this problem as well as flexibility to deal with it. Costa Rica has the strictest and most comprehensive legislation on noncompliance and also the highest percentage of participants who have contributed only once. Collections take place in one of two ways: centralized or through the pension funds. Argentina, Costa Rica, the Dominican Republic, Ecuador, Mexico, and Uruguay follow the centralized model, whereas Bolivia, Chile, Colombia, El Salvador, Nicaragua, and Peru rely on the pension funds. However, there seems to be no relationship between the way in which collections are made and compliance. The World Bank has stated that, after gaining the right to a minimum pension, most participants stop contributing because they prefer other less risky, less costly, and less liquid alternatives such as homeownership, investing in a family business, purchasing life insurance, or investing in the education of their children (Gill, Packard and Yermo 2005). If this is the case, research into incentives and disincentives to change this behavior is required.

Serious Flaws in Competition among Pension Funds

A cornerstone of the private system is competition, which ends the public system's monopoly and encourages efficiency, thereby reducing administrative costs and increasing returns on investments. It is assumed

Table 2.5	Competition among Funds in the Private System, 2002–03		
Model/Country	Participants (thousands) 2003	Number of pension funds 2003	Participants in the three largest pension funds (%) 2002
Substitutive			
Chile	6,883	7[a]	79
Bolivia	809	2	100
Mexico	30,381	12	44
El Salvador	1,034	3[b]	100
Parallel			
Peru	3,100	4	76
Colombia	5,013	6	66
Mixed			
Argentina	9,275	12	57
Uruguay	626	4	87
Costa Rica	1,104	9	82

[a] Reduced to six in March 2004.
[b] One of the funds went bankrupt by the end of 2003.
Sources: Participants and number of pension funds from AIOS 2003 and SBC 2003; participants in the three largest funds from BCU 2002; CONSAR 2003; SAFJP 2003; SAFP 2003; SBC 2003; SBS 2003; SPa 2003; SPb 2003; SPVS 2003.

that pension funds compete for workers and that workers, in turn, have adequate information and experience to select the best funds (that is, those charging the lowest fees and paying the highest return), implying that the individual account and pension would be higher. However, there is evidence that, in most countries, competition does not work or works inadequately.

To a large extent, competition depends on the size of the labor market: the greater it is, the larger the number of pension funds, and vice versa.[11] However, Costa Rica has 1 million participants but nine managers, a higher number than all countries except Mexico and Argentina, which have 30 and 9 times the number of participants, respectively, and 12 funds each. This may be partially explained by the fact that Costa Rica, as well as Colombia and Uruguay, have several private funds instead of only one, and by the fact that the Costa Rican system has been in place for only a few years. There is historical evidence showing that the number of funds grows at the beginning of the reforms and shrinks thereafter as mergers take place. For example, the number of funds in Argentina

---

[11] The Bolivian Government allocated all the participants between two pension funds, using the place of residence of participants as the allocation criterion, and prohibited changing participation between funds until 2002.

fell from 25 to 12; in Chile, from 21 to 7; in Mexico, from 17 to 12; in Colombia, from 10 to 6; in Peru, from 8 to 4; in Uruguay, from 6 to 4, and in El Salvador, from 5 to 2 (Mesa-Lago 2004).

Countries with a relatively small number of workers or participants in the pension system should not adopt the pension systems that work in large countries because they run a high risk that competition, which is the cornerstone of the private system, will not work. Small countries must also decide whether or not to establish privately managed funds or a combination of public and private funds. Choosing the privately managed funds affords workers access to a greater number of options.

Another important consideration for small countries is that the funds must invest in their own infrastructure (buildings, equipment, personnel), which can be extremely costly. To reduce costs and encourage greater competition, it has been suggested that countries with a small number of participants in the system should consider having the funds use the infrastructure of other institutions, such as banks, insurance companies, or financial institutions. This would require prudence and the strict separation of activities. The Dominican Republic adopted this approach. By the end of 2002, it had six approved funds and another three whose applications were pending, despite the fact that there are relatively few participants in that country's pension system (Mesa-Lago 2004).

Excessive concentration may impede competition even in countries with a considerable number of funds. The last column in Table 2.5 shows that, by the end of 2002, participants were concentrated in the three largest funds in most countries. Mexico had the lowest concentration (44 percent), reflecting the fact it has legislated limits on the number of participants per pension fund.[12] It can be argued that if the three largest pension funds are the best, concentration is not a bad thing. But a study of reforms in Chile shows that over time, the three largest funds were not the ones that charged the lowest fees and produced the highest returns.

There are three reasons why participants chose the largest three pension funds. First, many lacked an understanding of the market and/or information to be able to make an informed choice. Second, they were influenced by advertising, which put forth an image of security and financial soundness without providing comparative information on fees and return on investment. Third, many were swayed by sales representatives or promoters, who had a vested interest in convincing participants to switch funds because they were paid on commission. However, the switch was not necessarily in the best interest of the pension fund participant.

---

[12] The limits are 17 percent during the first four years and 20 percent thereafter.

The World Bank found that the region's pension systems have serious shortcomings in the area of competition. One of those shortcomings is that the industry is an oligopoly with a captive clientele whose pension contributions are withheld until retirement. In addition, industry concentration is high and growing. This is a worrisome development and could be even more so in the future. Another shortcoming is that, in order to reduce operating costs, restrictions were placed on the number of times that a participant may change pension funds during the course of one year.[13] These restrictions have become institutionalized. As a result, what was previously a de facto oligopoly is clearly developing into a powerful cartel. Moreover, evidence from Latin America clearly shows that competition among pension funds for relatively small portions of the market only generates higher fees. Finally, the pension fund industry in the region is anything but a good example of competition (Gill, Packard, and Yermo 2005).

This analysis implies that it is essential that market regulators play a more active role in encouraging competition in the pension funds market, reducing barriers to entry, and fostering the creation of new funds, as well as strictly regulating promoters' activities and establishing standards regarding truth in advertising. Both the regulator and the pension fund associations must commit more resources to improving information and making it understandable to potential participants. They must also publicize a ranking of funds according to their fees and net returns. Making this type of information public would allow participants to make informed and rational decisions. Reducing concentration through a limit on the percentage of participants per fund, as in Mexico, should also be studied.

High Administrative Costs

It is assumed that competition reduces the costs of administering pension funds, but this has not been the experience in many countries that lack adequate competition. Administrative costs have two components (fees and premiums), which are usually calculated as a percentage of wages (plus a fixed amount in some cases). In other cases, they are based on the individual account balance or return. Individual accounts, in-

---

[13] In Bolivia, Costa Rica, the Dominican Republic, El Salvador, Mexico, and Nicaragua, the switch can only take place once a year, while in three other countries it can take place twice a year. The countries with the greatest opportunities to switch among pension funds are Chile and Peru.

vestment funds, and old age pensions are financed through fees paid by participants (except in Colombia, where the employer shares the cost). A portion of the fee is the premium, which is transferred by the fund manager to a private insurance company to protect against the risks of disability and death (except in Mexico and Colombia, where the public system provides this protection).

Table 2.6 shows administrative costs (fee plus premium) as a percentage of wages. The comparison is complex because there may be a number of fees that are difficult to combine into one average. The lowest administrative cost is in the Dominican Republic, at 2 percent. However, in addition to the percentage that appears on the table, participants are also charged an amount that can reach up to 30 percent of the return, plus another 0.1 percent that goes to the regulator (LDSS 2001). Even without taking these additional charges into account, administrative costs in the Dominican Republic are among the highest as a percentage of total deductions from wages or deposits in individual accounts. At 2.21 percent, administrative costs in Bolivia are the second lowest. Low administrative costs in Bolivia can be explained by the lack of competition, which means that there are no advertising expenses. The pension fund fee is only 0.5 percent, but the premium of 1.71 percent is the second highest. The highest total costs are in Colombia (a 1.92 percent fee and a 1.58 percent premium). There is no percentage charged on wages in Costa Rica, but a fee ranging between 6 and 10 percent is calculated on the fund's investment return, to create an incentive for the pension funds to improve the returns. In El Salvador, the administrative cost of the public system before the reform (as a percentage of wages) was 0.5 percent. In 2003, establishment of the private pension system pushed it to 2.98 percent (Mesa-Lago 2004).

Fees and premiums have shown a number of trends over time. The fee ranges between 1.45 percent and 2.27 percent (except in Bolivia and the Dominican Republic) and is the major component of administrative costs. While the fee has varied over time, it has not exhibited a downward trend in the majority of countries. The premium fluctuates between 0.67 percent and 1.27 percent (except in Bolivia and Colombia). It is the lesser component and has decreased in almost every country. Thus fees represent a major portion of the total cost. The fact that they have not decreased significantly is one of the biggest challenges facing future structural reforms in the region. In Chile, after 22 years of reform, the fee as a percentage of total costs increased from 2.44 percent in 1981 to 3.6 percent in 1984, and then dropped to 2.26 percent in 2003 (Acuña and Iglesias 2001).

Table 2.6	Administrative Costs as a Percentage of Wages in the Private Pension System, 2003				
Model/ Country	Deposit in individual account as a % of wages	Administrative costs (fee plus premium)[a]	Total deduction from wages	Administrative costs as a % of	
				Total deduction from wages	Deposit in individual account
Substitutive					
Chile	10.00	2.26	12.26	18.43	22.60
Bolivia	10.00	2.21	12.21	18.10	22.10
Mexico	6.78	4.14	10.92	37.91	61.06
El Salvador	11.02	2.98	14.00	21.28	27.04
Dominican Rep.[b]	5.00	2.00	7.00	28.57	40.00
Nicaragua	7.50	3.00	10.50	28.57	40.00
Parallel					
Peru	8.00	3.51	11.51	30.50	43.88
Colombia	10.00	3.50[c]	13.50[c]	25.93	35.00
Mixed					
Argentina	4.75	2.25	7.00	32.10	47.37
Uruguay	12.19	2.81	15.00	18.73	23.05
Costa Rica	4.50	n.a.[d]	n.a.	n.a.	n.a.
Average[e]	8.52	2.87	11.39	26.00	36.21

n.a. Not applicable.

[a] Fee for the manager of the pension system and premium for the insurance company that covers death and disability risks (the latter paid to the public system in Colombia and Mexico).

[b] In addition to the cost shown, there is a 30 percent charge calculated on the surplus of the annual return on investment. The percentage for the individual account will gradually increase over five years to 8 percent, while administrative costs will not change. The total deduction will increase to 10 percent and the costs as a percent of the deduction will be reduced to 20 percent.

[c] The 0.5 percent goes to the Minimum Pension Guarantee Fund. The total deduction will be increased to 1 percent in 2004 for this fund and 1 percent more in 2005–06 for the individual account, for a total of 15.5 percent. It may be increased another 1 percent in 2008, if the economy grows.

[d] The administrative cost is not a proportion of wages but a percentage is calculated on the gross return on investment.

[e] Unweighted average of 10 countries (excludes Costa Rica).

Sources: AIOS 2003; except Colombia, based on SBC 2003; and Nicaragua and the Dominican Republic, based on LDSS 2001 and LSAP 2000. Average calculated by the author.

In mid-2003, the lowest administrative costs as a percentage of the total deduction on wages were in Bolivia, Chile, and Uruguay (in the neighborhood of 18 percent). The highest were in Mexico. In 2003, the unweighted average of administrative costs as a percentage of the total deduction in the 11 countries was 26 percent (next to last column). However, calculating administrative costs as a percent of deposits, the average charge increased to 36 percent (last column). Existing projections indicate that many participants will not be able to save sufficiently to finance their pensions, and that this problem is closely related to the high administrative costs. If administrative costs were reduced, pension participants would be able to invest a higher percentage and increase the value of the accumulated personal account at retirement, minimizing the cost of financing minimum pensions and hence lowering the fiscal burden (Uthoff 2002). Some supporters of structural pension reforms now recognize that administrative costs are high and that competition by itself (even when it works) does not ensure that costs will be reduced (Holzmann and Stiglitz 2001; Gill, Packard, and Yermo 2005). Marketing, advertising, and sales representatives' fees make up the bulk of administrative fees.

Although making administrative costs a percentage of payroll does not create incentives to lower costs, there are other options. Bolivia and the Dominican Republic, for example, have established ceilings on costs. If this proves to be an adequate alternative, the ceiling could be adjusted when it proves inadequate as an incentive. Another option for keeping costs low is to set them as a percentage of the individual account balance or the return on investment.[14] Regardless of the alternative followed, the regulator must ensure that the savings resulting from lower operating expenses are passed on to participants in the form of lower fees.

Growth in Pension Assets but not in Domestic Savings

It had been expected that structural pension reforms would result in a greater accumulation of savings in the pension fund investment accounts, and that this would lead to increased national savings (World Bank 1994). Table 2.7 shows that savings did grow, but with notable differences among countries.

The cumulative amount of fund assets in each country vary according to how long the system has been in place, the number of participants in the system, the size of the economy, the level of wages, and the return on investment. The Chilean reform was implemented 22 years ago, and not surprisingly, its pension investments are the largest. Yet while the Mexican reforms have been in place for only some five years, pension fund investments there are also large (reaching 88 percent of the Chilean fund).[15] The size of Mexico's fund reflects the fact that Mexico has the

---

[14] A study of Costa Rica's experience in this regard would be useful.

[15] The pension fund with the highest accumulated balance in Latin America is Brazil's, which reached $80 billion in 2003 (18 percent of GDP), although it is a voluntary complementary pension fund. This is explained by the fact that Brazil is the region's second largest economy and that both employers and employees contribute to the fund.

Table 2.7	Cumulative Fund Assets and Real Gross Returns on Investment, 2003		
Model/ Country	Cumulative fund assets, June 2003		Average real annual return on investment (%)[b]
	$ millions	% of GDP[a]	
Substitutive			
Chile	39,672	60.6	10.30
Bolivia	1,261	17.2	17.10
Mexico	34,963	5.6	10.40[c]
El Salvador	1,309	9.2	10.86[d]
Parallel			
Peru	4,541	8.2	6.57
Colombia	5,350[e]	6.2[e]	7.33
Mixed			
Argentina	15,607	15.6	10.45
Uruguay	1,149	12.7	15.00
Costa Rica	218	1.4	7.00

[a] The percentage of the cumulative fund to GDP depends not only on the amount accumulated but also on the size of GDP.

[b] From the start of the system until the end of 2002.

[c] CONSAR reports a net return of 7.95 percent.

[d] The author has estimated 8.36 percent, based on the nominal return and the annual average inflation rate.

[e] December 2002.

Sources: Accumulation and percentage of GDP from AIOS 2003 and author's estimates for Colombia based on SBC 2002; BCU 2002; CONSAR 2003; SAFJP 2003; SAFP 2003; SBC 2002; SBS 2002; SPa 2003; SPb 2002; SPVS 2003.

greatest number of participants in the region and that it is the largest economy in Latin America. Similarly, another large regional economy, Argentina, had the second highest number of participants in the region. In 2001 its pension assets reached 60 percent of Chile, despite the fact that its reform was, at the time, only about eight years old. However, by 2003, following the Argentine crisis, assets dropped to 39 percent of Chile's.

While these figures detail the accumulation of assets in individual pension accounts, they do not reflect the fiscal cost of the transition. In 1994, the World Bank maintained that structural pension reform would increase national savings, which in turn would boost economic growth, promote employment, and ultimately lead to more robust pensions. Chile is the only country where reforms have been in place long enough to test this assumption. Unfortunately, most of the studies reviewed for this chapter reach negative conclusions about the World Bank's hypothesis. Holzmann (1997), in a general equilibrium econometric exercise, deducted the reform's fiscal cost (negative) from the savings in private pensions (positive) and concluded that between 1981 and 1988 the reform had a negative impact on national savings. Moreover, he was unable to prove a positive direct impact for the period 1989–96, and advised Latin American countries against entertaining high expectations that the reforms would increase national savings.

Arenas de Mesa (1999) followed a similar methodology, but used a partial equilibrium analysis to measure factors and results in annual percentages of GDP between 1981 and 1997. He concluded that the capitalized savings in the individual pension accounts averaged 2.7 percent for the period, but that the fiscal cost averaged −5.7 percent, so that the average net result was −3.0 percent, a negative savings. However, Arenas de Mesa projected that, during the first five years of the 21st century, the situation would change and savings would be slightly higher than fiscal costs. This implies that the net impact will be positive and continue to grow, but it will probably take 20 years to offset the negative impacts of the first 20 years, meaning that it takes 40 years to achieve a net positive impact on national savings.

Acuña and Iglesias (2001) subtracted the "temporary social security pension deficit" from private pension savings (but excluded the deficit caused by assistance pensions, minimum pensions, and those of the armed forces). They also calculated an average negative net result between 1982 and 1997 (−2.7 percent), somewhat lower than that of Arenas de Mesa, who included all the fiscal costs of the reform.

Haindl Rondanelli (1997) concluded that reforms had a positive impact on national savings between 1990 and 1994, but based this conclusion on the general tax burden instead of the direct fiscal cost of the reform. If he had deducted the average cost of the public system deficit of −4.6 percent from the average private pension savings of 3.1 percent, he would also have obtained a negative result of −1.5 percent. Moreover this would not include other fiscal costs of the reforms.

Corbo and Schmidt-Hebbel (2003), taking into account only the operating deficit and the recognition bonds[16] and excluding the minimum pension, the armed forces' deficit, and the assistance pensions, estimated that national savings increased as a result of the reform, by 2.3 percent of GDP between 1981 and 2001 (for other opinions, see Kiefer 2004).

Although an increase in national savings would be desirable, it should not be a central objective of structural reform since, to date, there has been no solid empirical evidence to support that effect.

---

[16] Recognition bonds are like a compensatory benefit equal to the value of the contributions made before the reform.

Significant Long-Term Fiscal Cost of the Transition

Another expected result of reform is that it would gradually reduce or eliminate the fiscal cost in the long-term. This cost is difficult to measure and compare across countries because of the various components included and the methodologies used. Gross estimates as a percentage of 2000 GDP placed the cost at 6 percent in Chile (after 20 years of reform), 4.5 percent in Argentina and Uruguay, 2 percent in Bolivia, and 1.5 percent in Colombia. Figures for Mexico and Peru were unavailable (Mesa-Lago 2004). The World Bank has projected a fiscal cost in 2040 for Argentina, Bolivia, and Colombia much higher than the projections made by the countries before the reforms. For Mexico and Peru, the World Bank's projections indicate that the fiscal cost will grow between 2001 and 2040. Uruguay is the only country in which the World Bank's projections for 2040 are less than the national ones before the reform (Gill, Packard, and Yermo 2005). Each country has enacted different policies to deal with the fiscal cost. Chile took appropriate measures so that there was a fiscal surplus before the reform, and its economic policies have been mostly successful in the long term. Argentina, however, had no contingency plan. The country's projection of fiscal costs fell woefully short of actual costs, and its economic policies triggered the crisis of 2001–02.

There are three components of fiscal costs during transition periods: the public sector deficit, the recognition bonds, and the minimum pensions (see Table 2.8). All three, with a few exceptions, are financed by the government. Moreover, in some countries, the government provides certain guarantees and social assistance pensions that further increase fiscal costs (Mesa-Lago 2000). Since this section refers to legal rather than statistical aspects, the data provided are on the 12 countries that have enacted reforms.

Costa Rica is the only country in which the government does not have to pay the public pension system deficit; there is no deficit, as collective partial capitalization is sufficiently strong to cover costs. This fiscal burden varies according to the implicit pension debt: that is, the present value of long-term obligations, which include the payment of current and future pensions. Social security systems (PAYG) and collective pension programs contain an implicit pension debt, but the reform model can make this debt explicit, thereby generating a fiscal cost that could be either partially deferred or paid in full.

In the substitutive model, the public system is completely terminated and all implicit pension debt (IPD) is immediately made explicit; consequently, current pensions and those generated by the few workers

| Table 2.8 | Fiscal Costs of the Reform, 2004 |

Model/ Country	Financial responsibilities of the government		
	Covers public system deficit	Pays recognition bond	Guarantees minimum pension
Substitutive			
Chile	Yes	No ceiling, adjusted to inflation, earns 4 percent annual real interest, requires prior contribution	Yes
Bolivia	Yes	Has ceiling, adjustable, unclear if earns real interest, requires one month prior contribution	Yes
Mexico	Yes	No	Yes
El Salvador	Yes	No ceiling, not adjustable, earns real interest equal to inflation, requires prior contribution	Yes
Nicaragua	Yes	No ceiling, not adjustable, earns no interest, requires one year prior contribution	Yes
Dominican Rep.	Yes	No ceiling, adjustable, earns 2 percent real interest, requires prior contribution	Yes
Parallel			
Peru	Yes	Has ceiling, adjustable, earns no interest, requires 4 years of prior contributions	No. As of 2002, paid only to participants
Colombia	Yes	Has ceiling, adjustable, earns 3 percent real interest, requires 3 years of prior contributions	Yes (with restrictions)
Mixed			
Argentina	Yes	No ceiling, adjustable, earns no interest, requires 30 years of prior contributions (paid by first pillar-public system)	Yes (paid by first pillar-public system)
Uruguay	Yes	No	Yes (paid by first pillar-public system)
Costa Rica	No	No	Yes (paid by first pillar-public system)
Ecuador	Yes	No	Yes (paid by first pillar-public system)

Source: Legislation of the 12 countries.

remaining in the public system must be financed by the government. This is because 100 percent of participants (Bolivia and Mexico) or 91 to 98 percent of them (El Salvador and Chile, respectively) moved to the private system and stopped contributing to the public system. Thus the public systems were left with most of the pensions but with few or no contributors, and this generated a deficit.

In the parallel model, the implicit pension debt is made explicit in the private system, but not in the public system, whose implicit pension debt is deferred. Since the public system is left with contributing participants (for example, in Colombia and Peru), the fiscal cost is reduced, at least for a period of time. In the mixed model, the implicit pension debt is made partially explicit in the second pillar (private system) but not in the first pillar (public system) in which it is deferred.

In eight of the twelve countries, the government must pay a recognition bond to participants who switch to the private system. Costa Rica, Ecuador, Mexico, and Uruguay do not provide the bond. In Costa Rica, Ecuador, and Uruguay, following the mixed model, the participants of the public pillar remain in the first pillar, which pays them a basic pension. In Peru, a recognition bond was given to half the participants that had transferred, while in El Salvador, it was delayed five years (Mesa-Lago 2004).

In ten of the twelve countries, the government guarantees a minimum pension for participants in the private system if their capitalized contributions are less than the minimum pension. The Treasury must pay the difference. A minimum number of years of contribution (between 20 and 35 years) is required to qualify for the minimum pension. Bolivia does not provide a minimum pension. Since 2002, Peru has provided a minimum pension to participants in the private system. El Salvador imposes considerable restrictions on eligibility for the minimum pension (Mesa-Lago 2004).

In Argentina, Chile, Colombia, and Uruguay, the government offers two more guarantees. First, if a pension fund is unable to guarantee a minimum return for the individual account, the government makes up the difference in the minimum return. Second, in the event that a pension fund goes bankrupt, the government assumes responsibility for payment of the pensions. In Uruguay, these guarantees are given only to participants in the public pension system of the state-owned bank, Banco República, which to some extent explains why it has 38 percent of total participants. In the Dominican Republic, the law makes the government liable for any failure or noncompliance that occurs in the private system.

Every country faces a dilemma regarding fiscal costs. Governments have attempted to reduce these costs by not providing recognition bonds or minimum pensions, or providing them with restrictions (such as establishing a ceiling, requiring prior contributions, and excluding any adjustments for inflation). These restrictions have been introduced in the region since the Chilean reform. However, reducing fiscal costs in this manner has an adverse impact on retirees' pensions. Chile has had the most generous transitional benefits, but with the highest fiscal costs. Bolivia has had the lowest costs but, along with Peru, the most restricted benefits.

The fiscal costs of the transition period, as well as the present value of long-term obligations, must be projected carefully and professionally. This is particularly important since the transition period may span 40 to 70 years. The projections should be submitted to an outside actuary and published so that national experts and international agencies may examine them. A basic condition for the success of structural reforms is significant fiscal tightening, especially for governments that are already fiscally weak. Fiscal discipline and a budgetary surplus, or at least fiscal equilibrium, are preconditions for the financial sustainability of structural pension reform. To support the reforms, financial, banking, tax, and insurance reforms must be implemented in parallel. Sources of financing for fiscal costs must be identified and sound economic policies put in place. Finally, the impact of the fiscal cost on income distribution must be thoroughly investigated.

Potential for Financial Markets Development but Inadequate Portfolio Diversification

The pension reforms were supposed to contribute to the development of the securities market by creating new financial instruments and diversifying the fund's investment portfolio in order to offset risks. Holzmann's study on Chile (1997) concluded that pension reform had helped financial markets become more liquid and mature and that empirical evidence coincided with the assumption that reform had contributed to development and portfolio diversification. Nevertheless, he warned that the evidence was not proof that pension reforms had been the decisive factor in the development of these markets since the mid-1980s and that there might have been other factors unrelated to the reforms. The World Bank also maintains that market deepening may be partially attributable to pension reform. However, in countries such as Chile, where parallel macroeconomic reforms have occurred, it is extremely difficult to isolate the impact of specific reforms (Gill, Packard, and Yermo 2005). On the contrary, Corbo and Schmidt-Hebbel (2003) maintain that the contribution of pension funds to the development of Chile's financial markets was quite robust, and recommend the most radical structural reform possible, to maximize this effect.

There is an old debate about whether or not a securities market is a necessary precondition to structural reform, since it will have a positive impact on the development of such a market. Although this dispute cannot be resolved here, the fact is that small countries such as Bolivia, Costa Rica, El Salvador, and Uruguay had no securities markets before the reform, or the markets were small and incipient as well as highly concentrated, with few investment instruments. For instance, El Salvador promulgated a law creating and regulating the securities market just before beginning the reform. For the most part it is these countries that have the least portfolio diversification.

In mid-2003, the percentage composition of the portfolio by instrument indicates that the majority of countries are very far from achieving sufficient diversification (Table 2.9). In Uruguay, Bolivia, Argentina, El Salvador, Mexico, and Costa Rica, from 57 percent to 90 percent of each country's portfolio is in government bonds. Government bonds represent a minority share only in Peru and Chile. It should be noted that it took Chile 17 years to reduce that share from 46 percent to the current 29 percent, thanks largely to the actions of the regulator. The bulk of investments in most countries in the region are in government instruments. If these have produced good returns, it is because governments have paid high interest on debt securities, as in the case of Argentina until late 2001. However, this is costly for the economy, unsustainable in the long term, and risky.[17] Argentina is a case in point, when the economic crisis and currency devaluation caused a drastic reduction in the value of pension funds in 2002. An increased concentration in government debt ensued. The regulator took an active role, cooperating with the government through 2001, so that pension fund managers would agree to convert dollar-denominated instruments tradable on international markets into "guaranteed loans" with a lower interest rate. Moreover, subsequent government decrees forced pension funds to invest the proceeds of bank certificates of deposit and cash into debt paper. In 2002, the government converted the "guaranteed loans" into pesos, and the subsequent devaluation reduced the value of pension fund portfolios considerably (ILO 2002a; Hujo 2004).

Stocks are one of the favorite instruments for portfolio diversification. If the securities market is sufficiently developed, there are numerous stocks in which to invest. But only Argentina, Chile, and Peru have between 8 percent and 31 percent of the portfolio invested in stocks. In El Salvador and Colombia, equity investment is 0.4 percent and 2.9 percent, respectively. If there is insufficient potential for investment in domestic markets, an alternative is to invest in foreign instruments. However, this is prohibited in some countries. Chile invests 20 percent in foreign in-

---

[17] In El Salvador, the real return decreased from 14 percent in 1999 to 2.4 percent in 2002, mainly because of the dollarization of the economy and the reduction of the rate of interest paid by the government (Mesa-Lago 2004).

Table 2.9 Portfolio Distribution by Financial Instrument, 2003
(percent)

Model/Country	Government bonds	Financial institutions	Nonfinancial institutions	Stocks	Mutual funds and others	Foreign issuers	Other
Substitutive							
Chile	29.1	30.4	7.2	10.9	2.4	19.9	0.2
Bolivia	68.1	10.3	19.0	0.0	0.0	1.2	1.4
Mexico	85.4	3.4	11.3	0.0	0.0	0.0	0.0
El Salvador	84.0	12.0	3.6	0.4	0.0	0.0	0.0
Parallel							
Peru	13.0	33.2	13.1	31.2	0.8	7.2	1.6
Colombia	49.4	26.6	16.6	2.9	0.0	4.5	0.0
Mixed							
Argentina	75.9	3.5	1.3	8.2	1.6	8.3	1.1
Uruguay	57.2	37.1	3.4	0.0	0.0	0.0	2.3
Costa Rica	89.5	5.1	4.7	0.0	0.7	0.0	0.0
Average[a]	57.4	16.2	8.0	7.1	1.3	9.7	0.4

[a] Excludes Colombia.
Source: AIOS 2003, except Colombia, from SBC 2003.

struments; Bolivia, Colombia, Peru and Argentina, between 1 percent and 8 percent; and the remaining countries, zero.

Small countries with incipient capital markets must reinforce and consolidate these markets before undertaking pension reforms. It is essential to develop a securities market, regulate it, generate confidence in it, create new domestic instruments, and allow investments in foreign instruments. Countries that plan to invest pension funds primarily in government debt securities with the risk of default should not undertake structural reform because the risk would be ruinous for the private system. The regulator must play an independent and crucial role in fostering portfolio diversification, in collaboration with agencies that oversee the securities markets. Chile has had a positive experience and Argentina, a negative one.

Net Real Return on Investment

Another expectation of the pension reforms was that it would produce a higher return on investment. Statistics support this, although results vary by country and also according to the period used for calculation. Table 2.7 (page 63) shows average real annual returns adjusted for inflation from the start of the system until late 2002. These returns are gross: that is, without deducting the cost of fees. The net returns are considerably lower. For instance, in the case of Mexico, gross returns are 10.4 percent, while net returns are 7.95 percent. Between 1981 and 2000, the gross return on pension fund investments in Chile averaged 11.9 percentage points less than the return of the Selective Stock Price Index (or IPSA, in Spanish) of the Santiago stock exchange and 3.8 points more than the average interest rate on deposits, but with much higher volatility (Acuña and Iglesias 2001). Between 1993 and 2000, Peruvian pension funds averaged a lower return than interest on bank deposits and Brady bonds (Gill, Packard, and Yermo 2005).

These figures are averages for the entire time the reform has been in place. If the period up to the mid-1990s is considered, the average is much higher. Since 1995, it has been much lower, as a consequence of the economic and stock market crises of 1995, 1998, and 2001. For example, returns in Chile averaged 13.8 percent in 1981–94, compared with 4.4 percent in 1995–2002. Rates of return were negative in 1995 (–2.5 percent) and 1998 (–1.1 percent) (SAFP 2002, 2003). In Argentina, the average was 19.7 percent in 1994–97, compared with 7.2 percent from mid-1997 to mid-2001. Rates were negative from December 2000 to December 2001 (–13.7 percent) (SAFJP 2001, 2003). These fluctuations in return involve significant risk. If participants retire at the time of the stock market boom, their pensions will be good, but the funds accrued in their individual accounts may decrease considerably during a crisis and even more if the crisis is prolonged (as in Argentina in 2001–02).

The risk explained above is reduced in mixed models because they combine two systems: one with guaranteed defined benefits, and the other with undefined benefits. More time and research are needed to prove this point. In any event, it is evident that adequate portfolio diversification is necessary in both public and private pension systems. The portfolio diversification measures suggested in the previous section would pave the way toward reducing dependence of the fund's return on government bond interest rates, as well as doing a better job of offsetting risks.

Unclear Whether the Private Pension is Larger than that of the Public System

Pension reforms promised that the private system would pay better pensions than the public social security systems. However, it is difficult to verify this important effect because of the lack of up-to-date, statistical series comparing the two systems. Two Chilean experts make this point in a work in circulation in late 2001: "The latest information published by the regulator of the pension funds was dated June 1992," which was almost ten years old at that time (Acuña and Iglesias 2001, p. 27). They indicated that the average private pension compared with the average public pension was 43 percent higher than social security, 68 percent higher for disability, 42 percent higher for surviving spouse benefits, and 9 percent lower for surviving children benefits. However, these figures are contradicted by the statistics for average private pensions (March 2002) compared with average public pensions (December 2001), which show that old age pensions (which represent 63 percent of all pensions) were 24 percent less than the public ones; disability pensions (7 percent of the total) were 15 percent higher; survivors pensions (28 percent of the total) were 110 percent higher; and the weighted average of all private pensions was only 3 percent higher than the average for public ones (based on INP 2001; SAFP 2002).

In Argentina, the statistical publications of the pensions regulator do not include figures on the amount of the pensions in the private system. Furthermore, the changes introduced during the 2001–02 crisis (halving contributions, converting financial instruments from dollars into devalued pesos) are projected to reduce the pension of the average beneficiaries with 30 years of contributions by about 65 percent (ILO 2002a).

In Colombia, public pensions have a higher rate of return on capital than the private system, which is one of the reasons that most participants remain in the public system (Kleinjans 2004).

It is premature to predict whether future private pensions will be higher than public pensions because the private system is immature. (For example, by 2002 only 20 percent of the total pensions had been paid in Chile, the country with the longest standing reform.) The replacement rate of the closed public system is relatively easy to determine since it is based on a defined benefit. (It is estimated that this rate ranged from 61 percent to 80 percent in 2000 in Chile.) It is much more difficult to determine the future replacement rate in the private system, since this will depend on several variables: age at job entry, the growth rate of wages, the density of contributions, and the pension fund's rate of return. Simulations made in Chile and based on a number of assumptions about these variables show an enormous difference in results (Bertranou and Arenas de Mesa 2003). Furthermore, lifetime pension income in 1988–2001 showed substantial annual variations because of different replacement rates obtained by each cohort, caused by interest rate volatility in this period (Gill, Packard, and Yermo 2005).

In Chile, beneficiaries of the minimum pension in 2000 represented 43 percent of total pensioners in the two systems. The minimum pension averaged 70 percent of minimum wages and 24 percent of average compensation in the private system. The two percentages declined from 1990 to 2000. It is estimated that approximately half the private system participants (35 percent of men and 60 percent of women) will receive a minimum pension (Arenas de Mesa and Hernández Sánchez 2001). Surveys taken in Argentina in 2001 indicate that 33 percent of working-age men and 45 percent of working-age women had little or no expectation that they could meet the requirements for obtaining a minimum pension (Bertranou and Arenas de Mesa 2003). Based on surveys of the metropolitan areas of Santiago and Lima in 2000, the World Bank estimated that 30 percent of men and 50 percent of women participants in Chile do not meet the requirements for receiving a minimum pension. In Peru, the respective proportions are 30 percent and 60 percent, but with a wider gap to gain access than in Chile (Gill, Packard, and Yermo 2005). These percentages would be higher if the survey had been nationwide and included rural areas and smaller urban areas. Historical statistics comparing the averages for private and public pensions and broken down by category should be compiled and published. In addition, comparative research is needed on the replacement rates of the private and public systems.

Increase in Gender Inequality

Structural pension reforms have accentuated gender inequality. There is evidence from several countries that women have less social security coverage than men, and that their pensions are lower for both external and internal reasons. The external causes pertain to the characteristics of women's job: a lower labor force participation rate and a higher unemployment rate than men, wage discrimination, a greater proportion of work in unskilled jobs (domestic service, the informal sector, part-time work, and independent work, at home and without a contract). Furthermore, these jobs pay low wages and are usually not covered by social insurance. As a result, women's' contributions are lower than those of men. In addition, women live between four and five years longer than men, so they will require pension coverage for a longer period (Bertranou and Arenas de Mesa 2003; Mesa-Lago 2004).

The causes of gender inequality stemming from the social security system are found in both the public and private systems. A common problem of both systems is that women frequently retire at an earlier age than men (for example, five years earlier in five private systems). Combined with their longer life expectancy, women live on pensions an average of between 9 and 10 years more than men. The private systems accentuate gender inequality for three reasons. First, they require a minimum number of contributions to receive the minimum pension (for example, 20 years in Chile and 25 in El Salvador). Most reforms have increased the number of years of contribution required to obtain the pension (for example, from 15 to 25–30 years in the Dominican Republic), making it even more difficult for women to access this pension. Second, pension benefits are based on an entire active working life, instead of the final years, as in the public systems. This places women at a disadvantage because their contribution density is lower than that of men. Third, private systems rely on mortality tables that are differentiated by gender (in life annuities and in scheduled withdrawals). Because the accumulated sum in the individual account is divided by the average life expectancy, women's pensions are less than those of men, and even less if they retire early. (There is an offset for married women whose life annuities take into account their spouse's expected lifespan.)

It is argued that this treatment is fairer because it avoids subsidies between the sexes. However, it overlooks the fact that women, as a group, pay the cost of raising children, since Latin American pension systems do not provide credits for this work. (Legislation in Chile before the reform gave women one year of credit for each living child.) One positive measure of the reforms has been the enactment of the same normal retirement age for both sexes in seven countries (Bolivia, Costa Rica, Dominican Republic, Ecuador, Mexico, Nicaragua, and Uruguay). This encourages women to accumulate more contributions and a larger fund in their individual accounts, which is to be distributed in a retirement period reduced by five years. But this does not compensate women for their longer life expectancy.

The combined impact of the factors mentioned above on gender is evident in Chile. In 2001–02, the accumulated pension fund in a woman's individual account was between 32 and 46 percent of that accumulated in a man's pension fund. Also, the replacement rate for a female was between 52 and 57 percent, while that of a man was between 81 and 86 percent. Finally, the average pension for a woman who retired at age 60 was about 60 percent that of a man's, while if she retired at age 65 it was 87 percent (SAFP 2002; Bertranou and Arenas de Mesa 2003). A World Bank study concludes: "Women continue to earn lower rates of return than men in all countries that adopted the reform" (Gill, Packard, and Yermo 2005, pp. 62–64). Theoretically, the mixed systems would tend to compensate more for gender inequality than substitutive systems because the public first pillar would lessen this inequality, while the private second pillar would accentuate it (with variance determined by the importance of the two pillars). In Costa Rica, the compensatory effect would be greater than in other countries because the pension paid by the first pillar is the fundamental one and that of the second pillar is complementary. The opposite would occur in Argentina.

Policies to reduce gender inequality must address its causes. With regard to the external causes, suggested policies are encouraging productive and stable employment for women; ensuring more investment nationwide in company training of women; providing insurance coverage for occupations in which women are concentrated (domestic service, independent work); rigorously applying the "equal pay for equal work" principle; enforcing maternity leave and unemployment insurance (where this exists) and the payment of their contributions into the social security system during the leave period or compensation; and allowing women to reduce the pre-partum portion of maternity leave and lengthen the post-partum leave to provide more time to care for newborns. Other policies include the introduction of mandatory childcare at companies of a certain size or a public program set up with low fees and tax support. As for internal causes of inequality, two policy recommendations are standardizing the normal retirement age in those countries in which it still varies by gender, making women's retirement age increase gradually; and allowing early retirement at an actuarially calculated, lower pension.

Disappearance or Erosion of Solidarity

The solidarity principle is replaced in the private system by a principle of strict equivalence between the contribution and pension levels. This reproduces the existing inequalities of the labor market and wages and eliminates distribution between generations. It also restricts the redistribution and/or solidarity function to the government (external to the private pension system) through the guarantee of a minimum pension and through the provision of noncontributory assistance pensions.

The reforms have introduced or maintained redistributive mechanisms that are largely regressive. For instance, participants in separate programs like the armed forces (in virtually all countries) and civil servants (in some countries) do not contribute to the general system. These individuals generally have medium and high incomes and enjoy generous benefits and tax subsidies. Also, coverage remains low in the majority of countries for self-employed workers and other low-income groups in the informal sector, as well as the poor. Gender inequalities have increased. Employer contributions have been eliminated, while worker contributions have been increased. The tax reduction for high-income workers remains proportionately more powerful. Taxes on their accounts are deferred until the time of retirement (like all workers) but the tax benefit is greater because of their larger income. Administrative costs remain very high and are financed exclusively by participants. This generates a profit for pension funds but reduces the amount credited to the individual accounts—and thus to future pensions. This hits low-income workers hardest.

Moreover, pension funds charge flat fees, which take a higher proportion of the contributions of low-income workers than from those of high-income workers, resulting in proportionally larger reductions in the amounts credited to the individual accounts and thus lowering the pensions of low-income workers. Intergenerational inequalities have been created because the oldest participants have subsidized the younger participants by bearing the high cost of installing the new system. The fiscal cost of the transition implies a transfer to medium- and high-income workers, financed by taxes that are often imposed on consumption and paid by the entire population, including nonparticipants. This effect is aggravated as coverage declines (Arenas de Mesa 1999; SAFP 2002; Uthoff 2002; Gill, Packard, and Yermo 2005; Kiefer 2004; Mesa-Lago 2004).

The alleged solidarity aspects and progressive redistributive effects of the private system are usually exogenous to it. The minimum pension, guaranteed by the government and financed by taxes, does not produce redistribution among the participants in the private system but among taxpayers and workers that do not meet the entrance requirements. A large portion of those currently participating will receive the minimum pension. Moreover, usually it will not be adjusted to the cost of living. The assistance pension, which is also the government's responsibility, will be provided only in one-third of the countries with structural reform. It has a progressive impact in reducing poverty. However, it is not financed by the participants of the private system but by the entire population.

The lack of solidarity in private systems is evident from the distribution of Chile's fiscal costs related to the social security pension system. In 1981–2000, the average cost was 5.7 percent of annual GDP. Some 5.3 percent was allocated to cover the cost of the transition (operating deficit, recognition bond, and minimum pension) and only 0.4 percent for assistance pensions (Arenas de Mesa and Benavides 2003). There are two significant exceptions in the region. In Colombia, a participant whose wages are four times higher than the minimum pays a contribution of 1 percent to the Solidarity Pension Fund. There is an additional contribution of from 0.2 percent to 1 percent as income increases from 16 to 20 times the minimum wage. The first 1 percent goes toward extending coverage to self-employed workers and other groups whose socioeconomic circumstances prevent them from joining social security. The additional percentage goes toward the assistance pension (LRP 2002). In the Dominican Republic, employers pay 0.4 percent of wages to a Minimum Solidarity Fund that must finance the minimum pension of the contributive program (LDSS 2001). Standardization of entry requirements is positive, but has excluded some privileged groups that do not contribute to the general system while enjoying generous benefits and receiving tax subsidies. It has also excluded the large majority of independent workers and other low-income groups.

Integrating privileged groups into the general system or eliminating the tax subsidies that they receive may alleviate the absence of solidarity. These resources could then be used to help low-income workers join the system, extend assistance pensions, and implement some of the measures suggested above to reduce gender inequality. A solidarity contribution paid by high-income workers and/or employers (as in Colombia and the Dominican Republic) could also be introduced. An alternative would be to add a community-of-interests contribution to very high pensions (as has been proposed in Brazil). The funds generated by these contributions would go toward extending coverage to low-income groups and assistance pensions. The flat pension fees should be eliminated. The possibility of having fees shared by employers (as in Colombia) must be considered. The high fiscal costs of structural reform must be balanced with the need for resources to protect low-income groups and the poor.

Concluding Remarks

The challenges in undertaking pension reforms are complex and require careful consideration of aspects such as coverage, contributions, competition among pension funds, administrative costs, capital accumulation and the impact on national savings, fiscal transition costs, capital markets, portfolio diversification, investment returns, gender equity, and solidarity. Some countries copied what was thought of as a "universal model" for pension reform. Unfortunately, far from being universal, this model cannot function in the absence of certain essential basic conditions. This experience suggests that those countries that have not yet embarked on the process of reforming their social security system should carefully review the experiences of the 12 countries described in this chapter before deciding to go forward with structural or parametric reforms. Moreover, countries opting to undertake structural reforms should select a general model and carefully adapt it so that it meets their requirements.

References

Acuña, Rodrigo and Augusto Iglesias. 2001. Chile's Pension Reform After 20 Years. Social Protection Discussion Paper No. 0129 (December). The World Bank, Washington D.C.

Arenas de Mesa, Alberto. 1999. Efectos fiscales del sistema de pensiones en Chile: Proyección del déficit previsional 1999–2037: Unpublished work presented at the Seminar on Fiscal Responsibilities in the Pension System, Chilean Finance Ministry and Economic Commission for Latin America and the Caribbean, 2–3 September, Santiago.

Arenas de Mesa, Alberto and Paula Benavides. 2003. *Protección social en Chile: Financiamiento, cobertura y desempeño 1990–2000.* Santiago: International Labour Organization.

Arenas de Mesa, Alberto and Héctor Hernández Sánchez. 2001. Análisis, evolución y propuestas de ampliación de la cobertura del sistema civil de pensiones en Chile. In *Cobertura previsional en Argentina,*

Brasil y Chile, eds. Fabio M. Bertranou, Carlos O. Grushka, Hector Henández Sánchez, Vinicius Pinheiro, and Rafael Rofman. Santiago: International Labour Organization.

Barr, Nicholas. 2002. Reforming Pensions: Myths, Truths, and Policy Choices. *International Social Security Review* 55 (2) (March–June): 3–36.

Bertranou, Fabio and Alberto Arenas de Mesa, eds. 2003. *Protección social y género en Argentina, Brasil y Chile*. Santiago: International Labour Organization.

Bertranou, Fabio, Carmen Solorio and Wouter van Ginneken, eds. 2002. *Pensiones no contributivas y asistenciales: Argentina, Brasil, Chile, Costa Rica y Uruguay*. Santiago: International Labour Organization.

Central Bank of Uruguay (BCU). 2002. *Memoria trimestral del régimen de jubilación por ahorro individual obligatorio*. No. 26 (December). Montevideo.

Corbo, Vittorio and Klaus Schmidt-Hebbel. 2003. Efectos macroeconómicos de la reforma de pensiones en Chile. Paper presented at International Federation of Pension Fund Administrators Seminar, 15–16 May, Cancun.

Gill, Indermit, Truman Packard, and Juan Yermo. 2005. *Keeping the Promise of Social Security in Latin America*. Stanford, CA: Stanford University Press.

Haindl Rondanelli, Erik. 1997. Chilean Pension Fund Reform and its Impact on Savings. In *Generating Savings for Latin American Development,* ed. Robert Grosse. Boulder: Lynne Rienner.

Holzmann, Robert. 1997. Pension Reform, Financial Market Development and Economic Growth: Preliminary Evidence from Chile. Staff Papers, No. 44. International Monetary Fund, Washington, D.C.

Holzmann, Robert and Joseph Stiglitz, eds. 2001. *New Ideas About Old Age Security: Towards Sustainable Pension Systems in the 21st Century.* Washington D.C.: The World Bank.

Hujo, Katja. 2004. Reforma previsional y crisis económica: El caso argentino. In *¿Públicos o privados? Los sistemas de pensiones en América Latina después de dos décadas,* eds. Katja Hujo, Carmelo Mesa-Lago, and Manfred Nitsch. Caracas: Nueva Sociedad.

International Association of Pension Fund Supervisors (AIOS, in Spanish). 1998–2003. *Statistical Bulletin AIOS*. Available at htpp://www.safjp.gov.ar/DOCS/aios.htm

International Labour Organization (ILO). 2002a. Diagnóstico institucional del sistema previsional argentino y pautas para enfrentar la crisis. Buenos Aires: International Labour Organization.

————. 2002b. Panorama laboral. Lima.

Kiefer, Manfred. 2004. Evaluación de los 22 años del sistema privado de pensiones en Chile. In ¿Públicos o privados? Los sistemas de pensiones en América Latina después de dos décadas, eds. Katja Hujo, Carmelo Mesa-Lago, and Manfred Nitsch. Caracas: Nueva Sociedad.

Kleinjans, Kristin. 2004. La elección de un programa de pensión: La experiencia de Colombia. In ¿Públicos o privados? Los sistemas de pensiones en América Latina después de dos décadas, eds. Katja Hujo, Carmelo Mesa-Lago, and Manfred Nitsch. Caracas: Nueva Sociedad.

Madrid, Raul. 2003. Retiring the State: The Politics of Pension Privatization in Latin America and Beyond. Stanford: Stanford University Press.

Mesa-Lago, Carmelo. 2000. Estudio comparativo de los costos fiscales en la transición de ocho reformas de pensiones en América Latina. Financing of Development Series, No. 93, March. Economic Commission of Latin America and the Caribbean, Santiago.

————. 2002. Myth and Reality on Social Security Pension Reform: The Latin American Evidence. World Development 30 (8) (August): 1309–21.

————. 2003. La crisis del programa de pensiones en la caja de seguro social de Panamá. Friedrich Ebert Foundation, 5 February, Panama.

————. 2004. Las reformas de pensiones en América Latina y su impacto en los principios de la seguridad social. Financing for Development Series, No. 144. Economic Commission of Latin America and the Caribbean, Santiago.

Mesa-Lago, Carmelo and Fabio Bertranou. 1998. Manual de economía de la seguridad social latinoamericana. Montevideo: Centro Latinoamericano de Economía Humana.

Mesa-Lago, Carmelo and Eva Maria Hohnerlein. 2002. Testing the Assumptions on the Effects of the German Pension Reform Based on Latin American and Eastern European Outcomes. European Journal of Social Security 4 (4) (October–December): 285–330.

Mesa-Lago, Carmelo and Katharina Müller. 2004. La política de las reformas de pensiones en América Latina. In ¿Públicos o privados? Los sistemas de pensiones en América Latina después de dos décadas, eds. Katja Hujo, Carmelo Mesa-Lago, and Manfred Nitsch. Caracas: Nueva Sociedad.

Ministry of Labor, Employment and Social Security (MTESS, in Spanish) (Argentina). 2003. Libro blanco de la previsión social. Buenos Aires: Secretaría de Previsión Social.

Müller, Katharina. 2002. *Privatising Old-age Security: Latin America and Eastern Europe Compared.* Frankfurt: Frankfurter Institute for Transformation Studies.

National Commission on the Retirement Savings System (CONSAR, in Spanish) (Mexico). 2002, 2003. *Boletín Informativo SAR* No. 2 (March–April) and No. 6 (November–December).

National Social Security Administration (ANSES, in Spanish). 2002. *Informe de la seguridad social* 3 (4) (July – September) Argentina.

Orszag, Peter and Joseph Stiglitz. 2001. Rethinking Pension Reform: Ten Myths About Social Security Systems. In *New Ideas About Old Age Security: Towards Sustainable Pension Systems in the 21st Century,* eds. Robert Holzmann and Joseph Stiglitz. Washington D.C.: The World Bank.

Schwarzer, Helmut. 2004. La nueva reforma previsional en Brasil. In *¿Públicos o privados? Los sistemas de pensiones en América Latina después de dos décadas,* eds. Katja Hujo, Carmelo Mesa-Lago, and Manfred Nitsch. Caracas: Nueva Sociedad.

Social Security Standards Institute (INP, in Spanish) (Chile). 2001. Statistics provided to the author. Santiago.

Superintendency of Banking and Insurance (SBS) (Peru). 2002, 2003. Lima. Available at http://www.safp.gob.pe

Superintendency of Banking of Colombia (SBC). 1999–2003. Bogota. Available at http://www.superbancaria.gov.co

Superintendency of Pension and Retirement Fund Managers (SAFJP) (Argentina). 2001, 2003. *Boletín Estadístico Mensual* Vol. 9 (January) and Vol. 10 (June). Available at http://www.safjp.gov.ar

_____. 2002. Propuesta de fortalecimiento del sistema integrado de jubilaciones y pensiones. Buenos Aires.

Superintendency of Pension Fund Managers (SAFP) (Chile). 2002. *El sistema chileno de pensiones* (5th edition). Santiago.

_____. 1981 to 2003. *Boletín Estadístico* (December). Santiago.

Superintendency of Pensions (SPa) (Costa Rica). 2002, 2003. *Boletín trimestral,* (December and March). Available at http://www.supen.fi.cr

Superintendency of Pensions (SPb) (El Salvador). 2002, 2003. *Revista de estadísticas previsionales* (August). Available at http://www.spensions.gob.sv

Superintendency of Pensions, Securities and Insurance (SPVS) (Bolivia). 2002, 2003. *Boletín Informativo de Pensiones* No. 23 (December) and No. 25 (June). Available at http://www.spvs.gov.bo

Superintendency of Social Security (SSS) (Chile). 2002. Estadísticas de seguridad social 2001. Actuarial Department, Santiago.

Uthoff, Andras. 2002. Mercados de trabajo y sistemas de pensiones. *Revista de la CEPAL* 78: 39–53.

World Bank. 1994. *Averting the Old-Age Crisis.* New York: Oxford University Press.

Legislation

Colombia. *Ley de reforma de pensiones* (LRP). 2002. Bogota, December.

Costa Rica. *Ley de protección del trabajador* (LPT). 2000. Imprenta Nacional, San José.

The Dominican Republic. *Ley definitiva de seguridad social* (LDSS). 2001. Santo Domingo, 24 April.

Nicaragua. *Ley del sistema de ahorro para pensiones* (LSAP). 2000. Managua, 15 March.

Peru. *Ley de seguridad social* (LSS). 2001. Lima, 13 November.

Venezuela. *Ley orgánica del sistema de seguridad social* (LOSSS). 2002. Caracas, 30 December.

CHAPTER 3

Fiscal and Institutional Considerations of Pension Reform: Lessons Learned from Chile

Alberto Arenas de Mesa *

The structural reform of Latin America's pension systems has brought about perhaps the most sweeping and influential changes of any social policy implemented in the region over the past two decades. This reform process entailed the structural overhaul of the countries' old collective pay-as-you-go systems.

One of the chief objectives of the pension reform programs has been to resolve these systems' financial and fiscal imbalances—or prevent them for arising in the first place. The complete or partial replacement of public, collective pay-as-you-go defined benefit plans with privately run, defined contributions systems of individually funded accounts might appear to be quite radical. In the eyes of some, however, this was an inevitable reform, without which pension system deficits would eventually have triggered an extraordinary rise in contribution rates, a decrease in benefits, or a significant increase in public spending.

This chapter explores the institutional dimension and fiscal impact of the structural reform program in Chile, which has been the model followed by other countries in Latin America and the Caribbean. These

---

* Alberto Arenas de Mesa is Deputy Director of the Ministry of Finance of Chile, Office of the Budget, and has written extensively on social security and the fiscal effects of pension reform.

subjects have not figured in the policy debate or in policymaking because of an implicit assumption: that this reform would be neutral in terms of fiscal sustainability and a balanced management of public finances. Yet both play a role in the ultimate success or failure of the reform.

The institutional framework of pension systems consists of the array of organizational and regulatory arrangements directed at ensuring an adequate income for retirees, the disabled, surviving spouses, and orphans. The system's ability to achieve this public policy objective is a vital consideration in evaluating its institutional framework. In turn, government policy plays a key role in the institutional design of pension systems, not only in establishing a stable, sustained stream of financing for social programs, but also insuring that the institutional design is consistent with the country's financial and fiscal capacities and that it can efficiently provide basic pension coverage to the population. A country's success in optimizing its use of fiscal resources is influenced by the institutional framework of its pension systems. In most cases, the latter influences the efficiency of public spending, as well.

There have been high expectations regarding Chile's pension reform and its ability to have a positive impact on public finances over the long term by establishing a closer and more direct link between pension contributions and pension benefits. However, the transition from one pension system to the other tells a different story. Since the pension contributions deposited in the pension system's individually funded accounts are no longer being used to pay the pensions distributed under the pre-existing pay-as-you-go system, the State must finance those pensions. This will put a great deal of pressure on government finances for a number of decades. In addition, the rapid transition from defined benefits to a defined contributions pension system means that the public sector must cover the entitlements that workers have garnered by virtue of the contributions they have paid into the old system. As these implicit liabilities are acknowledged and paid off by the State, the financial gap associated with the fiscal/pension transition process begins to widen.

Within this context, the structural reform of Chile's pension system has generated considerable fiscal impacts, with the average annual State-financed pension system deficit amounting to 5.7 percent of GDP over the past two decades. The pension reform process, in conjunction with other factors, is strongly influenced by the institutional framework and its development. This institutional structure thus has had implications for the reform options open to Chile and other countries of the region. By the same token, it will have an influence on future options for any redesign of policies.

The Pension System before the 1980 Reform

The evolution of Chile's social security system can be divided into three stages. The first, between 1924 and the 1970s, was based on the Bismarkian model of occupationally segmented social insurance schemes. The second, from the 1970s to 1980, reflected the Beveridge Plan's proposal for universal social security coverage. The hallmark of the third, which began in 1980, has been the privatization of social protection instruments.

The development of the pension system as such began in the 1920s. By the mid-1950s, there were three main pension funds providing coverage for most salaried workers and two for the police and armed forces. As time went on, other funds were created. Within the three main pension funds, the array of regimes expanded, as well. The pension system grew to include a vast number of regimes (150) and suffered from institutional fragmentation (35 different funds). The Frei and Allende administrations attempted to standardize these pension regimes and to do away with the privileges enjoyed by some groups, but failed to achieve the necessary consensus. The military government carried the reform measures forward. In 1979 the most serious inequalities in the system were eliminated, retirement ages were raised and aligned, and contribution rates were increased. Then, in 1980, the third stage of the system's evolution began with the creation of a privately run system based on individually funded accounts.

Coverage

The core objective of a pension system is to ensure an adequate income for retirees, disabled persons, surviving spouses, and orphans. Its effectiveness in fulfilling this objective therefore hinges on its ability to bring members of the population into the system while they are still working and part of the economically active population (EAP). Thus a pension system's coverage of active members is an important consideration in its assessment.

The most commonly used indicators for measuring a pension system's coverage of active members are the number of contributing members in the workforce, effective coverage, and—for the working population—occupational coverage. Effective coverage increased during the 1960s and up to the early 1970s, rising from 69 percent in 1960 to 79 percent in 1973, and then began to steadily decline, falling to a low of 64 percent, according to Cheyre (1988) (see Table 3.1). Another study leads to the same conclusion for 1975–80, although the levels of coverage differ (Arellano 1985).

| Table 3.1 | Coverage of Contributing Members of the Public Civilian Pension System, 1960–80 (percent) |

	Occupational coverage (contributors/employed)		Effective coverage (contributors/labor force)		Ratio of active workers/retirees
Year	Cheyre	Arellano	Cheyre	Arellano	and pensioners
1960	75.0	n.a.	69.0	n.a	n.a.
1965	74.0	n.a.	69.0	n.a	4.5
1970	77.0	n.a.	73.0	n.a	3.6
1971	79.0	n.a.	73.0	n.a	3.6
1973	83.0	n.a.	79.0	n.a	3.3
1974	83.0	n.a.	78.0	n.a.	3.2
1975	86.0	71.2	74.0	61.9	2.8
1976	83.0	65.7	74.0	57.3	2.7
1977	79.0	62.2	73.0	54.8	2.4
1978	76.0	56.6	68.0	48.5	2.2
1979	75.0	56.2	68.0	48.5	2.2
1980	71.0	53.3	64.0	47.8	2.0

n.a. Not applicable.
Source: Cheyre (1988); Arellano (1985).

The downward trend in effective coverage that began in the early 1970s can be accounted for by increasing unemployment rates. This was not the only reason, however, since occupational coverage also began to decline in the mid-1970s, falling from 86 percent to 71 percent from 1975 to 1980 (according to Cheyre) or from 71.2 percent to 53.3 percent (according to Arellano). Cheyre (1988) contends that a considerable portion of the drop in coverage in the 1970s is attributable to increased evasion. This would indicate that the explanatory factors for the reduction in coverage between 1974 and the reform's implementation included higher unemployment, more precarious labor relations, and the incentives for evasion existing in a tight labor market (Marcel and Arenas de Mesa 1992).

A pension system's effectiveness in fulfilling its objective also hinges on its ability to ensure coverage and provide benefits to those members eligible to receive benefits. In Chile, the coverage of retirees and other eligible members climbed from approximately 500,000 in the late 1960s to over 1 million by the end of the 1970s. The average annual growth rate during that decade was 5.7 percent (Arenas de Mesa 2000).

Financing

The old system was for all intents and purposes a pay-as-you-go-system, since returns on investments amounted to just 2.5 percent of the system's

Table 3.2	Government Social Security Revenues and Expenditures, 1974–80					
Year	Revenues	Expenditures	Deficit	Revenues	Expenditures	Deficit
	(millions of 2003 pesos)			(percent of GDP)		
1974	344,523	698,866	−354,342	3.0	6.2	−3.1
1975	310,985	422,261	−111,276	3.4	4.6	−1.2
1976	360,509	662,877	−302,369	3.4	6.2	−2.8
1977	454,651	831,933	−377,282	3.6	6.7	−3.0
1978	556,642	1,027,681	−471,039	3.7	6.8	−3.1
1979	937,063	1,241,874	−304,811	5.2	6.9	−1.7
1980	1,017,362	1,336,172	−318,810	5.5	7.2	−1.7

Source: Marcel and Arenas de Mesa (1992).

total annual revenues. Thus, assuming constant conditions in terms of replacement ratios and contribution rates, the system's financial equilibrium depended on economic growth—since this is what determines wage levels and hence the level of revenues provided by contributions—and the trend in the ratio of contributing members to noncontributing members. This ratio, in turn, is determined by demographic factors such as the aging of the population, economic factors such as unemployment, the relative size of the informal sector in the economy, evasion rates, regulatory and policy-related factors such as the established retirement age, and pension eligibility requirements in such cases as early retirement options.

In Chile, the ratio of contributing members to noncontributing members trended downward during the review period, falling from 3.6 to 2.0 contributing members for every pensioner between 1965 and 1980 (Table 3.1). In the long run, under the existing conditions, the continued payment of pensions would have called for an increasing injection of State funds, had it not been for the parametric reform of the public pension system implemented between 1975 and 1980. Meanwhile, the State provided funding amounting to an average of 2 percentage of GDP per year (Table 3.2).

Overview of the 1980 Pension System Reform

The structural reform of the Chilean pension system carried out under Decree-Law 3,500 of 1980 addressed the problems raised by the public pay-as-you-go pension scheme. Chile's pension system, like those of many other Latin American countries that undertook reforms later, was institutionally fragmented and included a vast number of different regimes. It also exhibited problems with respect to finances, equity, and administrative efficiency (Arenas de Mesa 2000).

In 1980, Chile began to put into place the institutional framework of the structural pension reforms, including standardizing eligibility and benefit requirements.[1] The reform was based on a model involving the wholesale replacement of the public pay-as-you-go scheme by a pension system based on individually funded accounts. This new system can be described as a multi-pillar public/private system.

The first pillar has several components. The first is a noncontributory public system that provides welfare-based pensions (*pensiones asistenciales*, or PASIS). This component helps to alleviate poverty and indigence. The system is centralized in terms of both the allocation and determination of pension benefits.

The second component is a contributory public system that provides a State-guaranteed minimum pension (SGMP) for participants of the Administradoras de Fondos de Pensiones (pension funds, or AFPs) who have reached a set density threshold (20 years of contributions). This mechanism, which allows the State to ensure that all eligible plan members will have a basic minimum income during their old age, is one of the public sector guarantees provided under the country's social protection policy. The public benefit from this minimum pension is a transfer payment to the AFP, which have a more limited capacity for capital accumulation, because of low-income members and members with low contribution densities. This first pillar also encompasses the country's public sector contributory systems: the Instituto de Normalización Previsional (National Pension Fund, or INP), the public institution that administers the old public pension system and that was closed by the new pension reform program; and the pension systems for the armed forces (Caja de Previsión de la Defensa Nacional, National Defense Pension Fund, or CAPREDENA) and the police force (Dirección de Previsión de Carabineros de Chile, Chilean Police Force Pension Division, or DIPRECA).

The second pillar is an obligatory, contributory AFP pension system, which is a savings and insurance mechanism intended to provide members with coverage during their old age while optimizing their consumption path over their lifetimes. This system was designed with uniform entry conditions and became mandatory for all new salaried workers in May 1981. (It is optional for self-employed workers.) Workers must pay 10

---

[1] In 1979 some aspects of the civilian pension system were modified.

percent of their income into individual savings accounts managed by the AFPs. Each member has an individual account in which contributions are deposited, earning their share of the returns on the investments made by the AFPs with these funds. The AFPs charge a commission to cover their administrative expenses and the cost of taking out disability and survivors' insurance policies. The size of the pension that an individual ultimately receives is closely related to the amount that is built up in the account, and hence with the person's income level and payment history.

In contrast to a State-run, PAYG system in which risk is covered by all plan members regardless of gender, in this individually funded system, members' benefits are based on their individual risk levels, which are differentiated by gender. The decision to make this system compulsory has thus had unexpected ramifications, especially with regard to the potential fiscal and institutional impacts.

The third pillar, like the second, operates on the basis of individually funded accounts. However, it is a voluntary system. People who wish to pay more than the required amount into their pension accounts may do so. This third pillar provides tax benefits for its members.

The Pension System Transition

At the time of writing, 23 years into the reform's implementation, the transition is in full swing, with both systems—the one that is being replaced and the one that is being implemented—still in operation. The transition will last until around 2025 in relation to the retirement of the public system's current contributing members, and until about 2050 in relation to the payment of those members' pensions. Thus since 1981, when the AFP system began, four different pension systems have operated in Chile (Table 3.3). The AFP system covers nearly half as many pensioners as the INP system, more beneficiaries than the PASIS, and over three times as many beneficiaries as the public pension system for the armed forces (Arenas de Mesa 2004).

The reform was intended to confine the State's role in the pension system's management to that of a regulator, inspector, supervisor, and guarantor of the AFP system. However, the way in which the transition from one pension system to another has unfolded has reaffirmed the importance of the State's involvement in the administration of the system—in part because of the variety of institutions that continue to operate in the sector. Thus some of the problems that the transition was designed to resolve continue.

| Table 3.3 | Pension System Transition, 1981–2003 (number of people, as of December 2003) |

	Public pension system			Pension system administered by the private sector
	Noncontributory	Contributory		Contributory
	PASIS[a]	INP[b]	CAPREDENA and DIPRECA[c]	AFP
Active workers		160,868		3,618,995
Retirees and pensioners	371,782	887,554	152,792	421,884 40,569 (SGMP)[d]

a. PASIS = Welfare-based pensions.
b. INP= National Pension Fund.
c. CAPREDENA=armed forces and DIPRECA= the police force.
d. SGMP = State Guaranteed Minimum Pension.
Source: Arenas de Mesa (2004).

The State plays a significant role in the following five areas:

- the administration and payment of benefits under the old public pension system for civilians;
- the administration, calculation, and payment of "recognition bonds," which are the financial instrument used to certify the contributions made under the old system by people who then transferred to the individually funded system;
- the administration and payment of pension benefits under the public pension scheme covering the armed forces and the police;
- the administration and payment of the SGMP provided under the AFP system; and
- the administration of the public, noncontributory PASIS system that provides benefits to indigents and to other persons lacking pension coverage.

The first two of these governmental duties are time-bound, but the others are ongoing. Each of them places a financial burden on the State (Arenas de Mesa and Gumucio 2000).

Individually Funded, Contributory System

Since the pension reform was launched, the role played by these pension funds in the economy has grown considerably. As of 2003, they had come to represent roughly 60 percentage of GDP (Table 3.4).

Table 3.4	Cumulative Value and Rate of Return on Pension Funds and Individual Accounts, 1981–2003		
	Pension funds accumulated assets under management		Returns on fund assets
	Value	Percent of GDP	Average yearly real return
Year	(millions of current pesos)	(percent of GDP)	(percent)
1981	11,695	0.9	12.8
1982	44,495	3.7	28.5
1983	99,474	6.5	21.3
1984	159,576	8.4	3.6
1985	281,807	10.3	13.4
1986	433,377	12.7	12.3
1987	644,728	14.1	5.4
1988	885,875	14.7	6.5
1989	1,329,268	17.5	6.9
1990	2,244,481	23.3	15.6
1991	3,769,243	29.7	29.7
1992	4,736,462	29.4	3.0
1993	6,830,788	35.4	16.2
1994	8,983,563	38.8	18.2
1995	10,230,990	36.1	–2.5
1996	11,555,632	37.0	3.5
1997	13,405,826	38.6	4.7
1998	14,552,547	39.8	–1.1
1999	18,093,003	48.7	16.3
2000	20,343,371	50.1	4.4
2001	22,955,974	52.8	6.7
2002	25,227,058	54.4	3.0
2003	29,176,611	58.6	10.5
Average			
1981–1991			14.2
1991–2003			8.7
1981–2003			10.4

Source: Arenas de Mesa and Gumucio (2000); SAFP.

Pension funds have acted as an engine of growth for various sectors of the economy and for the capital and life insurance markets, among others. The AFPs are now the largest institutional investors in the financial market. They finance five out of every nine new mortgages (SAFP 2002).

The asset mix of these funds has changed considerably and has tended to become more diversified (Table 3.5). In 1981, the bulk of these investments were in financial paper (71.3 percent). By 1989, the share of such instruments dipped below 40 percent and by 2003 had fallen to 26 percent. Meanwhile, the share of corporate bonds (bonds issued by nonfinancial institutions) and equities expanded, rising to 7.7 percent

Table 3.5	Distribution of the Investment Portfolio, 1981–2003 *(percent of total investments)*						
Year	Government	Financial institutions[a]	Nonfinancial institutions[b]	Equities[c]	Mutual funds and others[d]	Foreign assets[e]	Other[f]
1981	28.1	71.3	0.6	0.0	0.0	0.0	0.0
1982	26.0	73.4	0.6	0.0	0.0	0.0	0.0
1983	44.5	53.4	2.2	0.0	0.0	0.0	0.0
1984	42.1	55.6	1.8	0.0	0.0	0.0	0.5
1985	42.4	56.0	1.1	0.0	0.0	0.0	0.5
1986	46.6	48.7	0.8	3.8	0.0	0.0	0.1
1987	41.4	49.4	2.6	6.2	0.0	0.0	0.4
1988	35.4	50.1	6.4	8.1	0.0	0.0	0.0
1989	41.6	39.2	9.1	10.1	0.0	0.0	0.0
1990	44.1	33.4	11.1	11.3	0.0	0.0	0.1
1991	38.3	26.7	11.1	23.8	0.0	0.0	0.1
1992	40.9	25.2	9.6	24.0	0.2	0.0	0.1
1993	39.3	20.6	7.3	31.9	0.3	0.6	0.1
1994	39.7	20.0	6.3	32.2	0.9	0.9	0.0
1995	39.4	22.4	5.2	30.1	2.6	0.2	0.1
1996	42.1	23.6	4.7	26.0	3.0	0.5	0.0
1997	39.6	29.3	3.3	23.4	3.2	1.1	0.1
1998	41.0	31.7	3.8	14.9	3.0	5.6	0.1
1999	34.6	33.2	3.8	12.4	2.7	13.3	0.0
2000	35.7	35.1	4.0	11.6	2.5	10.8	0.2
2001	35.0	32.4	6.2	10.6	2.5	13.2	0.1
2002	30.0	34.2	7.2	9.9	2.5	16.1	0.1
2003	24.7	26.3	7.7	14.5	2.9	23.8	0.1

[a.] Financial sector less the equities of financial institutions.
[b.] Business firms less equities and quotas of investment funds.
[c.] Stocks of financial institutions plus those of the business sector.
[d.] Investment funds of the business firms plus others from the external sector.
[e.] Foreign issuers less others from the external sector.
[f.] Disposable assets.
Note: Total of investment equals 100 percent.
Source: SAFP 2002.

and 14.5 percent (13.5 percent in business enterprises and 1 percent in financial institutions), respectively, by 2003 (about 13 percent of GDP). Investment in foreign assets began in 1993 although the law making this an option was passed in 1990. In that year, such investments amounted to 0.6 percent of the funds' total value; by 2003, their share had grown to 23.8 percent.

These changes in the portfolio have been made possible by the pension funds' growth and the development of the capital market, as well as by the relaxing of regulations that place limits on investments (SAFP 2002).

The State plays a crucial role in the AFP system by serving as the guarantor of last resort in the event of the bankruptcy or default of an AFP or insurance provider and by ensuring that the yields for plan members remain above an established floor rate. As mentioned, through the Superintendencia de Administradoras de Fondos de Pensiones (Superintendency of Pension Fund Managers, or SAFP), the State also regulates, inspects, and supervises the management of the AFPs. (For further information, see SAFP 2002.)

Pension Coverage

How has pension coverage fared under the new system? Tables 3.6 to 3.10 present data on pension coverage, broken down by occupation, type of employment, gender, and income quintile. Each break-down tells a different story. In interpreting these data, it is important to recognize that coverage indicators paint no more than a partial picture, because they do not provide information about the quality of coverage or about the types of people who are covered by the social security system. The quality of pension coverage is related to the benefits for which individuals are eligible based on their pension records or contribution density rates. Members' contribution density rates (that is, the percentage of an insured member's total working life during which the corresponding contributions to the system have been paid) are a fundamental factor in determining the level of benefits they are to receive, and hence the quality of coverage provided by the pension system.

Contributing Members

Occupational and effective coverage coefficients increased between 1981 and 2003, when they reached 66.7 percent and 61.8 percent, respectively (Table 3.6). In 2003, around 30 percent of the employed population was not covered.

One reason for the size of the uncovered population is that self-employment has grown relative to total employment, and the self-employed workforce has a lower rate of coverage than other workers. Another is that, judging from institutional records, the gap in coverage between salaried employees and self-employed persons has been widening in both relative and absolute terms (Arenas de Mesa, Llanés, and Miranda 2004). Whereas the coverage rate for salaried workers rose from 63.3 to 76.3 percent between 1986 and 2003, the rate for self-employed workers slipped from 12.2 percent to 6.5 percent (Table 3.7). In abso-

Table 3.6	Pension Coverage (contributing members), 1981–2003 (percent)					
	Occupational coverage (contributors/employed)			Effective coverage (contributors/labor force)		
Year	AFP	INP	Total	AFP	INP	Total
1981	n.a.	18.4	n.a.	n.a.	16.3	n.a.
1982	36.0	16.6	52.6	29.0	13.4	42.4
1983	38.2	14.9	53.1	33.5	13.0	46.5
1984	40.6	13.7	54.3	35.0	11.8	46.8
1985	44.0	12.8	56.8	38.8	11.3	50.1
1986	45.9	11.4	57.3	41.1	10.2	51.4
1987	50.6	10.9	61.5	45.7	9.9	55.6
1988	50.8	9.8	60.6	46.6	9.0	55.6
1989	50.6	8.7	59.3	47.2	8.1	55.3
1990	50.6	8.1	58.7	46.8	7.5	54.3
1991	53.7	7.6	61.3	49.9	7.0	56.9
1992	55.3	6.9	62.2	51.8	6.5	58.3
1993	54.6	6.0	60.7	51.1	5.7	56.8
1994	56.2	5.5	61.7	51.8	5.0	56.9
1995	57.2	5.5	62.7	53.5	5.1	58.6
1996	58.9	4.9	63.8	55.7	4.6	60.4
1997	61.3	4.2	65.5	58.0	4.0	62.0
1998	58.0	4.1	62.0	53.8	3.8	57.6
1999	60.4	4.2	64.6	55.0	3.9	58.8
2000	59.4	3.8	63.2	54.5	3.5	57.9
2001	63.0	3.3	66.3	58.0	3.1	61.0
2002	61.9	3.1	65.0	57.1	2.9	59.9
2003	63.8	3.0	66.7	59.1	2.7	61.8

AFP = Administradoras de Fondos de Pensiones (pension funds)
INP = Instituto de Normalización Previsional (National Pension Fund)
n.a. = not applicable
Source: Arenas de Mesa and Hernández (2001); Superintendencia de Seguridad Social (SUSESO); Superintendencia de Administradoras de Fondos de Pensiones (SAFP); Instituto Nacional de Estadística (INE).

lute terms, the number of self-employed workers not covered by the social security system climbed from 880,000 to around 1.58 million persons.

A bivariate analysis using information from the CASEN 2000 survey indicates that the low-income population is another group that is liable to remain outside the pension system. A characteristic trend in Chile is for the coverage rate for active members to decline as their household poverty level rises. In 2000, for example, the occupational coverage rate for workers belonging to households classified as indigent was 27.1 percent, whereas the rate for members of non-poor households was 64.7 percent. The rate for members of non-indigent poor households was 48.3 percent. This downward trend in social protection for the poorest mem-

| Table 3.7 | Pension System Coverage of Salaried Employees versus Self-employed Workers, 1986–2003 |

Year	Contributors (number of people)			Employed (number of people)	Occupational coverage (contributors/employed) (percent)		
	AFP	INP	Total		AFP	INP	Total
Salaried workers							
1986	1,445,218	367,188	1,812,406	2,861,390	50.5	12.8	63.3
1987	1,623,004	366,277	1,989,281	2,968,920	54.7	12.3	67.0
1988	1,721,642	351,332	2,072,974	3,142,790	54.8	11.2	66.0
1989	1,866,443	326,968	2,193,411	3,218,370	58.0	10.2	68.2
1990	1,913,625	303,996	2,217,621	3,289,630	58.2	9.2	67.4
1991	2,067,533	291,255	2,358,788	3,359,400	61.5	8.7	70.2
1992	2,246,132	279,170	2,525,302	3,541,460	63.4	7.9	71.3
1993	2,314,983	256,471	2,571,454	3,723,620	62.2	6.9	69.1
1994	2,380,946	229,947	2,610,893	3,687,460	64.6	6.2	70.8
1995	2,432,456	231,278	2,663,734	3,746,840	64.9	6.2	71.1
1996	2,497,019	206,845	2,703,864	3,849,860	64.9	5.4	70.2
1997	2,601,682	179,686	2,781,368	3,915,240	66.5	4.6	71.0
1998	2,560,158	173,549	2,733,707	3,887,660	65.9	4.5	70.3
1999	2,627,602	183,955	2,811,557	3,866,160	68.0	4.8	72.7
2000	2,685,772	158,550	2,844,322	3,861,380	69.6	4.1	73.7
2001	2,768,763	139,256	2,908,019	3,869,200	71.6	3.6	75.2
2002	2,793,697	130,326	2,924,023	3,903,530	71.6	3.3	74.9
2003	2,914,619	126,837	3,041,456	3,987,120	73.1	3.2	76.3
Self-employed workers							
1986	48,350	73,434	121,784	1,001,460	4.8	7.3	12.2
1987	52,611	71,545	124,156	1,032,370	5.1	6.9	12.0
1988	50,729	69,221	119,950	1,142,650	4.4	6.1	10.5
1989	51,186	61,104	112,290	1,245,050	4.1	4.9	9.0
1990	47,922	63,818	111,740	1,235,900	3.9	5.2	9.0
1991	50,840	59,311	110,151	1,271,270	4.0	4.7	8.7
1992	51,721	57,141	108,862	1,335,970	3.9	4.3	8.1
1993	52,657	52,257	104,914	1,385,670	3.8	3.8	7.6
1994	55,320	49,814	105,134	1,435,300	3.9	3.5	7.3
1995	57,077	51,393	108,470	1,427,570	4.0	3.6	7.6
1996	51,343	52,054	103,397	1,448,820	3.5	3.6	7.1
1997	59,923	48,971	108,894	1,464,950	4.1	3.3	7.4
1998	59,458	46,722	106,180	1,544,690	3.8	3.0	6.9
1999	62,999	45,319	108,318	1,538,320	4.1	2.9	7.0
2000	61,801	44,490	106,291	1,520,080	4.1	2.9	7.0
2001	66,731	42,318	109,049	1,610,200	4.1	2.6	6.8
2002	69,724	41,080	110,804	1,627,730	4.3	2.5	6.8
2003	68,186	40,990	109,176	1,688,020	4.0	2.4	6.5

AFP = Administradoras de Fondos de Pensiones (pension funds)
INP = Instituto de Normalización Previsional (National Pension Fund)
Sources: Arenas de Mesa and Hernández (2001); SAFP; SUSESO; INE.

bers of the population has grown steeper over the past decade, with the occupational coverage rate for indigent households dropping from 47.5 percent in 1992 to 27.1 percent in 2000. The trend is moving in the same direction for members of poor households, where the occupational coverage rate fell from 58 percent in 1992 to 48.3 percent in 2000 (Arenas de Mesa, Llanés, and Miranda 2004).

The two groups that are most likely to remain outside the pension system are self-employed workers and workers belonging to the country's poorest households. Women also have problems gaining coverage, as will be discussed below. The existence of these large groups that lack pension coverage has implications for the level of savings that the social security system can generate, and thus for how these groups' consumption needs are going to be financed when they are past retirement age.

These low coverage rates are of particular concern when evaluating the pension system's design, since the system's main function is to guarantee a basic minimum level of consumption for older persons, disabled persons, surviving spouses, and orphans. These low coverage indicators, especially for the vulnerable groups within the population discussed here, lessen the likelihood of achieving this objective.

Between 1992 and 2000, pension coverage for the population aged 65 years and over held fairly steady, at around 80 percent, the CASEN survey data indicate (Table 3.8). The breakdown of coverage by type of pension benefit varied considerably, however, with the share of PASIS pensions rising relative to social security retirement pensions. The relative share of survivors' benefits remained fairly stable, at around 13 percent. As of 2000, the coverage rates for the population over 65 years of age were 51.5 percent, 12.9 percent, and 14.7 percent for old-age pensions, survivors' pensions, and PASIS, respectively.

Pension Type and Gender

From 1992 to 2000, an average of 84.3 percent of the male population over the age of 65 was receiving some sort of pension (Table 3.8). For women, the figure was 74.9 percent, or 9.4 percentage points below the rate for males. This differential exists despite the fact that PASIS and survivors' benefits partly compensate for women's more limited access to old age pensions. In 2000, the male/female gap in old age pension coverage amounted to 34 percentage points. The gap in total pension coverage was just 7.6 percentage points, however, since 22.2 percentage points of the original gap were offset by survivors' pensions and 4.1 points were offset by PASIS pensions.

Table 3.8	Pension System Coverage by Gender, 1992–2000 *(percent of persons covered/persons aged 65 and over)*					
Type of pension		1992	1994	1996	1998	2000
Old age	Men	73.7	76.9	75.3	71.4	70.9
	Women	39.8	39.6	37.4	36.7	36.9
	Total	**54.5**	**55.8**	**53.5**	**51.5**	**51.5**
Survivors	Men	0.7	1.4	0.4	0.4	0.3
	Women	21.6	21.6	25.0	24.1	22.5
	Total	**12.6**	**12.8**	**14.6**	**14.0**	**12.9**
Noncontributory	Men	6.2	7.5	12.3	11.6	12.4
(PASIS)	Women	10.0	11.5	16.3	15.0	16.5
	Total	**8.3**	**9.8**	**14.6**	**13.5**	**14.7**
Total	Men	80.6	85.8	88.0	83.4	83.5
	Women	71.3	72.7	78.7	75.8	75.9
	Total	**75.4**	**78.4**	**82.6**	**79.0**	**79.2**

Source: Arenas de Mesa and Gana (2003).

These statistics confirm the fact that women are more likely to lack a pension or only have access to secondary benefits or such benefits as PASIS pensions (see discussion below).

Pension Type and Income Quintile

The information supplied by the CASEN survey shows little difference in coverage rates for noncontributing plan members based on the income quintiles to which they belong. In 2000, 63.5 percent of the people over 60 years of age in quintile I (the bottom income quintile) were receiving some sort of benefit, compared to 66.7 percent of those in quintile V (the top income quintile). The narrowness of the differential between the two rates is attributable to the fact that the poorest groups in the population are largely covered by welfare-based PASIS pensions, which offsets their lower coverage rates for old age retirement pensions (see Table 3.9). For quintile I, 63.4 percent and 26.8 percent of the total population of pensioners receive PASIS pensions and old age pensions, respectively, whereas in quintile V, the corresponding figures are 1.7 percent and 82.2 percent, respectively.

Age and Income Quintiles

The CASEN survey results clearly demonstrate that a positive correlation exists between the coverage of noncontributing members of the popula-

Table 3. 9	Pension Benefit Coverage by Income Quintile and Type of Pension 2000 (percent of the population receiving pension benefits)					
			Income quintiles			
Type of pension	I	II	III	IV	V	Total
Old age	17.0	40.4	50.3	54.7	54.8	45.3
Survivors	6.2	11.1	12.1	13.5	10.7	11.0
Noncontributory	40.3	15.7	6.8	3.2	1.1	11.6
Total	63.5	67.2	69.2	71.4	66.7	67.9

Source: CASEN (2000).

tion and the age of beneficiaries, both at the aggregate level and for all the income quintiles. At the aggregate level, the coverage rate, measured as the percentage of the population over 65 years of age, was 79.2 percent, while the rate, when measured as a percentage of the population over 60 years of age, was substantially lower, at 67.9 percent (see Table 3.9). The difference between the coverage rates for the population over 60 and 65 years of age is largely due to the fact that the legal retirement age for men is 65. Along the same lines, when the figures are broken down by income quintile, they indicate that the coverage of noncontributing members rises as the age cohort increases, with the rate for persons over 75 years of age averaging 50 points higher than the rate for those between the ages of 60 and 64 (see Table 3.10).

Contribution Density

The benefits obtained under an individually funded pension system are influenced by the amounts paid into the account, the length of time over

Table 3.10	Pension Benefit Coverage, by Age Group and by Income Quintile, 2000 (percent of the population receiving pension benefits)				
			Age group		
Income quintile	60–64	65–69	70–74	75+	Total
I	27.1	63.9	81.6	89.3	63.5
II	35.0	67.9	79.4	91.1	67.2
III	42.8	70.4	83.0	89.5	69.2
IV	46.1	70.5	79.9	90.9	71.4
V	42.7	69.0	78.6	83.3	66.7

Source: CASEN (2000).

Table 3.11	Distribution of Contribution Densities of Pension System Members, 1980–2002	
Percentiles (percent)	**Density of contributions (percent)**
5	0.0
10	1.1
15	6.0
20	12.9
25	19.8
30	27.1
35	34.4
40	41.3
45	47.6
50	54.2
55	60.3
60	66.4
65	72.4
70	78.5
75	85.2
80	92.6
85	99.3
90	100.0
95	100.0
Average	**52.4**

Source: Arenas de Mesa, Berhman, and Bravo (2004).

which payments are made, and the density of contributions: that is, the periods during which contributions are made, measured as a percentage of the individual's total working life. Plan members' contribution densities are a vital factor in determining the level of benefits they will receive, and hence the quality of coverage provided by the AFP pension system.

A basis for estimating members' contribution densities is provided by the first Social Protection Survey (Encuesta de Protección Social, or EPS), conducted in 2002 and 2003, which contains information provided by respondents concerning their work and pension histories.[2] This survey represents a major stride forward in the State's implementation of a basic information system on social protection in Chile (Bravo 2004).

The self-reported data supplied by the EPS (2002) indicate that the average contribution density for the pension system as a whole is 52.4 percent (Table 3.11). In other words, a person entering the labor market

---

[2] The survey was undertaken in 2002–03 and contains a representative sample of 17,000 participants in the pension system.

at 20 years of age and retiring at age 60 will have paid into the system for an average of 21 years.

Contribution densities tend to bunch up at the high and low ends of the scale, with 25 percent of the members having densities of under 20 percent and another 25 percent having densities over 85 percent. In addition, 10 percent have densities of 1.1 percent or less, while another 10 percent or so have a density of 100 percent.

The lowest contribution densities are concentrated in the lower-income quintiles. Contribution densities are also influenced by whether an individual is a salaried worker or self-employed. The average density for salaried employees at the time the survey was taken was 65.8 percent, which was 21 percentage points higher than the average density for self-employed workers (Arenas de Mesa, Llanés, and Miranda 2004).

Replacement Ratios

The replacement rate is an important indicator of the adequacy of the pension, showing the ratio of the pension to earnings. Studies that have calculated the replacement ratios for Chile's individually funded system have used a uniform contribution density of between 70 percent and 90 percent, depending on their degree of optimism (Arenas de Mesa and Gana 2003). Arenas de Mesa, Llanés, and Miranda (2004) recently estimated the system's replacement ratios based on information drawn from the EPS (2002).[3] The results furnished by this survey represent a major advance in this respect because they make it possible to compute replacement ratios on the basis of observed (rather than assumed) densities at the micro level; observed densities broken down by income level, gender, and other factors; and age-specific densities, which vary from one age group to another.

For purposes of comparison, the authors estimated replacement ratios using a uniform contribution density of 80 percent and age-specific densities derived from the EPS (2002) (see the last two columns in Table 3.12). When the EPS's age-specific contribution densities were used in

---

[3] To compute the replacement ratio, they used the model of Arenas de Mesa and Gana (2003) with the following assumptions: the worker (with no recognition bonds) enters the labor force at the age of 18 with a minimum wage that grows at a real annual rate of 2 percent until he reaches 50 years of age, after which the salary remains constant in real terms. The contribution density by age and gender is derived from EPS (2002). The annual real return on assets of the funds is assumed at 4 percent and the commission is fixed at $650. The base case takes contribution density by age and gender from EPS (2002).

Table 3.12	Replacement Ratios for the AFP Individually Funded System, by Gender *(percent)*		
	Authors and year of study		
	Arenas de Mesa and Gana	**Arenas de Mesa, Llanés, and Miranda**	
	2003[a]	**2004**	
Years of contribution (based on density)	**80**	**80 UNIFORM**	**EPS**[b]
Rate of return	4	4	4
Men 65 (18)	69	49	
Men 65 (18) — Women 60	57	41	
Men 65 (20)	66		
Women 60 (18)		41	22
Women 65 (18)		60	33
Women 60 (20)	39		
Women 65 (20)	57		

[a.] Estimates of replacement rate using unisex mortality tables.
[b.] Estimates of the replacement rate using specifics densities for each age.
Sources: Arenas de Mesa and Gana (2003); and Arenas de Mesa, Llanés, and Miranda (2004).

the simulations, the replacement ratios for all the groups covered in the study were between 16 and 27 percentage points lower than the rates estimated using a uniform contribution density of 80 percent. Women register the largest decrease, with the replacement ratio falling from 41 percent to 22 percent for women retiring at age 60, and from 60 percent to 33 percent for women retiring at age 65. For men retiring at age 65, with and without dependents, the rates decrease from 69 percent to 49 percent, and from 57 percent to 41 percent, respectively (Arenas de Mesa, Llanés, and Miranda 2004) (see Table 3.12).

The rates for women are 52 percent for those retiring at 60 and 75 percent for those retiring at 65. Thus a woman entering the labor market at 18 years of age who then pays regularly into her pension plan, without interruption, until the legal retirement age (60) will have a replacement ratio of about 50 percent. This simulation was calculated for a woman having a taxable income of 7 UF (Unidad de Fomento, the minimum rate for taxable income) but even for a high-income woman with an income of 60 UF (the ceiling for taxable income), the replacement ratio would not be substantially higher (54 percent).

The replacement ratios estimated for the different income groups and for salaried workers and the self-employed, using group-specific and age-specific contribution densities, yield the following results. There is

Table 3.13	Replacement Ratios for Taxable Incomes of 7 UF and 60 UF, and Pension Ratios *(percent)*		
	Wage replacement ratio		Pension ratio among those with an income of 7 UF and 60 UF
Participants	7 UF (percent)	60 UF (percent)	
MEN 65-s/c	36	53	12.97
MEN 65-c/c WOMEN 60	29	44	12.97
WOMEN 60	21	31	13.00
WOMEN 65	31	46	12.97

MEN 65 = Men 65 years of age.
WOMEN 60 and WOMEN 65 = Women 60 and 65 years of age.
s/c = Without dependents.
c/c = With dependents.
Note: Assumes the base case with the exception of the income levels in the case of 60 UF and of the contribution densities according to the households' per capita income — quintile I and quintile V.
Source: Author's estimates, based on the EPS densities (2002).

a positive correlation between income level and replacement ratio (see Table 3.13). Salaried workers have higher replacement ratios than self-employed workers (see Table 3.14 and Arenas de Mesa, Llanés, and Miranda 2004).

When estimates are based on contribution densities broken down by per capita household income quintiles, the replacement ratios for high-income members are over 10 points higher than the rates for their low-income

Table 3.14	Replacement Ratios for Salaried Workers and Self-employed Workers at the Same Income Level					
		Wage replacement ratio (percent)			Proportion with respect to the pension of H65[a] (percent)	
Participants	Base	Dependent	Own account		Dependent	Own account
MEN 65-s/c	49	55	35		111	70
MEN 65-c/c WOMEN 60	41	45	29		91	58
WOMEN 60	22	32	20		65	41
WOMEN 65	33	47	30		96	61

s/c = Men without dependents.
c/c = Men with dependents.
[a] H65 refers to men 65 years old and over. Assumes the base case, with the exception of the contribution densities that correspond to that of the dependent workers and to that of the independent workers.
Source: Author's estimates, based on the EPS densities (2002).

counterparts (Table 3.13). The 8.6 ratio between the earnings of high-income workers (60 UF) and low-income workers (7 UF) in the labor market rises to a multiple of 12 when their monthly pensions are compared.

The replacement ratios for male salaried workers exceed the rates for workers in the base case by 6 percentage points in the case of those with dependents and by 4 points for those without dependents (Table 3.14). The rates for self-employed workers are 14 points below the base case rates for those without dependents and 12 points below for those with dependents. For women retiring at age 60, female salaried workers have replacements rates 10 points above the base case rate, while female self-employed workers' replacement ratios are just 2 points below that rate. Female salaried workers retiring at age 65 have replacement ratios 14 percentage points higher than the rate for the base case, while the rates for female self-employed workers are just 3 points below it. The replacement ratios for men (base scenario) are more similar to the rates for salaried workers than to the rates for self-employed workers. By contrast, the rates for women (base scenario) are closer to the rates for self-employed workers (Arenas de Mesa, Llanés, and Miranda 2004).

Replacement Ratios and Coverage by Gender

As Chile's pension system matures, the issue of gender will occupy an increasingly central place in the debate concerning its future pension scheme. Women's growing participation in the labor market will earn them a larger share as direct beneficiaries in the pension market. Women's estimated future replacement ratios are low, even assuming a 100 percent contribution density (that is, even after isolating the effect of the lower contribution densities that women have because of their intermittent participation in the labor market). Given the conditions generally associated with women's participation in the labor market, which include, on average, lower pay levels and bigger gaps in contributions to the pension system, women will tend to have lower cumulative balances in their accounts and thus smaller pensions. Because of the impact of the demographic transition, especially in the case of women, a majority of tomorrow's older adults will be women, and they will have longer life expectancies than their male counterparts. The pension system's fiscal effects are concentrated among women, both during the transition and in terms of medium- and long-term projections (Arenas de Mesa and Gana 2003).

Institutional records indicate that in recent years, women's pension coverage has increased more than men's. Women's effective coverage expanded by 16 percentage points from 1986 to 2003, rising from

36.8 percent to 52.8 percent, whereas men's coverage rate climbed by 12.8 points (from 33.7 percent to 46.5 percent). This differential may be associated with the progressive increase in women's labor participation rates, which have outpaced male rates. In fact, while the female labor participation rate rose by 4.2 percentage points (from 30.9 percent to 35.1 percent) between 1990 and 2003, the male participation rate fell by 4.0 points (from 75.5 percent to 71.5 percent).

Institutional records also show that, on average, women's occupational coverage rate stood at 5.3 percentage points above the male coverage rate between 1986 and 2003. In the latter year, 57.6 percent of all working women were covered, whereas the coverage rate for men was 50 percent. However, EPS (2002) indicates that this ratio is reversed if certain variables are controlled. For instance, if the variables of income and education level are controlled, then women in the lower-income groups and women with levels of education below completion of secondary school have lower coverage rates than men. Women with no schooling at all are the most extreme case, with a rate 26.2 points below the corresponding male coverage rate. The EPS (2002) data yield lower occupational coverage rates for women than for men in all occupational categories except "employer" and "salaried employee" (Arenas de Mesa, Berhman, and Bravo 2004).

The EPS (2002) data indicate that the average contribution density for men is 16 percentage points higher than it is for women (59.8 percent for men versus 43.8 percent for women) (Table 3.15).

An analysis of contribution densities, broken down by gender, points to heavy concentrations of women in the lower ranges and of men in the higher ranges. Half the women have a contribution density of 40 percent or less, and 50 percent of this last group has densities of 11.3 percent or below (Table 3.15). Male contribution densities, on the other hand, are concentrated in the higher ranges, with 20 percent of the men having contribution densities of 100 percent or very close to that figure (Arenas de Mesa, Llanés, and Miranda 2004). Women's lower contribution densities are accounted for by the fact they have bigger contribution gaps than men. In the past, for example, women have had higher unemployment rates than men (a differential of 2.2 percentage points in 1990–2003) (see Table 3.16). Women are also more likely to work in the informal labor market (Gana 2002), which has negative implications in terms of their contribution densities.

Women face other drawbacks deriving from the pension system as such. These factors include the lower legal retirement age for women and the differential used in estimating their pensions because of their

Table 3.15	Distribution of Pension Contribution Densities of Pension System Members, by Gender, 1980–2002 (percent)		
Percentiles	Men	Women	Total
5	0.0	0.0	0.0
10	4.9	0.0	1.1
15	13.3	2.2	6.0
20	23.3	5.7	12.9
25	31.5	11.3	19.8
30	40.3	16.7	27.1
35	47.2	22.2	34.4
40	54.2	28.5	41.3
45	60.3	34.7	47.6
50	65.7	40.2	54.2
55	70.8	46.3	60.3
60	76.0	52.0	66.4
65	81.4	58.2	72.4
70	87.0	64.9	78.5
75	92.7	72.3	85.2
80	98.1	80.0	92.6
85	100.0	90.7	99.3
90	100.0	100.0	100.0
95	100.0	100.0	100.0
Average	59.8	43.8	52.4

Source: Arenas de Mesa, Berhman, and Bravo (2004).

Table 3.16	Unemployment Rates, by Gender, 1990–2003 (yearly averages, percent)		
Year	Men	Women	Total
1990	7.0	9.7	7.8
1991	7.3	10.3	8.2
1992	5.6	8.9	6.6
1993	5.4	9.0	6.5
1994	6.7	10.3	7.8
1995	6.3	9.0	7.3
1996	5.6	7.9	6.4
1997	5.4	7.7	6.1
1998	5.8	7.6	6.4
1999	9.4	10.7	9.8
2000	8.8	10.0	9.2
2001	8.9	9.7	9.1
2002	8.6	9.6	8.9
2003	7.9	9.7	8.5

Source: Arenas de Mesa and Gana (2003); INE.

greater average life expectancy. In view of these factors, the pensions to be received by a significant proportion of female AFP members are likely to be quite low. A recent study estimates that 45 percent of the women who are now between the ages of 45 and 50 will not have accumulated enough capital to qualify for the minimum pension. Among this group, only those who have at least 20 years' worth of contributions will be eligible for a State-guaranteed minimum pension (SGMP). A sizeable number of them may therefore end up receiving PASIS (provided that they meet the earnings requirements). The scale of this problem is all the greater because the number of older adult women will be increasing in the coming years. What is more, those women will be living longer than before and longer than their male counterparts (Table 3.17).

The Welfare-based, Noncontributory Pension System (the PASIS)

In addition to providing for the elderly, disabled, widowed, or orphaned, pension systems also fulfill a distributional function by alleviating the

Table 3.17	Projected Life Expectancy at Retirement Age, by Gender, 1955–2050 *(percent)*			
	60 years		**65 years**	
Period	**Women**	**Men**	**Women**	**Men**
1955–1960	17.38	14.95	14.19	12.16
1965–1970	17.83	15.36	14.56	12.57
1975–1980	19.29	16.25	15.69	13.20
1980–1985	20.17	16.76	16.36	13.57
1985–1990	21.00	17.56	17.14	14.21
1990–1995	21.73	18.25	17.82	14.78
1995–2000	22.66	19.06	18.67	15.53
2000–2005	24.00	20.34	19.91	16.71
2005–2010	24.52	20.71	20.38	17.03
2015–2020	25.44	21.35	21.22	17.59
2020–2025	25.84	21.63	21.58	17.84
2025–2030	26.20	21.87	21.91	18.06
2035–2040	26.82	22.30	22.48	18.43
2045–2050	27.34	22.64	22.94	18.73
Change in life expectancy (years)				
1980–1985 and 1995–2000	2.49	2.30	2.31	1.96
1995–2000 and 2045–2050	4.68	3.58	4.27	3.20

Source: CELADE (2004a, 2004b).

indigence or poverty of members of the population who fail to accumulate sufficient savings and who therefore find themselves in a vulnerable position during old age. In Chile, this function is performed by the PASIS pension system.

The PASIS pensions were created in 1975 by Decree-Law 869. They are intended for disabled persons and people 65 years of age or more who lack resources and are not covered by the social security system.

In 1987, eligibility requirements were modified to include persons with mental disabilities who lack financial resources, regardless of their age (Decree-Law 18,600). There are currently three types of PASIS pensions: disability, old age, and mental impairment pensions. The number of new PASIS openings per year is determined jointly by the Subsecretaría de Previsión Social (Office of the Under-Secretary for Social Insurance, or SPS), the Superintendencia de Seguridad Social (Superintendency for Social Security, or SUSESO), and the Dirección de Presupuestos (Budget Office, or DIPRES) during the formulation of each year's budget (see Gana 2002).

PASIS Coverage

Between 1990 and 2003, the total number of PASIS pensions granted and the unit value of those pensions rose by 19.7 percent and 94.2 percent, respectively. During that period, the total number of PASIS pensions went from 311,000 to 372,000 and the amount of those benefits rose from Ch$19,267 to Ch$37,412 (see Tables 3.18 and 3.19).

Between 1998 and 2003, the PASIS pensions' unit value was equivalent, on average, to 50 percent of the minimum pension, more than 9 percentage points higher than its average for the immediately preceding five-year period (1993–97) and about 20 points higher than the average for 1990–93.

Public Spending on PASIS Pensions

Public spending on PASIS pensions rose steadily throughout the review period, with the sole exception of 1993. This upward trend is in keeping with the expansion of PASIS coverage and with the stagnation, in real terms, of the funding for these pensions derived from the 1.5 percent allotment of taxable earnings collected by the INP, the CAPREDENA, and the DIPRECA. Public spending on PASIS pensions jumped by 112.5 percent during the period under study, with the sharpest upswings being recorded in 1994, 1999, and 2000 and a slowdown in the growth rate

| Table 3.18 | PASIS Pension Benefits Granted, 1990–2003 *(average number per month)* | | | | |

Year	Old age	Disabilities	Mental impairment[a]	Total	New annual quotas PASIS
1990	151,093	160,270	—	311,363	49,927
1991	141,151	158,181	—	299,332	68,374
1992	134,919	155,631	—	290,550	75,943
1993	138,374	157,847	—	296,221	103,113
1994	148,874	163,397	—	312,271	97,145
1995	152,449	166,343	—	318,792	24,611
1996	154,870	171,607	—	326,477	27,716
1997	160,800	169,450	9,390	339,640	30,409
1998	162,212	169,075	14,141	345,420	19,641
1999	163,338	170,404	17,003	350,745	20,000
2000	165,373	173,787	19,653	358,813	30,000
2001	167,358	177,507	22,522	367,387	26,070
2002	167,212	179,926	24,780	371,918	21,350
2003	165,150	180,921	26,641	372,712	15,000

[a.] Since 1997, data have been recorded for pensions granted for mental impairment.
Source: Gana (2002); SUSESO (1990–2002).

| Table 3.19 | Value of Welfare-based Pensions and Minimum Pensions, 1990–2003 | | | | |

| | Welfare-based pensions PASIS | | | Minimum pension | PASIS/minimum pension |
Year	Unit amount[a] (2003 pesos)	Index (1990=100)	Annual change (percent)	Unit amount[a] (2003 pesos)	(percent)
1990	19,267	100.00	43.00	49,863	38.6
1991	16,238	84.28	−15.72	55,898	29.0
1992	14,407	74.78	−11.27	57,066	25.2
1993	22,370	116.10	55.27	56,993	39.3
1994	23,324	121.05	4.26	56,970	40.9
1995	25,679	133.28	10.10	62,667	41.0
1996	26,194	135.95	2.00	62,619	41.8
1997	26,236	136.17	0.16	65,710	39.9
1998	35,836	185.99	36.59	65,469	54.7
1999	36,540	189.65	1.96	74,777	48.9
2000	35,828	185.95	−1.95	74,887	47.8
2001	36,482	189.35	1.82	75,203	48.5
2002	36,697	190.46	0.59	75,302	48.7
2003	37,412	194.17	1.95	75,211	49.7

[a.] Amounts as of December of each year.
Source: Gana (2002); SUSESO. (1990– 2002).

Table 3.20	Public Spending on PASIS Pensions in Chile, 1990–2003

				Public expenditure on PASIS		
Year	Public expenditure on PASIS (millions of 2003 pesos)	Annual change (percent)	Index (1990=100)	GDP (percent)	Public expenditure pensions (percent)	Social public expenditure (percent)
1990	78,450	100.0	0.3	5.0	2.5	2.5
1991	85,161	8.6	108.6	0.3	5.2	2.4
1992	89,436	5.0	114.0	0.3	5.2	2.3
1993	84,197	−5.9	107.3	0.3	4.5	2.0
1994	93,150	10.6	118.7	0.3	4.8	2.1
1995	98,068	5.3	125.0	0.2	4.8	2.0
1996	107,544	9.7	137.1	0.3	4.9	2.0
1997	112,310	4.4	143.2	0.3	4.9	2.0
1998	127,579	13.6	162.6	0.3	5.2	2.1
1999	155,884	22.2	198.7	0.4	5.8	2.4
2000	156,726	0.5	199.8	0.4	5.5	2.3
2001	162,128	3.4	206.7	0.4	5.4	2.2
2002	166,524	2.7	212.3	0.4	5.6	2.2
2003	166,681	0.1	212.5	0.4	5.3	2.2

Source: Gana (2002); Dirección de Presupuesto del Ministerio de Hacienda (DIPRES) (2000, 2004a, 2004b); SUCESO (1990–2003).

during the last four years (see Table 3.20). In real terms, this variable rose by 85.2 percent between 1993 and 1999, but its growth rate then slowed to 7 percent between 1999 and 2003.

In 2005, there will be around 400,000 PASIS beneficiaries, which translates into a budget for the welfare-based PASIS pensions of over Ch$197 billion (pesos at 2004 prices). Government spending on PASIS pensions has thus become a sizeable component of public sector pension and social spending, accounting for an average of 5.2 percent and 2.2 percent of the total amount spent on those items, respectively.

To ensure the financial sustainability of the PASIS, new sources of financing must be found to cover the system's future funding needs. To estimate the amount of funding required for this program, projections of the number of potential beneficiaries must be refined, using the detailed information on members' work histories that is now being compiled.

Impact on Indigence and Poverty

A recent study conducted by the International Labour Organization asserts that the PASIS scheme has brought about a sharp reduction in indigence and serves as a major redistributive tool for Chile's social protection. According to Gana (2002), indigence is down by 69 percent among households that receive a PASIS pension and by 83 percent in households where the PASIS recipient is over 65 years of age. These figures show how important a role a subsidy such as the PASIS pension can play in reducing poverty. In light of these results, it is vital for this program to be designed properly so that it can be targeted as accurately as possible on the corresponding group within the population (Gana 2002)

Institutional Effects of the Pension Reform

Chile's pension reform pursued the first pension objective (security) by designing the individually funded pension scheme. It sought to achieve the second (poverty alleviation) by setting a minimum income level for persons covered by the system. From a conceptual standpoint, this institutional arrangement is ideal in a system where everybody contributes, because it encourages people to save while at the same time providing a fiscally inexpensive way of guaranteeing a basic income during old age. However, if circumstances are such that not everyone can maintain a contributions record that will afford them access to that minimum level of income, then a considerable percentage of members may be left without benefits.

Although the welfare-based noncontributory scheme could mitigate the problem posed by such individuals' exclusion from the contributory scheme, at this time the system is not institutionally or financially equipped to cope with a problem of this magnitude.

The system was designed based on two basic, implicit assumptions. Those assumptions were that contribution densities and income levels would both be high enough that only a small fraction of plan members would need the State subsidy or PASIS. As noted, given the type of coverage provided to contributing plan members, many of the people who are now part of the active workforce may eventually become eligible for the GPME and PASIS pensions. Some people will not be able to afford an adequate level of consumption and will not qualify for any of the benefits provided by the State.

Even among the population groups for which the system was implicitly designed (that is, people with high contribution densities and high incomes), there will still be some members—primarily women—who will be left outside the system to some extent. In short, the existing institutional structure either does not address the income requirements of a very significant percentage of the members of Chile's pension system at all or does so only partially.

These findings attest to the fact that the design of Chile's pension reform program underestimated the role that the State would be called upon to play. In view of the pension system's current fiscal characteristics, it may be necessary to revamp what has come to be known as the pension system's first pillar, which comprises the noncontributory scheme and the SGMP. As noted earlier, the organizational, regulatory, and financial structure does not measure up to the magnitude of the problem to be resolved.

The implications that this overhaul of the first pillar will have for the second pillar (that is, the contributory system managed by the AFPs) will also have to be addressed. That the second pillar will be unable to perform its main functions for a large part of its contributors is unacceptable. Such a breakdown would generate a greater than expected fiscal burden and make it necessary to adopt policy measures not provided for in the reform program in order to deal with the shortfall in members' pension benefits.

The technical and political capacity of the State, in conjunction with other stakeholders, to identify, reach consensus on, and implement a redesigned pension system is crucial in maintaining the long-term viability of the advances made in organizing and consolidating the system and, in particular, of its very important role in the development of Chile's capital markets and its contribution to the country's development. On the other hand, if the system's redesign is postponed for too long, the deeper deficits that might well result could hinder the search for solutions and the stabilization of these achievements.

In terms of its place in the government's institutional structure, the pension system falls within the purview of the Ministry of Labor, which includes the SPS (Office of the Under-Secretary for Social Insurance), and is linked to SUSESO (Superintendency for Social Security) and the SAFP (Superintendency of Pension Fund Managers). The scope of the system, its impact on macroeconomic balances, its importance for the development and future status of the capital market, and the scale of its effects on public finances are such, however, that any redesign of systems in the sector will have to take account not only social protection issues but also issues of public finances and economic processes as a whole.

The economic authorities' responsibilities in terms of fiscal policy management are not limited to maintaining macroeconomic stability and providing a steady stream of financing for the social protection system. They also play an active role in the development and implementation of the public and semi-public institutional framework for social policies and programs. In other words, fiscal policy is not neutral in relation to the institutional structure underpinning social protection measures, nor will it be so in the future.

Before embarking on the redesign of any component of the pension system, it is crucial to have reliable, disaggregated, systematized information about that system. Even though Chile's pension reform program was introduced some 23 years ago, the data provided by its public information systems are still aggregated and are not broken down by plan member. In view of this situation, the SPS asked the University of Chile to administer the Social Protection Survey (EPS that will be used to monitor the pension status of a representative cohort of the system as a whole. This public database (www.proteccionsocial.cl) offers enormous potential and, when cross-referenced with other databases, will be one of the most valuable information systems for use in the design of pension and social policies.

Fiscal Effects of the Pension Reform

The way in which the pension system's deficit is financed during its transition from a public pay-as-you-go scheme to a fully funded system of individual accounts is one of the most important factors in determining the various capital accumulation paths and the system's inter- and intra-generational distributive effects (Arellano 1985; Arrau 1991; Kotlikoff 1995).

Components of the Deficit

The Chilean pension system's deficit consists of five components:

- the operating deficit occasioned by the need to pay out benefits under the old public pension system until its discontinuation;
- the recognition bonds used to certify the contributions made under the old system by people who then transferred to the AFP system;
- the PASIS noncontributory pensions paid to disabled persons and older adults (over 65 years of age) who are indigent and/or lack pension plans;
- the minimum pension payments made under the AFP system; and

- the deficit of the pre-existing pension scheme serving the military and police forces.

These components can be divided into short-run and ongoing fiscal obligations. The operating deficit and the recognition bonds are both short-term fiscal liabilities that stem directly from the 1980–81 pension reform. The transition will take until 2050 in the first case and until 2038 in the second (Arenas de Mesa and Marcel 1993).

The PASIS pensions and the deficit of the armed forces' pension scheme are fiscal obligations under the old pension system. The minimum pensions are obligations that the State has incurred under the new AFP system. The PASIS, the armed forces' pension deficit, and the SGMP are expenses that the Treasury will have to cover indefinitely.

Table 3.21 depicts the trends in the fiscal obligations from 1981 to 2003. During this period, the pension system's total deficit averaged 5.7 percent of GDP. The deficit of the pension system for the country's civilian population amounted to approximately 75 percent of the total deficit, while the military deficit accounted for the other 25 percent (4.3 percent and 1.4 percent of annual GDP, respectively).

Deficit from the Transition from the Previous System

During the transition from the government-run pay-as-you-go system to an individually funded model, the main cause of the deficit has been the financial imbalance stemming from the operation of the old system.

Between 1981 and 2003, the INP's operating deficit averaged 3.3 percent of GDP per year and represented around 58 percent of the total deficit. In 1980, the old public pension scheme was paying over 1 million pensions and had 1.7 million contributing members. This generated a deficit equivalent to 1.7 percent of GDP (Marcel and Arenas de Mesa 1992). With the introduction of the pension reform, nearly 1.2 million contributing members transferred to the new system between 1981 and 1982. This generated an operating deficit equivalent to 3.9 percent of GDP in 1982, which was covered with public funds. After 1984, the operating deficit rose more slowly than GDP because of the pace of economic growth and the slowly declining number of pensioners in the old system. As a result, the operating deficit shrank from 4.7 percent to 2.8 percent of GDP between 1984 and 1995. This trend should continue, but the pension benefits paid out by the administrations that have held office (backed by the political coalition known as the *Concertación*) have held the operating deficit fairly steady (around 2.9 percent of GDP in 2003) (see Table 3.21).

Recognition Bonds

Recognition bonds are a lump sum transfer that the State makes to pension plan members once they become eligible for retirement. These bonds certify the members' entitlements based on the number of years that they had paid their contributions into the old system before transferring to the

Table 3.21	Chile's Public Pension Deficit, 1981–2003 (percent of GDP)						
Year	Operational deficit[a]	Recognition bonds	PASIS pensions	Minimum pensions	Pension system deficit	Military system deficit	Total pension system deficit
	(1)	(2)	(3)	(4)	(5) = (1)+(2) +(3)+(4)	(6)	(7)= (5) + (6)
1981	3.6	0.0	0.2	0.00	3.8	—	3.8
1982	6.0	0.1	0.3	0.00	6.4	—	6.4
1983	6.5	0.2	0.4	0.00	7.1	—	7.1
1984	6.9	0.2	0.5	0.00	7.6	—	7.6
1985	6.0	0.2	0.5	0.00	6.7	—	6.7
1986	5.9	0.3	0.5	0.00	6.7	—	6.7
1987	5.2	0.4	0.5	0.00	6.1	—	6.1
1988	4.6	0.4	0.4	0.00	5.4	—	5.4
1989	4.7	0.4	0.3	0.01	5.4	—	5.4
1990	3.3	0.5	0.3	0.01	4.1	1.2	5.4
1991	3.3	0.5	0.3	0.01	4.1	1.2	5.3
1992	3.2	0.5	0.3	0.01	4.0	1.1	5.1
1993	3.2	0.6	0.3	0.01	4.1	1.2	5.3
1994	3.1	0.7	0.3	0.01	4.0	1.1	5.2
1995	2.8	0.7	0.2	0.02	3.8	1.1	4.9
1996	3.1	0.7	0.3	0.02	4.1	1.1	5.2
1997	3.0	0.8	0.3	0.02	4.1	1.1	5.2
1998	3.2	0.9	0.3	0.03	4.4	1.1	5.5
1999	3.2	1.1	0.4	0.04	4.7	1.2	5.9
2000	3.1	1.1	0.4	0.05	4.7	1.3	6.0
2001	3.1	1.1	0.4	0.06	4.7	1.3	6.0
2002	3.0	1.1	0.4	0.07	4.6	1.3	5.9
2003	2.9	1.1	0.4	0.06	4.5	1.3	5.8

— Not available

a. Data for 1981–89 includes an estimate of the military pension system. Data for 1990–2003 does not include the military pension system deficit.

Source: Arenas de Mesa and Benavides (2003); Arenas de Mesa (2004).

individually funded system. The bonds represent the State's obligation to contributors to the old pay-as-you-go system. This commitment had been implicit prior to the 1980–81 reform, but is now an explicit obligation. The most substantive change in this respect is not the existence of a financial commitment on the part of the State but rather the scale of that obligation and the time horizon for its fulfillment (Arenas de Mesa and Marcel 1993).

The deficit represented by these obligations rose from 0.1 percent of GDP in 1982 to 1.1 percent of GDP in 2003, for an annual average of 0.6 percent of GDP over that period. The status report on the public Treasury published in December 2003 notes that the State had paid off nearly 340,000 recognition bonds, leaving another 900,000 yet to be settled.

Welfare-based Pensions

Public sector spending on the PASIS pensions has been climbing steadily, for a cumulative increase of over 100 percent between 1990 and 2003. This rise is in keeping with the trend in the PASIS pensions' coverage and average unit value over this period (Table 3.21). Spending on the PASIS pensions averaged 0.4 percent of GDP per year between 2000 and 2003 (Table 3.20). Public spending on PASIS or the associated fiscal obligations have become a major item of current spending for the central government. By way of illustration, the PASIS budget for 2005 is 9.5 times the size of the budget for all the training programs conducted by the Ministry of Labor through the National Training and Employment Service, nearly three times as much as the total cost of Chile's Solidarity Program, and 30 percent more than the annual estimated cost of the health reform bill recently passed by Congress.

Minimum Pensions

The system of individually funded accounts offers a State-guaranteed minimum pension (the SGMP) for all members who have built up 20 years or more of contributions but who have not accumulated sufficient funds to finance what the State determines to be a basic minimum pension. The level of the minimum pension is the same under both the old and new systems and is adjusted periodically by the government based on past inflation. Table 3.20 shows the adjusted values of the minimum pension and how it compares to the value of the welfare-based PASIS pension. As may be seen from this table, the minimum pension rose more steeply than the PASIS in the 1990s, but this trend reversed itself between 2000 and 2003.

The State guarantee for the minimum pension is activated once the pension fund has been exhausted, so it takes a few years, once the member has qualified for the benefit, for this financial commitment to come into play. Table 3.21 shows that the public sector's spending on minimum pensions has risen steadily. As the AFP system matures, spending levels will continue to climb because of the increase in the number of pensioners. Spending on the SGMP rose steadily between 1989 and 2002, moving up from 0.01 percent of GDP to 0.07 percent of GDP during that period. This item of expenditure amounted to 0.06 percent of GDP in 2003, which is equivalent to US$35 million; the estimate for the 2005 budget is US$55 million.

As will be discussed below, the future nature of the government's financial obligations under the existing pension system will hinge upon the trend in SGMP expenditure. This is an ongoing commitment on the part of the State under the pension reform program that may generate fiscal liabilities on an unexpectedly large scale.

Deficit of Previous System

Given the low contribution densities of members of the current plan, more of them will presumably come to depend on the SGMP—or, if they do not have 20 years' worth of contributions, on the PASIS pensions. Almost half (45 percent) of the women who are now between the ages of 45 and 50 will not have accumulated enough capital to qualify for the minimum pension, estimates indicate. Among this group, only those who have at least 20 years' worth of contributions will be eligible for a SGMP, and a sizeable number of them may therefore end up receiving PASIS pensions (provided that they meet the earnings requirements).

Against this backdrop, the amount of pressure that the pension system will be exerting on government finances appears to have been underestimated because existing projections have been based on overly optimistic assumptions regarding contribution densities, especially in the case of women. These estimates are going to rise both because an increasing number of women will become primary beneficiaries of the pension system and because the demographic transition is more marked among the female population.

The Ministry of Finance's SGMP projections indicate that spending on these pensions will have increased fivefold by 2020 to Ch$200 billion (Table 3.24). The ministry has proposed the creation of a pension reserve fund for SGMP payments, to be financed with the savings generated by the rule requiring the country to maintain a structural surplus equivalent to 1 percent of GDP. This policy measure attests to the seriousness of this matter and to the precautions that must be taken in order to maintain a responsible, balanced fiscal policy. These steps place Chile at the forefront of the effort to find a suitable approach to the fiscal management of these types of long-term contingent liabilities. This kind of measure will also make it possible to create genuine social protection mechanisms backed up by sustainable, balanced, long-term financing.

The Total Deficit of the Pension System

The pension system deficit is composed of the civilian and military pension deficits. The former consists of the operating deficit, recognition bonds, PASIS pensions, and minimum pensions; the latter is generated by the pre-existing funds systems for the armed forces and the police force, which were not included in the 1980–81 pension reform and are still in operation. The armed forces' pension deficit has been estimated at an average of 1.5 percent of GDP per year between 1981 and 2003. This, plus the operating deficit of the civilian system, which averaged 3.2 percent of GDP, generated an operating deficit for that same period of 4.7 percent of GDP. By comparison, the pension deficit for the pre-reform period of 1974–80 amounted to 2.4 percent of GDP. Between 1981 and 2003, the Chilean pension system's total deficit averaged 5.7 percent of GDP per year (Arenas de Mesa 2004).

Deficit Generated by Pension Reform and Net National Savings

By comparing the savings generated by the pensions funds and the pension system's deficit (Table 3.22), a partial equilibrium analysis can be used to estimate the net effect in terms of the savings associated with the pension reform. Between 1981 and 2003, the reform of the country's pension system created a deficit that, on average, was double the size of the flow of private savings generated by the pension funds. This translated into an average net reduction in savings of nearly 3 percent of GDP. In the coming years, this net dissavings will surely give way to a positive net savings rate, once the AFP pension system has reached full maturity.

The country's success in achieving this trend in net savings in the future will hinge on the situation with regard to the pension system's deficit, since the net savings generated by the pension funds (measured

Table 3.22	Net National Savings/Pension Deficit in Chile, 1981–2003 (percent of GDP)			
Year	Total pension deficit[a]	Savings of the pension funds	Net national saving/deficit	Other saving of the central government
1981	3.8	0.9	−2.9	7.7
1982	6.4	1.8	−4.6	3.5
1983	7.1	1.7	−5.4	4.8
1984	7.6	1.9	−5.7	6.4
1985	6.7	2.0	−4.7	7.1
1986	6.7	2.2	−4.5	8.0
1987	6.1	2.3	−3.8	9.1
1988	5.4	2.7	−2.7	7.6
1989	5.4	2.9	−2.5	8.4
1990	5.4	3.0	−2.4	7.8
1991	5.3	2.8	−2.5	8.8
1992	5.1	3.3	−1.8	9.8
1993	5.3	3.6	−1.7	9.9
1994	5.2	3.9	−1.3	9.7
1995	4.9	4.4	−0.5	9.8
1996	5.2	4.3	−0.9	10.5
1997	5.2	5.1	−0.2	10.3
1998	5.5	5.0	−0.5	9.3
1999	5.8	5.3	−0.5	8.1
2000	5.9	5.5	−0.4	9.5
2001	5.9	4.8	−1.1	9.4
2002	5.8	—	—	8.6
2003	5.8	—	—	9.1

— Not available
[a] Includes estimates of the military pension system deficit.
Source: Arenas de Mesa and Gumucio (2000); DIPRES (2000, 2004a).

as a percent of GDP) will tend to level off once the new system's coverage stabilizes, among other factors.

Chile's pension system deficit was coupled with an effective adjustment in the central government's financial balance (excluding the pension system). Between 1981 and 1982, when the pension system's deficit jumped from 3.8 percent to 6.4 percent of GDP, the public sector's current surplus shrank from 3.9 percent to −0.9 percent of GDP. Thereafter, the public saving rate rose steadily, averaging 4.6 percent of GDP per year in the 1990s. This rate of increase has been heralded as an outstanding achievement on the part of the Chilean economy. However, if the public sector's financing of the pension system deficit is added into the picture (Table 3.22), then it is clear that the effort made by the government was even greater than the figures for public sector saving suggest. Non-pension public sector saving averaged 8 percent of GDP in 1981–96, with an increase of 2.5 percent of GDP being registered between the annual averages for 1981–89 and 1990–96. In other words, during the 1980s, public finances absorbed not only the impact of a deep economic crisis but also the financing of the deficit generated by the pension system. During the 1990s, public saving rose even further thanks to factors above and beyond the moderate decrease seen in the pension system's deficit (Arenas de Mesa and Marcel 1999).

Pension systems require more than 40 years to mature. Before then, it is difficult to determine a pension reform program's lasting effects on public finances and the economy. The figures given in the preceding paragraphs do, however, indicate that, alongside its beneficial effects in terms of the development of the country's financial and capital markets, the privatization of the pension system has, at least during this transitional period, generated a sizeable deficit, which is being financed by the State. Within this context, the increase in the Chilean economy's domestic savings rate during this period can be accounted for by the public sector's systematic absorption of the pension system's deficit. The reform's supposed success in boosting domestic savings rates in Chile can thus be attributed more to fiscal discipline than to the fact that the pension system has been placed under private sector management.

Pension System Deficit Projections, 2005–10

As the individually funded pension system matures, not only the size but also the composition of the system's deficit will change. The pension deficit's temporary components (the operating deficit and the recognition bonds) will, by definition, gradually disappear, but the deficit's permanent components, such as the State-guaranteed minimum pensions, will increase as the private system matures. Meanwhile, trends in the deficits of the armed forces' pension scheme and PASIS pensions will be determined by governmental policy decisions.

Table 3.23 shows the projected deficits of the these aspects of the pension system for 2004–10. These projections indicate that the level of the government's financial commitment under the pension system will remain high throughout this period. These results corroborate the conclusion that the estimates of the pension system's fiscal impact in Chile that were made at the time of the reform's introduction in the 1980s were fairly conservative and substantially underestimated that impact.

By the end of this decade, the operating deficit is expected to have declined by an additional percentage point of GDP, which would put it

Table 3.23	Projection of the Civilian Pension System's Deficit in Chile, 2004–10 (average annual rate, as a percent of GDP)			
Year	Operational deficit (1)	Recognition bonds (2)	PASIS pensions (3)	Minimum pensions (4)	Public pension deficit (5) = (1)+(2)+(3)+(4)
2004	2.7	1.3	0.4	0.1	4.6
2005	2.6	1.3	0.4	0.2	4.5
2006	2.5	1.3	0.4	0.2	4.4
2007	2.4	1.3	0.4	0.2	4.3
2008	2.3	1.3	0.4	0.2	4.2
2009	2.1	1.2	0.4	0.3	4.1
2010	2.0	1.2	0.4	0.3	3.9
2004–10	2.4	1.2	0.4	0.2	4.2

Source: Arenas de Mesa (2004).

at 2 percent of GDP in 2010 (Table 3.23). This means that the average deficit for the first decade of the twenty-first century is likely to amount to 2.4 percent of GDP.

The projections indicate that the deficit represented by recognition bonds will peak at 1.3 percent of GDP in 2004, will hold at that level until 2008, and will then begin to fall, disappearing altogether by around 2030. Thus for the first decade of this century, this deficit will average 1.2 percent of GDP.

The Ministry of Finance has estimated that the PASIS pension deficit for the first decade of the twenty-first century will remain at the same level as the average for the 1981–2003 period (0.4 percent of GDP) (Table 3.24). The SGMP deficit will average 0.2 percent of GDP per year for 2004–10 and is projected at 0.3 percent of GDP in 2010.

Conclusion

This chapter presents a detailed analysis of the Chilean pension system, aimed at determining its fiscal and institutional impacts. The main findings appear below.

1. The scope, institutional structure, and fiscal positioning of Chile's pension system go far beyond the bounds of a social protection scheme as such. They have a bearing on such factors as the financing of social policies in general, macroeconomic policy, and the financial status of the capital market. Today, pension funds represent the equivalent of

Table 3.24	Projected Spending on SGMP Pensions, 2005–20 (millions of constant 2004 pesos)	
Year	Expenditures (millions of 2004 pesos)	
2005	46,761	
2006	53,586	
2007	60,870	
2008	68,304	
2009	76,765	
2010	84,941	
2011	94,024	
2012	103,534	
2013	112,897	
2014	123,513	
2015	133,746	
2016	145,563	
2017	157,309	
2018	169,951	
2019	183,187	
2020	195,092	

Source: Dirección de Presupuestos (Budget Office).

60 percent of GDP, and the investments they generate have consolidated a capital market in Chile that simply did not exist two decades ago and that has become a mainstay of the economy's capacity for growth.

2. Along with the major role played by the pension system is a major unfulfilled challenge of providing quality coverage to a significant portion of the participants. Progress and achievements in the country's capital market should be matched by its social security policies. The country will have to strike a balance in this respect if its pension system is to be viable over the long term.

3. Chile and Uruguay have the highest pension system coverage rates in Latin America. Nonetheless, in Chile, the average, aggregated figures mask the much lower rates for vulnerable groups such as women, low-income workers, and self-employed workers. For the most part, the best option available to these groups is to qualify for an SGMP pension ($120 per month). It is likely that some will not succeed in meeting the SGMP eligibility requirements (20 years of contributions) and will be compelled to apply for welfare-based PASIS pensions in their old age.

4. The EPS survey (2002) has shown that contribution densities are actually around 52 percent for pension system members as a whole, with

much lower rates for women, low-income workers, and the self-employed. This contribution density is far lower than the assumptions on which the system's coverage and pension rates were projected, which were generally between 70 and 90 percent. Based on the contribution densities disaggregated by group and on estimated replacement ratios, projections of the pensions generated by this system indicate that half the members will depend upon State financing (see Arenas de Mesa, Llanés, and Miranda 2004). This may be an optimistic projection, given the increasing number of women who will be primary beneficiaries of the pension system and the fact that the demographic transition is more marked among the female population.

5. The fiscal cost of the transition has been substantial. Between 1981 and 2003, the pension system's total deficit averaged 5.7 percent of GDP, with 75 percent of the total being attributable to the pension system. Projections for the coming decades point to the continuation of high fiscal costs, with an average annual deficit for the system for 2004–10 of 4.2 percent of GDP. These figures outstrip the initial expectations for the Chilean pension reform by a wide margin.

6. Chile has a multi-pillar, public/private pension system. Its institutional structure lacks coherence, however, because its public sector component (its first pillar) is not designed to function as part of a mixed system and because the system does not provide the necessary resources to finance its welfare-based pension and minimum pension schemes.

7. The Ministry of Finance's SGMP projections indicate that spending on these pensions will have increased fivefold by 2020. The ministry has proposed the creation of a pension reserve fund for SGMP payments, to be financed by the savings generated by the legal requirement that the country maintain a structural surplus equivalent to 1 percent of GDP. This policy measure, which attests to the seriousness of this matter and to the precautions that must be taken in order to maintain a responsible, balanced fiscal policy, would also make it possible to develop genuine social protection mechanisms backed up by sustainable, balanced, long-term financing.

The above considerations indicate that pending reforms in Chile will entail the redesign of the first pillar of the pension system, which consists of its noncontributory subsystem and the SGMP. This component's organizational structure, regulatory scheme, and financing mechanisms are not commensurate with the scale of the issues to be resolved. The implications that this overhaul of the first pillar will have for the second pillar (that is, the contributory system managed by the AFPs) will need to be evaluated. Allowing the second pillar to fall short of its main responsibilities to its contributors is not a socially viable option for Chile. The price of such failure would be to generate a greater-than expected fiscal burden and raise the possibility that emergency policy measures might have to be adopted to address the shortfall in members' pension benefits.

References

Arellano, José Pablo. 1985. *Políticas sociales y desarrollo: Chile 1924–1984.* Santiago, Chile: Corporación de Estudios para Latinoamérica.

Arenas de Mesa, Alberto. 2000. Cobertura previsional en Chile: lecciones y desafíos del sistema de pensiones administrado por el sector privado. *Serie de Financiamiento del Desarrollo* No. 105 (Diciembre). Comisión Económica para América Latina y el Caribe, Santiago, Chile.

———. 2004. *El sistema de pensiones en Chile: principales desafíos futuros.* Santiago, Chile: International Labour Organization.

Arenas de Mesa, Alberto, and Paula Benavides. 2003. *Protección social en Chile: financiamiento, cobertura y desempeño 1990–2000.* Santiago, Chile: International Labour Organization.

Arenas de Mesa, Alberto, and Pamela Gana. 2003. Protección Social, Pensiones y Género en Chile. In *Protección social, pensiones y género en Argentina*, eds. Fabio M. Bertranou and Alberto Arenas de Mesa. Santiago, Chile: International Labour Organization.

Arenas de Mesa, Alberto, Gumucio Rivas, and Juan Sebastian. 2000. *El sistema de pensiones administrado por el sector privado en Chile: un analisis institucional a dos décadas de la reforma*, mimeograph, Santiago, Chile.

Arenas de Mesa, Alberto and Héctor Hernández. 2001. Análisis, evolución y propuestas de ampliación de cobertura del sistema civil de pensiones en Chile. In *Cobertura previsional en Argentina, Brasil y Chile*, eds. Alberto Arenas de Mesa, Fabio M. Bertranou, Carlos O. Grushka, Héctor Hernández Sánchez, Vinicius Pinheiro, and Rafael Rofman. Santiago, Chile: International Labour Organization.

Arenas de Mesa, Alberto and Mario Marcel. 1993. Reformas a la Seguridad Social en Chile. *Serie de Monografías No.5.* Santiago, Chile: Ministerio de Hacienda de Chile

———. 1999. Fiscal Effects of Social Security Reform in Chile: The Case of the Minimum Pension. Proceedings of the Second APEC Regional

Forum on Pension Fund Reforms, Ministerio de Hacienda de Chile and Asian Development Bank, 26–27 April, Viña del Mar, Chile.

Arenas de Mesa, Alberto, Jere Behrman, and David Bravo. 2004. Characteristics and Determinants of the Density of Contributions in Private Social Security System. Paper presented at the Annual Meeting of Economists of Chile. Sociedad de Economía de Chile, 23–24 September, Villa Alemana, Chile.

Arenas de Mesa, Alberto, María Claudia Llanés, and Fidel Miranda. 2004. *Protección social: cobertura y efectos distributivos de la reforma al sistema de pensiones en Chile*. Santiago, Chile: Economic Commission for Latin America and the Caribbean.

Arrau, Patricio. 1991. La reforma previsional chilena y su financiamiento durante la transición. *Colección de Estudios CIEPLAN* No. 32 (June): 5–44

Bravo, David. 2004. *Análisis y principales resultados, primera encuesta de protección social*. Departamento de Economía, Universidad de Chile, and Ministerio del Trabajo y Previsión Social, Santiago, Chile.

Ministerio de Planificación. 2000. *Encuesta de caracterización socio-económica nacional (CASEN)*. Santiago, Chile.

Centro Latinoamericano de Demografía (CELADE). 2004a. América Latina y el Caribe: estimaciones y proyecciones de población 1950–2050. Serie *Boletín Demográfico* No. 73, Santiago, Chile.

―――――. 2004b. América Latina y el Caribe: tablas de mortalidad 1950–2050. Serie *Boletín Demográfico* No. 73, Santiago, Chile.

Cheyre, Hernán. 1988. *La previsión en Chile Ayer y Hoy*. Santiago, Chile: Centro de Estudios Públicos.

Dirección de Presupuestos (DIPRES). 2000, 2004a. *Estadísticas de las Finanzas Públicas*. Ministerio de Hacienda, Santiago, Chile.

―――――. 2004b. *Informe de las Finanzas Públicas* (October). Santiago. Chile.

Departamento de Economía de la Universidad de Chile. 2004. *Encuesta de Protección Social* (EPS 2002). Available at www.proteccionsocial.cl. Ministerio del Trabajo y Previsión Social, Subsecretaría de Previsión Social and Centro de Micro Datos.

Gana, Pamela. 2002. Las pensiones no contributivas en Chile: pensiones asistenciales (PASIS). In *Pensiones no contributivas y asistenciales. Argentina, Brasil, Chile, Costa Rica y Uruguay*, eds. Fabio M. Betranou, C. Solorio, and W. Van Ginneken. Santiago, Chile: International Labour Organization.

International Labour Organization. 1998. La reforma estructural de pensiones en América Latina: tipología, comprobación de presupuestos y enseñanzas. In *Pensiones en América Latina, dos décadas de reforma*, eds. Alejandro Bonilla García and Alfredo H. Conte-Grand. Lima: International Labour Organization.

Kotlikoff, Lawrence J. 1992. *Generational Accounting: Knowing Who Pays, and When, for What We Spend*. New York: Free Press.

————. 1996. *Privatization of Social Security: How It Works and Why It Matters*. Boston: Boston University, Institute for Economic Development.

Marcel, Mario and Alberto Arenas de Mesa. 1992. Social Security Reform in Chile. Occasional Papers No 5. Inter-American Development Bank, Washington, D.C.

Ministerio de Hacienda (Chile). 2004. *Estado de la hacienda pública 2004*. Santiago, Chile.

Superintendencia de Administradoras de Fondos de Pensiones (SAFP) (Chile). 2002. *El sistema chileno de pensiones (Quinta edición)*. Santiago, Chile.

————. 2003. Statistical Bulletins. Santiago, Chile.

Superintendencia de Seguridad Social (SUSESO) (Chile). 1990-2003. Bulletins. Santiago, Chile.

CHAPTER 4

A Needs Assessment of Pension Systems in the English-speaking Caribbean

Stefano Pettinato and Javier Díaz Cassou[*]

Over the next few decades, old age pension systems—and, more broadly, national insurance systems—in English-speaking Caribbean countries are expected to face growing challenges, mainly because of external circumstances but also because of internal structural conditions. As a result, it may be extremely costly for many of these countries to maintain these systems unless changes are made. Such changes will require adapting to changing domestic policies and socioeconomic circumstances, as well as considering openness to international forces—features that are increasingly interactive and at times mutually reinforcing.

This chapter analyzes 11 English-speaking Caribbean countries (Antigua and Barbuda, Barbados, Belize, Dominica, Grenada, Guyana, Jamaica, St. Kitts and Nevis, St. Lucia, St. Vincent and the Grenadines, and Trinidad and Tobago) with a focus on how cyclical and structural conditions are affecting their pension systems, thereby undermining their medium- and long-term sustainability. Major concerns arise from:

---

[*] Stefano Pettinato is Program Manager at the Regional Bureau for Latin America and the Caribeean, United Nations Development Programme. Javier Díaz Cassou is an economist with the Bank of Spain. This chapter originally appeared in *Workable Pension Systems: Reforms in the Caribbean*, 2005, Inter-American Development Bank and the Caribbean Development Bank.

- Projected financial and actuarial difficulties that the systems will face due to changing demographics
- Neglect of large population groups at the same time that others have been granted special privileges
- An urgent need to rationalize management of the systems' funds and operations, increase efficiency and transparency, and reduce costs.

The first section describes the economic and social environments in which the region's pension systems operate. The second discusses the evolution and current structures of social security systems in the region, with an emphasis on old age pension systems. The final section identifies the main challenges facing these systems, and offers ideas on addressing them. Annex 4.1 provides detailed descriptions of the region's pension systems.

The analysis contained in this chapter is subject to a limitation stemming from the lack of reliable data about the performance of pension systems in some of the English-speaking Caribbean countries. There are few reliable sources of information, and data collection techniques and methodologies are often outdated and not uniform. In order to complete this needs assessment, this study has used a variety of primary and secondary sources that sometimes provided conflicting and incomplete data. The tables and indicators contained in this chapter should therefore be taken as an approximation.

Economic and Social Conditions in the Region

Before assessing the needs and challenges of pension systems in the English-speaking Caribbean, it is necessary to describe the environment in which these systems operate. This section first analyzes the recent evolution of macroeconomic conditions in the English-speaking Caribbean. It then examines the key structural social conditions of these countries.

Macroeconomic Conditions in the 1990s

During the 1990s, economic growth in the 11 English-speaking Caribbean countries analyzed in this chapter averaged 3.2 percent a year. Belize and St. Lucia were the strongest performers, while Barbados and Jamaica lagged behind (Table 4.1). Because of their size and close proximity to large markets like the United States and their wealthier South American neighbors, countries in the region have historically been and

Table 4.1 Economic and Structural Conditions in Various English-Speaking Caribbean Countries, 1990s

Country	GDP growth, 1990s (average annual percent)	Per capita GNP growth, 1990s (average annual percent)	Inflation rate, 1990s (average annual percent)	Per capita GDP, 1999 (PPPS)	Human Development Index, 1999
Antigua and Barbuda	3.3	3.6	—	10,225	0.798
Barbados	0.7	0.4	2.9	14,353	0.888
Belize	4.7	1.6	2.0	4,959	0.776
Dominica	2.2	1.7	2.3	5,425	0.776
Grenada	3.3	2.5	2.2	6,817	0.738
Guyana	4.8	7.6	7.0	3,640	0.740
Jamaica	0.8	0.4	27.8	3,561	0.757
St. Kitts and Nevis	3.9	3.8	3.6	11,596	0.808
St. Lucia	4.9	1.0	3.4	5,509	0.775
St. Vincent and the Grenadines	3.5	2.6	3.2	5,309	0.755
Trinidad and Tobago	2.7	2.3	6.2	8,176	0.802
Average	3.2	2.5	6.1	7,234	0.783

—Not available
Note: PPPS stands for purchasing power parity.
Source: World Bank data; UNDP (2003)

are increasingly exposed to regional and international economic and financial trends.

Toward the end of the 1990s and into 2000 and 2001 (a period not captured by available data), the international economic slowdown—driven by the sharp slowdown in the U.S. economy in 2001, as well as the terrorist attacks of September 11—weakened economic performance in the region. Among the most important causes was a dramatic reduction in exports to the United States, mainly in the form of reduced tourism flows from the United States, and lower revenues from sales of natural resources in international markets.

In terms of productivity growth (measured using as a rough proxy the growth in GDP per capita) the English-speaking Caribbean countries cover a wide range, with the best performance in St. Lucia, Guyana and Belize, and the worst in Barbados and Jamaica. With the exception of Jamaica, low inflation throughout the region indicates sound macroeconomic policies. Average annual inflation ranged from 2.0 percent in Belize and 2.2 percent in Grenada up to Jamaica's 27.8 percent, which was mainly driven by poor performance in the early 1990s (see Table 4.1).

Structural Socioeconomic Conditions

The last two columns of Table 4.1 present data on each country's level of economic development (expressed in terms of per capita GDP) and human development. Barbados and St. Kitts and Nevis are the richest countries, while Guyana and Jamaica are poorest. These and other structural differences must be considered when discussing policy options for the region, as they indicate extremely different realities among countries.

The United Nations Development Programme (UNDP) Human Development Index sheds some light on each country's relative level of development.[1] Among the region's countries, the index is lowest in Grenada and highest is Barbados (which is ranked 28th in the world in terms of the index). The indexes in the region are higher than the average for developing countries (0.647) and in line with the average for Latin America as a whole (0.760).

Demographics are also relevant when analyzing pension systems. Although the population of the 11 English-speaking Caribbean countries varies from 39,000 (St. Kitts and Nevis) to 2.7 million (Jamaica), the

---

[1] The Human Development Index is a composite measure based on per capita GDP, life expectancy, literacy, and school enrollment. It was designed and is updated yearly by the UNDP and published in the Human Development Report.

Table 4.2.	Demographic Features of Various English-Speaking Caribbean Countries, 2001				
Country	Population	Population group (percentage of total)		Life expectancy at birth (years)	Fertility rate
		16–64	65+		
Antigua and Barbuda	66,970	67.2	4.9	70.7	2.3
Barbados	275,330	69.4	8.9	73.8	1.5
Belize	256,062	54.4	3.5	71.2	3.4
Dominica	70,786	63.5	7.8	73.6	2.0
Grenada	89,227	59.0	3.9	64.5	2.5
Guyana	697,181	66.9	4.9	63.3	2.5
Jamaica	2,665,636	63.5	6.8	75.4	2.5
St. Kitts and Nevis	38,756	61.4	8.8	71.0	2.0
St. Lucia	158,178	62.6	5.3	72.6	2.4
St. Vincent and the Grenadines	115,942	64.0	6.4	72.6	2.1
Trinidad and Tobago	1,169,682	69.0	6.7	68.3	1.7
Average	509,432	63.7	6.2	70.6	2.3

Source: World Bank data; United Nations data; CIA (various issues); UNDP (2003)

region's population structures are more homogeneous (Table 4.2). (Only Belize is an outlier, with a younger population.)

Barbados and St. Kitts and Nevis have the largest elderly populations, with people over 65 accounting for nearly 9 percent of the population. (One major factor, especially for St. Kitts and Nevis, may be the migration of younger people to wealthier regions.) Jamaica has the highest life expectancy at birth among the countries considered, with 75.4 years. The fertility rate is also revealing, and is often used to predict future population structures. Women in Barbados and Trinidad and Tobago have the fewest children, indicating more gender-equal societies and smaller families. Belize, on the other hand, has a much higher fertility rate than the rest of the region.

In Barbados, the share of the population 65 and older went from 6 percent in 1960 to 9 percent in 2000. In 1990, almost a third of the 31,000 people over 65 were older than 80, and women accounted for two-thirds of elderly people. Other English-speaking Caribbean countries experienced similar trends during this period.

When demographic data are projected into the future, very different trends occur across the region. Old age dependency ratios (defined here as the ratio of people over 60 to people aged 20 to 59) are expected to increase in most countries between 1995 and 2040 (often falling over the

Table 4.3.	Old Age Dependency Ratios in Various English-Speaking Caribbean Countries, 1995–2040 (percent)									
Country	1995	2000	2005	2010	2015	2020	2025	2030	2035	2040
Barbados	28.0	25.3	21.2	22.8	26.5	32.5	40.9	48.0	54.2	54.9
Belize	16.1	14.7	12.1	11.6	11.1	11.9	15.5	19.4	24.2	30.0
Dominica	22.2	19.0	17.8	17.6	16.4	19.0	22.0	26.2	37.7	46.7
Grenada	22.5	20.8	21.2	21.1	21.0	19.4	18.9	22.1	28.6	36.4
Guyana	11.3	11.9	12.1	13.3	15.1	19.0	24.5	29.9	33.8	35.4
Jamaica	18.1	17.3	16.7	16.6	17.7	21.0	26.7	32.8	38.3	41.9
St. Lucia	22.1	22.7	21.4	17.4	15.2	12.8	16.0	20.0	27.9	36.5
St. Kitts and Nevis	42.1	31.8	24.0	18.5	13.3	16.1	27.6	34.5	31.0	32.3
St. Vincent and the Grenadines	16.7	17.7	19.4	19.7	20.0	26.0	31.6	35.9	41.8	48.1
Suriname	15.5	15.6	15.9	14.5	14.7	17.0	22.8	28.7	34.7	37.0
Trinidad and Tobago	17.6	17.3	17.2	19.0	22.5	27.4	32.5	35.4	38.8	43.5
Average	21.1	19.5	18.1	17.5	17.6	20.2	25.4	30.3	35.5	40.2

Note: The old age dependency ratio is defined as the population over 60 to the population age 20–59. Data for 2005–40 are projections
Source: Palacios and Pallarés-Mirales (2000).

next 10 to 15 years, and then rising). By contrast, St. Kitts and Nevis shows a declining trend (Table 4.3). The sharpest increases will occur in Guyana, where the old age dependency ratio is expected to more than triple in 45 years, and St. Vincent and the Grenadines, with a similar increase. Ratios in Barbados, Dominica, and St. Vincent and the Grenadines are expected to reach levels comparable to those in advanced OECD countries.

Unemployment levels and labor force structures also differ widely across the region (Table 4.4). Unemployment ranges from 5 percent in St. Kitts and Nevis to 22 percent in neighboring St. Vincent and the Grenadines. The composition of the labor force reflects countries' levels of economic development, with the richest countries (Antigua and Barbuda, Barbados, St. Kitts and Nevis, and Trinidad and Tobago) having the smallest shares of agricultural workers.

Levels of economic development are reflected in national poverty levels (see Table 4.4). As measured by the headcount poverty rate (calculated based on household surveys), poverty is highest in Guyana (with 43 percent of the population living below the national poverty line) and Belize (34 percent), and lowest in Antigua and Barbuda (12 percent) and Barbados (8 percent). But countries' income distributions (as measured

Table 4.4.	Labor and Poverty Indicators in Various English-Speaking Caribbean Countries			
Country	Unemployment rate (percent)	Labor force in agriculture	Poverty headcount	Gini coefficient
Antigua and Barbuda	7	11	12	0.53
Barbados	11	10	8	0.46
Belize	13	38	35	0.51
Dominica	20	40	33	0.49
Grenada	15	24	20	0.50
Guyana	12	30	43	0.42
Jamaica	16	21	34	0.43
St. Kitts and Nevis	5	<5	15	0.45
St. Lucia	15	39	25	0.47
St. Vincent and the Grenadines	22	26	17	0.45
Trinidad and Tobago	13	10	21	0.42
Average	13	25	24	0.47

Note: Data are the most recent available
Source: World Bank data; World Bank (1996); CIA (various issues).

by the Gini coefficient (a common measure of inequality) often do not reflect their economic development. The least equitable countries are Antigua and Barbuda (with a Gini coefficient of 53 percent) and Belize (51 percent). At the other end of the spectrum are Guyana and Trinidad and Tobago (42 percent in both).

The Region's Social Security Systems

This section describes the main features of the evolution and current state of pension systems in the English-speaking Caribbean.

Evolution of Public Pension Systems

Over the past several decades, social security in the Caribbean has generally evolved from social assistance to social insurance. Many countries began implementing public social insurance systems—including retirement pensions—in the 1960s and 1970s (see Annex 4.1 for details on each country's plan). Under these defined benefit systems, the benefits that workers receive upon retirement are based on their final salaries and predetermined replacement rates.[2]

Barbados has been one of the region's pioneers in social insurance. A social assistance plan was instituted in 1937, and a social insurance system was established in 1966. Similarly, in 1969 Guyana introduced a social insurance system to replace the social assistance plan of 1944. Further adjustments were made between 1981 and 1992. Trinidad and Tobago was also an early convert, introducing a social assistance plan in 1939, replacing it with social insurance in 1971, and amending it in 1999.

Jamaica introduced its social insurance system in 1958, though it covered only sugarcane workers, and evolved to a modern and comprehensive system in 1966. Belize introduced social insurance in 1979. Finally, Antigua and Barbuda departed from the model seen elsewhere in the region, introducing a social assistance scheme in 1993 on top of a social insurance system implemented in 1972.

In some countries social assistance was initially provided through provident funds: that is, publicly managed funds that pool workers' contributions and use them to cover those in need. Dominica, Grenada, St. Kitts and Nevis, St. Lucia, and St. Vincent and the Grenadines all followed this sequence, supporting provident funds around 1970 and shifting to social insurance between the late 1970s and mid-1980s. The main reasons for the shift away from provident funds were the widespread macroeconomic instability, inflation, and devaluation of the 1970s and 1980s, which produced large negative returns and widespread dissatisfaction with the funds' performance (ICSS 1995; Forde 2001).

The pension schemes of the English-speaking Caribbean are partially funded, and so entail a transfer of resources from current to retired workers. This approach is based on the notion of intergenerational solidarity and reciprocity. In actuarial terms such systems, when mature, are sustainable only if the ratio of pensioners to contributors remains at sustainable levels, given the growth in the wage rate and the parameters of the system (contribution rates, retirement age, and pension benefit formula).

An alternative approach is the pension scheme Chile introduced in 1981 (see Chapter 3). This revolutionary plan is fully funded, with benefits based on defined contributions and savings accumulated in indi-

---

[2] The replacement rate is an indicator used to reflect the relative generosity of a pension system in a particular country. It is usually calculated as the ratio between a worker's pension benefit and average pensionable earnings.

vidual accounts overseen by certified, carefully regulated pension funds. At retirement, workers are entitled to withdraw their savings and the accrued return on the investment and, among other options, purchase a life annuity. The sustainability of such a system depends on investment performance and pension fund regulation.

After more than three decades, many of the systems in the region are close to reaching maturity. Despite the difficulties facing some governments due to increasing ratios of pensioners to contributors, no Caribbean country has seriously considered introducing a system like that in Chile—with the exception of Trinidad and Tobago. In 1999, Trinidadian authorities sponsored discussions with various stakeholders about the possibility of shifting toward a pension model based on two tiers: a reformed social security system to play a welfare (redistributive) role; and a new mandatory, privately managed plan for the well-off. These discussions were still on the table when this chapter was written.

Current National Insurance Systems

In most public pension systems in the English-speaking Caribbean, benefits are based on predetermined formulas linked to average pensionable earnings: that is, a worker's final and highest salary levels. (Exceptions are Jamaica and Trinidad and Tobago.) In addition to this defined benefit approach, the systems do not operate on a fully funded basis, but only on a partially funded one. Most schemes are still building up funds, due to their relatively brief maturity, with contributors largely outnumbering beneficiaries.

When the systems mature, the ratio of contributors to beneficiaries will gradually decrease, creating financial pressure. As a result, a larger share of contributions will have to be used to cover benefits. When contributions become insufficient, investment income will have to be used. As a last resort, assets will have to be sold to finance the increased volume of benefits.

In other words, if contribution rates are not increased before funds are exhausted, when mature, the systems will operate on a pay-as-you-go basis.[3] For these reasons, current and future workers bear the risks from

---

[3] The reason behind this rests on the fact that most of these systems operate with cash-flow surpluses: income (from contributions and invested resources) exceeds expenditures. Because current benefits are also financed out of investment income from accumulated funds, in reality the schemes are partially funded (neither pay-as-you-go nor fully funded). The problem is that reserves are expected to be depleted over the next 20 to 40 years. For more details and projections on these trends, see Osborne (2001).

an underperforming economy or from increasing life expectancies (or both). Currently, most schemes operate with limited or no government financing or subsidies.

Rising old age and system dependency ratios have serious implications for the level of income support available through social insurance for the elderly.[4] Furthermore, countries with large informal sectors may experience additional pressure on their social assistance systems as more elderly people retire with little or no pension coverage and no alternative means of income support. Because of the rapid changes in population structures discussed above, many countries' pension schemes are under pressure both actuarially and financially.

In principle, all workers are required to participate in the national insurance schemes in all 11 English-speaking Caribbean countries. In practice, many workers are left out—especially those employed in the informal sector. It is difficult to establish the extent of the informality problem in the English-speaking Caribbean because few reliable data exist on this issue. The problem is aggravated by the fact that different countries apply different definitions of informal employment, making it difficult to draw any comparison (Mayers, Downes, and Greenidge 2002). Furthermore, research on this topic has been carried out only in the countries with the smallest informal sectors. Thus the results of these studies cannot be considered representative of the region.

The available data suggest that informality in the labor market is relatively high in the English-speaking Caribbean. In 1996, the World Bank estimated the importance of informal workers, unpaid workers, and self-employed workers in various Caribbean countries. In Antigua and Barbuda, this group was estimated at 9 percent of the labor force; in Dominica, 29 percent; in Grenada, 18 percent; in Guyana, 26 percent; in Jamaica, 39 percent; and in Trinidad and Tobago, 22 percent. Other studies estimate the size of the informal sector in Trinidad and Tobago at 2.6 to 6.8 percent of GDP, though this is considered an underestimation. In Barbados the hidden sector has been estimated at less than 1 percent of GDP (Mayers, Downes, and Greenidge 2002). The International Labour Organization offers yet another set of figures. It estimates informal employment in Barbados at 15 percent, and in Trinidad and Tobago at 19.4 percent.

Many observers believe that the informal sector has grown in most Caribbean countries in recent years, because of worsening economic per-

---

[4] The old age dependency ratio compares the number of elderly to the working age population. The system dependency ratio refers specifically to system beneficiaries and contributors.

formance. Belize, Jamaica, and St. Kitts and Nevis are good examples of this phenomenon, with large pockets of the workforce active in the informal labor market. Typically, school dropouts, housewives, and the disabled do not contribute to and are not covered by social security. As a result many individuals reach retirement age with no pension coverage.

In Belize and Grenada, less than 25 percent of the population of pensionable age receives pension income (World Bank 1996). At the other end of the spectrum, Barbados and Trinidad and Tobago have the highest coverage rates. In recent years, the problem of informality has been aggravated by a marked rise in unemployment, which is close to 20 percent in various countries in the region. The rising importance of the informal sector in the English-speaking Caribbean calls for further research on the informal networks that support informal workers upon retirement, and on possible ways of combining these networks with formal private or public programs to expand the coverage of pension systems.

Although in principle the self-employed are required to participate in the region's pension systems, in practice few of them do so (Table 4.5).[5] The low level of affiliation is mainly due to the myopia of large sectors of the population, many of whom do not attach enough importance to the reduction of income in old age. Despite the fact that the value of pensions exceeds contribution rates in almost every country in the region, young people seldom save for retirement.

Barbados and Trinidad and Tobago are often considered the region's star performers in terms of pension coverage. In Barbados more than 92 percent of people over 65 receive a pension, while in Trinidad and Tobago 82 percent do. Part of the reason for these countries' high coverage is their provision of noncontributory pensions to support antipoverty goals. This is especially true in Trinidad and Tobago, where noncontributory pensions are particularly important in relative terms. In other countries most of the elderly are left out of the social insurance system (see Table 4.5).

The proportion of elderly people with pension income is considerably lower elsewhere in the region. Jamaica's scheme covers only 27 percent of the country's elderly, while in Belize less than 10 percent of those over 65 receive pension coverage. Grenada is the worst performer, with less than 5 percent of those over 60 receiving pension income. It should not be surprising that, where data are available, spending on public pensions (as a percentage of GDP) generally rises with pension coverage (see Table 4.5).

---

[5] Making things worse, employers often fail to comply with their obligations for pension contributions, or omit information about contributors (partially or entirely), despite the threat of fines and even imprisonment.

Table 4.5	Pension Coverage in Various English-Speaking Caribbean Countries (percent)					
Country	Age of workers	Participation by self-employed workers	Contributors as percentage of working age population	Percentage of elderly receiving pension Income	Public pension spending as percentage of GDP	Pensioners as percentage of population
Antigua and Barbuda	16–59	Mandatory	—	—	—	—
Barbados	16–65	Mandatory	68	92	4.1	0.7
Belize	14–64	Excluded	70	10	0.2	—
Dominica	14–60	Mandatory	82	—	1.4	3.5
Grenada	16–59	Voluntary	60	<5	1.5	—
Guyana	16–59	Mandatory	—	37	0.9	3.3
Jamaica	18–65/60	Mandatory	33	27	0.3	1.7
St. Kitts and Nevis	16–62	Excluded	—	—	—	—
St. Lucia	16–65	Voluntary	—	—	—	—
St. Vincent and the Grenadines	16–65	Mandatory	—	—	—	—
Trinidad and Tobago	16–64	Excluded	61	82	3.4	3.5

— Not available

Source: World Bank (1996); SSA (2001); Palacios and Pallarés-Miralles (2000).

Although the region's average replacement rates of 30 to 60 percent are reasonable by international standards, the real value of pensions and contribution ceilings has been declining due to lack of indexation mechanisms. Governments increasingly rely on legislation aimed at periodically adjusting these levels to the cost of living, making such adjustments less frequent and more subject to delays from political debate. For example, high inflation in the 1980s eroded benefits in Belize and Trinidad and Tobago. Barbados is the only country in the region that has introduced automatic adjustments to correct for cost of living increases.

Ceilings on contributions are relatively high in the Organization for the English-Speaking Caribbean (OESC) countries. In other English-speaking Caribbean countries, current low ceilings on contributions tend to reduce the progressivity of the contributory structure of pension schemes. The schemes incorporate provisions for minimum pension guarantees. Full pensions are guaranteed with relatively few years of contributions, though requirements range from three years in Jamaica to fourteen years in Guyana and Trinidad and Tobago. Because benefits are generally based on average monthly earnings over the previous five to ten years, workers who experience higher earnings as they age (such as professionals and civil servants) reap most of the benefits.[6]

Although the level of benefits differs widely across the region, the range of benefits is relatively homogeneous. In every country national insurance schemes provide short-term benefits (maternity and sick leave) and long-term benefits (old age pensions and disability and survivor benefits). While some countries also provide benefits for on-the-job injuries, only Barbados covers the unemployed.

Old age pension coverage is the main long-term benefit. The retirement age is generally the same for men and women (except in Jamaica, where men retire five years later than women, at 60) and in most countries is 60 (except in Barbados, where it is 65, and St. Kitts and Nevis, where it is 62).

Some national insurance systems—in Barbados, St. Kitts and Nevis, and Trinidad and Tobago—include additional programs to alleviate poverty among those who have not contributed sufficiently or consistently enough to secure minimum pensions. Still, some population groups are entirely excluded from national insurance schemes. In particular, the unemployed are neglected because they lack the contributory power to reach eligibility conditions.[7]

A number that is difficult to obtain but important for gauging a scheme's maturity is the system dependency ratio, measured here as the number of pensioners per 100 contributors (Table 4.6). Among the six countries for which data are available, Barbados appears to have the most mature system, with 24.4 beneficiaries per 100 contributors. Grenada has the lowest system ratio, at 10.3. The costs of administration and operation also vary widely, with Jamaica having the lowest relative costs and one of the largest schemes.[8]

In addition to safety net, redistributive, and efficiency objectives, national insurance schemes throughout the region seek to provide long-term

---

[6] Although adopting a benefit formula based on average lifetime earnings would also be unfavorable to the underemployed and to workers in part-time positions or with interrupted earnings, one based on the highest 10 years of earnings (rather than the past 10) would be more progressive. However, such a system would require calculating earnings from earlier periods in current denominations.

[7] In Barbados, a notable exception to this rule, the unemployed receive partial coverage through an unemployment benefits scheme. Because of this scheme and the financial support it requires, the country's pension contribution rate is the highest in the region (see World Bank 1996).

[8] The Jamaican scheme makes full use of modern technology. In 1994 pensioners could already cash their vouchers at branches of the National Commercial Bank (World Bank 1996).

Table 4.6.	Ratios of Pensioners to Contributors in Pension Systems in Various English-Speaking Caribbean Countries		
Country	Year	Pensioners above the normal retirement age/contributors	Pensioners per 100 contributors
Barbados	2001	4.1	24.4
Dominica	2002	5.5	18.2
Grenada	2002	9.3	10.8
Guyana	2001	5.0	20.0
St. Kitts and Nevis	2002	9.7	10.3
St. Lucia	2001	14.9	6.7

Source: World Bank (1996)]; SSA (2001); Palacios and Parallés-Miralles (2000).

capital growth and investment income by investing funds in balanced, well-diversified portfolios (Bissember 2002). Even though as they reach maturity the systems will increasingly operate on a pay-as-you-go basis, the funds that are quickly accumulating could be used to foster domestic economic development. It is perhaps for this reason they are invested predominantly in domestic assets, limiting the often-required international diversification but also reducing dependence on foreign markets.

Private Pension Schemes

Complementary pension programs and retirement savings vehicles have been evolving alongside social insurance programs and are increasingly common in English-speaking Caribbean countries, though coverage is generally limited to better-off socioeconomic groups. These plans are more common in the region's more advanced countries. Such schemes are driven by growing concerns about the limited coverage provided by public systems, as well as by policies to promote alternative means of savings for old age.

These schemes, developed mainly within employer (occupational) plans, provide old age income in addition to the pension benefits that originate from public systems.[9] In these schemes, employers generally deduct contributions from wages. Occupational schemes are largely voluntary but can also derive from labor union treaties and collective bargaining.

---

[9] In some countries, civil servants receive additional employer-based pension coverage through State-owned companies that manage the funds (such as the Insurance Corporation of Barbados).

One of the main advantages of employer-based pension systems is the low public sector interference they require, due to their relative autonomy from the government. In addition, they are relatively cheap and provide incentives to reduce contributory evasion. On the flipside, the limited transferability of their benefits makes them limited and vulnerable to employment-related uncertainties. Furthermore, if workers change jobs frequently, these plans often fail to meet the long-term goal of saving for old age because many workers cash in the accumulated funds and use them for consumption.

Alternatively, voluntary pension schemes can be based on personal savings plans. In the past, some English-speaking Caribbean countries tried to implement such systems through provident funds—with little success and plenty of unhappiness among contributors, who saw most of their savings vanish. The collapse of the Jamaican financial market in the mid-1990s made many neighboring countries wary of the risks related to poorly regulated financial sectors.

Because of their limited coverage, most private and occupational pension plans have been developing within relatively weak legal frameworks. As concerns about pension coverage increase, along with the number of workers who can afford to contribute to complementary plans, these schemes are expected to experience rapid growth in terms of both contributors and beneficiaries. It would be advisable for the emerging pension funds market—as well as the one for annuities—to be regulated and supervised more coherently and rationally.

Most voluntary programs work on a defined contribution basis and pool worker contributions (along with employer contributions) into funds administered by specialized companies. The private pensions and annuities markets in the region tend to be dominated by a few large companies, including Sagicor, Clico, Guardian Life, and more recently some credit unions and other domestic and international financial institutions, such as the Bank of Nova Scotia. These companies provide markets for the large and increasing amounts of resources generated through the existing occupational plans.

One caveat is the lack of investments for these resources. Consequently, these companies have purchased vast amounts of real estate.[10] In the past this was a good investment for these companies, but the concentration of investments in real estate may pose significant risks for the future—es-

---

[10] Some of this information was obtained by interviewing pension fund market operators and regulators in Barbados and Trinidad and Tobago.

pecially if a decline in real estate prices occurs at the time of a rise in the number of retirees. This risk can be mitigated only by diversifying assets, for which regional financial integration might be the best option.

Unresolved Issues and Main Needs

Two General Models

Based on their underlying objectives and national characteristics, two models for social security seem to stand out in the English-speaking Caribbean: that of Barbados, and that of Trinidad and Tobago and Jamaica.

Among Caribbean countries, Barbados has one of the most extensive systems of social insurance and assistance. Pensions are paid to almost everyone over 65, putting pressure on the Treasury.[11] There is extensive unemployment compensation and insurance against injury and illness, as well as paid maternity leave, severance payments, and subsidized housing and funeral payments (for low-income families). In sum, the Barbadian system represents a model of broad coverage, pay-as-you-go intergenerational financing, and defined benefit pension calculation—with all the advantages and disadvantages of such a structure.

In many ways, the Barbadian system points to the future of systems on other islands. The relatively advanced economic and demographic development of Barbados makes it more advanced in time. The scheme requires the region's highest contributions from employees and employers, with a total contribution rate of 15.25 percent, with 7.25 percent coming from employees and 8 percent from employers (see Annex 4.1 for details).

In Trinidad and Tobago—and Jamaica, to some extent—social insurance systems have been set up largely on the basis of redistributive principles. The presence and impact of these systems are still limited, particularly because of low contribution rates. As a result, pension coverage can be granted only up to some maximum point beyond which the schemes' expenditures need to be covered by external funds, such as government funds or public sector employee contributions. Interestingly, public sector pay-as-you-go noncontributory benefits in the two countries

---

[11] Excluded are those people who worked for more than the number of years required to qualify for a pension but failed to contribute and who are not eligible for the country's noncontributory pension.

are partially funded by military personnel, as well as by parliamentarians in Trinidad and Tobago (Forde 2001).

Major Challenges for the Region's Systems

Demographic Pressures

As noted, populations in English-speaking Caribbean countries are rapidly becoming older, increasing demands for old age income security. Some countries in particular will begin seeing large groups of elderly citizens in the next few decades. St. Vincent and the Grenadines will have the sharpest increases in elderly population, eventually reaching levels of old age dependency comparable to those in advanced countries. Even though Barbados is starting from an older population structure, it will also experience demographic pressures that will likely exert financial pressure on pension systems.

Low and Unequal Coverage

Most of the systems examined cover only a small fraction of country populations—mainly people working in the public sector and, more generally, the formal sector. Even many self-employed workers not necessarily involved in the informal economy receive little coverage, despite mandatory provisions for their participation. High contribution rates are the main reason the self-employed avoid enrolling in pension systems and reporting their business activity. Such workers must provide the entire contribution—that is, what employees and employers pay separately—and are generally entitled to limited long-term benefits.

Poor Resource Allocation and Management

National insurance schemes are run like large nonbank financial institutions, levying taxes on workers and investing the resources for later use by contributors. But most of these institutions operate like unofficial public banks, providing different financial services for government and quasi-government agencies. The financial power of these institutions is so great that they could facilitate the development of capital market institutions not only in their domestic economies but also across the region. To do so, pension funds should use modern portfolio management techniques, including diversification in domestic and some international assets.

Preliminary Recommendations

This chapter does not pretend to offer solutions to all the challenges facing the region's pension systems. But it does identify some of the most compelling issues requiring careful examination. Over the next few decades, social insurance systems are going to experience serious cash flow shortages. Corrective measures must reflect the characteristics of each system and of each country's social, economic, and demographic environment.

The systems work by financing current expenditures, X, with current income, Y. The difference between the two is the pension surplus, S. Defining I as investment income, C as contribution income, P as pension benefits, and A as administrative costs leads to:

$$S = X - Y$$

$$Y = Y(I,C)$$

and

$$X = X(P,A).$$

Furthermore, I comes from current invested reserves, R, at the rate of return i. C is a function of the pool of contributors, W, and their wage, w, and the contribution rate, c. P depends on the number of beneficiaries, B, and the replacement rate, r. These definitions make it possible to describe the above relation as:

$$S = [I(R\ i) + C\ (W,\ w,\ c)] - [\ P(B,\ r) + A]$$

or, if $= 0$,

$$[I(R,i) + C(W,w,c)] = [\ P(B,r) + A].$$

Financial sustainability should be attained by increasing sources of income or by decreasing expenditures. The formula above shows the mechanisms that can be used to maintain a pension surplus, S.[12] Increasing income (raising the left-hand component) through higher

---

[12] Income from reserves will still decrease with time, however, because fewer resources will be accumulated as the ratio of beneficiaries to contributors increases.

contribution rates, c, could help mitigate the looming increase in the number of beneficiaries, B. Similarly, better management of pension fund investments could raise income by increasing returns, i, and future reserves, R.

On the other side of the equation, lowering benefit eligibility, B, or the pension formula, r, could help. But these measures will merely delay the deterioration of systems' cash flows, their move toward at best breaking even—and probably going into deficit. Other measures may be more effective in the long run. Some are described below.

Rationalizing Operating and Administrative Costs

In most Caribbean pension schemes, 10 to 20 percent of contributions are used to cover administrative costs (Osborne 2001). Most schemes operate under largely suboptimal conditions. Not only are staff underskilled and lacking in proper technology, but administrations are overstaffed—with more than half of administrative expenses going to staff costs. Thus existing administrative arrangements should be rationalized. Such efforts should include training staff (who are often the most opposed to structural reforms) and improving technology. In addition, given the small size of countries in the region, integration of part of the administration might be advisable (see Dowers, Fassina, and Pettinato 2001).

Increasing Public Pension Coverage

One reason why few self-employed and informal workers are willing to contribute to pension systems is the rapid loss of value of benefits, largely due to lack of automatic indexation mechanisms. As noted, Barbados appears to be the only country among those studied that provides automatic cost of living adjustments. Other countries rely on periodic reevaluations through legislative processes, an approach that inevitably delays changes and shifts decisions into the political arena. While this measure may increase financial costs because of the higher value of benefits, it can also have desirable effects through increased participation.

Introducing Legal Reforms to Encourage
the Development of Second and Third Pillars

As noted, the market for private pension funds has been developing steadily in the region. This has happened mainly in countries with sufficient demand and infrastructure for products such as deferred annuities and retirement savings plans. It is advisable, however, that such markets be strictly regulated and that transparency be made a priority. Doing so would foster the development of private schemes, providing important supplementary income for increasing numbers of individuals. Mandatory private pillars could ultimately be considered in more advanced countries, in a stable and fiscally sound macroeconomic environment with sophisticated capital markets, to complement and possibly to compete with reformed public pay-as-you go pillars.

Facilitating and Simplifying Provision of and Access to Pension Plans

Provision of (supply) and access to (demand) public pension coverage should be greatly simplified to allow the less privileged to get coverage. Several steps should be taken in this regard, including opening rural centers to collect contributions and distribute benefit checks, and maintaining constant information campaigns and periodic publications to explain how systems work, as well as the rationale for frequent (and often obscure) changes in rules. In addition, personnel in national insurance offices should receive better training. Supervision should be increased and improved to avoid corruption.

Involving Local Stakeholders, Public Pension Officials, Market Operators, and Sector Experts

It is often assumed that reform proposals are based on consensus by local experts, domestic academics, and operators of institutions (both private and public) involved in pension systems. But this process is not always the case—and even where it is, it should be more thorough. Thus this assessment proposes sending a questionnaire to such individuals to gather knowledge, ideas, and concerns, and to develop consensus on the direction of pension reforms (see Annex 4.2).

Promoting Dialogue and Negotiations with Governments

In line with the previous point, discussions concerning the reform of pension systems must involve business and labor organizations. It must also involve national and international policymakers and academia.

Annex 4.1 Social Insurance Systems in the English-Speaking Caribbean

Category	Antigua and Barbuda	Barbados	Belize	Dominica
First law	1972 (social insurance) and 1993 (social assistance)	1937 (assistance)	1979	1970 (provident fund)
Current law	Same	1966	Same	1975
Type	Social insurance system plus assistance program	Social insurance system	Social insurance system	Social insurance system
Coverage	Employed and self-employed (16–59), excluding family labor and those with wages less than $7.50 week	Employed and self-employed, excluding unpaid family labor	Employed persons 14–64 including public servants (compulsory with retirement at 65, with option at 60)	Employed, self-employed, apprentices age 16–60
Retirement age	M60, F60	M65, F65	M60,F65	M60, F60
Ceiling on annual insurable earnings	US$20,225	Minimum US$552; maximum US$18,788	US$8,320	US$22,305
Funding				
Public employee	3 percent of earnings	6.7 percent of earnings	1 to 3.5 percent of earnings	3 percent of earnings
Private employee	2 percent of earnings	7.25 percent of earnings	1 to 3.5 percent of earnings	3 percent of earnings
Self-employed	8 percent of earnings	125 percent of earnings	1 to 3.5 percent of earnings	7 percent of earnings
Voluntary contributions	—	—	1 to 3.5 percent of earnings	6.1 percent of earnings
Employer	5 percent of payroll	8 percent of payroll	3.5 to 6 percent of earnings	7 percent of earnings
Government	Only as employer	Only as employer	Only as employer	None

(continued on next page)

Annex 4.1 Social Insurance Systems in the English-Speaking Caribbean *(continued)*

Category	Antigua and Barbuda	Barbados	Belize	Dominica
Eligibility				
Full old age pension	Age 60+, 500 weeks of contributions	Age 65+, 500 weeks of contributions credited with at least 150 paid	Age 60+, 500 weeks of contributions paid or credited, with 150 paid	Age 60+, 300 weeks of contributions paid or credited (at least 150 paid)
Reduced pension	350 weeks of contributions	—	—	—
Transitional pension	156 weeks (starting before 1975)	—	—	—
Old age grant	Age 60+, at least 26 weeks of contributions (before 1975) or 52 weeks	Age 60+, 50 weekly contributions paid or credited	Insured person retiring after 60, not qualifying for a retirement pension; minimum 26 contributions	—
Old age assistance	Age 65+, age 60+ if blind or disabled	—	—	—
Disability pension	156 weeks of contributions	Less than 65, 150 weeks of contributions	150 weeks of contributions paid, with at least 110 weeks of contributions paid in last 5 consecutive contributing years	150 weeks of contributions paid or credited
Survivor pension	Insured, disability, or old age pension at death	150 weeks paid by deceased	Insurer was pensioner or eligible at death	Fully insured pension at death, married 3 years
Old age benefits				
Full pension	25 percent of covered earnings plus 1 percent for each 50 contributions above 500, up to 50 percent	40 percent of average earnings during best 3 years of at least 15, plus 1 percent of total earnings per 50 weeks of contributions after 500 weeks of contributions	30 percent of average weekly earnings, based on highest 3 years in last 15 years + 2 percent per 50 weeks of contributions above 500, and 1 percent above 750	30 percent of average earnings during best 3 of last 10, + 2 percent of earnings per 50 weeks contributions after 500, and 1 percent per 50 after 750 weeks of contributions

(continued on next page)

148

Annex 4.1 Social Insurance Systems in the English-Speaking Caribbean (continued)

Category	Antigua and Barbuda	Barbados	Belize	Dominica
Reduced old age pension or minimum benefit	Proportional to full pension	BD$105/week	—	—
Transitional pension/spouse supplement	25 percent of earnings, minimum - $136.50/month, maximum - $227.50/month	—	—	—
Old age grant	US$1,200	6 times average weekly earnings for each 50 weekly contributions paid or credited	Greater of 6 times average weekly earnings for each 50 weekly contributions paid or credited, or 2.5 times the sum of earnings divided by weeks of contributions	Lump sum of 3 times average weekly covered earnings for every 50 weeks of contributions paid or credited, if age 60 but ineligible for pension
Old age assistance	$136.50/month	BD$86/week	—	—
Delayed retirement	—	—	—	Increase of 6 percent of regular pension for every year of postponement
Institutional structure				
General supervision	Ministry of Finance and Social Security	Ministry of Finance and Social Security	Ministry of Finance	Ministry of Health
Administration	Social Security Board	National Insurance Office	Social Security Board	Social Security Board

(continued on next page)

149

Annex 4.1	Social Insurance Systems in the English-Speaking Caribbean *(continued)*			
Category	Grenada	Guyana	Jamaica	St. Kitts and Nevis
First law	1969 (provident fund, defunct)	1944 (old age assistance)	1958 (for sugar workers only)	1968 (provident fund)
Current law	1983	1969, 1981, 1986, 1989, 1992	1966	1977 (social security replaced provident fund); 1996
Type	Social insurance system	Social insurance system	Social insurance system	Social insurance and social assistance system
Coverage	Employed and self-employed (16–59), including public employees	Employees (public and private) age 16–59 and self-employed, voluntary contributions excluding employees earning less than GYD7.50/week, casual employees, family labor	Employees (public and private) and self-employed age 16 and below retirement age, voluntary contributions excluding casual employees, family labor	Employees (public and private) age 16 and below retirement age, voluntary contributions excluding unpaid family labor
Retirement age	M60, F60	M60, F60	M65, F60	M62, F62
Ceiling on annual insurable earnings	EU$36,000; US$13,483	US$5,064	US$4,464	US$29,213
Funding				
Public employee	4 percent of earnings	4.8 percent of earnings	2.5 percent of earnings	5 percent of wages
Private employee	4 percent of earnings	4.8 percent of earnings	2.5 percent of earnings	5 percent of wages
Self-employed	6.75 percent of earnings	10.47 percent of earnings	J$20/week plus 5 percent of earnings, up to J$6,570	10 percent of wages
Voluntary contributions	—	8.17 percent of average weekly including 2 years before stopping work	J$20/week	—
Employer	5 percent of coverage wage	7.2 percent of payroll	2.5 percent of wages up to J$6,570/year	5 percent of payroll
Government	None	Only as employer	Only as employer	Only as employer

(continued on next page)

Annex 4.1 Social Insurance Systems in the English-Speaking Caribbean *(continued)*

Category	Grenada	Guyana	Jamaica	St. Kitts and Nevis
Eligibility				
Full old age pension	Age 60+, 500 weeks of coverage (150 weeks of contributions paid)	Age 65+, 750 weeks of contributions paid or credited (150 weeks of contributions paid)	Age 65, men; Age 60, women. 1,248 weeks paid contributions and annual average 35 weeks paid or credited	Age 60+, 500 weeks of contributions paid or credited (150 weeks of contributions paid)
Reduced pension	Age 60, 260 weeks of coverage with at least 150 weeks of contributions paid	—	Annual average between 13 and 38 weeks	—
Transitional pension				
Old age grant	Age 60, ineligible for pension, at least 150 weeks of contributions paid or credited	—	Lump sum 52 weeks of contributions	For persons not qualified for pension
Old age assistance	—		—	Means-tested benefit
Disability pension	Under age 60, 50 weeks of contributions paid	Age 16–59 and permanently disabled, 250 weekly contributions credited (150 weeks of contributions paid)	Permanent disability from 156 weeks of paid contributions and annual average between 13 and 38 weeks	Under 62 years of age, 150 weeks contributions paid
Survivor pension	Deceased was pensioner or eligible for pension	Deceased was pensioner or eligible	1,248 weeks of paid contributions and annual average of 39 weeks paid or credited	150 weeks of contributions paid

(continued on next page)

Annex 4.1 Social Insurance Systems in the English-Speaking Caribbean *(continued)*

Category	Grenada	Guyana	Jamaica	St. Kitts and Nevis
Old age benefits				
Full pension	30 percent of average earnings plus 1 percent of earnings for each 50 weeks of contributions over 500 weeks	40 percent of average earnings during highest 3 years of last 5 years before age 60 plus 1 percent of earnings per 50 weeks of contributions after 750 weeks	Basic component, $10/week; earnings related component, $0.06/week. For every $0.34 of employer-employee contributions paid	30 percent of average wage (highest 3 of last 15 contributing years) + 2 percent of each 50 weeks of contributions credited or paid between 500 and 750 weeks, and 1 percent above
Reduced old age pension or minimum benefit	16 percent of average earnings + 1 percent for each 25 weeks of contributions over 150 up to 350 weeks	Minimum benefit of 50 percent of minimum wage	—	EU $200 month maximum, 60 percent of wages or EU $3,900 month (whichever is less)
Transitional pension/spouse supplement	—	—	$3.50/week for dependent's spouse age 55, women/age 60, men	—
Old age grant	Lump sum equal to 5 times average weekly wage for each 50 weeks of contributions	Lump sum equal to one-twelfth of annual insurable wage for each set of 50 weeks of contributions	$71 with 52 weeks of contributions paid	6 times average weekly wage for every 50 weeks of contributions, up to 499 contributions paid or credited
Old age assistance	—	—	—	—
Delayed retirement	—	—	—	—
Institutional structure				
General supervision	Ministry of Social Services and Labor	Ministry of Finance	Ministry Labor, Social Security and Sports	Ministry of Education, Labor and Social Security
Administration	National Insurance Board	National Insurance Board	National Insurance Division of	Social Security Board MISSS

(continued on next page)

Annex 4.1 Social Insurance Systems in the English-Speaking Caribbean *(continued)*

Category	St. Lucia	St. Vincent and the Grenadines	Trinidad and Tobago
First law	1970 (provident fund, defunct)	1970 (provident fund)	1939 (social assistance), 1971 (social insurance), 1999 amended
Current law	1978 (National Insurance Act)	1986 (social insurance)	Same
Type		Social insurance system	Social insurance and social assistance system
Coverage	Employed, self-employed, apprentices age 16–65; excluding civil servants	Employed, self-employed age 16–65	Social Insurance: employed person age 16–64, voluntary insurance available; excluding self-employed social assistance: residents age 65+, or 40+ if blind and needy
Retirement age	M60, F60		M60, F60
Ceiling on annual insurable earnings	US$22,472	US$16,944	US$6,873
Funding			
Public employee	—	2.5 percent of earnings	2.8 percent of earnings (12 wages classes)
Private employee	5 percent of earnings	2.5 percent of earnings	2.8 percent of earnings (12 wages classes)
Self-employed	10 percent of earnings	6 percent of earnings	n/a
Voluntary contributions	—	—	7.1 percent of earnings
Employer	5 percent of payroll	3.5 percent of payroll	5.6 percent of payroll (8 categories)
Government	None	None	Full cost of social assistance benefits

(continued on next page)

153

Annex 4.1 Social Insurance Systems in the English-Speaking Caribbean *(continued)*

Category	St. Lucia	St. Vincent and the Grenadines	Trinidad and Tobago
Eligibility			
Full age pension	Age 60 and 12 years of contributions, retirement necessary	Age 60 and 500 weeks of contributions	Age 60 or 65 (compulsory) with 750 weeks of contributions paid or credited, with increments if greater than 750
Reduced pension	—	—	—
Transitional pension	—	—	—
Old age grant	Age 60, lacking regular full old age pension	50 weeks of contributions	If ineligible for pension
Old age assistance	—	—	Means-tested pension: age 65+, 20 years residence, income below TT$5,000/year
Disability pension	Under pensionable age, minimum 5 years of contributions	Under age 60, 150 weeks of contributions disabled	10 weeks for contributions in preceding 13 weeks before onset of illness, payable after 26 weeks of illness
Survivor pension	Insured pensioner at death, widow over 55 or caring for deceased's children	150 weeks of contributions paid by deceased	Deceased insured, with 50+ contributions, or pensioner

(continued on next page)

154

Annex 4.1 Social Insurance Systems in the English-Speaking Caribbean *(continued)*

Category	St. Lucia	St. Vincent and the Grenadines	Trinidad and Tobago
Old age benefits			
Full pension	40 percent of average earnings in highest 3 of last 10 years plus 0.1 percent per month of contributions over 144 weeks	30 percent of average earnings; increased if over 500 weeks of contributions paid	Deceased insured, 30 to 48 percent of average weekly earnings, according to 12 wage classes
Reduced old age pension or minimum benefit		$50 per week	
Transitional pension/ spouse supplement		—	
Old age grant	Refund of contributions with interest plus 7.5 percent of average earnings per year of contributions	6 times average weekly wage for each 50 weeks of contributions	3 times total contributions
Old age assistance	—	—	Means-tested pension: TT$620/month
Delayed retirement	—	—	—
Institutional structure			
General supervision	Prime Minister's Office	No data	Ministry of Finance (social insurance system), Ministry of Social Development (public assistance and means-tested old age pension)
Administration	National Insurance Board	National Insurance Board	National Insurance Board (managed by tripartite board: government, labor, employers)

Source: SSA (2001); ICSS (1996); Plamondon (2001); World Bank (1996); Osborne (2001).

Annex 4.2. Questionnaire: Status of and Expectations for National Pension Systems

This questionnaire is designed to gather information on the status of pension systems in various English-speaking Caribbean countries. The information from this questionnaire is subjective because it comes from individuals and institutions involved with pension systems at different levels. Respondents should be chosen among policymakers, market operators, analysts, consultants, and any other institutions involved in and knowledgeable about pension systems in the countries being examined. The identities of respondents should be kept strictly confidential and not be made public under any circumstances. The questionnaire could also constitute the basis for a more extensive survey to study the factors of pension reform.

a. **What is the nature of your involvement with [country]'s pension system?**

☐ Policymaker, government
☐ Pension supervisor, government
☐ International specialist
☐ Private sector pension/insurance provider
☐ Private sector consultant/analyst
☐ Academic
☐ Other (specify) _____

I. *Current pension system*

b. **What is your general opinion of the current pension system in [country]?**

☐ Very satisfactory
☐ Satisfactory
☐ Unsatisfactory
☐ Very unsatisfactory

c. **Do you think that the pension system...**

☐ Doesn't need immediate adjustments

156

☐ Needs some adjustments (such as increasing the retirement age or contribution rates, changing the benefit formula, and so on)
☐ Requires major adjustments and possibly structural reform
☐ Requires major structural reform

d. What are the main problems with the pension system? (Indicate all that apply.)

☐ Actuarial unsustainability
☐ Mismanagement
☐ Fragmented structure
☐ Unfair advantages to special groups, inequities
☐ Low population coverage
☐ Other (specify) _____

_____

e. What do you perceive as the best/worst pension plans by provider type? Best:

☐ State
☐ Others

f. Do you worry about the adequacy of the current retirement system in [country] to provide old age security?

☐ No
☐ Sometimes
☐ Yes

II. *Pension system reform*

g. How should the responsibility and burden for old age pension provision be shared in [country] between individuals, employers, and government? (Indicate percentage.)

_____ percent individuals
_____ percent employers
_____ percent government

h. **What policy scenario do you consider most likely in the near future in [country]? (May choose more than one)**

☐ No changes
☐ Introduction of minor short-term adjustments (such as temporary reduction of benefits)
☐ Foreign
☐ Private

Worst case scenario:

☐ State
☐ Foreign
☐ Private
☐ Others
☐ Correction of some key parameters of the public system (such as retirement age or contribution rates)
☐ Establishment of new fully funded scheme, maintaining current public scheme (multipillar)
☐ Replacement of current public scheme with new fully funded one
☐ Creation of funded individual retirement accounts
☐ Other (specify) _____

---

i. **What policy scenario would you favor in the near future for [country]? (May choose more than one)**

☐ No changes
☐ Introduction of minor short-term adjustments (such as temporary reduction of benefits)
☐ Correction of some key parameters of the public system (such as retirement age or contribution rates)
☐ Establishment of new fully funded scheme, maintaining current public scheme (multipillar)
☐ Replacement of current public scheme with new fully funded one
☐ Creation of funded individual retirement accounts
☐ Other (specify) _____

III. *A fully funded pension system?*

j. Is some variation of the "Chilean model" (fully funded, defined contribution, privately managed, individual accounts) a desirable alternative for [country]'s pension provision arrangements and needs? Why?

☐ Yes, because _____
☐ No, because _____
☐ Don't know

If you answered "Yes" to (j), please complete the following questions:

k. How should supervision for private pension providers be structured in [country]?

☐ Autonomous specialized pension supervisory authority
☐ Autonomous insurance, banking, and pension supervisory authority
☐ Central bank as pension supervisory authority
☐ Ministry of Finance supervises market for pension providers
☐ Other (specify) _____
_____

l. What are the main obstacles to such reform? (May choose more than one)

☐ Political opposition (please explain) _____
_____

☐ Social resistance (please explain) _____
_____

☐ Labor organizations (please explain) _____
_____

☐ Employer organizations (please explain) _____
_____

☐ Other (specify) _____
_____

m. **What role do you think labor organizations should play in future discussions of pension reform?**

☐ Should play an active role throughout the process, as a major policy-making force
☐ Should be consulted throughout the discussions and provide feedback and monitoring
☐ Should be consulted only when broad policy decisions are made
☐ Other (specify) _____
_____

n. **Where should new pension fund administrators invest workers' contributions?**

☐ At first, they should be mandatorily invested in domestic markets, and only later should they be allowed to be diversified internationally
☐ They should be allowed to be diversified internationally from the start
☐ Don't know
☐ Other (specify) _____
_____

References

Bissember, Enid. 2002. The Role of National Insurance Schemes in CARICOM in the Transformation of the Financial System. Paper presented at the Senior Level Policy Seminar, Caribbean Centre for Monetary Studies, 2 May, Port of Spain, Trinidad and Tobago.

Dowers, Kenroy, Stefano Fassina, and Stefano Pettinato. 2001. Pension Reform in Small Emerging Economies: Issues and Challenges. Technical Paper (IFM-130). Inter-American Development Bank, Sustainable Development Department, Washington, D.C.

Forde, Penelope. 2001. Investing Social Security Reserves in the Caribbean. Paper presented at the Caribbean Subregional Tripartite Meeting on Social Security Financing and Investment Policies for Pension Funds, 24–25 October, Barbados.

Inter-American Conference on Social Security (ICSS). 1995. Social Security in the English-Speaking Caribbean. Monographic Series 19. Mexico City.

Mayers, Stuart, Darrin Downes, and Kevin Greenidge. 2002. Estimating the Size of the Hidden Economies in Barbados. Working Paper. Barbados Central Bank, Bridgetown, St. Michael.

Osborne, Derek. 2001. Financing Social Security: Options and Strategies. Paper presented at the Caribbean Subregional Tripartite Meeting on Social Security Financing and Investment Policies for Pension Funds, 24-25 October, Barbados.

Palacios, Robert and Montserrat Pallarés-Miralles. 2000. International Patterns of Pension Provision. Social Protection Unit, The World Bank, Washington, D.C.

Plamondon, Pierre. 2001. Financing Social Security Pensions. Paper presented at the Caribbean Subregional Tripartite Meeting on Social Security Financing and Investment Policies for Pension Funds, 24–25 October, Barbados.

United Nations Development Programme (UNDP). 2003. *Human Development Report 2003*. New York: Oxford University Press.

U.S. Central Intelligence Agency (CIA). Various years. World Factbook. Washington, D.C.: Central Intelligence Agency, Office of Public Affairs.

U.S. Social Security Administration (SSA). 2001. *Social Security Systems around the World*. Washington, D.C.: Government Printing Office.

The World Bank. 1996. Poverty Reduction and Human Resource Development in the Caribbean. Caribbean Group for Cooperation in Economic Development, Caribbean Country Operations Division, The World Bank, Washington, D.C.

SECTION THREE

Parametric Reforms as an
Alternative Model

CHAPTER 5

Public and Private Roles in Pension Reform: An International Comparison

Lawrence H. Thompson[*]

Most countries have or are developing retirement income systems with three basic elements:

- Programs that ensure a minimum adequate income to the elderly
- Mandatory programs that provide retirement benefits based on prior earnings or previous pension contributions
- Programs that encourage voluntary supplementation by individual workers and their employers.

The size of these elements and their reach throughout society vary widely, but the basic strategy of having three conceptually distinct elements has widespread appeal.

The financial strategy and management approach underlying the first and third elements are not particularly controversial; most controversy involves the second element. Programs supplying minimum incomes are invariably financed on a pay-as-you-go basis and are operated entirely or primarily by the public sector. Voluntary programs through which

---

[*] Lawrence Thompson is Senior Fellow at the Urban Institute. This chapter originally appeared in *Workable Pension Systems: Reforms in the Caribbean*, 2005, Inter-American Development Bank and the Caribbean Development Bank.

employers and individuals provide supplementary retirement incomes are usually financed on a funded basis and are almost always operated by the private sector. Mandatory, earnings-related programs are more varied. They can be either publicly managed or privately managed and can be financed on a funded or PAYG basis.

This chapter focuses on the debate about private management of mandatory, earnings-related programs. The debate arises most frequently in the context of proposals to shift from a publicly managed defined benefit program, financed on a pay-as-you-go basis, to privately managed individual defined contribution accounts, financed on a funded basis. The chapter first reviews the motives for reforming earnings-related retirement programs and the types of reform proposals being discussed. It then explores the issues surrounding current privatization and individual account proposals, including the merits of advance funding, private management, and defined contribution accounts.

Many approaches to pension management have evolved around the world, reflecting alternative ways that responsibility can be split between the public and private sectors. The different approaches reflect different philosophies about the role of the State, the role of social partners, and the importance of worker choice, and have different implications for the cost of administering pension programs and the predictability of pension benefits. This chapter reviews the various approaches to give a sense of the range of options that a country might entertain, to examine the link between management models on the one hand and administrative costs and benefit predictability on the other, and to discuss factors that might influence a country's decision about which model to adopt.

The Reform Debate

Although almost every country is reforming its pension system, the motivations for reform and the avenues it takes differ dramatically. In much of Asia, pension reform debates are dominated by concerns about broadening coverage and improving benefits. In economies in transition from socialism, reforms are largely motivated by the need to adjust pension programs and administering institutions to a market economy. Many Latin American reforms are partly motivated by a desire to insulate the pension system from political interference and to improve services for participants. Reform debates in North America, Japan, and Western Europe, on the other hand, tend to focus disproportionately on the costs of an aging society.

Reform proposals are sometimes characterized as being one of two types: parametric or systemic. Parametric reforms concentrate on changing key parameters that control the size and scope of the pension system. These involve extending coverage to additional industries or occupations, changing the age at which benefits become available, altering the average benefit (either by changing the size of the initial benefit or the procedure for indexing benefits after entitlement), and adjusting contribution rates. By contrast, systemic reforms concentrate on changing the basic structure of the pension system. In recent years the most common systemic reform has involved moving to advance funded, privately managed, individual defined contribution accounts. Why advance funded? Why privately managed? Why defined contribution?

Why Advance Funding?

Advance funding is commonly associated with private pensions, where it allows enterprises to match revenues and costs more accurately and provides assurance that pension promises will be met even if the firm that made them no longer exists when the worker retires. Neither objective is a particularly compelling reason for advance funding in a mandatory program sponsored by a central government. Rather, advance funding of public pension programs is advocated for a variety of different reasons, ranging from improving the macroeconomic environment to providing workers with higher returns on their pension contributions.

Economists and pension analysts generally believe that under the right circumstances, advance funding of pensions can:

- *Allow a given pension benefit package to be financed with a lower contribution rate.* The contribution rate will be lower under a funded approach than under a pay-as-you-go approach, provided that the rate of return earned on pension assets, net of administrative expenses, exceeds the growth rate of earnings covered by the pension system. Conversely, if the net return is below the growth rate of covered earnings, the contribution rate will be higher under a funded plan than under a PAYG plan (Aaron 1966). The link to the net rate of return underscores the importance of minimizing the risk of poor investment performance and avoiding excessive administrative charges when organizing a funded pension program.
- *Spread the cost of financing retirement income.* Financing for pay-as-you-go plans typically comes almost exclusively from taxes levied on

labor. Advance funding shifts a portion of financing responsibilities to capital, broadening the base of support for retirement income.

- *Increase national savings.* To the extent that a funded plan forces participating workers to save more than they would otherwise, it will raise personal savings. Increased personal savings are likely to come predominantly from average and below-average earners, since higher-income households are likely to be able to adjust the rest of their portfolios to offset any excess saving generated by mandated pension contributions. Whether an increase in personal savings translates into an increase in national savings partly depends on how transition costs are financed, a topic discussed below. Obtaining a positive effect on national savings also requires that financial markets channel funds accumulating in pension accounts into higher investment rather than higher consumer lending.[1]

- *Make capital markets more efficient.* Where capital markets exist but are not fully developed, funded pensions may help improve their efficiency and help the economy grow more rapidly. These improvements are thought to occur through encouragement of institutional reforms and creation of deeper markets for capital instruments. But the applicability of this argument to small countries (such as those in the Caribbean) or to individual countries that are part of an integrated financial system (such as the European Union) is not clear. The argument may be more relevant for relatively isolated, medium-size or large countries that can aspire to develop independent capital markets.

- *Increase workers' claim on future benefits.* Advance funding may reduce the odds of future benefit cutbacks by giving workers a moral claim to benefit promises. Benefit claims are particularly strengthened when advance funding is combined with individual defined contribution accounts. (For a longer discussion of advance funding expectations, see Thompson 1998.)

Discussions in the popular press about pension finance often suggest additional impacts of advance funding that are, in fact, unlikely. In particular, advance funding is *not* likely to:

---

[1] The lack of a clear link between pension asset accumulation and national savings rates is clear from the experiences of the United Kingdom and the United States on the one hand, and of France and Germany on the other. The United Kingdom and the United States have traditionally had low national savings rates, notwithstanding immense pension assets. In contrast, France and Germany have traditionally had higher savings rates, despite having virtually no advance funded pension plans (Thompson 1998).

- *Reduce the costs of an aging population.* In any given year, the retired population must be supported out of that year's national income, and the support will use resources that could otherwise be used for another purpose. Intelligent macroeconomic planning may make the pie larger, but if the retired are to be allowed to share proportionately in the general increase in living standards, the share of the pie going to their support will not change no matter how pensions are financed. Funds invested abroad might allow a country to consume more than it produces (that is, run a trade deficit) for an indefinite period, but using such a surplus to support the consumption of the retired population still denies its use for other purposes. Reducing the cost of supporting an aging population requires parametric reforms—changes in the retirement age or in the living standards of the retired population. Systemic reforms—changes in the structure and financing strategy of the retirement income system—will have little direct effect on the cost of supporting an aging population.[2]

- *Increase the return that workers receive from the retirement income system.* If a funded pension system can operate with lower contribution rates than a pay-as-you-go system, workers will experience a higher return on their pension contributions. As a group, however, they may be no better off, because the higher returns will likely be offset by changes in the costs of other activities. For example, unless a change in pension financing strategy produces significant macroeconomic benefits, the added cost of financing the transition from a PAYG to a funded system will equal or exceed the savings from lower pension contributions. (This point is developed more fully in Geanakoplos, Mitchell, and Zeldes 1998.)

Advance funding has two main drawbacks that have discouraged some countries from using it when organizing their pension systems or shifting from PAYG financing. These are:

- *Slow phase-in.* Advance funded pension plans—particularly those that take the form of individual defined benefit accounts—are not an adequate response to deficiencies in a country's retirement income system because they take so long to mature. Three or four

---

[2] A more sophisticated argument in favor of systemic reforms is that they can help reduce total pension costs by reducing political opposition to parallel parametric reforms. No systematic evaluation of this proposition has been undertaken. As noted below, a systemic reform that sharply increases administrative costs may increase the cost of the pension system.

decades will elapse between the inauguration of individual funded accounts and a significant change in the economic status of the retired population.

- *Transition costs.* Where a pay-as-you-go system is already operating, shifting to advance funding will likely involve substantial transition costs. These funds must be raised through increased taxes, reduced spending on other government programs, or borrowing from capital markets. To the extent that the transition costs are covered through additional borrowing, the change to advance funding will have a negative net impact on national savings. The funds accumulating in pension plans will simply be loaned back to the government to finance the transition, leaving society worse off by the amount of the administrative costs involved in the transactions. Chile's Ministry of Finance recently estimated that from 1981 to 1996, pension reform cost the government an average of 5.7 percent of GDP a year. It also estimated that pension funds experienced accumulations at an average annual rate of 2.7 percent of GDP—suggesting a negative impact on national savings equal to 3.0 percent of GDP a year (Arenas de Mesa 1999).

Why Privately Managed?

If there is to be advance funding of a pension plan, many analysts believe that the financial assets should be privately managed. It is generally believed that private sector management will help secure higher (gross) returns and produce better service. Specifically, the advantages of private management are seen as:

- *Insulation from political involvement in pension investment decision making.* Studies suggest that privately managed pension funds generally earn higher returns than do publicly managed funds (see, for example, Iglesias and Palacios 2000). Several factors seem to account for the difference. First, where public agencies are given fairly wide latitude in their investment activities, their portfolios become inviting political targets. The agencies may be required to purchase government bonds at below-market rates to facilitate government finance, to purchase particular securities to help well-connected people, or to invest in projects with greater political than economic appeal.[3] Second,

---

[3] Recent developments in Argentina and Bolivia show that these abuses are also possible where funds are privately managed if a government's fiscal problems are sufficiently serious.

to avoid unwarranted political interference in investment decisions and unwarranted influence over the private economy by a pension fund's investment managers, the investment activities of many national pension systems are restricted. For instance, a pension fund may be required to hold all its assets in bank deposits, government bonds, or housing bonds. Such restrictions tend to produce lower returns than would be earned by a portfolio more representative of the entire financial market. Canada recently changed the investment policy governing funds held by the Canadian Pension Plan, a government-managed defined benefit system. In the past these funds were invested exclusively in government bonds. In the future they will be invested more broadly in a portfolio that reflects the kind of investments held by private pension funds in Canada. It remains to be seen whether this move will allow the plan to earn investment returns equal to those earned by private managers without incurring the costs associated with decentralized, private management.

- *Better services.* Where public agencies have failed to provide decent services, a shift to private management is an attractive alternative. The relative service quality of public and private institutions varies widely from place to place, as does the applicability of this argument for private management.[4]

- *Greater operating efficiency.* It is assumed that a private firm will be a more efficient operator of pension programs under many circumstances, in that it will have stronger incentives to cut costs and be better positioned to implement technological improvements and streamline work practices. The impact of such efficiency gains needs to be weighed against the higher marketing costs incurred by private firms, as discussed below. In addition, pension fund management involves substantial scale economies. Particularly in small countries, the scale economies involved in monopoly public management may exceed the operating efficiencies from competing private firms.

- *Worker choice of providers.* Many recent systemic pension reforms provide workers with a choice among competing fund managers (although not necessarily among investment strategies). Worker choice is seen as an attractive feature in its own right and is possible only when competition is allowed among a variety of (presumably) private

---

[4] In 1995, Dalbar Financial Services of Boston rated the U.S. Social Security Administration (SSA) first in a survey of the quality of telephone services provided by financial service organizations. All the organizations except the SSA were private firms.

firms. Many view such competition as providing further insurance against political interference in investment decisions.

The experiences of some countries suggest that private management of pension funds also has drawbacks. Perhaps the two most important are:

- *Excessive marketing costs.* Many countries that have implemented private management of individual accounts have found that competition to acquire clients generates substantial marketing costs. High marketing costs lead to high administrative charges, offset the social gains from greater operating efficiencies among private firms, and reduce the return that would otherwise be earned in a funded pension plan. Administrative charges for fund management average around 18 percent of pension contributions in most Latin American countries and 25 percent in the United Kingdom.[5] Fees for converting fund balances into annuities add another 10 percent of the account balance. Combined, administrative charges in these countries consume more than 25 percent of total contributions, reducing the net rate of return on pension assets by 1.2 to 1.5 percentage points a year.[6] It is not unusual for aggregate pension benefits provided under a mature national pension plan to amount to 6 to 8 percent of GDP. If this level of benefits is produced by a pension system in which administrative expenses absorb 25 percent of contributions, the bill for administering the pension system will be 2.0 to 2.5 percent of GDP.
- *Need for effective regulation.* The Latin American pension reform model relies on close regulation of a limited number of specially licensed pension fund managers. In Argentina and Chile, for example, the pension regulator has about 10 employees for every licensed pension fund. Laws and regulations specify the allowable investment mix, the terms under which accounts can be switched from one manager to another, and many of the internal operating procedures of pension

---

[5] Whitehouse (2000) explores asset management fees in general, while Murthi, Orszag, and Orszag (1999) examine the full range of administrative charges in the United Kingdom.

[6] Well-run and mature national defined benefit pension plans typically have administrative costs of 1 to 3 percent of benefit payments. Administrative costs in the U.S. system are even lower, averaging 0.6 percent of benefit payments and 0.5 percent of contribution income. National plans that are not so well run or are relatively immature are likely to have somewhat higher costs, although they rarely exceed 6 to 8 percent of contributions or benefits. Costs of defined benefit pension plans are discussed more fully in Mitchell (1996).

agencies. Close regulation is seen as a necessary protection both for individual workers and the government as a whole. (As noted below, governments often retain a considerable contingent liability that would be triggered by poor investment performance or asset management by private pension fund managers.) The United Kingdom initiated a program of decentralized management of individual accounts without adequate consumer protection regulations. The results were additional costs to consumers, estimated to average 15 percent of contributions from termination and transfer fees, and a major "misselling" scandal.

Why Defined Contributions?

Almost all the funded accounts introduced in recent pension reforms have been defined contribution accounts.[7] Pension programs typically operate on the basis of defined benefits or defined contributions. Under a defined benefit system, the retirement benefit is calculated using a formula that sets a monthly payment that may be uniform for all recipients or that may reflect the pre-retirement earnings and work history of the individual retiree. Under a defined contribution system, the contribution rate is specified but the retirement benefit is not. Rather, the pension benefit is simply the annuity value of the amounts that have accumulated in the worker's account.

The defined contribution approach has several advantages in a system that relies on private management and advance funding, including:

- *Facilitating portability*. Decentralization of responsibility for managing pensions creates portability problems under a defined benefit system, but not under a defined contribution system.
- *Fostering competition among fund managers and choice about investment strategies*. The defined contribution approach is necessary to any system that offers worker choice, either in terms of fund management or investment philosophy.
- *Reinforcing political insulation*. Workers are presumed to be more reluctant to allow political interference in pension investment decisions when they understand that poor returns on their portfolios mean lower retirement incomes.

---

[7] Saudi Arabia provides an example to the contrary. Its public pension plan is defined benefit and is essentially fully funded. Some assets are managed by the central bank. Others are managed by one of three private firms—two of which are located outside the kingdom.

But the defined contribution approach also has drawbacks, including:

- *Requiring workers to assume more risk.* Retirement benefits are much less predictable under the defined contribution approach because they depend both on the long-run relationship between average wage growth rates and investment returns (which cannot be known when the contribution rate is set) and on annual changes in wage levels and investment returns over a worker's career. Even in the unlikely event that average wage growth and investment returns over a worker's life are predicted perfectly, annual variations in each introduce a random element into the pension calculation. The impact of this variation on retirement benefits is explored later in this chapter.
- *Contingent liabilities for the government.* Where the government guarantees a minimum income level, such variation in pension amounts creates contingent liabilities. Government payments for minimum pensions will rise whenever an unlucky cohort reaches retirement age. The government's fiscal commitment is asymmetric, however, because lucky cohorts are not required to help finance the subsidy to unlucky cohorts.
- *Difficulties in providing annuities.* Defined contribution accounts must be converted into life annuities to provide assurance that retirement incomes will last the lifetime of the recipients. Such conversions raise both policy and technical issues. One policy issue is whether annuitization should be voluntary or mandatory. The individual account programs established in Europe tend to mandate annuitization, while it is optional for those with sufficiently high account balances in many Latin American countries. Another issue is whether annuity providers should be required to index annuity amounts to price or wage changes after retirement. In most countries private firms do not issue indexed securities. As a practical matter, then, if the government wants to require that annuities be indexed, it will probably have to issue price-indexed bonds. (Even a retirement system based on individual funded accounts must rely on pay-as-you-go financing for inflation protection.)

Some proponents of the defined contribution approach argue that it links benefits more closely to lifetime contributions. But such a link can be just as close under a defined benefit system, if so desired. The link is likely to be looser in a defined benefit system because departures from a close link are easier to implement than under a defined contribution system. Whether this feature is an advantage or disadvantage depends on whether one favors certain departures from a strict benefit contribution link, such as gratuitous credits for years spent in school, in the military, in unemployment, or in raising children.

Private Management Models

A variety of individual account models have evolved in the past quarter-century, illustrating different ways to divide responsibilities between the public and private sectors, select asset managers, and give workers a voice in their account management. The descriptions here illustrate the range without attempting to cover all the approaches that have developed. (For more complete descriptions, see Thompson 1999.)

Latin America

Under the Latin American model (also adopted, with variations, in Hungary, Kazakhstan, and Poland) workers select one of a limited number of authorized pension funds. Any worker can select any fund and is free to change funds from time to time, moving the entire account balance from one to the other. For a variety of reasons, all pension funds hold similar portfolios, so workers are selecting funds rather than investment philosophies.[8]

In many countries, the government collects contributions and allocates them among the pension funds. But in a few (such as Chile), collection responsibility is also decentralized. Pension funds are responsible for maintaining account records. Upon retirement they pay benefits by allowing periodic withdrawals or by transferring the account balance to insurance companies to finance the purchase of annuities.

United Kingdom

In the United Kingdom, workers have the option of setting up a personal pension in lieu of the State-managed plan or their employer's plan. (They can also opt back into the State system after having opted out.) They can select from a wide array of personal pension providers offering a variety of investment instruments. They can also change providers each year, and can leave their previous account balance with their old provider. The

---

[8] Chile requires firms to offer multiple portfolios that differ in their mix of equities and bonds, on the assumption that equities should have a lower weight in the portfolios of older workers.

government collects contributions and allocates them to the personal pension providers that individuals have selected. Personal pension providers are then responsible for maintaining account records. Accounts must eventually be converted into annuities, which may be sold by the pension provider or by a separate insurance company.

Sweden

Sweden's approach offers a wide selection of investment instruments while keeping administrative costs well below those in Latin America and the United Kingdom. In Sweden, funded individual accounts are based on a relatively small contribution rate (2.5 percent of wages) and supplement a more generous system run by the State on a pay-as-you-go basis. Any firm licensed to sell mutual funds is allowed to participate in the mandatory funded account system—provided it agrees to a schedule of rebates of its normal administrative charges. Workers select one or more of 400-odd funds eligible to participate. The government collects contributions and maintains all the individual accounts.

Participating mutual fund managers know the aggregate volume of business coming from the State pension system but do not know the identity of individual workers whose investments are being managed. It is hoped that this feature will eliminate the marketing costs found in other individual account models. Upon retirement, accounts are converted into annuities by one or two insurance companies selected by the State through competitive bidding.

Switzerland

Switzerland requires employers to contribute, at specified rates, to industry-wide pension funds. The funds are managed jointly by worker and employer representatives, and upon retirement pay benefits in the form of annuities. Workers do not have a direct choice of pension funds or investment philosophies. Other than general policy oversight, all aspects of the Swiss system are privatized, including contribution collection, account maintenance, asset management, and pension payment. A similar arrangement has evolved in Denmark.

U.S. Thrift Savings Plan

The U.S. government has developed a thrift savings plan for its employees that provides an institutional model attractive to many pension reformers, although the plan has not been instituted nationwide. Under the model, the government selects a few market indexes calculated by private firms. The indexes track the performance of domestic and international equities, corporate bonds, and government bonds. The government contracts with other private firms to manage asset portfolios—with the goal of matching the behavior of each index—and lets workers allocate their account balances among the funds. Workers have a choice of investment philosophy but not fund manager, the opposite of the choice offered in the Latin American model. In the U.S. model, the government is responsible for all functions except asset management and annuities payment, although it selects the annuity provider. The model's main attraction is its potential to reduce administrative costs to a fraction of those under the Latin American model.

Management Models and Contribution Rates

As discussed, advocates of advance funding often note that it holds potential for allowing a given pension to be financed with a lower contribution rate. As a general rule, contribution rates will be lower under advance funding as long as the rate of return earned on the asset portfolio, net of administrative expenses, exceeds the rate of growth of wages covered by the pension program (also less administrative expenses). Because the different pension management models outlined above differ substantially in terms of administrative costs, the probability of realizing lower contribution rates will partly depend on the model chosen.

Table 5.1 shows real (inflation-adjusted) portfolio returns and wage growth rates in four major industrial countries from 1953 to 1995.

Table 5.1	Annual Investment Returns and Wage Growth Rates in Four Industrial Countries, 1953–95 *(geometric average percent, adjusted for inflation)*				
Country	Equity returns	Bond returns	Mixed portfolio	Wage growth	Gap between mixed portfolio and wage growth
Japan	8.1	3.8	6.6	5.0	1.6
Germany	7.4	3.9	6.3	4.8	1.5
United Kingdom	7.8	1.8	5.6	3.6	2.0
United States	8.2	2.2	5.6	1.0	4.6

Source: Thompson (1998).

Equity returns refer to the combination of dividends and capital gains for a broad market index in each country. Bond returns are returns on 10-year government bonds. The mixed portfolio is one in which half the portfolio is equities and half is bonds. Wage growth reflects changes in average manufacturing wages in each country.

The data in Table 5.1 give an idea of the room for absorbing administrative costs in advance funded pension systems. As a first approximation, the ceiling on administrative costs is the figure in the final column, showing the gap between the mixed portfolio and wage growth. If administrative costs exceed this level, advance funding will probably require higher contribution rates than would pay-as-you-go financing. Since the calculation is based on changes in average wage levels, technically it applies only when total employment is constant. If total employment under the pension program is growing, the gap would be reduced by the rate of growth of employment. To get a complete picture, the costs of administering a pay-as-you-go system must be added to this gap.

There was a major difference between the experience in the United States and that in the other three countries, largely as a result of slower U.S. wage growth. As a result, the room for administrative expenses was more than twice as large in the United States as in the other countries—where the gap ran from 1.5 to 2.0 percent a year.

Estimates of the administrative costs associated with some of the individual account models discussed previously are shown in Table 5.2. The second column shows estimates of administrative costs of maintaining each account and managing the money, while the third column reflects the additional cost of converting the account balance into an annuity. Costs are expressed as percentages of assets under management, to allow direct comparisons with the estimated gaps between investment returns and wage growth shown in Table 5.1.

Models based on decentralized management of pension accounts have substantially higher costs than models based on centralized management. Where account management tasks are centralized and competition among pension managers is restricted, costs run 0.5 percent of assets or less. Where pension funds are allowed to compete freely for workers' business, costs can be much higher. Indeed, in parts of Latin America, in some funds in Australia, and in the United Kingdom, administrative costs equal or exceed the gaps estimated in Table 5.1. Workers participating in some of these programs are likely to receive less generous pensions from their funded accounts than they would have received had the same contributions been used to support a PAYG regime. Thus, those planning pension reforms must pay careful attention to the structure of the

Table 5.2	Administrative Costs of Different Fund Management Approaches (percentage of assets under management)		
Type of approach/system		Accumulation phase	Both phases
Centralized approaches			
Denmark			0.3
Switzerland			0.5
U.S. Teachers Insurance Annuity Association			0.3
U.S. Federal Thrift Savings Plan		0.1	0.4 [a]
Decentralized approaches			
Australia		0.5–1.9	1.0–2.4
Latin America		0.6–1.4	1.1–1.9
U.K. personal pensions		1.2–1.3	1.7–1.8
U.S. 401(k) plans		0.8–1.9	1.3–2.5

Note: For Australia, Latin America, and the U.S. 401(k) plans the additional cost of annuitization was assumed to be 0.5 percent of assets, an estimate consistent with Mitchell, Poterba, and Warshawsky (1999). Murthi, Orszag, and Orszag (1999) reach the same result in their analysis of the United Kingdom. The cost of annuities for the U.S. Federal Thrift Savings Plan was set at 0.3 percent of assets to reflect the fact that it has negotiated an exclusive contract with an annuity provider. But annuitization is not required under the plan, and presumably few annuities are actually sold. In addition, except for the U.S. 401(k) program these estimates do not include the transactions costs associated with buying and selling assets. Conceptually, those costs should be added to these figures.

[a] Author's estimate.

Source: Danish Financial Supervisory Authority (flnet.dk/engdefault.asp); Federal Social Insurance Office of Switzerland (bsv.admin.ch/statistk/ f/svs/pp_1_1.pdf); Teachers Insurance Annuity Association (tiaa-cref.org/pubs/html/AR.01/fin_02.html and 03.html); U.S. Federal Thrift Plan Annual Report (tsp.gov/forms/financial-stmt.pdf); Whitehouse (2000); Murthi, Orszag, and Orszag (1999); James, Smalhout, and Vittas (2001).

reformed system if one of the goals of reform is to produce lower contribution rates.

Management Models and Benefit Predictability

Another area where the models differ is the predictability of the income provided by a pension program. As noted, benefits under defined contribution pension systems are difficult to predict because they are determined by the pattern of wage changes and investment returns over a beneficiary's work career—something that cannot be known in advance. Some management models involve greater uncertainty than do others, however.

Conceptually, the uncertainty associated with projecting benefits under a defined contribution system can be divided into two components. One involves the uncertainty associated with not knowing in advance the average growth rate of real wages and average investment returns that will prevail over a lifetime. The other involves the impact on each retirement cohort of the particular pattern of annual wage adjustments

179

Table 5.3	Contribution Rates Required to Produce a Pension Equal to 50 Percent of Final Pay under Different Annual Investment Returns and Wage Increases *(percentage of wages)*				
		Average net investment return (percent)			
Average wage increase (percent)	1	2	3	4	5
3	12	14	17	20	
4	9	11	13	16	18
5	7	8	10	12	14
6		7	8	10	11
7			6	7	9

Note: Assumes an uninterrupted 35-year work career with constant earnings growth and constant investment returns. Upon retirement the final account balance is converted into a 15-year annuity. Blank cells are combinations that are unlikely to occur.
Source: Author's calculations.

and investment returns, even when the long-run average wage trend or investment return is known. Tables 5.3 and 5.4 give an idea of the degree of uncertainty from each of these sources.

Table 5.3 shows the contribution rate required to produce a retirement pension equal to half (50 percent) of final pay under different assumptions about average wage growth rates and net investment returns over a worker's career. The challenge for workers planning their retirement is that the amount they must contribute annually to produce a given pension varies substantially with relatively modest changes in net returns and wage growth rates.

With a wage-return gap as large as that in the United States after World War II and a cost-effective pension management model such as the U.S. Federal Thrift Savings Plan, contributions of about 7 percent of pay will be sufficient. A wage-return gap of the size experienced in Germany and Japan over the same period would require contributions of almost twice that level to produce the same pension—even with the most cost-effective pension management model. With a more expensive pension management model and the Japanese or German wage-return gap, contributions would have to be at least 17 percent of pay. Should workers now entering the labor force contribute 7 percent of wages, assuming that the 1953–95 U.S. experience will repeat itself and that they will be able to participate in a very cost-efficient pension management

Table 5.4	Mean and Standard Deviation of Replacement Rates *(percent)*		
Model	Model	Standard deviation	Standard deviation as percentage of mean
Traditional defined benefit (sponsor absorbs all variation)	55	0	0
Swiss model (sponsor absorbs investment and annuity variations)	56	5	9
Swedish model (sponsor absorbs annuity variation)	55	21	38
Chilean model (worker absorbs all variation)	57	26	45

Note: Figures are simulations using historical U.S. values. The calculations assume continuous work for 35 years, a contribution rate of 10 percent, a benefit equal to a 15-year annuity, a portfolio of half equities and half 10-year government bonds, administrative costs equal to 1 percent of assets, and annuities at the 10-year government bond interest rate. The annual mean and standard deviation (in parentheses) were 0.99 percent (2.44 percent) for wages, 5.6 percent (9.4 percent) for a balanced portfolio of half equities and half bonds, and 2.25 percent (2.89 percent) for government bonds. These calculations ignore administrative costs.
Source: Author's calculations.

model? Or should they contribute 17 percent, assuming a narrower gap and a less efficient management model?

Table 5.4 quantifies the impact of annual variations in actual rates of wage increases and investment returns. The table was constructed using a Monte Carlo approach: random numbers were used to construct annual estimates of investment returns and wage growth from a distribution that had the same mean and standard deviation as the actual 1953–95 U.S. data. The results of 35 such random draws from each distribution produced a simulated wage growth pattern and pattern of annual investment returns for an illustrative cohort of workers, from which the wage replacement rate afforded these workers was calculated. For each model, the simulation was run 1,000 times to calculate the variance in replacement rates that can be attributed simply to the random pattern of annual variations.

The various models differ in the degree to which pension benefits can be predicted, particularly in this stylized experiment where average returns are known with certainty. The differences come from the way the models handle worker choice and provide annuities. The Swiss model, described earlier, locks workers into a particular account provider. Because of this, pension managers use a longer-run average rate of return to calculate each worker's account balance each year. In effect, annual variations in investment returns are smoothed, with higher returns from luckier retirement cohorts used to raise lower returns from unluckier cohorts. This practice is not possible, however, where workers have the right to change their account from one manager to another. If workers can transfer at any time, variations in market returns must be immediately reflected in variations in each worker's account balance.

A second source of variation involves the strategy for providing annuities. The differences are similar. Where workers are locked in to one annuity provider, the provider can smooth out annual fluctuations in the price charged for a given annuity. Where a variety of providers compete for the business of each worker, prices must adjust more quickly to changes in interest rates.

As shown in Table 5.4, under the assumptions used to make these calculations, all the pension models produce a benefit equal to about 55 percent of final pay, which is the amount that a defined benefit plan would always pay.[9] Under the Swiss model, unpredictable wage growth patterns introduce uncertainty. Cohorts experiencing relatively rapid wage increases early in their careers fare better than those with more rapid wage increases later in their careers because the earlier growth increases the relative size of the earliest contributions and generates larger final balances. The simulation suggests that as a result of this source of uncertainty, the standard deviation of the actual pension will be 9 percent of the mean.

Under the Swedish model, workers can change pension fund managers at any time during their working years. Upon retirement, however, they are required to convert their account balance into an annuity to be provided by a monopoly supplier. Since the annuity provider is a monopoly, it can afford to offer annuities based on average bond yields, rather than constantly adjusting the price of its annuities. In this case, uncertainty about the size of one's pension comes from both the variability in annual wage changes and the variability in annual returns during the work career.

The simulation suggests that this increases the inherent variability of the actual pension, so that the standard deviation rises to 38 percent of the mean.[10]

---

[9] Slight differences in the average replacement rate reflect the impact of the random numbers used in the exercise. Presumably, with a large enough sample, they would all approach 55 percent.

[10] Using a different methodology, Alier and Vittas (1999) find that the annual variation in investment returns in a balanced portfolio produces a standard deviation equal to about 25 percent of the mean benefit. However, the authors did not consider the additional variability introduced by unpredictable annual wage increases or changes in the interest rate used to calculate annuities, however. Thus their results appear consistent with these.

In Chile, workers can select from competing pension fund managers as well as competing annuity providers. Competition among annuity providers introduces additional uncertainty into the pension benefit calculation through uncertainty about the cost of purchasing an annuity when an individual worker retires. The simulations suggest that this feature causes the standard deviation of the ultimate pension to rise to 45 percent of the mean.

This final simulation may overstate pension variability by assuming that annuity prices adjust rapidly to changes in interest rates, although no studies address that issue. Even if a better estimate is a standard deviation of just 40 percent of the mean, the model introduces substantial uncertainty in pension planning. If pensions replace an average of 55 percent of final pay but the standard deviation is 40 percent of that, or some 22 percentage points, the actual benefit will be less than 33 percent of final pay for one-sixth of retirees and more than 77 percent of final pay for another one-sixth of retirees. The other two-thirds of retirees will receive benefits equal to 33 to 77 percent of final pay.

Comparison of Models

The various approaches outlined here are compared in Table 5.5 and 5.6. Table 5.5 rates each approach on four attributes: insulation of investment decisions from political interference, choice offered to workers, administrative costs, and pension predictability. No single approach is superior on all four dimensions.

Table 5.6 shows how the various responsibilities are divided between the government and the private sector under each model. In all cases, asset management is assigned to the private sector and policy development to

Table 5.5 Comparative Strengths of Different Funded Account Models				
Model	Political insulation	Worker choice	Low cost	Predictable pensions
Latin America	*	*		
United Kingdom	*	*		
Switzerland	*		*	*
Sweden	*	*	*	
U.S. Thrift Plan	*	*	*	
Canada			*	*

Source: Author comparisons

Table 5.6	Allocation of Responsibilities under Different Funded Account Models				
Responsibility	Latin America	United Kingdom	Switzerland	Sweden	U.S. Thrift Plan
Set policy	Government	Government	Government	Government	Government
Collect contributions	Varies by country	Government	Private	Government	Government
Maintain records	Government	Private	Private	Government	Government
Manage assets	Private	Private	Private	Private	Private
Pay benefits	Private	Private	Private	Government	Government

Source: Author's comparisons.

the public sector. The models differ in their assignment of other responsibilities. The particular strategy adopted in any country will depend on its preferences, priorities, and traditions. For example, it appears possible to develop models that produce relatively predictable pensions and insulate the funds effectively, without having high administrative costs, provided one is willing to sacrifice worker choice (as in Switzerland). Alternatively, it is possible to provide worker choice and low costs, provided one is willing to allow the government to play a major role in selecting investment options and maintaining worker accounts (as in Sweden and under the U.S. Thrift Plan). Finally, it is possible to insulate the government and offer wide choice, but the result may be high administrative costs and less predictable pensions (as in the United Kingdom).

Those interested in introducing funded individual accounts into a particular pension system will need to consider carefully the situation in their country. Is the institutional environment more conducive to the successful implementation of one of the models than the others? Which of the possible objectives are the most important to pursue in designing an approach? What is the best way to reduce the uncertainty in defined contribution approaches? Careful considerations like these can make a major difference in the success or failure—perceived and actual—of particular pension approaches in particular countries.

References

Aaron, Henry J. 1966. The Social Insurance Paradox. *Canadian Journal of Economics and Political Science* 32 (3): 371–74.

Alier, Max and Dimitri Vittas. 1999. Personal Pension Plans and Stock Market Volatility. Paper presented at the World Bank conference,

New Ideas about Old Age Security, 14–15 September, Washington, D.C. Available at http://www.worldbank.org/ knowledge/ chiefecon/ conferen/secagend.htm

Arenas de Mesa, Alberto. 1999. *El sistema de pensiones en Chile: resultados y desafíos pendientes*. Paper presented at the United Nations Economic Commission for Latin America and the Caribbean conference, Latin American and Caribbean Symposium on Older Persons, 8–10 September, Santiago, Chile.

Geanakoplos, John, Olivia Mitchell, and Stephen P. Zeldes. 1998. Would a Privatized Social Security System Really Pay a Higher Rate of Return? In *Framing the Social Security Debate: Values, Politics and Economics*, eds. R. Douglas Arnold, Michael J. Graetz, and Alicia H. Munnell. Washington, D.C.: National Academy of Social Insurance.

Iglesias, Augusto and Robert Palacios. 2000. Managing Public Pension Reserves. World Bank Pension Primer, Washington, D.C. Available at www.worldbank.org/pensions

James, Estelle, James Smalhout and Dimitri Vittas. 2001. Administrative Costs and the Organization of Individual Account Systems: A Comparative Perspective. In *New Ideas About Old Age Security*, eds. Robert Holzmann and Joseph Stiglitz. Washington, D.C.: The World Bank.

Mitchell, Olivia S. 1996. Administrative Costs in Public and Private Retirement Systems. Working Paper 96-4. Wharton School, Pension Research Council, Philadelphia, Penn.

Mitchell, Olivia S., James Poterba, and Mark Warshawsky. 1999 New Evidence on the Money's Worth of Individual Annuities. *American Economic Review* 89 (5): 1299–1318.

Murthi, Mamta, J. Michael Orszag, and Peter R. Orszag. 1999. The Charge Ratio on Individual Accounts: Lessons from the U.K. Experience. Working Paper 99-2. Berbeck College, London.

Thompson, Lawrence H. 1998. *Older and Wiser: The Economics of Public Pensions*. Washington, D.C.: Urban Institute.

———. 1999. Administering Individual Accounts in Social Security: The Role of Values and Objectives in Shaping Options. Occasional Paper 1. Urban Institute, The Retirement Project, Washington, D.C.

Whitehouse, Edward. 2000. Administrative Charges for Funded Pension: An International Comparison and Assessment. World Bank Pension Primer, Washington, D.C. Available at www.worldbank.org/pensions

CHAPTER 6

The Politics of
Pension Reform in Brazil

*Vinícius C. Pinheiro**

Brazil's pension reform strategy differs from that of many other Latin American countries that emulated the Chilean reform model. The Brazilian strategy centered on strengthening the basic public pay-as-you-go scheme and on developing the existing private voluntary pension scheme to supplement it. The reform's main measures tightened eligibility rules, reduced replacement rates, ended special regimes, homogenized rules for private and public sector workers, and increased coverage. At the same time, successive governments improved the regulatory framework to set the stage for development of private pension funds based on personal and occupational savings. In sum, Brazil has chosen to modify the first pillar (public, mandatory PAYG) and further develop the third pillar (voluntary supplementary savings) without creating a second pillar (private, mandatory individual savings plans).

Brazil's pension reform process took place over two distinct periods. Between 1998 and 2001, the Cardoso administration proposed a package of reforms that covered all existing social security plans; that is, the general plan for private workers, the civil servants plan, and the private pension plan. While most of the measures affecting civil servants did not

---

* Vinícius C. Pinheiro was the Secretary of Social Security in Brazil (1999–2002) and the main policymaker responsible for the elaboration and implementation of the Brazilian pension reform. He currently works as Social Protection Senior Programme Officer for the International Labour Organization, in Italy. This chapter is an update of Weyland (2004).

go forward, reform of the general and supplementary schemes did succeed. In 2003, despite the political change, the Partido dos Trabalhadores (PT), which assumed power, followed the policies of the previous government. The PT focused its reform efforts on the pension plan for civil servants.

At the end of the 1990s, discussion centered on the alternative of introducing a mandatory individual capitalization regime to replace the pay-as-you-go system, but it was considered politically and economically unfeasible because of its fiscal implications. At the same time, strengthening the public PAYG system was supported by the notion that pensions are one of the pillars of social stability in the country. The National Social Insurance Institute (INSS) pays benefits to more than 22 million beneficiaries a month and 65 percent of them are equivalent to the minimum wage. For each person receiving a pension, there are 2.5 additional individuals who benefit indirectly, according to the Brazilian Institute for Geography and Statistics (IBGE). As a result, Brazil's existing system reaches more than 76 million people, or 45 percent of the Brazilian population. Recent estimates show that the poverty rate among the elderly in Brazil (18 percent) is the lowest in Latin America. Moreover, Brazil is the only country where the percent of the elderly below the poverty line is smaller than all other age groups (Table 6.1).

This performance is largely explained by the old age rural program, which pays rural workers benefits equivalent to the minimum wage when they reach the age of 60 for men and 55 for women. Maternity, disability, and survivor pensions are also guaranteed. The program is mainly

Table 6.1	Population Below the Poverty Line by Age Group, Selected Latin American Countries, 1998 (percent)				
		Age group			
Country	TOTAL	0–14	15–39	40–64	65+
Bolivia	30.5	34.4	24.1	31.0	47.5
Brazil	24.6	33.4	22.3	18.7	18.5
Chile	20.8	24.4	19.2	18.5	23.9
Colombia	24.0	27.1	20.6	23.8	32.9
Costa Rica	21.7	23.6	19.4	21.0	29.1
Guatemala	19.1	21.6	16.6	15.0	27.1
El Salvador	27.4	31.3	22.8	26.5	38.0
Mexico	22.1	27.4	18.3	19.6	37.6

Source: Gill, Packard, and Yermo (2005).

Table 6.2	Total Pension Deficit, 2003 *(percent of GDP)*	
Pension scheme		**2003**
General regime		1.74
Urban		0.57
Rural		1.17
Public sector systems[a]		3.04
Federal		1.79
States and municipalities		1.25
TOTAL		4.79

[a.] Employer contribution is two times the employee contribution.
Source: Ministerio da Previdência Social (MPS).

financed through sales taxes on rural transactions and payroll taxes, but evasion is extremely high and the program's deficit reached 1.17 percent of GDP in 2003 (Table 6.2).

The main source of the overall fiscal imbalance in Brazil is the public sector pension plans, including those that cover federal, state, and municipal civil servants and the armed forces (the army and state military police), which account for 2.6 percent of GDP. Moreover, the beneficiaries of these plans tend to have relatively higher incomes, making the allocation of public resources to this group unfair. Reform efforts conducted in 2004 mainly affected future generations of workers. Current civil servants have succeeded in blocking reform initiatives that would have reduced their benefits. In addition, supreme court decisions have annulled some reform efforts and contributed to maintaining the status quo.

This chapter discusses why the result of the pension reform process was different in Brazil than in other Latin American countries. It argues that, in spite of the inconclusiveness of the pension privatization debate (Stiglitz and Orszag 2001; Barr 2002; Mesa-Lago 2002), many Latin American countries adopted structural pension reforms following the logic of a collective action approach based on the Chilean model. Pension privatization directly benefits organized groups that have strong interests and take political action to push forward the reform agenda using the privatization rhetoric.[1] By contrast, adjustments in the PAYG system

---

[1] The arguments used by the proponents of this type of model were based on a privatization rhetoric that identified an inherent trend toward crisis in PAYG systems and believed that simple adjustments would merely delay the inevitable adoption of a permanent solution. This privatization rhetoric tried to prove the superiority of the capitalization

promise diffuse benefits to the population as a whole—mainly to future generations that are not even represented in the political process—and impose costs on specific groups whose lobbying actions can paralyze the policymaking process.

Radical pension reform schemes were first proposed in Brazil during the administration of Fernando Collor de Mello (1990–92). However, his political weakness and lack of an organized political base became an insurmountable obstacle and the proposal stalled. When similar plans resurfaced in 1997–98 under President Fernando Henrique Cardoso (1995–2002), the country's impending financial crisis made it impossible to carry out any changes of this type. At that time, the country could not afford the substantial transition costs inherent in privatizing pensions.[2]

The option that was eventually adopted involved strengthening the PAYG system and developing voluntary private pension plans, and paved the way for changes introduced by President Luiz Inácio "Lula" da Silva, which focus on the civil servants schemes. In sum, political and economic obstacles in Brazil blocked the logic of collective action that was at work in other Latin American countries. However, today, rival political forces have embraced a modified version of the same project.

The next section explains how the logic of collective action operates in parametric and structural pension reforms. This is followed by an application of this theoretical framework to the historical evolution of the pension system and to the recent pension reform process in Brazil. The Brazilian experience raises significant issues that argue in favor of a gradual, well-targeted, and incremental reform of the PAYG system.

The Logic of Collective Action in Pension Reform

A Historic Overview of Pensions in Brazil

The historical process that led to the creation of pension systems in Latin America was characterized by a gradual extension of coverage to orga-

---

system over the distribution system, invoking its positive impact on domestic savings, capital markets, and the labor market, and its capacity to accommodate demographic changes. According to its advocates, this was a definitive model that would not require any further reforms and that could function as a pillar for development. However, these claims were not based on solid technical and empirical data. Only anecdotal evidence, derived especially from the Chilean case, was offered to demonstrate its success.

[2] Privatization would have forced the government to continue to pay existing pension benefits without continuing to collect social security contributions.

nized labor that reflected each sector's bargaining power. Some organized groups worked within the political system to obtain special eligibility or contribution conditions (Mesa-Lago 2002). The cost of expanded coverage and special group benefits was passed through to consumers as price increases. As a result, few limits were established on the growth of pension expenditures. Indeed, special interests benefited from the lack of transparency in the relationship between contributions and benefits. The resulting imbalance between them strained public finances.

Brazil's pension system has three components. The General Social Security Regime (Regime Geral de Previdência Social, or RGPS) is a public, mandatory pay-as-you-go plan, managed by the National Social Insurance Institute, which covers all private sector workers up to a pension ceiling of approximately $800. The Pension Regime for Government Workers (Regimes Próprios de Previdência Social, or RPPS) covers civil servants who fall under specific pension provisions. Although the eligibility criteria are the same for all government workers, there are over 2,400 specific pension systems managed by the federal government, states, and municipalities, each with its own financing rules. The regimes are mostly PAYG, with some allocated funds in a few states and municipalities. The armed forces and similar groups at the state level have a career-based scheme that is mostly financed through the general budget. The Complementary Pension Regime (Regime de Previdência Complementar, or RPC) includes funded employee and personal pension plans that are privately managed by closed and open pension funds and insurance companies. Affiliation is not mandatory and reform efforts have focused on modernizing the rules and extending coverage.

The Need to Reform the Public Pension System

The PAYG system has undergone frequent reforms to respond to demographic changes in the labor market. When there is no sustainable balance between revenues and expenditures, any combination of the following measures can be used to make periodic adjustments to the system: raising the contributions rate; changing eligibility requirements; modifying the benefits formula and the rules for cost-of-living increases; restricting coverage; and eliminating special pension schemes. Cost increases resulting from these measures are concentrated on specific groups of workers, employers, and pensioners. Regardless of the measures adopted, these organized interest groups are generally able to oppose any changes that would reduce their benefits or increase their contributions. However, the benefits of these changes (namely, the financial and actuarial sustainability of pension system) are similar to a public good and accrue to society as a whole, including future generations. Because those who would benefit are such a large group and individual gains are relatively quite small, it is unlikely that a constituency in support of reforms to strengthen the system would organize and lobby for such changes. In other words, since the costs are tangible, short term, and concentrated on specific groups, while the benefits are intangible, long term, and diffuse, reforms to the PAYG system are politically difficult to carry out—despite the fact that in the long run, the interests of pensioners and contributors tend to meet (Mebane 1994).

Further complicating the issue is the likelihood that rather than preventing reform, pressure from the organized opposition may lead to a watering down of the needed measures and no real solution to existing problems. This could create a cycle of relatively frequent reforms, further reducing their political viability.

The Rationale for Introducing the Private Pension System

Privatization of the pension system also faces political challenges, but they are not as severe as the changes discussed above because the costs of privatization are concentrated among groups with little political clout, such as future pensioners (whose accumulated contributions would not be sufficient to cover their benefits) and lower-income persons (who cannot be included in the capitalization scheme). In contrast, privatization produces clear beneficiaries in the financial sector, who can be expected to lobby aggressively for reform in order to broaden their market opportunities. In addition, it is possible to win the political support of entrepreneurs and workers by offering to decrease or even eliminate payroll taxes (as was the case in Chile) or by allowing unions to create their own pension funds (as was the case in Argentina). Some sectors of the public bureaucracy can also be co-opted by offering to create independent regulatory agencies, which would have considerable financial resources and power since they could be financed by contributions from the pension funds.

Pension reform privatization proposals promise to ensure the long-term financial balance of the system. In addition, their advocates expect that the resulting increase in savings in personal accounts in the pension funds will lead to higher economic growth. By contrast, they depict the PAYG system as a zero-sum game that limits savings because contributions are spent immediately to cover current pension benefits. In fact, their endorsement of privatization feeds on the criticisms of the PAYG system: the worse its condition, the stronger the argument in favor of structural reform and the more seductive the promises of generating savings and economic development, even without sufficient theoretical or empirical evidence.

Advocates of privatization also claim that pension fund savings eliminate the dichotomy between capital and labor because they turn workers' contributions into the basis for capital accumulation. According to Piñera (1996), who describes Chile as a country of capitalists, the capitalization system eliminates social conflict because taxpayers, pensioners, and entrepreneurs become stakeholders in the economic development that is anticipated to result from privatization of the pension funds. Privatization would also neutralize collective action and state interference because of the system's increased visibility and the fact that workers would acquire property rights over their contributions.

The argument is that privatization means that reform occurs "once and for all." Under a privatized system, any changes in payroll taxes, years worked, retirement age, and eligibility are borne by the individual and are no longer subject to political interference. Political influence will be limited to the system's regulatory framework (control over profitability of fund investments, management fees, migration between funds, and so on), and to guaranteeing a social safety net. Those who have the most to lose from this type of structural reform generally are pensioners, retirees, and low-income persons. The latter will depend entirely on the fiscal budgets for their retirement income, and will have to compete with other budget items, including the enormous transitional costs of pension privatization. However, as can be surmised, the "losers" have the least political clout.

Summing up, reforms whose aim is capitalization are generally able to garner more favorable collective action than those that are geared to making changes in the pay-as-you-go system. PAYG reform imposes costs on a relatively limited and vocal number of people, while its benefits (especially the improved financial viability of the system) are widely distributed among constituents who are less likely to organize in its favor. The system's actuarial balance is a public good that benefits everyone but raises little individual concern. In contrast, organized groups will always engage in collective actions to defend their privileges. For these reasons, PAYG system reforms have no allies and face strong adversaries.

By contrast, the creation of a capitalization system finds support among powerful social and political forces that have interests in the private pension fund market. These groups include financial sectors, productive enterprises that foresee the possibility of reducing their tax burdens, certain groups of workers that want to organize their own pension funds, and sectors of the bureaucracy that aspire to positions in new regulatory agencies. The adversaries of privatization are people who will certainly be harmed by the process—current retirees who will lose the backing of new contributions to guarantee their benefits, and sectors of the population that have no capacity for capital accumulation and therefore need a social safety net.

Theoretically, one would expect that the drive toward pension privatization that affected so many Latin American countries during the last decade would also have taken hold in Brazil. The section that follows explains why this has not happened.

Concentrated Benefits and Diffused Costs: The Evolution of Brazil's Pension System

The initial framework for the development of the Brazilian pension system was the creation of the Caixas de Aposentadoria e Pensões (Retirement and Pension Credit Unions, or CAPs) during the 1920s.[3] CAPs were collective capitalization systems that also offered health care services to members. They included railway workers, stevedores, and employees in the maritime, telegraph, and radio industries. The credit unions were inspired by Bismarck's social security model, which granted rights to organized workers in certain industries that had bargaining power. During the early years, social security policies played a double role by responding to workers' claims while allowing the government to co-opt and control the fledgling union movement (Cohn 1980).

During the 1930s, the system was restructured along a corporatist model as part of a comprehensive program of state-led industrialization. In addition to the CAPs, there were many retirement and pension institutes (Institutos de Aposentadoria e Pensões, or IAPs) with membership restricted to urban workers. While in the 1920s the social security system was made up of private organizations created within companies, the IAPs had a different legal status and were directly dependent on the Labor Ministry, becoming parastatals in nature. They were part of the corporate structure. Unions were organized vertically and placed under the supervision of the State as a means to buffer conflicts between

---

[3] The credit unions provided infrastructure financing that played a role in promoting exports of primary materials.

capital and labor and to encourage a cooperative strategy for development.

Politically, corporatism served as a means to guarantee the pact between
urban workers and national entrepreneurs to support an authoritarian,
centralized, and interventionist State. From an economic standpoint, the
creation of a social protection system restricted to urban workers served
to concentrate income and helped consolidate the purchasing power of
relatively better-off social strata (which, in a poor country like Brazil, included organized labor). As a result, this strengthened domestic markets,
facilitating a process of industrialization based on the substitution of im-
ports. Social security also contributed to industrialization by becoming a
forced savings mechanism that supplied resources to facilitate state intervention in the economy.

Government initiatives to unify and universalize social security
programs were influenced by Britain's Beveridge Report, which advocated guaranteed social protection as a universal right of citizenship.
The technical experts who worked for the Labor Ministry, especially in
the Instituto de Aposentadoria e Pensões dos Industriários (Institute for
Retirement and Pension of Industries, or IAPI), played a fundamental
role in these efforts (Malloy 1976). But corporatist structures had already
taken root. The IAPs controlled enormous financial resources and many
jobs, which were an important source of leverage in Brazil's system of
patronage politics. In the post-1945 period, those corporatist structures
attained an unexpected degree of autonomy and blocked all attempts to
unify the social security system.

After the military coup of 1964, the government took complete control of social security, removing workers' and employers' representatives
from the management of the system. In 1966, the IAPs were merged
into the new Instituto Nacional de Previdência Social (National Social
Security Institute), which covered all workers except civil servants.
The 1966 reform implied a victory for the IAPI experts, inspired by
the Beveridgean paradigm, over corporatist interests. The reform was
possible only because of the authoritarian environment, which led to
an increase in administrative judiciousness and a decrease in societal
participation in decisionmaking. At the same time, the new institution
unified the sources of funding, using surpluses and reserves of some
IAPs to cover the deficits of others. This consolidated PAYG regime was
financed through payroll taxes paid by employers and employees, as
well as state contributions.

Social security policies played an important political and economic
role in the 1970s as a result of an increase in coverage and expansion

of social assistance benefits. On the one hand, social security helped to cushion the social costs of the military regime's economic development strategy. On the other hand, through the centralized distribution of benefits, it facilitated the concentration of power in the federal government and ensured political support for the military regime (for example, when the pension system added special social welfare schemes for rural and domestic workers). It also started to include the self-employed and entrepreneurs by means of compulsory and regular individual contributions. This made the social security system more comprehensive, and permitted the distribution of income derived from payroll taxes and individual contributions not only among social classes and generations, but also among social security pensions, health care, and safety net functions.

The 1980s were a period of chronic economic crisis for Brazil that manifested itself in low GDP growth rates, high rates of inflation, increased income concentration, and the inability of the State to meet its domestic and foreign debt obligations. This period also saw the return to democracy, which put an end to the bureaucratic authoritarian regime of the 1970s and introduced new actors into the decisionmaking process regarding public resources, giving an outlet to new demands for additional social benefits. The 1988 constitution institutionalized a concept of social security inspired by the European postwar experience, which is understood as the implementation of multiple programs to meet retirement, health care, and social welfare assistance needs.

From the point of view of social security, the most important development was the creation of the Regime Geral de Previdência Social (General Social Security System, or RGPS), which gave urban and rural workers the same legal status. This change brought the entire formal private sector workforce into the general social security system. But the constitution maintained especially generous rules for specific categories of workers and thus preserved the historical distortions inherent in the RGPS. Under both systems, public sector workers and groups with greater bargaining power received better entitlements in terms of eligibility and benefits. Furthermore, those whose incomes were above the RGPS ceiling could also join complementary private systems. Consequently, despite the unification, different social security schemes continued to co-exist, and the special privileges of relatively narrow sectors were financed with greater contributions paid for by broad segments of the population, including future generations.

Between 1988 and 1994, inflation became the key tool to make the promises enshrined in the 1988 constitution compatible with the limited availability of resources. Constant price increases reduced the real value of benefits and the system's costs. In effect, inflation hid the system's distortions, which became apparent with enactment of the monetary stabilization plan (the Real Plan) in the second half of 1994. The resulting fiscal pressures strengthened the calls for fundamental reform.

Concentrated Costs and Diffused Benefits: Pension Reform

The first reform proposals for radical privatization emerged at the beginning of the Fernando Collor administration in 1990. These were spearheaded by small academic think tanks and/or financial sector representatives, such as the Instituto Liberal and the Instituto Atlântico, which recommended implementation of the Chilean model. Since these organizations did not have ties to any particular social group, their proposals acquired a certain degree of feasibility during the prevailing reformist mood of the Collor administration, a government marked by drastic reform initiatives. But the Collor government was fully occupied with its eventually unsuccessful efforts to bring down inflation and stabilize the economy. Also, the president lacked organized support and thus a strong political base to push forward the comprehensive reform of the pension system.

After the initial push, the creation of the Special Social Security System Commission in 1992 and the initiation of a constitutional review process in 1993 rendered the debate over pension reform more systematic and wide-ranging. Interestingly, the reform proposals were not designed or presented by political parties but by professional associations.

At this stage, the major obstacles to privatizing the pension system were the fragmentation of social forces and the weakness of political parties, combined with a lack of internal cohesion inside the government. Although groups who commanded great economic clout aggressively advocated privatization, they were not able to transform their economic resources into political power (Weyland 1996). The proposals they put forth were vague and fundamentally ideological. There was no adequate quantification of the effects of a systemic transformation nor a detailed outline of the transition from PAYG to a capitalized system. The rhetoric of these groups was based on extolling the Chilean model. Social security reform along Chilean lines was part of the comprehensive set of neoliberal reforms proposed earlier by the Collor administration, which also included trade liberalization, reducing the size and scope of the federal bureaucracy, privatizing public services such as education and health care, and greater labor market flexibility.

Enactment of the proposed social security reform ran into several problems under Collor's successor, Itamar Franco (1992–94). First, the reform agenda was packed with other priorities, such as monetary stabilization, trade liberalization, and fiscal reform. The constitutional review of 1993–94 took place during difficult times that were characterized by political instability after Collor's impeachment on corruption charges, a bribery scandal that shook Congress, the implementation of an economic stabilization program (the Real Plan), and the 1994 elections, all of which limited the attention paid to social security reform. The necessary room on the political agenda for a discussion of social security reform opened up only after the stabilization of the economy in the second half of 1994.

Second, the pension reform was an issue about which the general public, as well as politicians and academics, knew very little. Technical discussions were restricted to specialists. The ideas they discussed were not properly disseminated, and there was little or no transparency in the statistics and information available about the topic. Even the studies conducted by international financial organizations, such as the World Bank and the International Monetary Fund (IMF), were of limited use because of the lack of a clear diagnosis of Brazil's social security system.

Third, social security had not yet become a fiscal problem. In fact, Brazil's inflationary spiral had postponed the system's financial collapse. Chronic inflation had created additional resources through the investment of social security reserves at high interest rates, while it artificially reduced costs by decreasing the real value of benefits.

The most recent reform of the pension system was initiated at the beginning of the Fernando Henrique Cardoso administration (1995–2002). This coincided with the deterioration in social security accounts, which had started to lose value in 1994 following the launching of the Real Plan. A proposal for a constitutional amendment to modify the pay-as-you-go system was sent to Congress in 1995. The proposal called for striking details regarding eligibility criteria and formulas for calculating and modifying benefits from the nation's constitution. The aim was to facilitate reforms and make it possible to carry it out through ordinary legislative changes, which required only a simple majority, not a super-majority as in the case of constitutional amendments.

During consideration of the proposal in the Chamber of Deputies in 1995 and 1996, several changes were made to the constitutional amendment, making it significantly different from the government's original proposal. In 1997, when the amendment was being considered in the Senate, the Cardoso administration and its congressional supporters tightened some of its provisions, including the introduction of stricter eligibility rules for the PAYG system. Seven main issues were being debated at the time, including:

- Replacing the option of retiring after a certain number of years of work with the obligation to prove the same number of years of contributions to the system
- Introducing a minimum age for retirement based on years of contribution (a rule that was approved only for public employees)
- Removing the formula for benefit calculation from the constitution
- Establishing an income ceiling equivalent to ten times the minimum wage for the general retirement plan, but not linking the ceiling to future minimum wages
- Capping benefits for public servants earning more than the income ceiling
- Introducing taxes on retiree earnings above the ceiling, and
- Eliminating the special retirement plan for university professors, judges, and members of congress.

The government lost support in the lower house of congress for some of these proposed changes: namely, the proposals to establish a minimum retirement age for private sector workers, to limit pensions paid to public servants, and to tax public sector retirees and pensioners.

Although all the proposed changes were not enacted, the constitutional amendment was approved by the Senate at the beginning of 1998 and by the Chamber of Deputies in December of that year, making it possible to enact sweeping changes in social security by means of ordinary legislation.

The burden of these changes were borne by specific, concentrated groups, while the resulting improved financial stability of the system was more widely distributed among the populace. As a result, organized interest groups did not mobilize to support this important reform. But a number of organized groups, which would be affected by specific provisions of the amendment, did organize to lobby against those provisions. In fact, opposition was widespread because some groups asserted that it was too modest, whereas others attacked it as a neoliberal package that would hurt workers and sell the country to foreign capitalists.

As the constitutional debate wore on, the government set up a working group in 1997 to discuss more radical reform options, including privatization. The group was made up of well-known specialists from such institutions as the national development bank (Banco Nacional de Desenvolvimento Econômico e Social, or BNDES), the national statistical institute (Instituto Brasileiro de Geografia e Estatística), and the government's planning think tank (Instituto de Pesquisa Econômica Aplicada, or IPEA). The group's mission was to plan the second phase of the reform, which would include the creation of a mixed private/public system to be implemented following the constitutional reform. Given Brazil's stark social inequalities and widespread poverty, most social and political stakeholders agreed that following the Chilean model of complete privatization was out of the question. Such a radical measure would have left large segments of the population (and voters) without adequate social protection. Therefore, even advocates of privatization accepted that it was necessary to preserve a public pension system with a redistributive component for people at the lowest income levels.

But beyond this basic agreement, the working group never managed to reach a consensus on the specifics of the new reform plan. Initially, during the first half of 1998, a model was proposed that reduced the income ceiling in the PAYG system to three times the minimum wage and created a mandatory privately managed personal savings system in the bracket between three and ten times the minimum wage. People with incomes above that level would contribute to a voluntary savings account.

The working group's final proposal consisted of a basic pillar that would function as a publicly administered capitalization system (Oliveira, Beltrão, and Pasinato 1999).[4] In addition, there would be the mandatory and voluntary fully funded private pillars managed by private pension fund administrators.

The Politically Active Groups

Employer associations linked to financial markets, such as the Brazilian Banking Federation and the Brazilian Stock Market Institute, had de-

---

[4] This is a combination of pay-as-you-go and an individual capitalization system. As in a PAYG system, workers' social security taxes are used to pay for current pension benefits for older generation. But these social security contributions are recorded in individual estimated accounts and "remunerated" according to a set interest rate. After retirement, individuals are entitled to pension benefits that correspond to the estimated funds accumulated in their notional account. Thus, as in an individual capitalization system, the value of pension benefits is determined by the (implicit) accumulation of individual contributions. However, since the State uses actual revenues from social security contributions to pay current pensioners, the system of virtual capitalization avoids the transition costs that make the establishment of a Chilean-style private pension system so economically difficult. While according to the proposal of the working group, the State would administer the notional accounts, the mandatory and voluntary pillars in this mixed system would be managed by private pension fund.

fended reduction of employer payroll taxes and a benefit cap for public sector workers since 1992. However, these groups opposed the constitutional reform because they thought it did not go far enough. The National Confederation of Industry also advocated a reduction of payroll taxes and a lowering of the income threshold for coverage under the public PAYG system—a measure that would open up greater opportunities for private pension funds. It also felt that the reform should eliminate the special plan for public sector workers, and that retirees and pensioners should pay taxes.

Pension fund associations emphasized their importance for increasing domestic savings. Therefore, they advocated privatizing the pension system by decreasing the income ceiling in the general plan, which would greatly increase the demand for their own services. Like the other business associations, they considered the government's proposal insufficient because it did not stipulate such a drastic change.

At the opposite extreme were organizations that represented the interests of public workers, such as the Movement of Retired Public Servants, the Association of Auditors of Social Security Contributions, and the National Confederation of Social Security Workers. These associations opposed changes to the special retirement plan for public servants, especially taxing retirees' income, reducing benefits, and introducing an age threshold for retirement. These organizations did not agree with the government's diagnosis and believed that the problems of social security lay in tax evasion, fraud, diversion of resources, and lack of investment in human resources. Stressing difficulties on the revenue side, they resisted cuts in entitlements.

The Brazilian Federation of Retired Workers and Pensioners, which represented members/beneficiaries of the general plan, defended the public, state-managed social security system and rejected any move to privatization. It advocated a cost-of-living adjustment for benefits and the implementation of a four-party administration for the social security system, comprised of the government, workers, entrepreneurs, and retired workers.

The leftist Confederação Geral dos Trabalhadores (General Workers' Confederation, CGT) and the socialist Central Única dos Trabalhadores (United Workers Confederation, CUT) similarly opposed the reform. They submitted proposals to strengthen and expand State-managed social security, making eligibility conditions more flexible, especially for lower-income workers; increasing the value of benefits, which were to be indexed to the minimum wage; and democratizing the social security administration through the introduction of group representation. CUT was against any type of restrictive measures and advocated the maintenance of the existing social security rules for public servants. This group argued that the financial problems were a consequence of tax evasion, fraud, and the mismanagement of social security resources, including their misuse to finance other types of expenditures as part of the government's economic stabilization policies.

By contrast, a more conservative private sector union, Força Sindical, proposed the unification of the retirement plans for private and public sector workers, stating that the special conditions enjoyed by public servants were an "unacceptable privilege." Força Sindical was against any adjustments to the PAYG system that would be restrictive for private sector workers. It also proposed the structural reform of the social security system, decreasing the income ceiling to the equivalent of three times the minimum salary, and implementing a capitalization system for those interested in higher benefits. It took this position because it expected to create its own pension funds.

New Factors in Play: Speculative Attacks Against the Real and the Government's Response

Beginning in September 1998, the direction of social security reform shifted as a result of the Asian and Russian financial crises. At the time, Brazil was seen as the next potential victim of a speculative attack on its overvalued currency. In that same month, the government started negotiations with the IMF, the World Bank, and the Inter-American Development Bank for loans to guarantee the level of international reserves and avoid a currency crisis.

The speculative attack hit Brazil in January 1999, right after the reelection of President Cardoso. It resulted in a devaluation of the currency, the replacement of the head of the central bank, and a deepening of the economic adjustment program. Generating a sufficiently large surplus to ensure the payment of the government's voluminous debt was crucial to the success of this stabilization effort. This made reforming the social security system extremely important. Priority was given to changes that would yield immediate fiscal gains, while any measures that could cause further public debt or declines in the fiscal surplus were blocked.

This led to a shift in the debate regarding privatization and collective action. The provisions of the constitutional amendment modifying the PAYG system promised immediate financial gains.[5] There also was a

---

[5] For example, taxing retirees would increase revenues to the social security system.

generalized feeling among politicians, government experts, and representatives of international organizations that only the approval of tough measures by congress would send a positive signal to international markets. Yet while privatization promised economic development in the long run, the costs of a transition to a capitalization system would place a huge burden on public accounts in the short term. Estimates of the increase in public debt resulting from the transition ranged between 188 and 250 percent of GDP (see Pinheiro 1998; Bravo and Uthoff 1999).

Given the high fiscal costs involved and the economy's weakness, representatives of the government's economic institutions, led by the technical staff of the Finance and Planning ministries, expressed their opposition to the planned social security reform. The MPS (Ministério da Previdência Social) supported the opposition by stressing the high transition costs experienced in Chile and Argentina. As a result, and because of the need to reduce fiscal outlays, the technical group working on pension reform submitted an alternative proposal at the beginning of 1999 that maintained the PAYG system but included virtual capitalization mechanisms, or notional accounts, based on the Swedish model, which was submitted to the MPS to prepare a draft bill.

Implementation of the notional accounts model faced political and operation obstacles. The political problems revolved around the debate over the interest rates to be used to adjust individual accounts. The long practice of high, very short-term interest rates had eliminated long-term references. The only existing reference was the minimum rate from an actuarial analysis of complementary pension funds, which was (and is) 6 percent a year in real terms. Thus, congressional debates over interest rates began from a minimum level of 6 percent a year. However, this rate increased the new system's anticipated costs relative to those of the existing system. The operational problems had to do with the lack of long-term records for contributions, which prevented any restoration of accumulated benefits for persons close to retirement. Furthermore, high inflation during the 1980s and the first half of the 1990s reduced the quality of existing data and made the system vulnerable to legal challenges over the indexes used to adjust for inflation.

The problem of selecting an interest rate was resolved by putting it into the formula used for calculating benefits. This implies that the system continues to operate as a PAYG system where the current generation of workers finances current retirement payments. However, the value of benefits is closely correlated with contributions, which are capitalized based on a rate that is a function of the length of time during which contributions were made and the age of the beneficiary. The issue of the lack of records was resolved by using the average salary for the years since 1994 to calculate an estimated salary for contributors' entire work history contributors. This solution was part of the bill approved in November 1999, which introduced a special readjustment factor to calculate the value of social security benefits.

The formula can be expressed as follows:

$$\text{Pension} = [(W \times c \times P) / LE] \times \text{Bonus}$$
$$\text{Bonus} = 1 + [\text{retirement age} + (c \times P)]/100$$

where,

$W =$	average of 80 percent for highest contribution salaries contributed to the pension system between July 1994 and the retirement date, adjusted for inflation
$c =$	contribution rate = 0.31
$P =$	contribution period
$LE =$	residual life expectancy at retirement, updated annually by the Instituto Brasileiro de Geografia e Estatística (IBGE).

The numerator of the first component of the equation (average contribution salary, W, times the contribution rate, c, times the length of contribution, P) shows the amount accumulated by each contributor in his/her individual account. Dividing this notional fund by life expectancy after retirement yields the value of the pension benefit at an interest rate equal to zero. The second component of the equation functions as an implicit interest rate that rises based on increases in the retirement age and the contribution period, P. When the premium defined by age is added to the product of the length of contribution and the contribution rate ($T \times c$), the result represents an endogenously determined interest rate. This number should have a positive correlation with the number of years worked: that is, it increases as retirement age increases. This methodology means that the retirees themselves determine the interest rate because they decide when to retire. Thus, those who retire early could potentially cause a negative impact on the system's cash flow, but must accept a lower rate of return compared to those who work for a longer period of time (and thus contribute to the system longer).

The changes brought about by the reform slightly improved the financial situation of the general pension regime. The measures were intended to improve collections from private sector workers, increase their coverage, and strengthen the link between contributions and benefits. To this end, the main changes included a gradual elimination of early retirement provisions, placing restrictions on special rules for some professional categories, and changing the benefit calculation.

Prior to the reform, retirement benefits were calculated based on the inflated average salary of the last three years worked, which resulted in generous pensions for workers retiring before the age of 50. By establishing a lower replacement rate, the new formula provides incentives to postpone retirement. Life expectancy calculations are adjusted annually following annual updates of the mortality table published by the official statistics agency. This works as an automatic benefits adjustment mechanism based on demographic dynamics.

The immediate impact of reform was to raise the average retirement age from 48.9 years in 1998 to 54.1 in 2001 for those retiring under the new rule. Because there are still workers with vested rights retiring under the old rules, the effective retirement age is around 53 years. Retirement benefits are also being paid to persons who accumulate 35 (men) and 30 (women) years of contribution without age limit requirements.

Forecasts of the deficit of the general pension plan are very sensitive to two variables, GDP growth and changes in benefits. Assuming that GDP grows at 3.5 percent and that benefits adjustments are linked to annual inflation, the RGPS deficit will double in the next decades reaching 3.5 percent of the GDP by 2050. However, the lackluster economic performance of the last few years means that if GDP growth averages 3 percent in the next several decades, the deficit could reach 5 percent of GDP by 2050. The most important assumption for carrying out these calculations is the one for adjusting benefits. Ideally, to protect the purchasing power of retirees, benefits would be adjusted annually based on the prior year's rate of inflation. But in Brazil, the minimum pension is linked to the minimum wage, this means that, in recent years, pensions have experienced impressive real increases.

Despite its positive redistributive impact, the fiscal burden is enormous. Assuming real increases in benefits corresponding to changes in GDP, the deficit could reach 7.5 percent of the GDP by 2050 (with GDP increasing 3.5 percent per year) (Figure 6.1).

Reform of the Civil Service Pension System

The reform of the pension system for civil servants was intended to adjust the pensions of the current workers and retirees in order to reduce the gap between pension rules for government workers and those for

Figure 6.1. Scenarios for the General Deficit, 2004–50

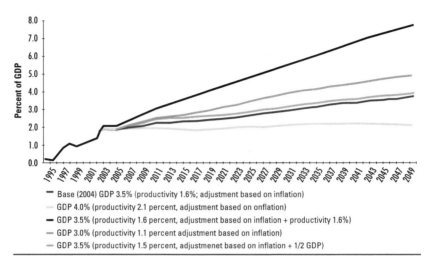

- ▬ Base (2004) GDP 3.5% (productivity 1.6%; adjustment based on inflation)
- ▬ GDP 4.0% (productivity 2.1 percent, adjustment based on onflation)
- ▬ GDP 3.5% (productivity 1.6 percent, adjustment based on inflation + productivity 1.6%)
- ▬ GDP 3.0% (productivity 1.1 percent adjustment based on inflation)
- ▬ GDP 3.5% (productivity 1.5 percent, adjustmenet based on inflation + 1/2 GDP)

Source: LDO (2005), MPAS (2002) and author's estimates.

future generations of private sector workers. The complete unification of the two pension regimes was proposed in 1995 when discussions were started, but this idea was met with strong resistance from the business sector. Several measures were proposed in 1998–2002 that would have removed the link between changes in salaries and benefits, increased the minimum retirement age, reduced the income replacement rate, rescinded special regimes and early retirement options, and established a benefits ceiling. However, most of these proposals were blocked in congress or judged unconstitutional by the supreme court.

In concrete terms, the minimum retirement age proposed (60 years old for men and 50 for women), was approved only for civil servants entering the public sector after the reform. A transition rule was established for current workers that set the minimum retirement age at 53 for men and 48 for women. In addition, a "toll" of 20 and 40 percent, respectively, was levied over the difference between age at retirement and the minimum age established in the new legislation. In addition, government workers are required to contribute to the RPPS for at least 10 years to be eligible to retire by the time they reach the minimum retirement age or reach the minimum years of contribution under this regime.

Special retirement rules that accorded privileged treatment to congressmen, magistrates, and university professors were eliminated; however, those for primary and secondary school teachers and the armed forces were maintained. The contribution rate for active duty and retired military personnel was increased from 1.6 to 7.5 percent at the end of 2001. An additional contribution of 1.5 percent was established to finance the lifetime pensions awarded to the unmarried daughters of members of the armed forces. As a result of the political negotiation, the retirement and pension benefits relative to the salary and the parity of the adjustments between civil servants in activity and retirees were kept for current workers. The introduction of the general regime ceiling depended on the approval of legislation pertaining to the pension plans for civil servants. The bill was not approved.

It is worth noting that important progress was made during this period in raising public awareness about the problems surrounding the pension plan for government workers. Approval of legislation on public sector pensions as well as legislation on fiscal responsibility contributed to this process by requiring that financial statements and actuarial projections be made public, thus improving the system's transparency. The establishment of the National Council of Public Pension Managers (Conselho Nacional dos Dirigentes de Regimes Próprios de Previdência Social, or CONAPREV) promoted a public debate about these issues that helped to create a consensus around local initiatives, which later led to changes in political positions on a national level. The cultural shift regarding pensions that took place during this period was fundamental to the success of the reforms because it helped overcome ideological barriers.

This is not to say that the proposals met with resounding success. Indeed, despite the approval of many important measures and increased public awareness of the issues, progress was much less than expected and a final solution to the problem of reforming civil servant's pensions was postponed.

Approval of the constitutional amendment in 1998 gave rise to the enactment of legislation to revise the existing regulatory framework, which had been established in 1977 and no longer properly reflected new market practices and techniques. The new regulatory framework improved flexibility, reduced operational costs, and expanded the system's coverage. In order to adapt to market dynamics and take advantage of economies of scale, the new regulations made it possible to aggregate management of several types of plans (multiplans) or sponsors (multiemployer). This rendered the complementary pension system more attractive to small and medium-size companies that previously faced relatively high operational costs. The new regulatory framework also created the figure of the *instituidor*. Trade unions and professional associations were allowed to establish defined contribution plans for their members. These measures would help improve pension coverage under these programs.

In addition to these measures, the reform also put into place a new disciplinary program and improvements to the fund's governance, such as ensuring professional management, transparency, and the involvement of plan participants in its management.

However, regulatory advances have not been accompanied by institutional improvements to implement the new rules. Indeed, a regulatory and supervisory body has not yet been established. This entity, which can be an autonomous body or integrated into other financial or insurance organizations, is necessary to protect participants' interests and promote stability.

Although there were significant improvements in the national social security system between 1995 and 2002, significant problems remain. The most important is the lack of approval for establishing a minimum retirement age that is a function of the length of time that a worker has made contributions to the system. The same is true of the pension plan for government workers, which experienced substantial improvements but still fell short in key areas (such as the contributions of retired civil servants, ending the parity with wages, and establishing a benefits ceiling). Perhaps the main legacy was the dissemination of information about the pension reform process, which is likely to make future reform efforts easier to implement. While much progress was made to update the legal framework of the complementary pension, the needed institutional changes have yet to take place.

The 2003 Reform of Civil Servant Pensions

The government of President Luiz Inácio "Lula" da Silva reignited discussions about pension reform by focusing on those issues where the previous administration had failed to make progress because of lack of political support (namely, the plan covering government workers). The 2003 reform of the civil servant pension plan combined an adjustment of the PAYG system to the current generation of workers and proposed a new regime for future civil servants. Changes to the existing plan include:

- Establishing a tax on the portion of the pension that exceeds R$1,440 for federal workers and R$1,200 for states and municipal workers[6]

---

[6] In September 2004, the supreme court decided that benefits above the general regime's ceiling should be taxed.

- Setting retirement age at 60 years for men and 55 for women, with an early retirement penalty equivalent to a 5 percent reduction in the value of the pension
- Reducing the survivors pension by 30 percent for the part of the benefit that exceeds R$2,400
- Establishing an exemption of 11 percent on the retirement contributions of workers who postpone their retirement beyond the normal age of retirement.

The proposal included other important measures affecting the current generation of workers (such as a reduction in the replacement rate and changes in the wage indexation benefit), but these measures were removed from the discussions and will apply only to future generations of workers. Workers retiring at age 60 (men) and 55 (women) who have 35 years of contributions (30 years for women) and 20 years of working as civil servants may retire with a benefit equivalent to their last full salary. The contribution of retirees was possibly the most controversial item in the reforms and is still being reviewed by the courts.

To reduce resistance to the establishment of a benefits ceiling and to raise revenues for the RGPS in the short run, the authorities proposed adjusting the RGPS ceiling by 30 percent in real terms, or R$2,400. While this will have a short-run positive impact on INSS accounts, it will also increase the long-run deficit and discourage the accumulation of resources in the complementary pension funds. Because the ceiling defines the boundary between the national pensions (RGPS and RPPS) and the complementary pensions, any expansion in one of them means a reduction of the other. This proposal opts for expanding the INSS actuarial deficit by raising long-run fiscal obligations and potentially reducing the resources accumulated in pension funds. In other words, the higher public deficit is replacing private savings. This step goes against the international trend that was discussed earlier, whose aim is to increase private participation and reduce the top pensions paid by the public sector.

For future generations of public employees the reform was deeper, and includes the following measures:

- Benefits will be calculated based on average salaries during a person's entire working life, pro-rating the period of contributions to the INSS.
- Benefits will no longer be indexed to wages; they will instead be adjusted to inflation.
- The introduction of the RGPS ceiling for civil servants is pending on the implementation of civil servants complementary pension funds.

Figure 6.2. Impact of the Civil Servants Pension Reform on the Federal Public Pension Deficit, 2004–32

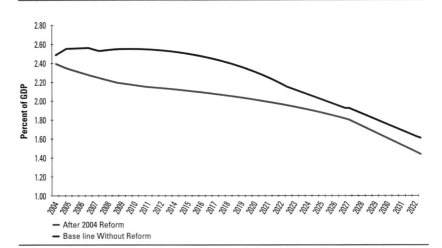

Source: Brasil (2004); LDO (2005); author's estimates.

Adjustment to the pay-as-you-go system may result in a reduction in actuarial liabilities. The MPS estimates that the economy will grow by R\$49 billion in the next 20 years.[7] Estimates made by the economics department of the University of São Paulo show a 10 percent reduction in the implicit debt of the entire pension system in the next six decades, from 302 percent of GDP to 272 percent (assuming a discount rate of 3 percent a year). However, while significant progress has been made, uncertainties about the design of the capitalized pension system remain.

Under the new system, civil servants will be subject to the same ceiling applied to private sector workers and would have the option of joining the complementary pension funds to increase their retirement income. The complementary pension funds will be public and operate on a defined contribution basis. Establishment of these pension funds is not mandatory and depends on a federal, state, or municipal government initiative. Once the fund is established, the employer's contribution should be, at most, equal to that of the civil servant and all existing rules should apply. The funds should be open to current civil servants in case they opt for the new model.

---

[7] O Estado de São Paulo, August 2003.

Although the reforms are expected to have a positive social redistributive impact, the fiscal burden is enormous. Assuming real increases in benefits in line with increases in GDP, the deficit could reach 7.5 percent of GDP by 2050 (assuming that GDP increases at 3.5 percent per year).

The deficit trend in the civil servant's pension is very sensitive to the benefit adjustment hypothesis. The government baseline scenario assumes that, in the long term, benefits and wages will be indexed to inflation. However, policy decisions are very vulnerable to political demands or judicial decisions in favor of increases in salaries and benefits in line with productivity improvements. If civil servants' earnings grow at the same pace as GDP, the federal workers' pension deficit could reach 4 percent of GDP by 2032.

Brazil's 2003 pension reform continued the reform agenda of previous periods, which had been partially blocked by congress. The strategy includes a deep adjustment in the pay-as-you-go system for active workers and retirees of the current generation. For future workers, the new system implies rules similar to those applied to private sector workers. Ideally, rules for the public and private sectors should be unified, reducing costs and improving equity. However, this would result in huge fiscal costs for states and municipalities. The proposal approved by congress has positive and negative aspects. Among the positive ones are the adjustments

Figure 6.3. Scenarios for the Public Sector Pension Deficit, 2004–50

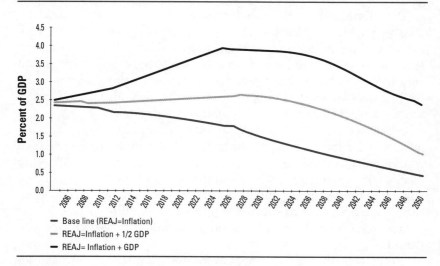

Source: Brasil (2004); LDO (2005); author's estimates.

in the parameters of the PAYG system: retired civil servant contributions, reductions in pensions, immediate application of the pension value to current workers, and of the parity between the salary adjustments of active workers and retirees. Among the more negative aspects is the proposed organization of the new funded complementary pension system. Its potential growth was reduced because of the increase of the RGPS pension ceiling that will also be applied to the regime for government workers.

Conclusions

Brazil's pension reforms did not follow the region-wide trend toward privatization. Instead of a radical change in the social security system, the government adjusted the existing PAYG system in significant ways. The reform of a PAYG system is a political process whose costs are concentrated on some groups and whose benefits are more diffuse. The costs of the reform affected groups that enjoyed special privileges under the existing system (public sector workers, teachers, high-income earners with the option of early retirement, and workers in state-owned enterprises) and participated in government-subsidized pension funds. By contrast, the main benefit of the reform—guaranteeing the long-term sustainability of the system—was diffused both within and between generations.

The reform of the PAYG system required a change in the constitution, which necessitated the approval of three-fifths of congress. To that end, in March 1995 the government sent a proposed amendment to congress. Lawmakers deliberated for over three years until passing a watered-down version of it in November 1998. The government's proposal was wide-ranging, seeking to alter the general social security regime, the special scheme for public workers, and complementary regimes.

The debate over the constitutional amendment exacted a very high political cost for the Cardoso administration. The reform process imposed concentrated, immediate costs on specific sectors, which mobilized to block it. The incentives for these minorities to act were tangible, and the costs of not participating in the political process were high. By contrast, there were few incentives for other groups to mobilize in favor of the reform, given that the benefits of doing so would be generic and dispersed.

The complexity and comprehensiveness of the proposal provoked adverse reactions from a vast range of political actors. The result was that no particular group agreed completely with the proposal. The positive aspects that could be used as an incentive for specific groups to mobilize in favor of the proposal were cancelled by other stipulations that the same group could consider as negative. Each group attacked specific points, thus creating a generalized sense of obstruction. There were no pro-reform movements; all sectors, for different reasons, worked against it.

In 1997, at the same time that the social security legislation was making its way through congress, a group of experts began to study the creation of a mixed system. The resulting proposal sought to reduce the income ceiling coverage under the public PAYG system to three times the minimum wage, institute mandatory savings for people with incomes equivalent to between three and ten times the minimum wage, and provide for voluntary savings above the top income bracket.

These proposals faced opposition within the government because of the high transition costs that privatization would entail. The issue of financing these transition costs became especially relevant after the financial crises in southeast Asia and Russia. At the end of 1998, Brazil negotiated a loan with the IMF, the World Bank, and the IDB to buttress its monetary and foreign exchange policies. The social security reform that had been debated in congress since 1995 became one of the fundamental elements in the adjustment program adopted by the government, because it allowed for short- and medium-term fiscal gains. By contrast, the bid to privatize the system lost momentum because the transition costs became impossible to finance.

Thus, the international economic situation restricted any initiative to change the social security system in ways that could decrease the fiscal surplus or increase public debt. These concerns were shared by the international organizations that were monitoring Brazil's fiscal adjustment program. The preference was for adjustment measures with positive short- and medium-term effects on the social security system, to the detriment of measures that entailed transition costs such as a capitalization system.

Once the constitutional amendment was passed, it was necessary to enact complementary laws and regulations. As an alternative to privatization, a proposal was made to create individual notional accounts. This idea had been disseminated in courses and seminars organized by the World Bank, with the participation of Brazilian technical staff. However, the adoption of such a system was hindered by the problems of properly defining the rates of capitalization for the funds accumulated in individual accounts, and the criteria to be used to recognize prior contributions to these accounts under the old system. These problems were resolved through an innovative formula that made the return on contributions dependent on the length of contribution and the age at retirement, thus giving people an incentive to delay retirement.

The comparison between the reform periods of 1995–2002 and 2003 yields some important conclusions concerning the political strategies used.

First, while efforts in the initial period were directed at the entire pension system, the 2003 reform focused on the pension regime for government workers. In attempting to enact a comprehensive reform, many fronts for dispute were opened at the same time, leading to strong efforts at blocking the process.

The 1995–98 constitutional reform process was slow because the proposal was too comprehensive and led to the creation of a coalition of opposition groups. A more successful policy was adopted in 1999–2001, during the process of enacting regulations to implement the constitutional reform measures, which separated the various measures as well as the laws to change the complementary pensions, the national regime, and the regime for government workers.

Similarly, during the constitutional reform of 2003, affected groups were carefully identified. The government built a coalition of political groups directly interested in the process (state governors and private sector groups) that might benefit from increased fiscal resources.

Second, while President Cardoso's pension reform efforts took place at the same time that other important matters were occurring (reelection, administrative reform, privatization, tax reform, and efforts to achieve fiscal responsibility), President da Silva's reform had the almost exclusive attention of congress. This helped avoid political negotiations on other issues and made it easier to build coalitions, increasing the effectiveness of the political process.

Third, the communication and marketing strategies of the 2003 reform were managed better than in the previous reform period. The contributing factors were the improved social awareness of the problems that resulted from years of discussions and the focus on the civil servants' pension scheme. During the constitutional reform of 1995–98, lack of information among leaders was high and there was a lot of confusion concerning the measures proposed for each regime. For example, RGPS retirees often expressed their opposition to contributions by retired workers, which was being proposed only for civil servants.

Brazil's recent experience shows the advantages of a gradual, incremental, and specialized process of pension reform, and a relatively high level of social awareness of the topic. Reforming pensions is as inevitable as the aging process itself. Most measures are tough and unpopular and should be well explained and gradually implemented. The Brazilian experience shows that political and ideological obstacles that may seem impossible to overcome can be surmounted.

References

Anexo de Metas Fiscais da Lei de Diretrizes Orçamentárias (LDO). 2005. Brazil.

Barr, Nicholas. 2002. The Pension Puzzle: Prerequisites and Policy Choices in Pension Design. *IMF Economic Issues* No. 29. International Monetary Fund, Washington, D.C.

Bravo, Jorge and Andras Uthoff. 1999. Transitional Fiscal Costs and Demographic Factors in Shifting from Unfunded to Funded Pension in Latin America. *Serie Financiamiento del Desarrollo* No. 88 (October): 40pp. Economic Commission for Latin America and the Caribbean, Santiago, Chile.

Cohn, Amélia. 1980. *Previdência Social e Processo Político no Brasil.* São Paulo: Editorial Moderna.

Diamond, Peter. 1994. Privatization of Social Security: Lessons from Chile. *Revista de Análisis Económico* 9 (1): 21–33.

Gill, Indermit, Truman Packard, and Juan Yermo. 2005. *Keeping the Promise of Social Security in Latin America.* Stanford, CA: Stanford University Press.

Lieberman, Trudy. 1997. Social Insecurity: The Campaign to Take the System Private. *The Nation* (January 27).

Malloy, James M. A. 1976. Política de Previdência Social no Brasil: Participação e Paternalismo. *Revista Dados* (13), Rio de Janeiro, Brazil.

Mebane, Walter R. Jr. 1994. Fiscal Constraints and Electoral Manipulation in American Social Welfare. *The American Political Science Review* 8 (1):pp. 77–94.

Melo, Marcus André B. C. 1997. As Reformas Constitucionais e a Previdência Social (1993–1996). In *Reforma do Estado e Democracia no Brasil*, ed. Sérgio de Eli e Azevedo Diniz. Brasilia: Universidad de Brasilia/Escola Nacional de Administração Pública.

Mesa-Lago, Carmelo. 2002. La reforma de pensiones en América Latina. Modelos y características, mitos y desempeños, y lecciones. In *¿Públicos o privados? Los sistemas de pensiones en América Latina después de dos décadas de reformas*, eds. Katja Hujo, Carmelo Mesa-Lago and Manfred Nitsch. Caracas: Nueva Sociedad.

Ministério de Previdência Social (MPS). 2002. *Livro Branco da Previdência Social*. Brasilia, D.F.: Ministério de Previdência Social, Gabinete do Ministro.

Oliveira, Francisco, Kaizô Iwakami Beltrão, and Mônica Guerra Ferreira. 1997. Reforma da Previdência. Texto para Discussão No. 508. Instituto de Pesquisa Econômica (IPEA), Brasilia.

Oliveira, Francisco, Kaizo Beltrão, and Maria Tereza Pasinato. 1999. Reforma Estrutural da Previdência: Uma Proposta para Assegurar Proteção Social e Equidade. Texto para Discussão No. 690. Instituto de Pesquisa Econômica (IPEA), Brasilia.

Piñera, José. 1996. Empowering Workers: The Privatization of Social Security in Chile. CATO *Letters*, CATO Institute, Washington, D.C.

Pinheiro, Vinicius. 1998. *Instituições Previdenciárias e Modelos de Desenvolvimento no Brasil e Argentina*. Tese de Mestrado defendida no Instituto de Relações Internacionais e Ciência Política da Universidade de Brasília, Brasília.

Stiglitz, Joseph and Peter Orszag. 2001. Rethinking Pension Reform: Ten Myths About Social Security Systems. In *New Ideas About Old Age Security: Toward Sustainable Pension Systems in the 21st Century*, ed. Robert Holzmann and Joseph Stiglitz. Washington, D.C.: The World Bank.

Weyland, Kurt. 1996. How Much Political Power do Economic Forces Have? Conflicts Over Social Insurance Reform in Brazil. *Journal of Public Policy* No.16 (I).

————. 2004. *Learning from Foreign Models in Latin America Policy Reform*. Washington, D. C.: Woodrow Wilson Center Press.

SECTION FOUR

Reinforcing Reforms in the Region

Enhancing the Success of the Chilean Pension System: The Addition of Multiple Funds and Annuities

Guillermo Larraín Ríos *

The Success of Chile's Model

In many respects, the Chilean pension reform introduced in 1981 has been a success. Total accumulated assets reached $60.6 billion, about 64 percent of GDP, as of the first quarter of 2005 (Figure 7.1). Measured by this standard, pension funds in Chile rank fourth in the world, after the Netherlands, the United Kingdom, and the United States. Chilean pension funds are by far the biggest investors in domestic capital markets and their investment portfolios are increasingly diversified.

Pension funds have put pressure on the domestic financial market and the authorities to improve and update financial regulation, adopt better corporate governance standards, and increase transparency. They have stimulated specialization in investment decisionmaking and promoted the emergence of new financial instruments while increasing the size, depth, and maturities of the financial market. Positive secondary

---

* Guillermo Larraín Ríos is the Regulator of Chile's Pension Funds (Superintendente de Administradoras de Fondos de Pensiones, SAFP) and President of the International Association of Pension Fund Supervisors (Asociación Internacional de Organismos de Supervisión de Fondos de Pensiones, AIOS).

Figure 7.1. The Importance of Pension Funds in Chile
(US$billions, and funds as a percent of GDP)

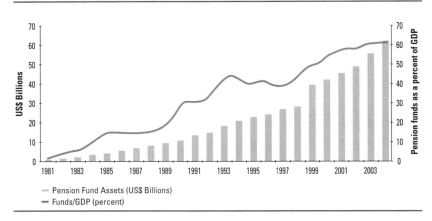

Source: SAFP (1981–2004).

effects have spilled over to other markets such as banking, insurance, and mortgages.

The outcome has been a significant stimulus to capital market development and thus has had a statistically significant and positive effect on total factor productivity and growth. One-ninth of the average rate of per capita growth in Chile between 1981 and 2002 is related to pension reform, directly or indirectly, Corbo and Schmidt-Hebbel (2003) estimate.

The high rate of GDP growth, partially explained by the pension reform itself, has delivered a high rate of return on capital—and in particular on pension assets. The average yearly rate of return between 1981 and 2004 has been 10.2 percent (after controlling for inflation), with only two years of mildly negative rates of return.

Aspects of the Reform that Merit Special Attention

Two issues associated with the Chilean model of pension reform deserve special consideration: the demographic transition and the fiscal situation. The old Chilean pay-as-you-go system was in crisis by the 1960s. There was a growing consensus that reform was needed. The administration of Frei Montalva sent a reform proposal to congress, but it was not approved (see Larraín Ríos 2005). The basic problems that led to calls for reform were the irrationality with which pensions were granted and the chaos generated by the 32 different pension regimes, some of which ignored actuarial criteria and generated regressive benefits.

The Chilean model was launched just before the current demographic transition began to emerge. There is no evidence that special considerations were given to the demographic change while designing the model. But from an actuarial point of view, defined contribution systems are better prepared to adapt to the new demographic paradigm than defined benefit systems. The reason is simple. In defined benefits systems, benefits reflect the dynamic of politics—not of demographics. Obviously, these two dynamics need not coincide.

Transition Costs

An important aspect of the reform concerns the transition costs. Chile chose a drastic type of reform; it forced all new entrants into the labor market to join the new system and provided strong incentives to older workers to move to it as well. These *nominal* incentives affected both workers and employers. Under the old system, contributions were mixed and made by both workers and employers. They were also very high. The contribution to the pension component alone reached more than a quarter (26 percent) of wages and amounted to half (50 percent) of wages by 1974, including contributions for health services and job-related accidents (SAFP 2002).

There were two main incentives to move to the new system. Contributions were cut by half, leading to a substantial increase in real wages for workers. The employer contribution was discontinued. So there was a big incentive to move to the new system.[1] Indeed, there is some evidence that the reduced costs of payroll taxation to firms appear to have been fully passed on to workers in the form of higher wages.

But that left the old system without contributors and with a large number of pensioners. Hence the change induced a fiscal deficit, which has had two characteristics. First, it has been persistent. The associated deficit started in 1981, at the time of reform, and has increased steadily since. It is forecast to last until around 2030, even though its composition is changing. Initially, the main component was the operational deficit of the old system. Over time, the operational deficit started to shrink, while

---

[1] Today, total participation is about 7 million workers, 1 million more than the current labor force.

Table 7.1	Implicit Public Debt in Select Countries with Defined Benefit Systems
Country	**Implicit public debt at a discount rate of 4%**
Brazil	330
Slovenia	298
Poland	261
Ukraine	257
Romania	256
Hungary	203
Argentina	85
Mexico	65
Chile	60
Colombia	56

Source: Holzmann, Palacios, and Zviniene (2004).

the deficit associated with recognition bonds has grown, and has now reached 1.3 percent of GDP.[2]

Second, the fiscal deficit has been significant. It peaked at around 4.5 percent of GDP in 1999 (excluding the armed forces) and has gradually been decreasing (Arenas de Mesa 2004; Bennett and Schmidt-Hebbel 1999).

To contain this huge deficit, expenditures were cut in other areas. These actions cannot be understood without considering the special political situation of Chile at the time. A strong dictatorship was in power and was able to restructure public outlays, cutting social expenditures to finance the pension deficit in the middle of the worst macroeconomic crisis since 1930.

The transition from a defined benefit to a defined contribution system is expensive for any State—at least on a cash basis. Chile has had fiscal deficits associated with the pension reform on the order of 4 to 6 percent of GDP for two decades. To balance the budget, a huge fiscal effort must be made to cut or reallocate fiscal expenses. This is not easy for a democracy to absorb, especially in the context of so many urgent needs, including education, health, infrastructure, and poverty alleviation. On an accrual basis, the picture is not that clear, as implicit public debts associated with defined benefit systems are also quite huge, as shown in Table 7.1.

---

[2] Recognition bonds are issued in acknowledgement of the previous contributions made by workers under the old PAYG system.

Why does the market not accept the trade-off? There are several reasons, related to the lack of financial integration of Latin American countries to world markets, the weaknesses of the institutions in some countries, and market failures in world capital markets. These factors and the high transitional costs explain why some Latin American countries now face difficulties in proceeding with their reforms and, to some extent, why some countries, are talking about reversing them.

But as in any process in which a country takes the lead, the successes mentioned above coexist with failures in other areas. In the case of pension reform, the Chilean reform introduced a totally new concept with respect to the paradigms of the pay-as-you-go or defined benefit systems.

Difficulties with the Reforms

A successful reform must be in accord with the underlying economy. Over time, the dynamism of the economy and the pension system itself gradually unveil problems that were probably marginal at the beginning but increase in importance as time passes. The main problems that have appeared in the Chilean system arise from the dynamics of factors that are both external (exogenous) and internal (endogenous) to the pension system.

Four exogenous factors are particularly important. The first pertains to changes in the labor market. When the pension system was first launched 25 years ago, lifetime employment was much more prevalent. That era has ended in Chile. Modern labor markets require more flexibility, with greater job rotation. As a result, episodes of unemployment are more frequent. This does not affect people equally, as employability differs according to such factors as education, family linkages, and economic sector. In practice, poorer workers are generally more exposed to these uncertainties—although not all of them. Among low-income workers in Chile, there is a wide distribution of average lifetime profiles of density of contributions,[3] Berstein, Larraín Ríos, and Pino (2005) found, using administrative data of current workers. In addition, the labor market appears to have a significant degree of turnover. Since August 2002, more than 3 million new labor contracts have been signed, but only half a million jobs have been created on net; the rest were short-term jobs. Workers work for short periods of time, only to be faced with another

---

[3] The concept of density is defined as the ratio of actual contributions relative to potential contributions in a given period of time.

episode of unemployment of uncertain length. Confronted with these risks, many workers are naturally reluctant to contribute to pensions.

The second important development in the labor market is the proliferation of formal self-employed workers. Today, one out of three workers is an independent worker. Those workers require savings to be liquid in case they need them. However, pension assets are extremely illiquid. Thus this category of workers is naturally reluctant to contribute to pensions, as well. [4]

In both cases, such reluctance would be even greater in a PAYG scheme. The reason is simple. The worker's contribution would be used to finance someone else's benefit. The worker's net income would be cut, but no new right would be granted. In the defined contribution system, the contribution goes directly to the worker's own personal account. Even if that money is totally illiquid in the short run, at least it belongs to that individual. Accordingly, incentives to contribute are greater in the Chilean system.

Much of the coverage problem of the Chilean pension system lies in the structural changes of the labor market. Given these changes, new and imaginative mechanisms are needed to increase the contribution density. Other directions for public policy are also called for, notably unemployment insurance.

A third exogenous factor relates to the characteristics of women in the labor market. Generally, women start working later, earn less, retire earlier, and live longer. Given these considerations, it is not surprising that pensions are particularly low for women.

This situation is gradually changing, at least for some portions of the population. In 1981, female participation rates were at around 20 percent of the respective labor force. By 2004, it had grown to 35 percent. Nevertheless, Chile has one of the lowest female participation rates in Latin America.

The characteristics of the female labor markets are complex around the world and the solutions are far from obvious. There is a 20 percent wage gap between males and females in Chile, correcting for other determinants of wages, according to Berstein and Tokman (2004). Problems and solutions probably require a broader approach to the issue, including such matters as child care for working women, the role of men at home, and greater flexibility in labor contracts and working arrangements.

---

[4] To see how crucial this point is, consider that in the highest quintile of the population there are 1.9 persons per wage earner. In the poorest quintile, there are 4.7 persons per wage earner

The fourth exogenous factor is the increase in life expectancy. In Chile, as elsewhere in the world, people are living longer, thanks in part to progress in medical science. This means that at the end of their lives, a given amount of accumulated savings must finance more years. The natural consequence is that pensions are smaller.

In striking contrast with these developments, in the last decade many Chilean pension plan participants have retired well before their legal retirement age. Indeed, workers are allowed to retire early if they fulfill two prerequisites. One is that the pensioner must be able to buy the equivalent of an annuity greater than 110 percent of the minimum pension. The other is that the replacement ratio must be 50 percent above the last salary. In practice, these prerequisites were too lenient. The outcome was that many people retired earlier than they should have: 64 percent of men and 18 percent of women retired early. The average age of early retirement is 56 for men, nine years earlier than the legal retirement age of 65, and 54 for women, six years earlier than the legal retirement age of 60.

Not only are people living longer, but at any given age they are feeling better. Many retirees in Chile continue working. They do so both because they are in better health and because their pensions are smaller as a result of early retirement.

In addition to these exogenous factors, endogenous factors are also at work. These are linked to design problems in the pension system. One such problem is the interface between the accumulation and disbursement phase of the system. Originally "the system" was conceived mainly to accumulate savings. Indeed the Chilean model is known worldwide thanks to the success of the AFPs, which manage savings in the accumulation phase. But little attention was given to the workings of the disbursement phase and, in particular, to the transaction costs between both of them. Moreover, when the problems linked to the disbursement phase became apparent in Chile and the government proposed some solutions, significant political opposition arose. It took nearly a decade to pass legislation to improve this situation.

Two problems of design have had an impact on competition in the Chilean system. The first is inelasticity of demand, which arises mainly because the system is mandatory and participants contribute because they are required to do so. Hence, the pension market is artificial; there is no spontaneous demand for it and competition is artificially restricted.

The second is that economies of scale, while typical in financial sectors, are not realized by the pension funds because to a large degree, they are exclusive in a mandated system in which participants are required to contribute. Eliminating switching costs might promote greater competition by enabling participants to switch from one fund to another, creating an environment in which pension funds would need to compete to keep clients and market share.

In recent years, Chile has implemented two important complementary reforms to the original model: multiple funds (*multifondos*), and the electronic market for annuities (known as SCOMP). These two reforms are examined in the next part of the chapter.

Multifondos:
Better Risk Profiles, More Valuable Information

When the Chilean system began, each AFP could offer only one portfolio to its participants. That portfolio was shaped by two forces. The first was the way regulation evolved. While pension fund regulations have always been strict, they have contained sufficient leeway to enable the funds to adapt to financial innovation and market conditions. Currently, regulations are totally based on fulfilling clearly defined quantitative limits on investments. Those limits are set for issuers, groups of issuers, instruments, groups of instruments (asset classes), related parties, and foreign assets. In addition, limits on individual types of investments are corrected according to liquidity factors and other coefficients. Figure 7.2 illustrates the evolution of some relevant limits.

Over and above this complex system of limits, the minimal return relative to average market performance has been regulated. Each AFP is required to guarantee participants that their return will be at least 200 basis points below the average market performance. This represents a strong incentive not to deviate significantly from the average market portfolio, creating herd behavior.

It was argued that this set of limits would minimize the likelihood of individual errors of judgment by AFPs and thus amount to a built-in safety element for the system. However, the effect was that portfolios did not vary significantly, nor did their returns. Thus not only were AFPs offering only one portfolio, but that portfolio was very similar to the one offered by alternative AFPs. The comparability of the portfolios made it immaterial for the participant to have accurate market information on their accounts and pension funds performance. Given the nature of the pension market and its inelastic demand (that is, its mandatory nature), the management of pension savings started to look more and more like a commodity, inducing further indifference. People periodically received

Figure 7.2. Evolution of Investment Limits in Chile

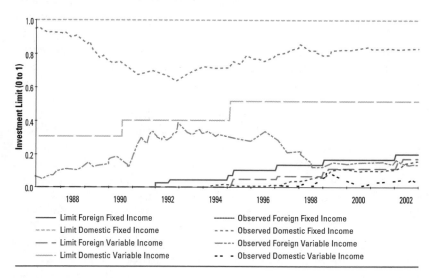

Source: AFP (1998–2002).

Figure 7.3. Multiple Funds: Portfolio Composition

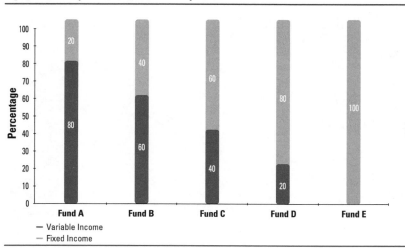

Source: SAFP (2002).

their statements, but the statements were immaterial. People did not read them. The outcome was disinformation and further inelasticity. Some 93 percent of the people declared that they did not know the price of their pension service and 56 percent declared that they did not know the balance in their personal accounts. The system was also characterized by inertia. More than half the men (54 percent) and nearly two-thirds of women (64 percent) declared that they have never changed from one AFP to another.

The multiple reforms undertaken in 2002 allowed AFPs to offer five portfolios differentiated by the share of variable income instruments in each. Fund A has 80 percent of its investment in variable income instruments; Fund B has 60 percent; Fund C has 40 percent; and Fund D has 20 percent. The balance of each fund is in fixed income instruments. Fund E is restricted to a purely fixed income instrument. The underlying idea was to allow people to take a life cycle approach to risk in a very simple structure.

Figure 7.4 suggests that, in general, people understood this. Younger people chose the riskiest fund while older people opted for more conservative portfolios. Contrary to the indifference and inertia that characterized the prior single fund system, about 50 percent of pension fund participants chose a new fund within six months.

Figure 7.4. Age Distribution by Class of Fund in Chile

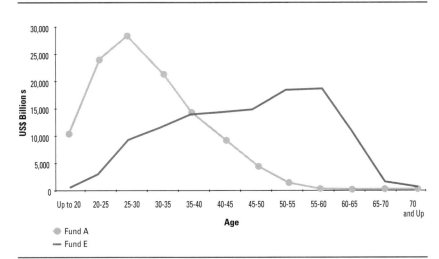

Source: SAFP (2002).

Figure 7.5. A System Improving? Why Participants Say They Changed Their AFP

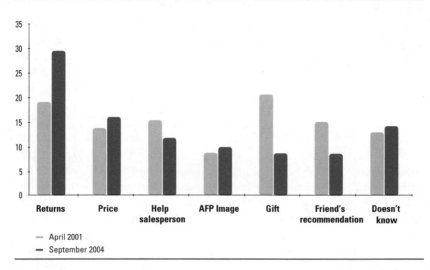

Source: SAFP (2002).

The multiple fund reform has created a greater awareness among participants of the importance of current asset management and performance, even though their retirement age is distant. It now pays to be informed, as at any time people may change funds. With more informed participants, the system as a whole improves. Figure 7.5 shows the results of two surveys, one before and one after the multifondos reform. Contributors report giving greater consideration to return and price as reasons to justify the decisions they make. The huge drop of influence of gifts given by salespersons is particularly noteworthy.

While the addition of multiple funds gave participants options, it did not change the herd behavior of the funds in that their returns on investment performance remained undifferentiated. Rather, participants passed from one big herd to five different kinds of herds, all differentiated in their preference for return and risk.

The Annuities Law and the SCOMP

When individuals are able to retire (because they have reached retirement age or have made sufficient contributions to qualify for early retirement)

Table 7. 2	Quantity and Types of Pensions Paid in 2003						
	Programmed withdrawal		Annuity		Total		
	Number	Percent	Number	Percent	Number	Percent	
Pension = Minimum pension at age 65	97,778	26	221,190	85	263,983	50	
Pension < Minimum pension at age 65	274,178	74	38,531	15	245,156	50	
Total	371,956	100	259,721	100	509,139	100	

Source: Berstein, Larraín Ríos, and Pino (2005).

the Chilean system used to provide two options for withdrawing assets: programmed withdrawals or annuities. Table 7.2 presents the breakdown between the two methods, according to the pension level. Some 85 percent of pensioners whose pension level exceeds the minimum pension chose not to face the risk of longevity (living longer than their pension benefits) and bought an annuity. Those who are eligible for the State guarantee must take programmed withdrawals. Those who can choose generally prefer annuities (for more on annuities, see Chapter 10).

But the functioning of the annuities market was far from satisfactory from the perspective of social security. As mentioned, the previous law required that participants wishing to retire before the legal age of retirement must comply with the criteria that their replacement ratio (contributions to pension) be 50 percent above the last salary, and the pensioner must be able to buy the equivalent of an annuity greater than 110 percent of the minimum pension. Eventually, the criteria proved to be too lenient and early retirement began at increasingly earlier ages. On average, each year of early retirement reduces the pension by 7 percent. Thus people have been retiring with significantly smaller pensions. Early retirement is partially a matter of legal requirements and partially the outcome of the workings of the annuities market.

As noted, the pension industry is an artificial one. Figure 7.6 shows the commissions paid by insurance companies to insurance brokers or to their sales force. In principle, the insurance company pays these commissions. In practice, they are taken out of the retiree's capital.

Commissions reached a peak of 5.9 percent of the accumulated capital by 1999, and then decreased. It is remarkable that in 1999 retirees were willing to pay such a large amount of money for this service. Basically people are short-sighted and do not give adequate weight to the reduction in savings that such a large commission implies, which argues well for making social security mandatory. In 1994 legislation was introduced

Figure 7.6. Commissions Paid for Annuities
(percentage of the person's pension fund, annual average)

Source: SCOMP.

in congress to lower this commission. It was not approved until 2000, when a new government took office. The mere announcement that discussions would resume induced commissions to fall.

Another aspect of the commissions market is the role of brokers and the sales force. Many pension participants did not know the balance in their personal accounts, so they could hardly have known or calculated whether they complied with the early retirement requirements. The AFPs obtained this information and transmitted it to the sales force of insurance companies. Potential early retirees were contacted not by a pension advisor but by a salesperson interested in selling an annuity, who convinced them to retire early. Arguments were not linked to maintaining income in old age but how to solve current problems through instant cash rebates (paid by the pensioner themselves, as explained) and/or with a second salary, if they returned to the workforce.

The Annuities Law passed in 2004, after 10 years of congressional debate. It created the Sistema Electrónico de Consultas y Ofertas de Montos de Pensión (SCOMP), an electronic consultation system that generated pension offers (annuities) from insurance companies and the AFPs market for programmed withdrawals, which has drastically improved information. Every potential pensioner is enrolled in this market. The AFP sends the participants' information anonymously to life insurance companies that offer different kinds of annuities and AFPs that offer programmed withdrawals. At a given date, the pensioner receives offers from the entire market, along with information that would enable him to make the best possible decision. Pension offers are adjusted for inflation because they are expressed in Unidad de Fomento (UF), a measurement unit indexed to consumer prices. Offers are ranked in descending order. There are five options once the potential retiree receives this information:

- choose one of the offers in the sheet
- postpone any decision without time limit
- bargain with a salesperson for a better offer
- ask the system for another round of offers
- call for an auction (in this case, the person must choose the best offer).

The system started on August 19, 2004. To date, 86 percent of the pensioners have paid commissions of 2.1 percent, on average. The other 14 percent have paid no commissions at all The weighted average of commissions fell from 5.9 percent before the law was proposed, to 2.7 percent during the interim period before the law was approved, to a mere

Figure 7.7. Real Value of Annuities Sold and Interest Rates
(percent)

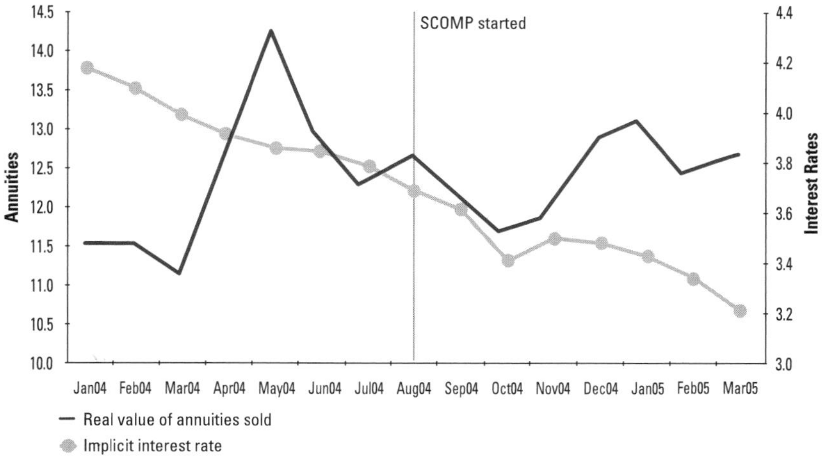

Source: SAFP (2004–05); SVS (2004–05); SCOMP.

1.8 percent thereafter. The entire decrease in commissions is passed on to the retiree in the form of higher pensions.

Evidence to date indicates that this is happening. Figure 7.7 shows the real value of new annuities sold compared to the implicit interest rate at which annuities are calculated. One would expect that both variables should behave alike. An exception was the period from April to June 2004, when life insurance companies carried out an aggressive policy to induce early retirement before the new law took effect. While the implicit rate has declined consistently, the average pension has increased. It is too early to draw a conclusion, but the indication is that this is where the market is heading.

The Ongoing Reform Agenda

The reform agenda that has unfolded from 2004 to 2005 has three components, all related to the endogenous problems of the Chilean pension system.

Recommendation 1: Improve Competition

The Chilean system lacks competition. Thus participants in the pension system pay high commissions to the AFPs. Fees are paid as a percentage of the worker's salary, unlike in other asset management industries, where fees are paid as a percentage of assets under management. One reason for this peculiar manner of collecting fees is that workers can more closely see the price they are paying for the service. However, many participants lack financial sophistication, as several surveys have shown. People have difficulty reading the regular financial statement they are given. However, when workers receive their salary receipt every month, the commission paid to the AFP is clearly shown. This creates greater transparency for the participant and must be encouraged in a mandatory system.

However, there is a drawback to this arrangement. Price comparability with other industries is diminished. To compare prices, the monthly fees on income must be transformed to lifetime fees as a share of assets under management. A proxy for that measure is to take all fees charged by AFPs in a particular year as a share of assets under management that particular year.

In 2004, the average fee charged by AFPs was 0.64 percent of assets. This can be compared to the fees paid to foreign mutual funds, the main vehicle to invest abroad. Fees charged by Chilean AFPs are estimated at

Figure 7.8. Return on Equity in Chile, 1991–2020 (percent)

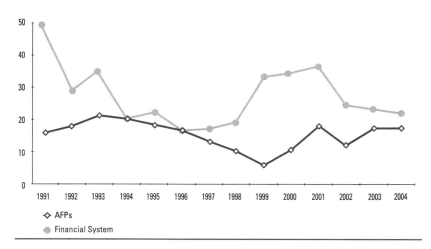

◇ AFPs
● Financial System

Source: SAFP and SBIF.

0.78 percent of assets. By contrast, Chilean mutual funds charge 2.3 percent of assets as management fees and U.S. mutual funds charge 1.38
percent. Thus the fees charged by AFPs appear to be relatively inexpensive. However, they are higher than fees charged by certain U.S. pension
funds, even though the U.S. government absorbs some of their costs. The
critical point is that if prices were set at their appropriate level, then pension industry profits should be comparable to profits in similar financial
industries, adjusted for risk. Figure 7.8 shows the return on equity in the
pension fund industry in Chile compared to the entire financial sector,
excluding pension funds. Profits for the AFPs seem abnormally high. This
suggests that prices in this particular industry are too high.

The point of this exercise is to find a mechanism to reduce prices. The
discussion below is totally market-based because the underlying problem is the poor definition of some industrial organization features of this
market.

Supply-side View

Under the current norms, AFPs are required to fulfill several functions,
some of which could be dealt with more efficiently if they were out-
sourced. Economies of scale in functions such as record keeping and
revenue collection could thus be achieved. These economies of scale are

the impetus toward concentration in this industry. Good policy measures should *include incentives to outsource.*

Demand-side View

From the demand perspective, the main problems arise from the fact that consumers in these markets have very limited information and little knowledge about pensions and financial matters. The main implication of this is that people are not sensitive to price incentives. Moreover, as discount rates appear to be high, people seem to be sensitive to short-run incentives such as gifts or other promotional devices that the AFPs provide, rather than the inherent characteristics of the pension provider, such as return, risk, and service.

All this implies that there are important non-legal barriers to entry in this industry. As new entrants, pension funds cannot attract new clients by offering them low prices. They must "visit" clients, client by client, offering something else: a gift. This is a very costly and slow strategy. Moreover, given that efficient scales of operation are large, new entrants need to "visit" a lot of potential clients.

Thus, beyond improving financial literacy and making information clearer and more transparent, it is crucial to *expand the aggregate demand or density of contributions.* One way to do that is by creating a bidding process in which all pension funds, new and old, make offers to manage pension savings (subject to rules designed to avoid dumping). Pension funds would therefore compete in pricing.

Recommendation 2. Improve Coverage

Extending the coverage of the pension system to reach a wider proportion of workers is a major concern for future reforms. Recent research by Berstein, Larraín Ríos, and Pino (2005) forecasts pension levels in Chile over the next three decades using a sample of 24,000 participants for which monthly administrative data were available from 1981 to 2003. The study found that:

- Between 40 to 50 percent of participants will not accumulate enough savings for a minimum pension. At the same time, they will not have made the required number of contributions for the minimum pension guarantee. As pension savings belong to them in any event, they will have access to their savings plus the returns. On average, people would be able to finance three to four years at the minimum pension level. Most of these people would not have the right to any pension had they remained in the old system

- About 10 percent of participants might require a minimum pension guarantee and have the right to get it. These participants would be financing almost half their retirement life with their own funds, in the case of men, and a third, in the case of women. From the perspective of public finances, this does not seem to be a heavy burden.
- The remaining participants will get a pension that is above the minimum pension level and will not require the minimum pension guarantee.

These results improve significantly if a larger rate of return on investments is assumed, if wages grow faster, or if the unemployment rate is lower. In terms of the fiscal budget, the rate at which the government increases the minimum pension level turns out to be crucial. If it grows by less than wages, State liabilities might decrease significantly over time. The opposite might happen if increases are greater than the growth rate of wages.

This outcome is less encouraging than expected. One crucial aspect is unemployment rates. Because average unemployment rates have fallen and this analysis used historical data, it may be overstating bad scenarios. But these results are an important reminder that the coverage issue must be addressed soon.

Under the old pension system, coverage was around 60 percent of the labor force. The new system has converged gradually to those levels. Because of the major financial crisis that occurred in 1982, in which unemployment peaked at almost 20 percent and remained in double digits until 1988, coverage suffered significantly, initially. As unemployment rates have improved, coverage has been closer to past trends except for the 1999–2001 period. Moreover, as Figure 7.9 shows, the deficit in terms of coverage varies greatly by type of worker. Some 80 percent of salaried workers are covered by the system. The other 20 percent is probably linked to informal activities, as informality is estimated at that same rate. This means that coverage of formal dependent workers is close to 100 percent.

Accordingly, two problems remain. One, as mentioned, is informality. The solution to that lies more with labor and tax policies than pension policies. The second is self-employed workers. As Figure 7.9 shows, the current rate of coverage for those workers is close to 4.5 percent. Those workers are not required to contribute in Chile. One alternative is to adopt a symmetric approach compared to dependent workers. However,

Figure 7.9. Coverage of the Pension System, by Type of Worker
(percent of self-employed or salaried workers)

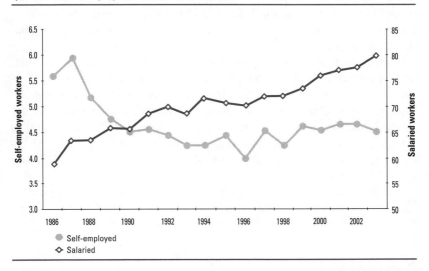

Source: SAFP.

as contributions to social security, including health, are expensive (amounting to some 20 percent of the worker's income) there is a risk that some of them may switch into informality.

With informality estimated at about 20 percent of the labor force in Chile, compared to 7 percent in the United States, it seems more reasonable to induce self-employed workers to participate. Given the current pension structure, the main measure would be to immediately decrease the transaction costs associated with voluntary contributions. In addition, self-employed workers should be provided with information on the consequences of not making contributions. These two measures seem appropriate because evidence shows that self-employment is not always a permanent option for the worker. New data arising from the newly created unemployment insurance scheme show that the labor market has a huge turnover between formal and informal workers, and dependent and independent ones.

Recommendation 3: Improve the Investment Framework

The Chilean investment regime has been very successful. Returns in real terms have averaged 10.2 percent a year for the better part of a quarter-century. No scandals have erupted in that time. Assets have undergone significant diversification. The share of State securities is now much lower: close to 20 percent of the assets of all the funds. Foreign investment is approaching 30 percent of all assets and is properly diversified by region, currency, and asset class.

This good performance, however, hides potential weaknesses. Each fund is subject to 94 limits, which introduces unneeded complexity. This overregulated system has several drawbacks. One is that it does not encourage self-regulation by fund managers. Thus high-level executives are probably making less effort than desirable. Also, board of directors do not always involve themselves in the definition and surveillance of investment policies. Overall, risk control mechanisms differ significantly among managers.

Greater flexibility in investment decisions is needed, along with investment policies sanctioned by the board of directors. At the same time, risk-based-supervision should be gradually adopted.

Conclusion

The Chilean pension system is about a quarter-century old. Its strengths and weaknesses can now be measured. Its major strengths are linked to financial management and its macroeconomic impact. Through financial development, the pension reform has improved productivity, growth, and all related variables.

The main weaknesses seem to be coverage issues, followed by industrial organization concerns. However, one of the main lessons to be drawn from the Chilean experience is that pension reform itself cannot solve all problems. Pension reform must embrace an overall reform agenda that reflects the development challenges facing the country. Such an agenda must be broad, include the expansion of some markets, especially financial markets, and improving others, such as the labor market.

References

Arenas de Mesa, Alberto. 2004. Presentation to the International Labour Organization, Santiago, Chile.

Bennett, Herman and Klaus Schmidt-Hebbel. 1999. Déficit previsional del sector público y garantía estatal de pensión mínima. *Notas de*

Investigación, Economía Chilena 4(3): 87–95. Central Bank of Chile, Santiago, Chile.

Berstein, Solange, and Andrea Tokman. 2004. Sistema de pensiones en Chile y diferencias de género: ¿perpetuadas o exacerbadas durante la vejez? Unpublished paper. Superintendence of Pension Funds Administrators, Santiago, Chile.

Berstein, Solange, Guillermo Larraín, and Francisco Pino. 2005 Coverage, Density and Pensions in Chile: Projections for the Next 30 Years. Unpublished paper. Superintendence of Pension Funds Administrators, Santiago, Chile.

Corbo, Vittorio, and Klaus Schmidt-Hebbel. 2003. Macroeconomic Effects of Pension Reform in Chile. In *Pension Reform: Results and Challenges,* ed. International Federation of Pension Funds Administrators. Santiago, Chile.

Holzmann, Robert, Robert Palacios, and Asta Zvienne. 2004. Implicit Debt: Issues, Measurement, and Scope in International Perspective. Social Protection Discussion Paper No. 0403. The World Bank, Washington, D.C.

Larraín Ríos, Guillermo. 2005. *Chile, fértil provincia.* Santiago, Chile: Random-House Mondadori Editors.

Superintendencia de Administradoras de Fondos de Pensiones (SAFP). 2002. *El sistema chileno de pensiones (Quinta edición).* Santiago, Chile.

———. 1981–2004. Quarterly Reports. Santiago. Chile.

CHAPTER **8**

Mexico's Second-generation Reforms: Strengthening Financial Regulation and Risk-based Supervision

Isaac Volin Bolok Portnoy *

The Mexican Pension Reform

In the mid-1990s, Mexico began a comprehensive reform of the social security system for workers in the private sector. This entailed a structural transformation of the old pension system for workers who participated in the Mexican Social Security Institute (Instituto Mexicano del Seguro Social, IMSS), which had existed since 1943.

The system, which was reformed in 1997, includes only those workers in the formal private sector. Nevertheless, it is the most important system in the country, covering the entire territory of Mexico and one third of the participants in the labor force: almost 13 million workers. The second most important system is the State Workers Social Security Institute (Instituto de Seguridad y Seguros Sociales de los Trabajadores del Estado, ISSSTE), which includes around 2 million federal government workers. Other, smaller pension plans encompass various decentralized government agencies, state governments, the armed forces, and state universities.

* Isaac Volin Bolok Portnoy was Vice President of Planning for the National Commission for Retirement Savings (CONSAR) of Mexico until December 2004. The author expresses his gratitude to Gabriel Ramírez Fernández, Antonio Mora, Jorge Tejeda, and Paloma Silva for their assistance and valuable comments in producing this chapter.

Since July 1, 1997, workers in the formal private sector have been required to participate in the new pension system and to make contributions to their individual accounts. These accounts are administered by specialized financial institutions, the Administradoras de Fondos para el Retiro (Afores). These companies, in turn, invest in financial markets through specialized retirement investment funds, the Sociedad de Inversión Especializada de Fondos para el Retiro (Siefores).

In the new pension system, the contribution level is established by law, and the pension that the worker receives at retirement will depend on the balance accrued in his or her individual account. Funds accrued will be based on the contributions deposited in the worker's individual account throughout his or her productive life, as well as the yield generated through the investment of savings. If the worker does not meet the requirements for obtaining a pension, the savings in the individual savings account will be paid to the account holder or beneficiaries of the account.

As a result of the reform, three independent insurance programs now cover pension-related benefits:

- Life and disability insurance (*invalidez y vida*, IV)
- Worker's compensation insurance (*riesgo de trabajo*, RT)
- Retirement, early retirement, and old age insurance (*retiro, cesantía en edad avanzada y vejez*, RCV)

Life and disability (IV) insurance covering death and disability is administered by the IMSS under a defined benefit plan. Contributions to this program are made by three parties (the worker, the employer, and the government) and total 2.5 percent of the wage. Illness and work-related accidents are covered through worker's compensation (RT) insurance, which is financed by employers through contributions managed by the IMSS.

Old age and early retirement pensions are financed through contributions made by workers, employers, and the government, which are deposited in individual accounts administered and invested by the Afores and Siefores.

Importance of Retirement Saving and its Regulation

As of year-end 2004, the value of the private sector retirement savings system was nearly 11 percent of Mexico's GDP, some 851 billion pesos.

Table 8.1	Investments in Financial Market Securities, June 2004 *(percent)*	
Financial intermediary		**Share**
Siefores[a]		29.0
Commercial banks		26.1
Investment funds		25.1
Insurance companies		13.9
Development banks		5.6
Limited purpose financial institutions (Sofoles)[b]		0.3
Factoring companies		0.0
Leasing companies		0.0
TOTAL		**100**

[a.] Includes 24-, 48-, and 72-hour investments and settlements.
[b.] Sociedades Financieras de Objeto Limitado.
Source: CONSAR, with data from the Mexican Banking and Securities Commission (CNBV) and the Mexican Insurance and Surety Commission (CNSF).

The pension funds (Afores) manage more than half this total, or about 471 billion pesos, through the specialized retirement investment funds (Siefores). The funds pertaining to retirement savings systems existing before the reforms were administered by the central bank.[1]

Within seven years after the reform, the Siefores, managing retirement assets, had become the leading holders of financial debt instruments in the Mexican financial system. They have outstripped commercial banks and traditional investment funds (see Table 8.1).

Given the importance of the pension funds to individuals' old age security, as well as the significant impact they exert on the growth of the financial system and the economy, it is essential that financial regulations insure that funds are invested under the highest standards of safety and control while still providing adequate investment returns. To establish financial regulations that meet these goals, the National Retirement Savings Commission (Comisión Nacional del Sistema de Ahorros para el Retiro, or CONSAR) uses two tools: the investment framework and prudential regulations.

The investment framework followed by the Siefores establishes the types of assets that funds may invest in, as well as the limits by type of

---

[1] The retirement savings system, Sistema de Ahorro para el Retiro (SAR), includes private sector workers and workers affiliated with the IMSS and ISSSTE systems created in 1992 (SAR92). SAR92 in addition to providing a pension, provided housing finance, funded by employer contributions made regularly in parallel with pension contributions.

risk, including market risk, credit risk and the risk of concentration. The prudential regulations are used for both investment management and risk management and control. The main objective of prudential regulation is to set minimum quality standards for the pension industry. The goal is to create an institutional infrastructure so that their investment management decisions are on par with the best fund managers worldwide.

The Investment Framework

Mexico's retirement savings system differs from other forms of savings and investment in the country and requires a different, and sometimes unique, form of regulation. First, it is a mandatory savings system. Private sector workers are obligated by law to save for retirement in the system. Second, these funds serve an important social purpose in that they represent the only savings that the majority of workers have to cover their financial needs once they retire from the labor force. For many workers, this may be the only income they will receive in their old age. Third, after 25 years of contributions, some participants may not have succeeded in saving enough to retire with a pension equal to the 1997 minimum wage, adjusted for inflation. These workers are entitled to a federal government subsidy, which is invested directly into their accounts until it becomes sufficient to provide them with a minimum pension. In this way, the government provides these participants with a minimum guaranteed pension. These features make this system unique. Thus its regulation must be specific. In particular, the investment framework must prevent excessive exposure to risk.

While other savings and investment vehicles also have investment rules, these are determined by their own managers and are voluntarily accepted by their clients. However, the retirement savings system is mandatory, with a government guarantee of a minimum pension (which could generate moral hazard). Moreover, most participants do not have the high level of financial sophistication needed to make complex investment decisions, thus leading to information asymmetries. This is the justification for the federal government assuming fiduciary responsibility and limiting exposures by issuing overall mandatory guidelines for the pension funds.

The need for the State to set investment guidelines through the competent authority—CONSAR—does not imply a disregard for the requirement that an investment framework be modern, flexible, and in keeping with the development of the financial markets.

Accordingly, CONSAR's work is to provide an investment regime that allows returns to be maximized at every risk level, without exceeding the maximum risk allowed. To that end, it must avoid certain restrictions that may impede the optimal mix of risk and return: that is, the optimal point known as the "efficient investment frontier" (see Figure 8.1).

An investment framework that allows suitable diversification of the funds offers two main benefits. First, investment risk is reduced. Second, expected returns are increased. Thus the increase in the worker's wealth can be used to finance his or her pension.

The investment framework serves to guide each pension fund in defining its investment strategy. This strategy must be designed by each pension fund management company to meet its fiduciary responsibilities, which stipulate that when management companies invest workers' funds, they must take every step required to obtain suitable profits and insure the security of the investment. Thus, in fulfilling their duties, these companies must pay exclusive attention to the workers' interests, making sure that all transactions to invest workers' funds are carried out to that end.

Once it determines the investment regime, the pension fund must work to achieve the efficient frontier with the investments under its control, given the risk level desired. This risk level will depend on the specific features of the participants in the pension fund's particular portfolio, including their age, wage level, financial sophistication, and tolerance for risk. Each pension fund must decide on the fund risk level most suitable for its clients.

Figure 8.1. Efficient Investment Frontier for Each Pension Fund

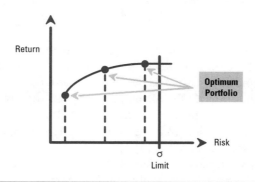

Mexico is not the only country that has had to establish an investment framework or guidelines. Indeed, every country with a system similar to Mexico's has detailed regulations about these matters. In Latin America, the regulatory philosophy is implemented through a series of precise rules about what one can and cannot do in the investment arena. This translates into guidelines consisting of quantitative limits based on certain measurable parameters.

This form of quantitative regulation contrasts somewhat with the guidelines commonly used in more developed countries, which are known as the "prudent person rule." Under this guideline, the fund manager makes investment decisions about the funds entrusted to him or her as if they were the manager's own funds. This places a premium on fiduciary responsibility and fosters the avoidance of excessive risk and conflicts of interest.

Countries where the prudent person rule is used have a legal system based on Anglo-Saxon common law. Such a legal system has a conceptual and interpretative nature, providing its judicial authorities with the flexibility to judge whether or not a given action is prudent.

By contrast, the legal system of Mexico and the rest of Latin America is based on the Napoleonic code. This legal system is less conceptual and interpretative. It starts from the premise that anything not strictly prohibited is allowed. This is a barrier to the region's adoption of the prudent person rule. The Napoleonic code makes quantitative investment regulations a more suitable guidance in Latin America than the prudent person rule.

Moreover, in Mexico, the new pension system for private sector workers started operations under two constraining circumstances. One was the 1995 financial and banking industry crisis. The other was the lack of savings and investment instruments for long-term portfolio management. These constraints, along with the priority set on getting the system started, explain why some very strict, conservative quantitative regulations were issued initially.

Some of the impediments to a broader and more conceptual investment regime have been overcome in recent years, including the financial and banking industry crisis and the lack of long-term fund management. This is why, in 2002, CONSAR began to change the investment guidelines to provide a more modern framework. In doing so, it provided pension funds with tools that are indispensable for managing the risks inherent in investments.

CONSAR has turned to the task of modernizing the investment framework with a clearly defined, double-pronged strategy:

- Make the investment regime more flexible, eliminating unnecessary or inefficient parameters.
- Create an institutional infrastructure in the pension funds for managing investments and controlling risks, adhering to international best practice.

The strategy represents a significant turnaround in Mexico and in Latin America. The traditional diversification model, consisting of establishing quantitative limits by *type of instrument* in the investment regime, has been abandoned (see Srinivas, Whitehouse, and Yermo 2000). The transition toward limits by *type of risk* is under way. This allows a better composition of the portfolio, since the contribution of each asset class to the total portfolio risk is evaluated, rather than treating each asset individually. At the same time, risk management and control capability is strengthened at the pension funds through policies and procedures based on international best practice.

Within this strategy, certain quantitative limits, as established by the international association of pensions regulators, the Asociación Internacional de Organismos de Supervisión de Fondos de Pensiones (AIOS), are observed by Mexico and other member countries. In addition, quantitative limits that should not be included in an investment regime must be defined: those that do not allow achievement of the best risk-adjusted returns, that generate unsuitable incentives, or that do not efficiently control investment risk. A quantitative investment framework may be efficient if the guidelines are designed to establish asset classes as well as currencies and transactions allowed. It must also define limits for market risk, credit risk, and concentration risk.

On the other hand, inefficient parameters are those that do not regulate any specific or conceptually valid risk; make a pointless distinction within a given class of asset by type of instrument or issuer; introduce undesirable conduct into portfolio management on the part of the managers or in the market valuation of the portfolios; or reduce incentives for competition in the industry.

The Regulators

CONSAR is an independent agency linked to the Ministry of Finance. It has two governing bodies that oversee a variety of matters, including the definition of the investment framework: the Board of Governors and the Consulting and Surveillance Committee.

Board of Governors

The Board of Governors is CONSAR's highest governing body. It has the authority to:

- Grant/revoke authorization to operate a pension fund
- Order an administrative/management takeover by the participants in the system
- Issue rules related to the investment framework, subject to the prior approval of the Consulting and Surveillance Committee (CSC)
- Determine the fee schedule, subject to the prior approval of the CSC
- Be aware of violations by participants in the retirement savings system and impose sanctions
- Remove personnel who provide services to participants in the retirement savings system in violation of certain provisions.

This governing body has representatives from the federal government, labor unions, and employer organizations (Figure 8.2).

Figure 8.2. CONSAR's Board of Governors

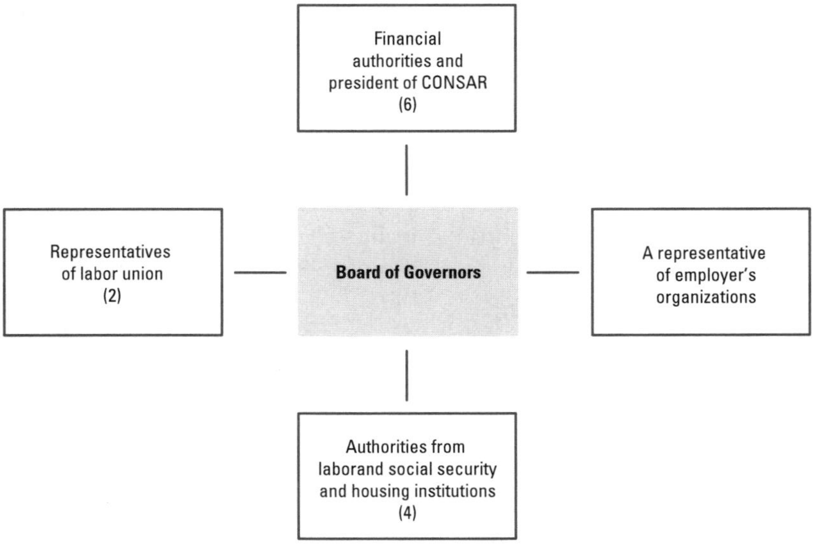

Consulting and Surveillance Committee

The Consulting and Surveillance Committee (CSC) has the authority to:

- Approve the rules related to the investment framework and the fee schedule
- Oversee the development of the system to prevent conflicts of interest and monopolistic practices
- Recommend preventive measures for the healthy development of the system.

In addition, the CSC is required to be familiar with matters submitted to the Committee head regarding adoption of criteria and policies generally applicable to the retirement savings system; special authorizations provided to the Afores and Siefores and any revocation; and removal of the compliance controllers and independent advisors of the pension funds and retirement investment funds.

The CSC is also tripartite, but the representation of the three sectors is more equal in terms of the number of members and thus votes (Figure 8.3).

Figure 8.3. CONSAR's Consulting and Surveillance Committee

	3 Financial authorities	
6 Representatives of labor unions	**Consultation and Vigilance Commitee**	6 Representatives of employer's organizations
	4 Authorities from labor and social security and housing institutions	

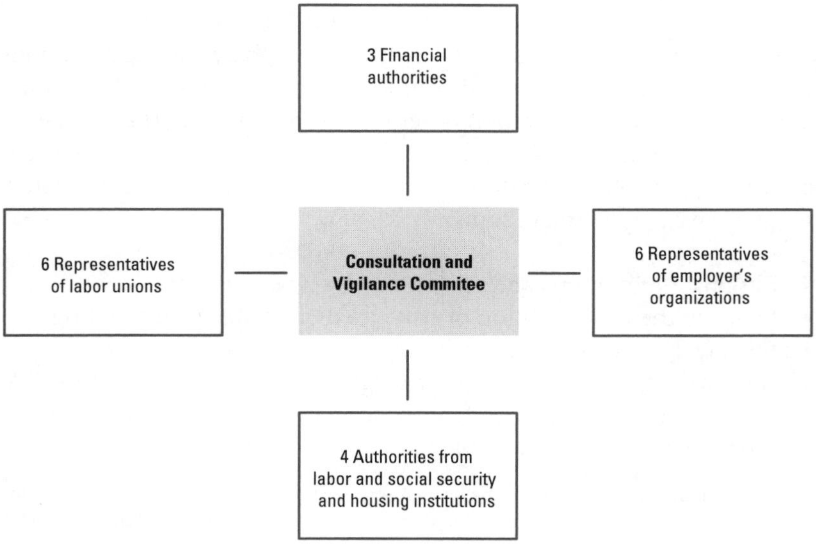

To change the investment framework, the approval of both bodies is required. Thus it is indispensable for the CONSAR management team that drafts proposals regarding the investment framework to stay in constant communication with members of the Board of Governors and the CSC. A frank dialogue between both bodies is based on their common objective of designing rules with the sole purpose of protecting and advancing workers' interests.

Reforming the Investment Framework

During the early years of the system, the investment framework was very restrictive and based on investment categories. This was a response to the adverse conditions under which the new pension system started operations. At that time, operating aspects were the priority for CONSAR. Initially, CONSAR and the pension funds had the following operating goals:

- Assure that a high standard for information quality was upheld in the operating systems for recording worker information in the pension funds
- Guarantee the security of funds flows and of information related to collecting contributions (this meant overseeing the operations of 4,000 payment counters and the receipt of more than 600,000 employer contributions and more than 11 million worker contributions)
- Strengthen the systems related to the oversight of the retirement savings system.

Once the system had passed through its initial phase and the conditions were right for broadening the investment framework, the modernization process and second generation of reforms were initiated. The guidelines governing investments were adjusted, based on well-defined policies for improving portfolio diversification. The following policies were pursued to open up the investment framework.

- Eliminate minimums and restrictions by type of issuer
- Regulate the concentration of risk based on credit quality (ratings)
- Effectively control market risk
- Allow the use of derivatives to manage the portfolio in a more flexible way under the concept of "complete markets,"[2] taking advantage of arbitrage in favor of the workers

---

[2] To operate in complete markets means that once a class of assets is permitted, the pension administrators can operate on a cash basis or with derivatives to obtain the desired exposure.

- Broaden the investment choices by class of asset, currency, and nationality of the issuer
- Offer the workers different risk/return choices.

One of the first reforms of the system was to eliminate the restrictions on debt instruments, which was the most basic element of the asset classes. This approach was taken since it made sense to update the basic class of local debt (Mexican debt) before opening the framework to other classes of assets.

The main initial changes in the investment framework are summarized in Table 8.2.

Despite these changes, the investment framework continued to be limited to a single asset class: "Mexican debt." Thus in the next step, new asset classes had to be added to better diversify investment portfolios (Figure 8.4).

In April 2004, the three most important changes to the investment framework to date were approved. They added new asset classes and risk/return alternatives. These changes are summarized in Table 8.3.

Table 8.2	Changes in the Investment Framework, 2001–03	
Policy	**Prior investment framework**	**New investment framework**
Eliminate minimums and restrictions by issuer	Government (minimum 65%). Private (maximum 35%) Financial intermediaries (maximum 10%)	No limits on government, private, state, municipal, State-controlled, and financial intermediaries
Regulate concentration risk in accordance with credit quality	10% per issuer. Issuers AAA and AA	Per issuer: 5% in AAA; 3% in AA; 1% in A
Broaden opportunities to invest in bonds, in foreign currency	Only dollar-denominated government bonds	Government and private bonds in dollars, euros, and yen
Allow the use of derivatives	Cash	Cash and derivatives with allowed underlying assets
Efficiently control market risk	Minimum 65% in bonds with maturities or rate changes in less than 183 days	A weighted-average term-to-maturity (WATM) of 900 days was used temporarily. Later, it was replaced by VaR.

Table 8.3	Changes in the Investment Framework, 2004	
Guideline	**Before**	**After**
Asset classes allowed	Debt securities only	Debt securities and equity instruments (stock)[a]
Nationality of the issuers	Mexican issuers exclusively	Mexican issuers and international issuers[b]
Investment funds (Siefores)	Only one Siefore per Afore	Two Siefores mandatory, offering different investment alternatives based on risk and asset class

[a] Through instruments with principal protected to maturity linked to stock market indices.
[b] Listed or placed in countries that are members of the European Union or the Technical Committee of the International Organization of Securities Commissions (IOSCO).

Equity Investment and International Securities

The recent changes in the investment framework have three basic objectives:

- Increase expected returns
- Reduce the risk of concentration in investment portfolios
- Provide differentiated investment alternatives, based on the characteristics of the workers.

Equity instruments and international securities were added to increase the expected returns and reduce portfolio concentration, particularly their dependence on bonds issued by Mexican institutions.

Figure 8.4. Conceptual Framework of the Opening of the Investment Framework

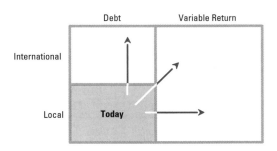

Figure 8.5. Siefores

	New Basic (SB1)	Current Basic (SB2)	
Workers who are 56 or older can choose to be transferred to the New Basic Siefore (SB1)	Current regime without variable interest 51 percent indexed for inflation and international equities	Current regime +15 percent invariable interest instruments and international equities	The option by default for all workers, except those who are 56 or older, is Current Basic (SB2)

Pension funds were approved to offer two investment funds, or Siefores. One would invest portfolios in fixed-income securities (basic Siefore 1, or SB1). The other would invest in fixed-income securities, but also up to 15 percent in equity instruments (basic Siefore 2, or SB2).[3]

The current basic Siefore (the only retirement investment fund available before the recent changes) was designated as SB2 and was considered profitable for all workers. Those near retirement age were given some exposure to equity instruments to increase their expected returns and so improve their future pensions.

If the current Siefore had not been designated as SB2, the signatures of all the workers would have had to have been obtained in order to invest in equity instruments. This would have been a slow, expensive, and inefficient process.

The system that was approved (equity instruments, international securities, and families of funds) is shown in Figure 8.5.

Each Siefore is designed for specific types of workers, following the strategy of "life-cycle funds."[4]

Basic Siefore 1 (SB1). This fund is designed for workers near retirement age (56 years, or older). It has no equity instruments, since the greater

---

[3] Through dated Financial Protected Notes linked to equity indexes. The 15 percent limit refers to the exposures at variable returns and not to the notes. The exposure is estimated through the derivatives (deltas) or the stocks.

[4] The "life cycle" fund is the ideal strategy when investors lack financial sophistication to adjust the characteristics of the risk-return of their portfolios, according to their nearness to retirement.

volatility of these instruments may represent a risk for workers who will draw on their savings in the near term to finance their pensions. For this reason, it is better for workers near retirement to have an investment framework whose returns have a low level of volatility.

Workers who are 56 years or older and have funds invested in SB2 may transfer funds to SB1 through twice-yearly transfers over five years. In this way, when the worker reaches age 60, the retirement age, 100 percent of that worker's funds will be invested in SB1.

Workers under 56 years of age who decide that their savings should not be invested in equity instruments, given their personal preferences, may transfer their funds to SB1, if they state their intent in writing. In this way, the worker's right to choose is respected at all times.

Finally, the funds of workers who do not choose a pension fund will be invested in this fund. Every two months, CONSAR will assign them to the pension fund with the lowest costs in the system. This is because there is no personal information on these workers; therefore, it is impossible to send them forms for them to choose the retirement investment fund in which they would like to invest.

Basic Siefore 2 (SB2). This fund is designed for workers up to 55 years of age, since the years of work that remain before retirement allow them to assume greater risk. That is, they have time to recoup losses from more volatile investments. Thus, they may take advantage of the profitability of investing in equity instruments and longer-term bonds.

CONSAR's governing bodies (BG and CSC) agreed that investment in equity instruments and international securities would adhere to the five basic principles of the system.

1. *Daily market valuation of all instruments in the portfolio.* Create suitable incentives in the administration of savings, provide full transparency on each worker's balance at all times, and avoid cross-subsidization among workers entering and leaving the retirement investment fund (Siefore).[5]
2. *Daily transparency of all the securities in the portfolio.* Allow daily verification of compliance with the Siefore investment framework.

---

[5] Even though some people had argued that this policy could generate volatility in the markets and encourage "herd" behavior, these arguments have not proven true. Furthermore, even in cases where they are true, it would be useful to evaluate these effects compared to the distortions that would result without a daily market valua-

Figure 8.6. Probability Analysis: Returns of Stocks vs. Bonds

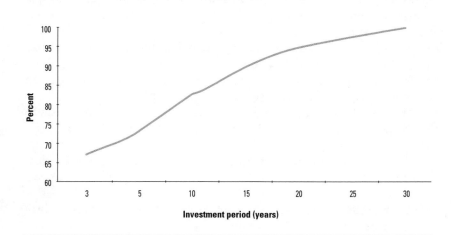

Source: Federal Reserve Bank of Minneapolis (1996).

3. *Collect only indispensable management and brokerage costs from workers.* Avoid collecting double fees for investment of workers' savings.
4. *Operations through the complete market.* If investment is opened to certain instruments, such instruments may also be used as underlying assets in derivatives to avoid regulatory arbitrage and provide the retirement investment funds with the greatest operating flexibility.
5. *General regulations.* The regulator must not be involved in approving individual managers or vehicles to carry out investment of funds in the international markets since this makes the regulator jointly responsible for events out of its control.

One of the reforms to the investment framework was to allow investment in *equity instruments.* This was based mainly on empirical evidence that shows, over the long term, that stock portfolios provide better returns than bond portfolios (Figure 8.6).

Over time, Fund SB2 is estimated to generate an average of 100 basis points of real annual return over Fund SB1.[6]

tion of the portfolio in a system where the workers change pension administrators frequently.

Moreover, equity investments would be made through *structured notes,* which are debt instruments tied to stock market indices with principal protected until maturity.

- It has been proven in various countries that the concept of "guaranteed principal" has a high value for risk-averse persons.
- In Mexico, people are averse to investing in equity instruments, given the history of stock market crashes.
- The capitalized coupon protects the principal, since it is equivalent to the portion invested in equity instruments.

The *indices* were important to this asset class for the following reasons:

- An index is a pre-diversified instrument, which reduces the risk of concentration.
- As a passive investment strategy, it entails low transaction costs to be charged against the workers' savings.
- It is commonly used in structured notes.
- There is no conflict of interest between an issuer and an Afore in terms of an equity interest or relationship.

However, investing in equities through structured notes has two disadvantages:

- High structuring costs, which can reach 5 percent of the value of the issue, based on the need to establish a specific vehicle to issue them, as well as the costs of registration and sale of the issue.
- Low liquidity, because they are issues made to order for a specific client, and the issuer is not obligated to repurchase them.

To avoid these disadvantages, the retirement investment funds are also permitted to buy the notes, which they structure within their balance sheet by mixing bonds with equity instruments (options, stocks, or vehicles that contain stock) based on approved indices.

This allows them to replicate the behavior of the structured notes while eliminating the structuring costs, by avoiding the cost of registering the

---

[6] This number is the result of multiplying the exposure in variable returns of 15 percent for an expected yield in pesos over the free risk rate of 600 base points (including Mexico's extra risk rate).

issue and having to set up a specific vehicle for this. Moreover, the structured note created within the Siefore is as liquid as its components since the components may be split off, and, for the most part, they have their own secondary markets already developed. In this way, the retirement investment funds (Siefore) need only purchase equity instruments and combine them with bonds already in its portfolio. In this case, the only costs incurred are the brokerage costs for acquiring the components.

Figure 8.7 shows how the combination of equity and fixed income instruments through a vehicle gives rise to a structured note. The figure also shows the two ways of structuring: directly through stock, or through derivatives.

It was decided to limit these instruments to the indices of countries that are members of the IOSCO Technical Committee or the European Union, after assessing their regulation in terms of information disclosure, transparency, and liquidity. Those markets were deemed to offer conditions suitable for the investment of Mexican workers' savings. The approved indexes are listed in CONSAR Circular 15-12, Annex H (CONSAR 2004a). This and other CONSAR Circulars can be accessed at CONSAR's webpage: www.CONSAR.gob.mx.

In the event that the notes are structured with stock that replicates the approved indices, the pension fund may change the official weight of each issuer in the reference index in a range not to exceed plus or minus 1 percent. This is permitted to reduce the transaction costs and administration costs caused by rebalancing portfolios with respect to the

Figure 8.7. Structuring of Notes

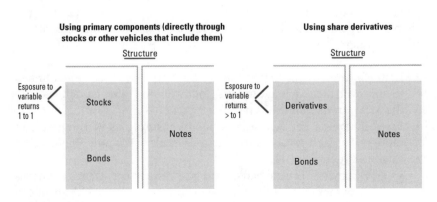

The first alternative allows long exposures, while the second one allows a combination of long and short exposures.

indices. Working within this range, the pension fund may avoid acquiring stock more likely to fluctuate out of the indices and/or stock that is less actively traded.

If the Siefores structure notes with different vehicles, such as ETFs or mutual funds, that replicate the behavior of the approved indices, the Afores must absorb the costs for handling or managing the funds.

There were two underlying reasons for liberalizing the investment framework to permit investment in *international securities:*

1. It serves as a safeguard against the potential scarcity of instruments if the Siefores grow more rapidly than the country's financial market. If new investment alternatives are not available, the retirement investment funds could end up purchasing instruments that have lower credit quality or artificially low returns.
2. It provides greater portfolio diversification, thus improving returns and reducing risk.

Based on an internal working paper, CONSAR concluded that if the investment framework did not open up to international securities, it would run a significant risk that the Siefores could purchase the entire stock of both existing and new federal government debt—which would be detrimental to the portfolio's diversification. Against this backdrop, the opening up of the investment framework to international securities was a necessity for the retirement savings system, as it has been for other systems in Latin America. The upper limit approved by the Board of Governors for investment in international securities is 20 percent of each retirement investment fund, in both equities and fixed-income securities.

The guidelines governing investment in international securities describe what asset classes are allowed and the nationality requirements for eligible issuers.

- Equities: Investment may be made through structured notes linked to approved stock market indices, following the same guidelines as in the Mexican market (SB2s only).
- Fixed income: Debt securities issued by institutions with high credit ratings of at least A- on an international scale (SB1s and SB2s).
- Eligible issuers:
  - Governments, central banks, and government agencies of countries that are members of the European Union or the IOSCO Technical Committee. The regulations of these markets guarantee suitable information disclosure and transaction transparency.

- Institutions that issue securities under the regulation and oversight of countries that are members of the European Union or the IOSCO Technical Committee.
- Multilateral financial institutions such as the World Bank and Inter-American Development Bank.

The retirement investment funds may carry out transactions in the international markets directly or through financial services providers. These providers are persons or institutions authorized to conduct operations in securities for third party accounts. They are also authorized to offer other securities-related services, such as investment advice and asset administration/management. They are subject to the regulation and oversight of government agencies of countries that are members of the European Union or the IOSCO Technical Committee.

Before a Siefore can operate in the international market through a financial services provider (FSP), it must sign an agreement enabling the provider to act on behalf of the Siefore. For transactions in the international market, it must be stipulated that the FSPs will maintain the investments they make for the account of the retirement investment fund in separate accounts. To guarantee absolute transparency, they must be separate from investments they make for their own account or for any other third party.

Furthermore, the Siefores and the provider are prohibited from carrying out certain transactions that entail possible conflicts of interest. Avoiding conflicts of interest is essential for the transparency of the system and to ensure that the workers' interests are always placed above any other interest.

Changes in the investment framework of this magnitude and significance require considerable work on regulatory and operational aspects, which in turn require time for implementation For this reason, although the investment framework was approved in April 2004, it went into full effect only as of January 17, 2005.

Moreover, a significant portion of the funds were transferred to SB1s. Thus it was necessary to design a mechanism for transferring these funds without altering the order and price formation in the financial market.

The transfer mechanism consisted of moving instruments from SB2 into SB1 without selling them in the markets. This was carried out through a proportional cut in each of the positions in every security in the current Siefore (SB2). This was done in such a way that on the day of this cut (January 14, 2005), the two Siefores (SB1 and SB2) had the same portfolio structure. The idea was that the event of moving funds would neither be favorable or detrimental to any worker.

VaR as a Regulatory Parameter of Market Risk

Market risk may be defined as the probability that the price of assets in the financial markets will fluctuate adversely, resulting in a decrease in value. Various factors may cause this type of risk, depending on the type of financial instrument affected. The most important are:

- Interest rate risk (both nominal and real rates)
- Surcharge or premium paid for liquidity reasons
- Inflation risk
- Exchange rate risk
- Corporate risk

Various methodologies have been designed to monitor and control market risk, including:

- Weighted-average term-to-maturity (WATM)
- Sensitivity analysis: duration and convexity
- Scenario analysis
- Stress testing
- Value at Risk (VaR)

Thus CONSAR issued various circulars that began to regulate market risk through investment categories based on length of maturity or rate change. According to these directives, at least 65 percent of the portfolio must be invested in securities with maturities or rate changes of less than 183 days. While this provision limited the risk rate of only two-thirds of the portfolio, the remaining third could be invested in very long-term instruments.

When this rule was established, there were no fixed-income securities with terms of more than one year. Because of the lack of variety in the instruments available, the risk exposure of the uncontrolled third of the portfolio was limited. However, because this provision applied only to a portion of the portfolio, it did not allow the risk of the entire retirement investment fund portfolio to be controlled.

As the financial market in Mexico evolved, fixed-rate bonds with maturities of 20 to 30 years were issued, along with 10-year and 20-year bonds with fixed nominal rates. Thus the need for risk measurements that would include the entire portfolio became evident.

This is why Weighted-Average Term-to-Maturity (WATM) was implemented as a regulatory measurement to replace the prior rule. This tool was adopted on a temporary basis, while the infrastructure required for measurement through Value at Risk (VaR) was being put in place (see discussion below).

The WATM is a weighted average of the days to elapse until the portfolio asset review. The WATM includes all the securities in the portfolio, and it is very easy to calculate. However, it presents some problems. While the daily movements in financial markets based on fluctuations in interest rates and rates of exchange do not affect the behavior of the WATM, they do determine losses of value in the portfolio. This factor is even more important for derivatives.

The Siefores with the greatest WATMs are not always those that have the greatest risk of possible loss of value. This is the case because the term structure of interest rates is more volatile in short-term instruments than in long-term instruments. Thus CONSAR deemed it necessary to establish an effective control measurement for losses in value. To this end, it selected the best-known and most effective tool yet developed for this purpose, the "VaR limit."

VaR estimates the maximum loss a portfolio could record in an interval of time, with a defined level of certainty or confidence. There are different methodologies for calculating the VaR, based on the assumptions and the method used to construct a distribution of returns. Two of the best known methodologies are the historical and the Monte Carlo methods. The historical method simulates the future performance of all instruments in the portfolio as a function of the changes observed in historical interest rates, exchange rates, stock market indices, and other relevant factors. The Monte Carlo method simulates future scenarios of interest rate and exchange rate behavior and other factors affecting the valuation of the instruments in the portfolio. This is based on a specific structure involving the average, the volatility, and the relationship between these variables (matrix of variances and covariances).

While the VaR is a commonly accepted risk measurement method, when it is used as a regulatory parameter, it must be borne in mind that a portfolio's VaR may increase for three reasons:

- The securities position (risk profile) may increase, with no increase in the volatility of the risk factors.
- The risk factors (volatility) may increase, without a significant increase in the securities position.
- Both the securities position and the volatility of the risk factors may increase.

Given that one principle of good regulation is to provide the entities supervised with parameters that are within their control, it is very important to establish a more predictable measurement tool.

Therefore, the historical method was chosen because it minimizes the effects of "volatility" and emphasizes a portfolio's "risk profile," which is also under the control of the pension fund. Under the historical method, all scenarios are known a priori (except that of the next day). This makes it a predictable measurement tool and allows the pension fund to anticipate and control the risk of violating the VaR limit.

With the Monte Carlo method, however, it is difficult to anticipate changes in the VaR, since it is calculated through a matrix of variances and covariances that is updated daily. Thus one or more highly volatile event that disrupts the correlations can lead to an unexpected increase in the regulatory VaR.

Historical VaR is the ideal choice because it can be easily applied across the board to the entire industry, since it does not require formulation of assumptions. The supervisory bodies can thus avoid the serious problem of having to calibrate and harmonize both the models and assumptions used and the entities regulated.

However, it is important that the pension funds not react to volatile events by selling securities with greater VaR, and thus generating a pro-cyclical chain of events. To this end, the regulations provide that sanctions for exceeding VaR limits will be applied only when a violation was for reasons attributable to the fund manager. In other words, sanctions are applicable for purchasing or selling instruments that increase portfolio risk, not for volatility bubbles that increase VaR. The circular on restructuring portfolios Circular 45 (CONSAR 2004b) establishes a simple methodology for determining these instances.

Finally, whenever the VaR limit is exceeded, the Afore must submit an action plan for restructuring the portfolio to reduce its VaR and bring it back under the limit. The pension fund will have up to six months to carry out such a restructuring. The objective of this long period is to prevent herd behavior: that is, selling, which accentuates market volatility and creates a vicious circle.

Impact of the Reforms

Changes in the investment framework have allowed the retirement investment funds to achieve greater returns, assuming the same risk level. In other words, they allow the efficient frontier to be moved upward. To demonstrate this point, CONSAR analyzed the trend of the efficient frontiers based on the various changes made to the investment framework. Five different efficient frontiers were calculated. The most relevant changes to the investment regime were then incorporated. Four main assumptions were used. First, the complete set of instruments available up to August 31, 2004 was used. Second, the return of each instrument in the portfolio was estimated using the expected annual yield at maturity, as provided by the Integral Price Provider (PIP). Third, to calculate the portfolio risk, the regulatory VaR methodology was used with PIP as described in CONSAR Circular 15-12 (CONSAR 2004a). Fourth, returns were maximized subject to different levels of VaR. The actual calculations used a program that optimizes the portfolios using the Mat lab tool.

The first efficient frontier was calculated under the investment framework in effect through December 2001. To begin with, the investment framework included the following six parameters:

1. Minimum of 65 percent in instruments with maturities or rate changes not to exceed 183 days
2. Minimum of 51 percent in instruments with protection against inflation
3. Minimum of 65 percent in government securities
4. Maximum of 10 percent per issuer
5. Maximum of 10 percent applicable to financial institutions, as a group
6. Maximum of 20 percent of the amount issued by each private instrument.

As noted, the investment framework in effect at that time did not control risk efficiently because it controlled only one portion of the portfolio (the 65 percent minimum), through an indicator that was not very efficient.

Given these facts, the first significant change in the investment framework, in December 2001, was to introduce market risk controls based on the maturities of the portfolios. This change eliminated the 65 percent minimum of the portfolio in instruments with maturities or rate changes of more than 183 days. Instruments with a maximum maturity of 900 days of Weighted-Average Term-to-Maturity of the entire portfolio could now be used. Moreover, the 65 percent minimum in government securities was eliminated, thus freeing up a section in the portfolio for nongovernmental issuers. In addition, the makeup of the portfolio was regulated by credit quality (ratings). With this change, market risk is better controlled because it truncates the portion of the efficient frontier that added the least return by risk level.

In November 2002, the WATM was replaced by a VaR limit (0.60 percent of the total assets of a retirement investment fund), and investments in derivatives were allowed. Permitting derivatives made it necessary to control the risks of preventing potential losses using the VaR limit, instead of a duration parameter (which would be ineffective for derivatives).

Because of the potential of derivatives, including them contributed to a shift in the efficient frontier of the retirement investment fund. The shift of the efficient frontier translates into an increased return of up to 80 basis points in some parts of the curve.

In August 2003, another change was implemented that allowed a shift in the efficient frontier: the elimination of the 10 percent cap on investments in financial institutions. This change provided more opportunity to invest in financial institutions and to transact a greater number of derivatives outside the stock exchanges (OTC derivatives).

In April 2004, further reforms of the investment framework were approved. These became effective in January 2005. These reforms will allow the retirement investment funds to include equity instruments and international securities in their portfolios. It also eliminates the 51 percent minimum limit on equities with inflation adjustmnent of SB2 portfolios when transferring to an SB1. This will contribute to greater diversification and will also increase returns.

If the implied efficient frontier as of December 2001 is compared with the current frontier, an average shift of more than 130 basis points in the return is apparent, assuming the same risk level (Figure 8.8). Moreover, by maintaining the 130 basis-point difference in the estimated return, the worker's projected balance will increase up to 32 percent at the same risk level and assuming a portfolio with a VaR of 0.4 percent of the net assets.

The changes in the investment framework will significantly improve workers' pensions. In the coming years, the investment framework will continue to be adjusted as financial markets develop and the risk management capabilities of the pension funds evolve.

Future Reforms

In this regard, CONSAR must continue to foster regulatory changes that translate into benefits for the workers. Some changes that would be suitable for implementation in the near or medium term are the following:

Figure 8.8. Impact of Reforms between December 2001 and April 2004: Shift in the Efficient Frontier

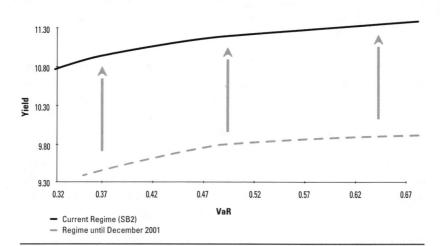

— Current Regime (SB2)
— Regime until December 2001

- Include credit-based derivatives as an alternative to synthetic investments with corporate issuers, or to hedge this type of risk.
- Extend the risk/return continuum for the workers through new retirement investment funds, following the mutual funds life-cycle model. In this regard, a new Siefore (SB3) could be set up for the youngest workers, in order to improve the risk/return of the investment strategy for each group of workers in accordance with their age.
- Incorporate new asset classes that have a low correlation with those currently allowed, such as real estate investment trusts (REITs) and commodities.
- Review the current risk limits.

Prudential Regulation

Before investment regulations could be relaxed, it was necessary to ensure that the pension funds had an institutional infrastructure suitable for investment and risk management. Thus CONSAR concentrated on the following objectives in its prudential regulation.

- Generate basic competence in pension funds in investment and risk management.

- Instill international best practices.
- Reduce major disparities in the competence of pension funds.
- Ensure that the pension funds avoid inappropriate conduct, such as incurring excessive risk or engaging in transactions that involve conflicts of interest.

The prudential regulations issued by CONSAR cover three areas: investment management, risk control, and derivatives transactions. The first two are mandatory for all pension funds, including those just starting up their operations.

The regulation of derivatives transactions is voluntary. Nonetheless, the pension fund must demonstrate that it is in full compliance with this rule before transactions in these instruments can begin. Failure to verify compliance with this regulation will result in suspension from using derivatives. Noncompliance with the other regulations will trigger a process of sanctions and correction of the irregularities found.

Regulation of Risk

CONSAR's risk regulations contained in Circular 51 (CONSAR 2004c) have the following specific objectives:

- Promote a culture of risk management among pension fund managers.
- Establish basic guidelines to identify, measure, monitor, limit, control, and disclose the different types of risks that Siefores may face.
- Protect workers' assets through continuous measurement of Afores' risk exposure.
- Strengthen best practices that Afores and Siefores must adopt in order to diminish the operating risk in trading, settlement, and allocation of resources.
- Standardize operating logistics, decision making, and execution of the financial transactions known as derivatives, as well as any other transactions that the Investment Committee deems necessary. Such procedures are meant to ensure the participation of the Investment and Risk Committees in the areas of investment, control, and transaction record-keeping.
- Measure and control the risk exposure of Siefores under extreme market conditions (stress testing).

In order to practice integrated risk management, Afores must:

1. *Develop policies and procedures for integrated risk management.* Siefores must develop policies and procedures for managing the different types of risks to which they may be exposed, whether quantifiable or not.
2. *Form a Risk Committee.* Each Siefore must form a Risk Committee, whose objective is to manage the risks to which they are exposed, and to ensure that transactions conform to the limits, policies, and procedures issued by the Committee.[7]
3. *Create an Integrated Risk Management Unit.* The Siefores Risk Committees must be supported by an Integrated Risk Management Unit. The Unit's objective is to identify, measure, monitor, and report on the quantifiable risks the Siefores face. It must use risk assessment models and systems that incorporate market information accurately, reflecting the value of investment positions and their sensitivity to a range of risk factors. In addition, for analytical purposes, it must consider quantifiable risks (market, credit, and liquidity). Whether the Unit is created within the Afore or its services are contracted out, the Afores must designate an officer who will be responsible for risk. This officer must be at least a second-tier executive within the organizational hierarchy, reporting directly to the pension fund's chief executive officer.
4. *Prepare a manual of policies and procedures for integrated risk management.* Each Siefore must have such a manual. CONSAR will track its implementation and dissemination, and will monitor for strict adherence to the manual.
5. *Disclose information concerning risk management.* In the notes accompanying their financial statements, Afores and Siefores must disclose information on the policies, procedures, methodologies, and other measures that they adopt for risk management.

Among the future challenges in integrated risk management will be ways to deal in greater depth with such matters as the accurate assessment of the Afores' risks associated with credit, counterparties, and liquidity.

Regulation of Investment

CONSAR issued its prudential regulations in Circular 55–1 (CONSAR 2004d) to improve investment decision making by pension funds and re-

---

[7] The Risk Committee is composed of the General Director of the pension fund, at least one independent member, one non–independent member, and the member responsible for the Risk Management Unit.

tirement investment funds and to encourage pension funds to adopt best practices in investment matters. Best practices for investment include:

1. *Automation of Afores' operating systems.* Minimum standards are established for Siefores operating systems.
2. *Compliance with minimum requirements for the Investment Director and certification of personnel involved in the investment strategy.* Because of the volume of assets managed by Afores, it is advisable to make ongoing efforts to enhance the professionalism of staff responsible for carrying out the investment strategy. To this end, the following minimum requirements were set for the staff responsible for investment who participate in the Investment Committee:

    * At least three years of experience in operations with financial instruments.
    * Demonstration of moral integrity, as well as technical and managerial ability, to the Commission.

    Certification of certain staff must also be obtained from an independent third party widely recognized in matters of financial education and designated by the Commission. Personnel to be certified are those responsible for executing the investment strategy, the UAIR, the regulatory controller, and those responsible for recording, allocation, and settlement of investment transactions. Certification must be renewed every three years to guarantee that staff remain up-to-date in investment matters.
3. *Makeup of the Investment Committee.* The Investment Committee must have at least five members, including an independent director, the chief executive officer, and the director of the pension fund manager's investment division. Participation by an independent director is mandatory, to ensure that investment-related decisions and transactions take place without conflicts of interest. Among the objectives of the Investment Committee are determining portfolio composition and designation of traders and other employees responsible for the investment process, as well as approval of replenishment programs.
4. *Other best practices in investment matters.* The Afore is required to establish the following in an investment manual:

    * Procedures for reviewing the quality of private securities in which the Afore invests, including minimum disclosure standards for parties issuing instruments available for purchase by a Siefore and the

minimum requirements that must be met by common representatives handling the issuance of securities that may be purchased by the Siefore.

- Internal policies for the selection of counterparties.
  Establishment of an internal code of conduct for members of the Investment Committee governing their personal investments, in order to avoid conflicts of interest with their fiduciary responsibilities.
- Mechanisms necessary to ensure that the best interest rates and best spot market prices are obtained at the time when workers' funds are invested.
- Fiduciary accountability required for the management of third party funds.

Regulation of Derivatives

Derivative transactions by the Siefores are regulated jointly by CONSAR and the Central Bank of Mexico. Both financial authorities have issued prudential regulations determining the types of operations that may be conducted, with what parties, and in which markets they may take place. Central Bank regulations state that:

- Siefores may take long-term and short-term positions in swaps, futures, and options so long as the underlying securities are permitted in the investment framework.
- Derivative trades may take place in securities markets (derivatives markets) or over-the-counter markets (OTCs).
- Trading in derivatives whose underlying security is another derivative instrument is not permitted. Therefore, credit derivatives are forbidden. CONSAR will be the competent authority to issue prudential regulations and authorize Siefores to trade in derivatives.

CONSAR studied the best-known market cases that led to problems for derivative holders. These cases reveal that there are three major risk factors in derivative transactions:

1. Operational failures due to errors in the execution and recording of derivatives.
2. Excessive or uncontrolled positions, such as those arising from conflicts of interest between the front and back office, untrained staff,

inefficient measurement and risk control systems, and inadequate or nonexistent limits.
3. Failures of a legal nature (flawed contracts).

CONSAR's prudential regulations for derivative transactions in Circular 53 (CONSAR 2004e) seek to mitigate these risks. Before they can be authorized to engage in derivative transactions, pension funds must meet certain requirements regarding their investment processes, personnel, measurement and risk control, and legal requirements. Afores investment processes must be ISO 9000-certified to reduce operating risk to a minimum and ensure that:

- An overall operating strategy on derivatives is in place.
- Risk limits are established for transactions.
- Transactions have legal backing.
- The risk of each transaction and its contribution to portfolio risk are known before trading.
- Trading and settlement of transactions are consistently and properly recorded.
- A daily valuation of instruments is made.
- A daily monitoring of risks is made.

In addition, persons involved must have the necessary knowledge to carry out these types of transactions and must be certified by an independent third party. Afores must also fulfill minimum requirements in the areas of measurement and risk control systems. To this end, pension funds must have systems for the recording and valuation of positions and guarantees. They must also have risk measurement systems and incorporate an early-warning system in contingency planning to anticipate violations of both their own limits and legal regulations. Finally, they must calculate the marginal VaR of each new transaction and its contribution to total VaR.

The legal requirements define the general framework for derivative transactions and specify the counterparties with which Afores may trade. In securities markets this includes standard contract with the clearinghouses of the authorized markets and letter of confirmation for each transaction carried out. In OTC markets it implies trade with IOSCO member country intermediaries that qualify under the investment regulations and international Swap and Derivatives Association (ISDA) agreements or ISDA-type agreements (as the case may be).

To date, five Afores have met the regulatory requirements and are now authorized to trade in derivatives. In the near future, several more Afores may request authorization, given that investment in structured notes is more versatile and efficient through derivatives.

Finally, it should be emphasized that under CONSAR's prudential regulations on matters of investment, risks, and derivatives, it is CONSAR that defines *what* must be done, and each pension fund that determines *how* it shall be done. Both aspects should be reflected in the manuals on investments and risks.

Risk-based Supervision

In recent years, there has been a worldwide consensus on the need to conduct risk-based oversight of financial systems. The greatest progress has been made in the commercial banking sector, following the guidelines of the Basel Committee and lessons gleaned from the failures of major banks.

Pension fund supervision has progressed only recently, based on a set of best practices agreed upon and issued by the Working Group on Pensions of the Organisation for Economic Co-operation and Development (OECD). To facilitate their universal application, these best practices are general in nature and based on broad principles.

In the case of Mexico, it has been possible to establish a meticulously detailed risk-based oversight model because the retirement savings system (SAR) is regulated by a single authority that issues mandatory rules governing all pension fund managers.

Because oversight basically consists of ensuring compliance with current regulations by all participants at all times, the key to the Mexican risk-based oversight model has been designing regulations to control investment risks and strictly monitoring compliance with these regulations. In accordance with this approach, this oversight model is centered along three basic lines:

1. *Compliance with the investment framework.* Verification that regulatory limits are respected and that prohibited transactions or those involving conflicts of interest do not occur.
2. *Enforcement and compliance with prudential regulations.* Verification that regarding investment matters, the pension fund Afore is managed in a culture that has fully integrated risk management and best operating practices.

Figure 8.9. Financial Oversight

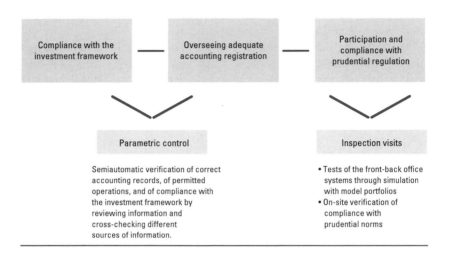

3. *Review of appropriate accounting records.* Ensure that on a daily basis, the price of Siefore shares reflects a fair value, to avoid undesirable or involuntary transfers among workers who are affiliated with the Afore or who switch to another pension fund. Depending on the nature of the matter under review, this oversight is conducted through monitoring actions or on-site inspections. Monitoring actions focus on investment portfolios, transactions, and account activity and are carried out based on information received daily by CONSAR. In addition, on-site inspections are conducted at the Afore's physical facilities and are geared to a review of everything that cannot be supervised through regular monitoring. A key aspect of the visits is to verify that the pension funds comply with the policies and procedures set forth in their investment and risk manuals. Figure 8.9 shows which aspects are overseen through monitoring and which are overseen through on-site inspections.

Risk Monitoring

CONSAR also performs risk analyses on Siefores' portfolios, in order to conduct proactive—rather than reactive—oversight. It is extremely useful for CONSAR to know the different risks in the portfolios to be able to identify the likelihood of their occurrence.

Moreover, through risk analyses, CONSAR serves as a laboratory for testing future investment and risk regulations. Some outcomes of this responsibility are:

- Analysis and monitoring of risk assumed by Siefores: mainly financial risks (market, credit, and liquidity) that could result from possible losses in financial markets
- Generation of information to be used by CONSAR and in aggregate form by the Afores: Reports on variables that affect the value of the investment portfolio, such as interest rates and exchange rates, are regularly generated to measure risk in the retirement investment funds' portfolios and the behavior of financial markets.

Concluding Remarks

CONSAR has spearheaded a set of regulatory changes that have generally loosened investment regulations while creating the infrastructure within the pension funds required for appropriate investment and risk management.

One of the hallmarks of investment deregulation is the elimination of various investment prohibitions and limits that had hampered the ability to cut risk and/or boost yields on savings deposited in individual accounts. Among the most noteworthy advances in this area are:

- The 35 percent ceiling on private sector bonds and the 10 percent ceiling on debt from financial intermediaries were eliminated.
- Both derivatives and bonds issued by states, municipalities, and government-controlled businesses were included in the scope of permissible securities.
- Foreign securities and equity instruments through structured notes were included in retirement investment funds' portfolios.
- Two types of Siefores retirement investment funds were formed, with different risk/return profiles to better suit the preferences and needs of affiliates.
- A VaR was introduced as a regulatory measure to control market risk.

In addition, there has also been significant improvement in the pension funds' infrastructure for handling investment and risk:

- A Risk Committee and Integrated Risk Management Unit were created.
- Best practices in investment matters have been implemented.
- The pension funds that have requested authorization to engage in derivative transactions have complied with prudential regulations on such transactions.

The bases for the institutional infrastructure to manage risk and investments were created within the pension funds before deregulation. This ensured that workers' pension funds would be managed appropriately, given the broader range of investment opportunities.

Finally, CONSAR's financial oversight was redirected toward compliance with new investment and risk regulations. Specifically, it sought to verify compliance with investment regulations and prudential rules and ensure that appropriate accounting records were maintained at the retirement investment funds. CONSAR thus developed its risk-based oversight of pension funds in tandem with commercial banking sector oversight.

The potential growth of the funds managed and the use of their funds are just two of the factors that pose significant challenges to financial authorities and the pension funds. The main challenges will be in developing three areas in parallel:

- Local financial markets with sufficient depth and sophistication to permit efficient investment of the ever-increasing pension fund savings
- World-class skills of the pension funds in investment of savings and controlling risk
- Investment regulations that promote the efficient creation of portfolios with high yields adjusted by risk level.

The various participants in the retirement savings system also face specific challenges. These challenges will require actions by CONSAR, the Afores, and other financial entities, including the Ministry of Finance (Secretaría de Hacienda y Crédito Público), the central bank (Banco de México), and other regulators such as those of the banking and securities (Comisión Nacional Bancaria y de Valores).

Challenges for CONSAR include:

- Adding new types of assets to improve diversification at a slow but steady pace, depending on the development of the pension fund managers' capabilities.

- Broadening the range of retirement investment funds to offer workers more investment options according to their age and risk/return preferences.
- Shifting from investment regulations, with certain constraints on the allowable classes of assets, to more effective regulations that set limits only by type of risk (market, credit, liquidity, and so on).
- Updating prudential regulations for investments, risk management, and conflicts of interest, as best international practices continue to evolve.
- Boosting competitiveness among pension funds through incentives to maximize absolute yields (as opposed to relative yields).

Challenges for the Afores include:

- Becoming institutional investors with world-class capabilities.
- Using the full potential of investment regulations to generate high yields for workers.
- Spreading the concept of fiduciary responsibility and the culture of risk management to all levels of the organization.

Challenges for the Mexican financial authorities include:

- Maintaining the framework of stability and economic growth conducive to long-term investment.
- Strengthening stock market regulation to protect investors, promote the disclosure of information, and reduce transaction costs.
- Resisting pressure from certain interest groups to use the regulation of institutional investors to engage in political grandstanding.

References

Federal Reserve Bank of Minneapolis. 1996. *Quarterly Review*, Vol. 20, No. 3, Summer 1996, pp.11–23.

National Retirement Savings Commission (CONSAR). 2004a. *Circular CONSAR 15–12* (May). Mexico D.F.

———. 2004b. *Circular CONSAR 45* (June). Mexico D.F.

———. 2004c. *Circular CONSAR 51* (June). Mexico D.F.

———. 2004d *Circular CONSAR 55–1*. (January). Mexico D.F.

———. 2004e. *Circular CONSAR 53* (January). Mexico D.F.

Srinivas, P.S., Edward Whitehouse, and Juan Yermo. 2000. Regulating Private Pension Funds' Structure, Performance and Investments: Cross-country Evidence. Social Protection Discussion Paper No. 0113. The World Bank, Washington, D.C.

CHAPTER 9

The Impact of Argentina's Economic Crisis on its Pension System

Rafael Rofman[*]

The pension system in Argentina is over a hundred years old and has developed into the most important social program in the country. It accounts for nearly 30 percent of public expenditures and pays benefits to nearly 3 million people. The system has undergone many reforms and has weathered several economic and political crises. The role of the pension system in the 2001–02 economic crisis—which resulted in serious political instability, a default in sovereign debt, and a 300 percent devaluation of the national currency in a few months—has been the subject of many debates in the last few years. This chapter explains the interrelationship of the crisis and the pension system, disentangling short-term problems from structural faults that need to be addressed in the near future.

Since the first occupational pension schemes were organized in Argentina in the early twentieth century, there have been many changes in design and regulations. However, during all these years, a guiding rule was always that benefits were granted to those who made contributions before retirement. The amount and duration of these contributions varied

---

[*] Rafael Rofman is a Senior Economist, Social Protection Unit, Latin America and the Caribbean Region, The World Bank. All comments and opinions expressed herein are the sole responsibility of the author.

widely, but the principle of requiring contributions to qualify for a benefit survived almost one century. The rationale behind this was that most workers were part of the formal labor force. Thus requiring contributions was a simple way to identify workers and, at the same time, ensure that those who would benefit from the system would also finance it.

While Argentina has always had one of the largest coverage rates in Latin America,[1] demographic aging, fiscal pressures, and declining formality in the labor markets resulted in successive crisis and reforms. The 1994 reform introduced a funded scheme, creating some new opportunities to solve the long-term problems but, at the same time, generating new challenges to the sustainability of the system. The 2001 crisis affected nearly all activities in the country, including the pension system. In addition, the dynamics of the labor market in the last 25 years have resulted in a declining proportion of formal workers, a problem that has been compounded by the increase in unemployment rates.

This chapter reviews the situation before the crisis, the effects the crisis had on the system, and the challenges that will continue to affect it after many of the short-term problems are resolved. The discussion is organized in seven sections. Following this introduction, the second section briefly describes the history of the pension system in Argentina, the 1994 reform, and its performance since then. The third section presents a short description of the economic crisis, discussing some of its fiscal and financial aspects in some detail. The fourth section notes some of the effects the crisis had on the pension system, and the fifth section assesses some of these effects in the short and long term. The sixth section discusses some ideas on pension policy strategy for the future, aiming to reconsider the design of the system. The seventh section presents a few conclusions.

The History of the Argentine Pension System

The System Before the 1994 Reform

The first pension system in Argentina was created in 1904 and covered civil servants. In the years that followed, many occupational schemes

---

[1] Coverage among the elderly peaked at more than 75 percent in the early 1990s, and then began to decline. This high coverage among retirees has not been matched by active workers, as contributors rarely exceeded half (50 percent) the labor force at any point in time.

were introduced, although they usually covered few workers. By the mid-1940s, only 7 percent of the labor force was protected by social security. A wide range of heterogeneous schemes also existed, where retirement age could be as low as 47 years, contributions totaled around 8 percent of salaries, and benefits were as high as 90 percent of the last salary. Most of these schemes claimed to be funded, but in most cases their long-term financial condition was weak. During the late 1940s and most of the 1950s, the system rapidly expanded and became more homogeneous. A 1958 law established that benefits should be 82 percent of the wage of active workers in similar jobs, but no significant increase in contribution rates or retirement age was enacted.

As a result of the 1958 parametric changes, the various funds faced serious financial problems by the mid-1960s. This led to the enactment of legislation that consolidated most previously existing funds into only three at the national level: civil servants; self-employed; and manufacturing, commerce, and others. The legislation also increased the minimum retirement age to 60 years for men and 55 for women and increased contribution rates to a total of 20 percent (5 percent from the employees, 15 percent from the employers). Other schemes run by the provincial governments for civil servants and special independent activities continued operating with variable financial outcomes.

The structure adopted in the late 1960s remained financially sound for approximately 15 years. By the early 1980s, the system had increasing deficits, financed in part by illegal manipulations of cost-of-living adjustments to benefits. This strategy resulted in massive lawsuits against the government, which were systematically won by the retirees.

By the early 1990s, the need for reform was undeniable. The deficit of the national system, which had never exceeded 1 percent of GDP in the previous years, escalated to 1.7 percent by 1993. The provincial systems and other special schemes added another 2 percent to the consolidated balance deficit. The strategy of avoiding benefit increases was backfiring, and the accumulated debt to pensioners was estimated at 3 percent of GDP. Moreover, increasing informality and unemployment resulted in insufficient collections. At this point, with the ability of the system to pay benefits seriously weakened, the fiscal situation deteriorating, and the institutional structure of the pension system seriously deficient, the government prepared a proposal to reform the system and introduced it to congress in 1992.

The Reform[2]

After a lengthy discussion in congress, a new law was passed in October 1993 and the new system started operating in July 1994. The main reforms included changes in the parameters of the system and in the institutional arrangements. The most relevant parametric reforms were an increase in employee contribution rates (from 10 to 11 percent), an increase in the minimum retirement age (from 60 to 65 years for men, and from 55 to 60 years for women), an increase in the number of years of contributions required to qualify for retirement benefits (from 20 to 30 years), and a reduction in the expected replacement rate (from 70 to 82 percent of the average of the last three years of wages to an average of approximately 60 percent of the last ten years of wages, with a strong redistributive formula). All these changes were to be introduced gradually, with the first one fully enacted by 2001, the second one by 2007, and the last one after approximately a forty-year transition period.

Institutionally, the new system is organized in two pillars. A first pillar, financed with employer contributions of 16 percent, grants a flat defined benefit of around 28 percent of average wages to those who satisfy requirements regarding minimum age and years of contributions. The second pillar provides a benefit linked to previous contributions, and is managed by the State (through a pay-as-you-go scheme) or by a private pension fund manager (through an individual account). Workers are allowed to choose. However, those who do not make an explicit choice are assigned to the private funded scheme. Expected benefits from this pillar are at around 30 percent of the last salary (with some variance on the funded scheme, depending on actual contributions and returns on investments). A transitional benefit was created to compensate for years of contributions before 1994, and paid to all retiring workers, as long as they had a minimum of 30 years of contributions to any system (Figure 9.1).

The System After the Reform

The reform enacted in 1993–94 was made to confront the growing crisis of the pension system. The main goals of these reforms were to promote formality in the labor market (to expand coverage and increase collection), contain the growing fiscal cost of the system, and create the basic conditions for a strong development of the local capital market. The outcome for each of these three areas is described below.

---

[2] For a detailed description of the new system, see Rofman (2000).

Figure 9.1. The Pension System in Argentina after the 1994 Reform

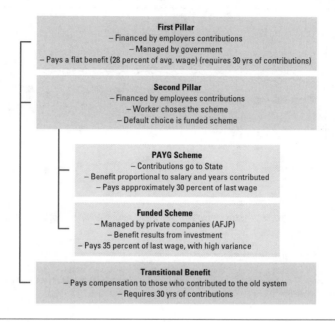

Formality and Coverage

The new system was strongly promoted, both by the government and by the new pension fund managing companies (known as AFJPs, for their Spanish acronym). When the system first went into effect, active workers were given the choice of joining the new PAYG scheme or the funded scheme, which was the default choice. The AFJPs undertook an important marketing effort, mobilizing a sales force of almost 30,000, and spending more than half a billion dollars in marketing and sales commissions in the first few months. This effort resulted in an enrollment of 2.2 million workers in the AFJPs, while 270,000 workers chose the PAYG scheme. Approximately 800,000 workers who made no choice were randomly assigned to an AFJP, for a total of 5.7 million workers registered in the new system. Even considering enrollment in provincial and other special systems, coverage was low given a labor force of 14 million people. However, the number of pension fund members continued to grow, reaching 8.8 million by the end of 2001 and almost 9.5 million

Figure 9.2. Labor Force, Individuals Enrolled in the Pension System and Contributors, 1994–2003

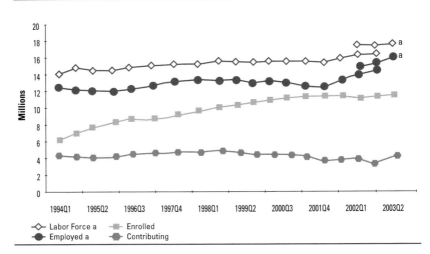

a. Beginning in late 2002, a new labor force survey produced higher estimates of the labor force and those employed.
Source: Author's calculations based on data from the Superintendencia de AFJP (SAFJP) and the Permanent Household Survey (EHP).

by the end of 2003, and bringing the total number of enrolled workers to 11.5 million by the end of 2003. Of the 5.8 million workers who joined the reformed system, nearly 4 million did not make an explicit choice to join the funded scheme but were randomly assigned to an AFJP.

The increase in the number of registered workers was not accompanied by an increase in the number of actual contributors,[3] which remained around 4 to 4.5 million from 1993–94 to the present, with a sharp decline during the 2001 crisis and a later recovery (Figure 9.2). The analysis of individual compliance with the system indicates that most of the workers enrolled after the reform have very short periods of formal employment and then move to the informal sector or leave the labor force altogether.

While participation in the system among younger workers did not increase after the reform, stricter requirements for obtaining benefits re-

---

[3] This problem appears to be common in most Latin American countries, and is caused by the high rotation between formality, informality, unemployment, and inactivity among working age individuals. As a result, the number of registered workers tends to increase over time (for example, in Chile it reaches more than 120 percent of the labor force), but that does not imply increases in the number of contributors over time.

Figure 9.3. Population 65 and Older Without Coverage, 1990-2003

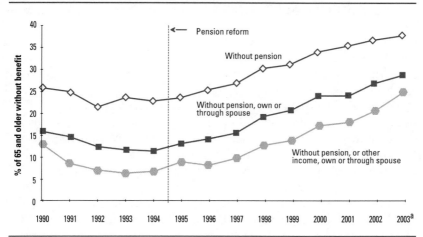

a. Data for 2003 are provisional.
Source: Bertranou and Rofman (2002); author's calculations based on the Household Survey (EHP).

sulted in a decline of coverage among older individuals. By 1993, 23 percent of the population over 65 was not covered by the pension system. Ten years later, that percentage had increased to 37.3 percent. Similarly, only 12.5 percent of the elderly population had no benefit at all, either through their own account or their spouses. Ten years later, that percentage had risen to 26.5 percent. A related indicator, the proportion of the elderly population with no pension and no other source of income, increased dramatically from 7.4 percent in 1993 to 23.8 percent in 2003 (Figure 9.3).

The Fiscal Situation

While most workers joined the funded scheme (either by choice or default), the government still paid most benefits. Benefits to all workers who retired prior to the reform, plus the first pillar and the transitional benefits for all new retirees, were financed by the government and paid through the government pension agency (ANSES).[4] There were also other pressures on the fiscal deficit, which caused it to increase. One

---

[4] Workers retiring after 1994 from the new funded scheme receive part of their benefit from it but, in the first two decades, most of the benefit will come from the first pillar and the transitional benefit.

of these was a policy to integrate provincial schemes into the national system, which resulted in increased federal expenditures. Another was lower revenue as a result of reductions in employer contribution rates, which was part of a labor market competitiveness policy adopted by the government. As a result, ANSES was able to finance less than 30 percent of pension benefits through contributions. The rest was covered with general revenue and other earmarked taxes.

The fiscal effect of the reform can be ascertained by estimating the revenue lost in personal contributions that used to go to the PAYG scheme but are now financing the funded scheme.[5] Using this approach, the fiscal cost by the year 2003 was close to 1 percent of GDP (Table 9.1). However, it is important also to take into consideration the effect of the parametric reforms, which reduced expenditures.[6] Assuming that expenditures should have grown by 3 percent a year,[7] benefit payments in 2003 should have been approximately 1 percent of GDP—more than was the case. Thus the net effect of the reform was close to zero. Other policies, such as the reduction in employer contributions (0.9 percent of GDP by 2003) and the cost of transferring the provincial systems to ANSES (0.4 percent of GDP), had an impact on ANSES finances.

In short, by 2003 the 1994 reform was causing ANSES a loss of approximately 1 percent of GDP, but it was also resulting in an equivalent saving in expenditures and, therefore, an overall neutral effect. On the other hand, ANSES had an additional deficit of 1.3 percent of GDP resulting from other policies, which should not be attributed to the pension reform.

The Funded Scheme

The funded scheme, created in 1994 has had a short history, making it difficult to assess its performance. About 80 percent of formal workers are enrolled in this scheme, but actual contributors are well below 25 percent of the labor force. Funds have accumulated since the system started and by the end of 2003 represented 11.8 percent of GDP. Real

---

[5] The estimate of this "loss in revenues" results from applying a 10 percent contribution rate (the rate applied to all workers before the reform) to the salaries of workers enrolled in the funded scheme. Actual rates for these workers have varied from 11 percent in 1993–2001 to 5 percent in most of 2002 and 7 percent since early 2003.

[6] Benefits were scaled down in 1995. Law 24.463 limited total payments to retirees to the amount budgeted each year by congress and also capped the amounts paid.

[7] This estimate is based on an increase in the retirement age population of 1.5 percent a year and an increase in average benefits of 1.5 percent a year.

Table 9.1 Fiscal Effects of Pension Reform and Other Related Policies. 1993–2003

(percent)

Year	Transition cost			Other policies affecting the pension system			TOTAL EFFECT
	Losses in revenues	Savings in expenditures	"Pure" transition cost	Reduction in employers contributions	Costs of transferred provincial systems	Total other policies	
1993	0.0	0.0	0.0	0.0	0.0	0.0	0.0
1994	0.3	0.1	0.1	0.4	0.2	0.6	0.8
1995	0.8	0.3	0.6	0.4	0.2	0.6	1.2
1996	1.0	0.4	0.6	0.8	0.6	1.4	2.0
1997	1.2	0.5	0.7	0.8	0.6	1.4	2.1
1998	1.3	0.6	0.7	0.8	0.6	1.3	2.0
1999	1.4	0.8	0.6	1.1	0.6	1.7	2.3
2000	1.4	0.9	0.4	1.5	0.6	2.0	2.5
2001	1.5	1.2	0.2	1.6	0.6	2.2	2.4
2002	1.1	1.0	0.1	1.0	0.4	1.4	1.5
2003	1.0	1.0	0.0	0.9	0.4	1.3	1.3

Source: Author's calculations based on data from ANSES and AFIP.

annual average returns on these funds have been higher than expected (10.5 percent). Both the actual value of funds and the returns have been the object of a controversy surrounding the valuation criteria for some assets, as will be discussed later. Although the scheme is still relatively young, the number of beneficiaries has grown, and by the end of 2003 reached almost 150,000, including retirees, disabled, and survivors. This figure is approximately 5 percent of the number of beneficiaries under the old PAYG system.

Two of the most serious problems in the funded scheme have been the operating costs (and commissions charged to workers) and the exposure to sovereign risk from holdings of bonds issued by the Argentine government. From the creation of the system until 2001, commissions averaged 3 to 3.5 percent of taxable wages, a level considered too high by many observers. Commissions were reduced in late 2001, partly as a result of a change in insurance regulations, but they have increased since then. In addition, about 50 percent of the assets of the AFJPs have been invested in government bonds since the system was established (Table 9.2). The only exception was 1997, when term deposits grew quickly in the form of stocks derivatives and investments in stocks were also large. The concentration of risk, usually explained by the lack of alternatives and the high yields of government bonds, made the pension funds extremely vulnerable to the government's fiscal problems. The crisis of 2001 and subsequent valuation problems pushed this percentage to a much higher level, although it began to decline again in 2003.

The Crisis

Even though the purpose of this chapter is to discuss the relationship between the pension system and the economic crisis in Argentina, it is necessary to consider the context in which the crisis developed. Argentina's fiscal and financial problems in late 2001 and 2002 had important links to the pension system. This section provides a basic description of these aspects. The role or final outcome of some factors described here is not yet clear. Nevertheless, the discussion provides a reasonable review of the most relevant processes taking place in Argentina's economy since 2001.

The Fiscal Crisis

Argentina has had serious fiscal problems for many years. The different levels of government (federal, provincial, and municipal) have been unable to

Table 9.2	Investment Structure of Pension Funds, 1994–2003

(percent)

	Dec 94	Dec 95	Dec 96	Dec 97	Dec 98	Dec 99	Dec 00	Dec 01	Dec 02	Dec 03
Cash accounts	6.33	1.68	1.83	0.98	1.52	0.97	0.28	2.23	1.26	1.54
Government debt	49.83	52.68	52.70	43.36	49.99	52.30	54.62	67.97	76.69	68.15
Corporate debt	5.84	8.71	7.78	2.86	2.50	2.13	2.80	1.69	1.06	1.54
Term deposits	27.55	24.76	14.19	24.44	18.83	15.47	15.63	10.89	2.56	3.22
Stocks	1.53	5.85	18.74	21.46	18.36	20.54	12.26	10.24	6.54	11.82
Mutual funds	5.01	1.74	2.34	4.47	6.59	6.28	8.21	1.97	1.10	2.37
Foreign investment	0.08	0.73	0.16	0.37	0.25	0.37	4.47	1.84	8.92	9.71
Other	3.82	3.86	2.26	2.06	1.97	1.93	1.73	3.16	1.87	1.65
TOTAL	100.00	100.00	100.00	100.00	100.00	100.00	100.00	100.00	100.00	100.00

Source: SAFJP (2004).

balance their budgets, partly because of increased expenditures and, more importantly, because of their inability to collect taxes efficiently.

During most of the 1990s, the deficits were financed with revenues from privatization and an increasing federal and provincial debt. The situation was difficult but manageable until an economic recession seriously affected revenues, interest on the accumulated debts increased the debt burden significantly, and international emerging financial markets became tighter. Figure 9.4 shows that aggregate public expenditures were very stable during the 1990s, reaching 30 to 32 percent of GDP, and that after 1998 they began growing, reaching 35 percent of GDP in 2001. Most of the growth was due to debt servicing, which rose from 1.6 percent of GDP in 1990 to 5.3 in 2001. However, pension expenditures (including ANSES expenditures, as well as those of the provincial and municipal schemes) remained very stable at around 8 percent of GDP (although this figure was larger than the 5.3 percent average of the 1980s).

In 2001, when the Argentine economy slipped into recession, fiscal pressures became unsustainable. Federal tax revenues declined by 9 percent, forcing the government to attempt a severe cut in expenditures, while promoting better tax compliance and increased consumption to spur economic growth. These policies were not always consistent. For example, in November 2001, the contributions of employees to the pen-

Figure 9.4. Aggregate Public Expenditures, 1990–2002

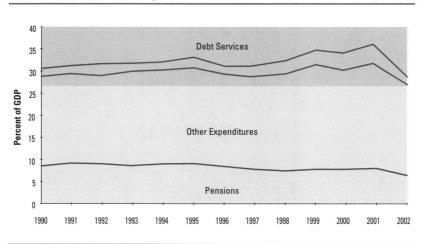

Note: The figure includes federal, provincial, and municipal expenditures.
Source: Ministerio de Economía (2003).

sion system were reduced from 11 to 5 percent of wages in an attempt to increase consumer demand. Unfortunately, this led to a reduction in social security revenues and had to be reversed for those in the PAYG scheme one month later.

Tax collections fell rapidly in the second half of 2001 and the first few months of 2002. The drop in collections was particularly large for the value added tax (VAT), which is the country's most important source of tax revenues. Social security revenues also fell, but less significantly. The lack of resources prompted reductions in civil servants' salaries and pension benefits. In July 2001, pensions higher than $500 were reduced by 13 percent, and the nominal wages and pensions of civil servants were barely adjusted for inflation in 2002, when that indicator reached more than 40 percent.

The fiscal crisis ended in a formal default of government debt payments in late December 2001 and the abandonment of the peso/dollar exchange rate. The federal and most provincial governments were not able to finance their current expenditures and started to issue low denomination bonds, to be used as cash. These bonds, issued by 14 of the 24 provinces, became standard currency in some areas of the economy but were not accepted in others, further deteriorating tax collection and reinforcing a negative circle. All in all, tax revenues in the last quarter of 2001 and first quarter of 2002 were 23 percent below those of a year earlier, and per capita GDP was almost 25 percent lower than four years earlier.

The Financial Crisis

While the fiscal problems were growing, the banking sector in Argentina suffered an increasing run on deposits. Total deposits fell 22 percent between February and November 2001. This decline prompted the government to strongly limit cash withdrawals and international transfers of funds in December 2001. Even so, deposits continued to decline, with a total loss of nearly 47 percent by April 2002. The default in government debt, the devaluation of the peso (which fell almost 70 percent in three months), and the "pesification"[8] of all local deposits and loans accelerated the crisis. Thousands of individual account holders have sued the banks and the government in order to reassert their deposits in dollars.

---

[8] After the devaluation, the government decided to convert U.S. dollar-denominated deposits into pesos at an exchange rate of 1.40 pesos per dollar, and convert loans at an exchange rate of 1 peso per dollar. This asymmetric conversion and the fact that external debt was not affected put most banks in an extremely vulnerable position.

Figure 9.5. Per Capita GDP, Unemployment, and Poverty
(Headcount Index, 1992–2004)

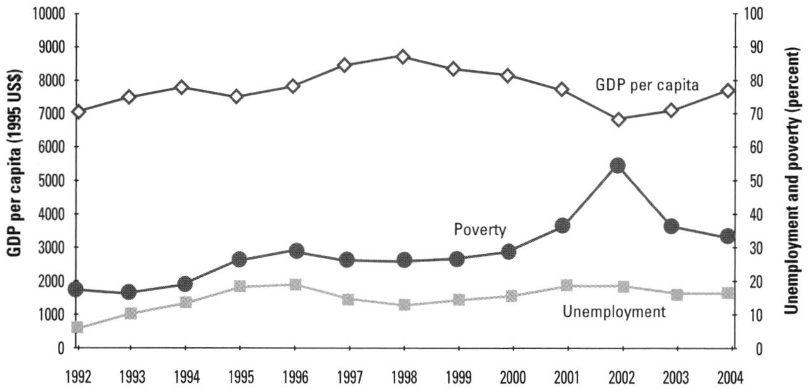

Source: INDEC (2001); Ministerio de Economía (2003).

In many cases, banks were forced to return the deposits in hard currency. While deposits recovered in 2003 and 2004,[9] the financial system is still under serious stress and lacks public confidence.

The Economic and Labor Market Crisis

During the past few decades, the Argentine economy has fluctuated widely between periods of growth, deep recessions and crises. After growing rapidly in the early 1990s, the tequila crisis of 1995 pushed it into a short recession. Growth recovered and continued until 1998, when per capita GDP reached a peak of $8,670 (in constant 1995 U.S. dollars). Since then, what began as a slow decline became a major crisis in 2001–02 that resulted in a plunge in per capita GDP to only $6,840, a peak-to-trough decline of 21 percent (Figure 9.5). The economy recovered in 2003 and 2004, but per capita GDP in 2004 is still expected to be approximately 11 percent below the 1998 peak.

The labor market closely mirrored overall economic activity, falling when the economy declined and recovering when GDP improved. The

[9] Deposits grew by almost 40 percent per year. They reached the early-2001 level by the end of 2003 and by mid-2004 were 20 percent higher.

incidence of poverty also followed the same pattern, although the recovery phases were much weaker than the periods of decline, resulting in a significant increase in long-term poverty.

The Effect of the Crisis on the Pension System

The deep fiscal and financial crisis affected the pension system several ways. It weakened the institutions and performance of the system, worsening the problems that existed before the crisis and creating new ones. Two types of impacts can be considered: those directly produced by the downturn in the fiscal, financial, and labor markets; and those resulting from the many regulatory changes implemented as a reaction to the crisis.

Fiscal, Financial, and Labor Market Impacts

The combination of growing unemployment, increasing informality, and declining tax compliance resulted in a reduction in the number of contributors and total funds collected. The number of workers contributing to social security declined by approximately 25 percent from its 1998 peak. Part of this decline can be attributed to changes in the regulatory framework (beginning in late 1999, some workers were excluded from contributing), but the decline was also caused by the crisis. Another very important effect was the loss in the value of government bonds that took place when Argentina defaulted on part of its debt. The default affected two-thirds of the government bonds held by the pension funds, or approximately half (50 percent) of their total assets. However, because most government bonds were not valued at market prices but followed a technical criterion for daily valuation, the immediate effect on pension funds value was small. Valuation problems and lack of liquidity had other important effects, especially when transfers of funds were involved. Insurance companies faced restrictions in paying benefits and switching among pension funds became controversial. Pension managers were supposed to transfer cash when workers switched funds, but they did not always have access to enough liquid resources to do so.

Regulatory Impacts

Government attempts to limit the effects of the crisis on the pension system or elsewhere also created problems of their own. Many "urgent" measures were adopted, weakening the basic framework of the system. Pension schemes are designed to operate in the medium and long term, and short-term adjustments usually have long-lasting negative effects. The institutional design of the system was damaged when established roles and procedures were abandoned or disrupted during the crisis. For example, the Superintendency of AFJPs (SAFJP), whose main responsibility was to supervise the private managers and enforce the pension legislation, became a de facto intermediary in the financial negotiations between pension funds and Ministry of Finance officials—ignoring, at least at the highest levels, the needs and interests of participants. At the same time, the Secretary of Social Security, who is formally in charge of designing pension policy, had a limited role in the design and implementation of most measures.

A large number of "urgent" policies implemented in the last few months of 2001 and early 2002 had a direct impact on the pension system. Most of these policies required a change in basic legislation, but instead of being studied and publicly approved by congress, they were enacted by decree due to "exceptional" circumstances. These exceptional procedures made the system highly volatile. The changes affected many aspects of the system, including the value of current benefits, contribution rates, investment rules, and pension fund commissions. While some of these issues needed to be reviewed and revised or improved, the procedures established to do so rarely involved adequate analysis and proper normative tools. In several cases, important changes were "hidden" within larger decrees. In others, major reforms were enacted by lower regulatory authorities, using technicalities to justify them. Some of the most important changes introduced in the system dealt with benefits, contributions, insurance costs, government debt, and funded scheme costs.

Benefits

- Benefits in the PAYG scheme were reduced by 13 percent in mid-2001 to reduce public expenditures. This reduction was eliminated in September 2002, and funds were reimbursed to beneficiaries.
- A new maximum benefit for current pensioners was established, reducing it from AR$3,100 to AR$2,400 a month in December 2001. It was eliminated in February 2002.
- Benefits in the PAYG scheme were not adjusted between December 2001 and September 2004 (when they were increased by 10 percent). During this same period, inflation increased by 50 percent. This large loss in real value resulted in a rapid improvement of the system's fi-

nances, as revenues increased. While benefits in general were not adjusted, the minimum was increased by slightly more than 100 percent in the same period. As a result, the percentage of beneficiaries receiving the minimum benefit rose from 10 to 44 percent.

- In January 2002, new beneficiaries in the funded scheme were banned for 60 days from buying annuities denominated in U.S. dollars, due to the lack of clear valuation criteria for pension fund assets. This restriction has been extended at least 10 times since then, and in October 2004 a new resolution established a permanent prohibition on issuing annuities in foreign currencies. However, no requirement to use a transparent indexation criterion has been incorporated into the system, leaving beneficiaries exposed to high inflation risks.

Contributions

- Beginning in November 2001, employees' contribution rates were reduced from 11 to 5 percent for a period of one year. After a few weeks, the fiscal limitations made it necessary to increase the rate back to 11 percent for workers in the PAYG scheme. The reduction in funded scheme fees was extended for another year, changed to 7 percent in early 2003, and then extended again at that level until July 2005.
- In November 2001, the government created the National Institute of Social Security Collection (INARSS), a new organization in charge of collecting social security contributions, with private participation in its board. INARSS was dissolved in July 2003 and collections assigned back to the tax authority.

Insurance Costs

- A technical change in the insurance policies brought the cost of insurance premiums for the year 2001–02 to almost zero, as payments were postponed. This was approved in November 2001 and made retroactive to July 2001. However, payments made to insurance companies between July and October 2001 (approximately $200 million) were not reimbursed.

Government Debt

- In November 2001, a swap of government bonds held by domestic investors, mostly banks and pension funds, was approved. A "guaranteed loan" was issued in exchange for the old bonds (which had market value and were regularly traded in the local stock market and in New York). These new instruments had a lower interest rate and no secondary market, making their valuation more subjective. The swap was voluntary, but with strong political pressure from the government and the pension funds supervisor.

- In October 2001, the government issued a decree ordering that all money invested in CDs by pension funds had to be used to buy Treasury bills directly from the government.
- In March 2002 the government decided to convert the guaranteed loans (denominated in U.S. dollars) into pesos at an exchange rate of 1.4 pesos per dollar. These new loans are indexed to inflation and yielded an annual interest rate of between 3 and 5.5 percent. The first scheduled interest payment was made in April 2002 and the Supervisor of Pension Funds applied the 1.4 exchange rate to valuation on April 15, resulting in an instant return of the funds of about 30 percent. All but one of the pension funds refused to accept payment, citing a breach of contract.
- In August 2003, the government issued a new decree canceling the conversion for those that had not accepted it. Consequently, pension fund assets that had rejected the conversion reverted to the defaulted bonds and stopped accruing interest (although they continued to be valued at technical values).
- In October 2004, as part of the government debt renegotiation process, the pension fund managers and the Ministry of Finance agreed on a program to swap all defaulted obligations for new bonds. This agreement establishes that all defaulted government assets owned by pension funds or managing companies will be exchanged for peso denominated bonds, with a face value of approximately 70 percent of the face value of original assets and a maturity period of 42 years. (In the case of Treasury bills bought as a consequence of the October 2001 decree, the bonds will have a maturity of 10 years.) The agreement also establishes that the new assets will continue to be valued at technical prices, to avoid sudden shocks to quota values.

Funded Scheme Costs

- In November 2001, an Urgent Decree modified the fee structure of the funded scheme, eliminating flat fees and authorizing funds to charge an insurance fee to workers with no contributions in a given month (this applies under limited circumstances), and a fixed fee on annual returns over 5 percent.

- The fee on returns created in November was "suspended" sine die in February 2002.

Short- and Long-Term Effects of the Crisis

The crisis in Argentina had clear effects on the pension system. Some of them were short-term, and their influence was felt only during the crisis or shortly afterward. Others were long-term, in the sense that they affect the basic design aspects of the system and, as such, need to be addressed as part of a review of the fundamentals of the model.

Short-term implications of the economic crisis on the PAYG system include reductions in current benefits for some retirees and in real benefits for most retirees, except those who were receiving very low benefits. Adjustments in PAYG benefits were discretionary because there is no indexation rule in place—a problem that was only theoretical during most of the 1990s, when there was no inflation, but became relevant after the devaluation.

Valuation problems and low liquidity had serious effects on the funded scheme because authorities suspended new annuities contracts, forced pension funds to accept in-kind financial transfers, and produced undesired wealth transfers among workers, beneficiaries, insurance companies, and pension managers. As the new government bonds are issued and they begin to be traded, supervisory guidelines should bring the valuation of these assets closer to their actual market value. Private estimates indicate that, at the time of the exchange, the new assets in the pension funds portfolio will be overvalued on average by approximately 50 percent. Because these bonds represent approximately 50 percent of the portfolios, the total overvaluation of the pension funds is approximately 25 percent. Once the new bonds start trading, if their perceived value increases as Argentina concludes default negotiations satisfactorily and economic recovery continues, the overvaluation should be reduced and, eventually, disappear.

The economic crisis created some serious new problems. The recovery is slowly solving some of them, but also deepened preexisting one, which are not likely to be easily solved by economic recovery. Correcting these problems will require deeper policy actions. The low and declining coverage of the pension system is probably one of the most critical issues facing the system today. Since the creation of the new system in 1994, the number of contributors has been very stable, at around 4 to 4.5 million workers (the figure would be about 1.5 million higher if those contributing to provincial or special schemes were included). During the crisis, the number of contributors fell by as much as 20 percent. By late 2003, the number of contributors was back to the historical level, yet continued growth in the labor force resulted in a decline in the coverage rate (from about 30 percent to less than 25 percent).

The recovery in economic activity in 2003–04 has brought down unemployment, but the experience of the 1990s indicates that a rapid reduction in labor market informality should not be expected. Low participation appears to be a structural economic problem and not directly linked to Argentina's labor market policies.[10] This situation is similar in most countries in Latin America, where coverage rarely exceeds 50 percent of the labor force.[11]

Projected old age pension coverage for the next 20 years highlights the seriousness of the situation. The proportion of the population older than 65 without benefits is anticipated to grow from the current level of 33 percent to more than 50 percent (Figure 9.6).

The fiscal situation was one of the positive outcomes of the crisis. Expenditures on pensions in Argentina have declined since 2001, when aggregate spending (including provincial and municipal spending) reached slightly over 8 percent of GDP. It is estimated that total spending in 2004 will be below 6 percent of GDP. This provides an opportunity to design and implement policies.

The most serious problems that will remain in the funded scheme once the defaulted assets are exchanged are similar to those present before the crisis. These include inadequate financial risk diversification, high administrative costs, poor competition and transparency, delays in granting benefits, and lack of independence of the supervision. Even though much has been said, these issues need to be addressed because the crisis appears to have exacerbated some of their worst aspects.

---

[10] It is interesting to consider the evolution of the number of contributors to the system between 1993 and 1999, before the financial crisis started. In this period, regardless of major changes in the pension system, including large reductions in employers' contributions, the enactment of several policies to promote employment, and significant economic cycles, the number of contributors remained almost constant, indicating that changes in the labor market in Argentina occur mostly in the informal sector (Rofman 1999). This explanation does not seem to be applicable in other Latin American countries, where econometric studies have found a stronger link between individual account contributory systems and worker participation (Packard 2001; Valdes-Prieto 2001).

[11] Chile is the only Latin American country where more than 50 percent of the active population contributes regularly to the pension system, with a rate estimated at 58 percent for 1999 (Arenas de Mesa and Hernández Sánchez 2001).

Figure 9.6. Population 65 and Older Without Coverage, 1990–2025

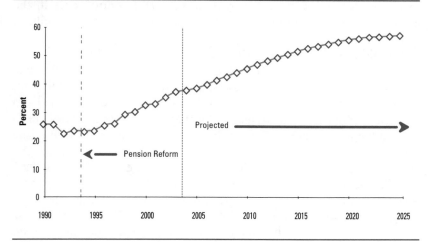

Source: Author's estimates, based on the Permanent Household Survey (EPH) and Rofman, Stirparo, and Lattes (1997).

Overall, there seems to be a serious, and worsening, institutional problem. The roles of various government agencies have slowly begun to overlap as power struggles led some agencies to take over the responsibilities of others. This is particularly the case with the Secretary of Social Security. Despite the fact that the secretary holds a rank similar to that of vice-minister, reporting directly to the minister of labor, his/her role has been diminished by the direct involvement in policy debates of the director of the Social Security Administration (who reports to the secretary) and officials at the Ministry of the Economy (who are not supposed to have a role in pension policy design).

An Agenda for the Future

The previous sections presented a quick review of the design and performance of the pension system before the economic crisis in Argentina and an overview of the main aspects of this crisis and its consequences. While understanding the causes of the problems is very important, effort should now be concentrated on building a stronger, more efficient pension system.

The basic rationale of pension systems is to provide a reasonable income for those who are too old to continue working. Definitions of what is a "reasonable income" and what is the best institutional organization to provide it are, of course, subject to important controversies in the academic and political arenas. Finding the best technical and political solution is a complex task.

Policymakers who design pension systems are limited by three competing goals: to provide the highest possible benefit to the largest possible number of beneficiaries at the lowest possible cost. Before the 1994 reforms, Argentina had a system that provided medium to low benefits to a large share of the population at a cost that was increasing and increasingly difficult to finance. The reform was clearly aimed at solving the problem of cost in the medium term, mostly by reducing coverage. At the same time, it shifted part of the risk of future cost increases from the State to individuals by moving from a government-financed, defined benefit scheme to a mixed scheme with an important private sector role and a design that included defined contribution elements. This change was expected to promote compliance (because it strengthened the link between contributions and future benefits), which would, in turn, compensate for the loss of coverage due to stricter requirements.

As discussed earlier, some, but not all, of the reform's goals were successfully achieved. As Figure 9.4 shows, fiscal costs acted as a drag on growth. In addition, instead of improving, participation deteriorated, and coverage declined. This is critical, since a pension system that fails to cover a large proportion of the population is not doing its job and becomes questionable.

Argentina needs a new, more stable pension system that maintains the multipillar approach, but differentiates the roles of each pillar more clearly and makes them more efficient. While maintaining fiscal and social costs under control, the new system should provide minimum income security to all retirees and income replacement (with some proportionality to pre-retirement income) to the largest possible share of the population.

The aim of the first pillar should be to provide minimum income security. This pillar should be non-contributive and have universal access based on age. For example, each resident aged 65 or older would receive a flat benefit of close to 25 percent of the average wage. This benefit would be structured in such a way that it would guarantee that all beneficiaries would receive an income above the poverty line.

This type of universal benefit faces opposition for two reasons. First, some question whether it is reasonable to pay a flat benefit to individuals with higher incomes. A means-tested benefit that would be easier to finance is proposed as an alternative. Yet there are reasons to prefer universal coverage to a means-tested benefit. First, the income distribution curve among the elderly is strongly skewed to the left, meaning that most older individuals have little or no income of their own, and the number that could be excluded because they are relatively rich is too small. This is not necessarily the case of the wealth distribution, but measuring wealth is complicated and raises practical considerations. For example, older individuals may not be able to easily convert their stock of wealth into cash flows.

The second argument against the universal benefit has to do with its operational simplicity, since eligibility would be only a matter of age. In addition, universal benefits are likely to be more politically popular than a program aimed only at poorer individuals. Finally, fiscal concerns regarding universal benefits can be addressed through a well-designed income tax program to recover benefits to relatively more well-off individuals.

The third argument against the universal benefit is a fiscal one. It refers to whether the government will be able to pay the benefits and how it will obtain the resources to do so. Table 9.3 presents an estimate of the number of beneficiaries and the potential cost of a flat benefit as of 2004. If a monthly benefit of AR$225 (the poverty line as of mid-2003) were to be paid to every citizen aged 65 and older, the total cost, as of 2003, would be slightly more than 9.8 billion pesos, which is equivalent to 2.5 percent of GDP or 61 percent of current pension expenditures. While it is not legally or politically possible to replace the old system immediately, it is important to point out that the potential total cost would be less than current costs. Nevertheless, establishment of a new system would require a transition period. A very proactive approach, granting this benefit immediately to every individual over the age of 65 who currently has no benefits, would cost 3.6 billion pesos, or 0.9 percent of GDP.

A smoother transition program that starts immediately but covers those aged 75 and older would cost slightly more than 1.2 billion pesos, or 0.3 percent of GDP. A phased-in change in the system where universal coverage is available for those 65 and over is also possible. The second panel of Table 9.3 shows that by the year 2025 the flat benefit would cost 1.8 percent of GDP (assuming an annual GDP growth rate of 3 percent a year from 2003 on) although, since almost 44 percent of those older than 65 will still receive pension benefits from the current scheme, the actual incremental cost would be of only 1 percent of GDP.

While the first pillar would provide basic income security to the elderly, a second pillar would offer income replacement at a reasonable rate. Both are also necessary if the system limits income and consumption levels decline as middle-income individuals retire. This pillar should be strictly contributive, reducing cross subsidies as much as possible. Argentina's

Table 9.3 Beneficiaries and Cost of a Universal Flat Benefit, 2002–25

Panel 1. Data as of 2003

| Age Interval | Population | Population without pension | | Cost of a flat benefit of AR$225 | | | | | |
| | | Percent | Number | Universal | | | For those without pension | | |
				Million AR$	Percent of current pensions	Percent of GDP	Million AR$	Percent of current pensions	Percent of GDP
65 and older	2,633,140	36.9	1,340,629	9,809	61.3	2.5	3,620	22.6	0.9
70 and older	2,509,539	32.8	823,129	6,776	42.3	1.7	2,222	13.9	0.6
75 and older	1,523,031	29.2	444,725	4,112	25.7	1.0	1,201	7.5	0.3

Panel 2. Data as of 2025

| Age Interval | Population | Population without pension | | Cost of a flat benefit of AR$225 | | | | | |
| | | Percent | Number | Universal | | | For those without pension | | |
				Million AR$	Percent of current pensions	Percent of GDP	Million AR$	Percent of current pensions	Percent of GDP
65 and older	5,034,332	56.2	2,829,295	13,593	85.0	1.8	7,639	47.7	1.0
70 and older	3,368,566	50.0	1,682,786	9,095	56.8	1.2	4,544	28.4	0.6
75 and older	2,463,720	44.5	1,095,681	6,652	41.6	0.9	2,958	18.5	0.4

Source: Author's calculations based on INDEC (2001) and CELADE (2002).

current pension system should operate as described here. However, a number of problems have significantly reduced its efficiency.

Participation in this second pillar would be compulsory for workers who earn above a minimum level. This minimum would be linked to the benefits received through the first pillar. Participation would therefore be compulsory for all workers earning, say, more than 50 percent of the mean wage. Contributions would be 10 percent of the income above that threshold (plus 1 percent for disability and survivors benefits), so that the benefit is close to 40 percent of the last salary (after deducting administrative fees). Thus the combination of both pillars would generate a replacement rate that starts very high and declines with income to a minimum of 40 percent (see Figure 9.7).

A number of regulatory changes should be introduced to make the second pillar more efficient, as well as increase competitiveness, reduce costs, and increase investment security. This would require enactment of the following measures:

- Increase the personal contribution rate, from the current level of 7 percent to 10 percent, plus 1 percent for disability and survivors benefits.
- Promote market transparency and simplify the commssion structure.

Figure 9.7. Replacement Rate for Different Income Levels Under the Proposed Pension Scheme

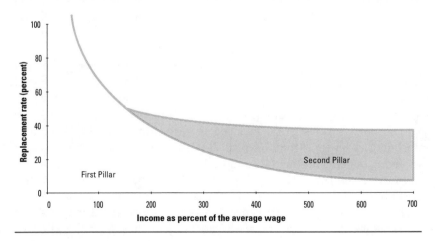

Source: Author's calculations.

- Develop an active approach to fight cartelization among pension fund managers, especially with regard to marketing strategies.
- Reduce the possibility of cross-subsidies among related companies, especially in commercial expenditures.
- Replace the current disability and survivors insurance scheme with a single provider model that can be run by the government or a private organization selected through an open bid process, or through a PAYG scheme run by the government.
- Set strict limits on investment strategies, requiring wide diversification of risks.
- Strengthen the independence of the supervisory authority, both from political interference and from industry influence.

The ideas developed in this chapter refer to the pension system in the long term. It is also critical to establish the steps necessary during the transition to that model. As mentioned, fiscal, legal, and political reasons make it impossible to implement the proposed model immediately. The rights of retirees and the expectation of those close to retirement cannot be affected. The transition can be administered using current tools (the compensatory benefit). In addition, an indexation rule should be established to reduce government discretionary actions.

Conclusion

This chapter presented some of the most important impacts that Argentina's political, fiscal, and financial crisis of 2001–02 had on the pension system, as well as the pension system's role in the crisis. It was shown that the pension system did not have a critical impact on Argentina's fiscal balance and that while the 1994 reform carried transition costs, this can hardly be considered a critical cause of the crisis. However, the crisis had several short-term impacts from which the system is still recovering. It also worsened some serious structural problems that must be addressed.

The most serious problem faced by Argentina's pension system is declining coverage. From 1993 to 2003, the proportion of the elderly receiving benefits declined by almost 20 percent. This seems to be a medium-term tendency. Having a pension system based exclusively on a contributive scheme in a society whose labor market is mostly informal, and financing it with general revenue, is not a reasonable social policy, since it is probably regressive and very inefficient. In this context, a pure contributive scheme is not consistent with the goal of providing basic protection to all aged individuals. Instead, a basic flat benefit for everyone older than a certain age would provide poverty protection, and the fiscal cost could be controlled. A second pillar, strictly contributive and aimed at income replacement for formal workers, should be maintained to provide income replacement to middle-class workers. A funded scheme is the soundest way to achieve this. Maintaining the current system, where funds are administered by competing private managers, is reasonable as long as market rules and supervision principles and practices are reviewed and improved.

References

Arenas de Mesa, Alberto, and Héctor Hernández Sánchez. 2001. Cobertura del sistema de pensiones de capitalización individual chileno: diagnóstico y propuestas. *Revista Sociales* No. 4. Rosario, Argentina

Administración Nacional de la Seguridad Social (ANSES). 1995. *Series Financieras del Sistema Nacional de Previsión Social. Período 1962–1994.* Buenos Aires.

Bertranou, Fabio and Rafael Rofman. 2002. Providing Social Security in a Context of Change: Experience and Challenges in Latin America. *International Social Security Review* 55 (1): 67–82.

Centro Latinoamericano y Caribeño de Demografía (CELADE). 2002. *Boletín Demográfico* No. 69. Santiago, Chile.

Instituto Nacional de Estadísticas y Censos (INDEC). 2001. *Encuesta Permanente de Hogares. Base Usuarios Ampliada.* Buenos Aires.

Ministerio de Economía. Secretaría de Política Económica. Dirección de Gastos Sociales Consolidados (Argentina). 2003. *Series de Gasto Público Consolidado por Finalidad-Función* (1980–2001). Buenos Aires.

Packard, Truman. 2001. Is There a Positive Incentive Effect from Privatizing Social Security? Evidence from Latin America. Background paper for Regional Study on Social Security Reform. Office of the Chief Economist, The World Bank, Washington, D.C.

Rofman, Rafael. 1999. El costo laboral como explicación del desempleo en la Argentina: un análisis de los efectos de las reducciones en las contribuciones patronales sobre el desempleo entre 1994 y 1999. Paper presented at the V Jornadas Argentinas de Estudios de Población, Buenos Aires.

_____. 2000. The Pension System in Argentina Six Years after the Reform. Social Protection Discussion Paper No.15. The World Bank, Washington D.C.

Rofman, Rafael, Gustavo Stirparo, and Pablo Lattes. 1997. *Proyecciones del Sistema Integrado de Jubilaciones y Pensiones. Estudios Especiales* No. 12. Superintendencia de AFJP, Buenos Aires

Superintendencia de AFJP (SAFJP). 2002. *Memoria Trimestral* No. 31. Buenos Aires.

————. 2004. *Memoria Trimestral* No. 41. Buenos Aires.

Valdes-Prieto, Salvador. 2001. *Social Security Coverage in Chile 1990–2001.* Background paper for Regional Study on Social Security Reform. Office of the Chief Economist, The World Bank, Washington, D.C.

Annuities and Pension Reform: Main Issues in Developing Countries

*Pietro Masci, Stefano Pettinato, and Kenroy Dowers**

Populations are aging rapidly in both industrial and developing countries, reflecting falling fertility rates and rising life expectancies. As a result people will spend larger portions of their lives in retirement. This trend has wide-ranging implications in industrial countries, as is evident in current efforts to restructure pension systems in the United States and other G-8 countries. But in the developing world this old age crisis is in some ways more severe because about 80 percent of the world's elderly are expected to live in these countries by 2030. At the same time, inefficient management and underfunding of pension systems in developing countries reduce the chances of providing the income security needed for the elderly—exacerbating the old age crisis.

In most countries facing an old age crisis, pensions are publicly managed. Benefits are allocated using a formula based on the retiree's highest past salary. Pension contributions by employees and employers (payroll taxes) are perceived as taxes (World Bank 1994). This principle is associated with pay-as-you-go pension systems where funds are not

---

* Pietro Masci is Chief of the Infrastructure and Financial Markets Division at the Inter-American Development Bank. Stefano Pettinato is Program Manager at the Bureau for Latin America and the Caribbean of the United Nations Development Programme. Kenroy Dowers is Senior Financial Specialist at the International Finance Corporation.

accumulated, but transferred intergenerationally from current contributors to pensioners. Tightening the link between workers' contributions and old age pension benefits is generally considered a sensible option for policymakers because it enhances a pension system's transparency and performance. Thus most countries are implementing this approach, along with a pay-as-you-go publicly managed pillar that covers those unable to accumulate enough for a minimum pension.[1]

Hence it is becoming increasingly important for workers to have access to financial instruments that help them insure against the risk of outliving their assets after they retire (longevity risk) and against the risk of depleting their assets while still alive (overconsumption risk). These instruments need to reduce risks both during the accumulation phase (when assets are building up) and during the payout period (when resources are being withdrawn). One such product is an annuity.

This chapter views annuities as critical tools for retirement income security and as complements to publicly provided pensions. The main purpose of this chapter is to examine how life annuity products operate in developing countries, concentrating on the constraints on the expansion of such products.[2] Emphasizing the need for a comprehensive approach to pension reform, the chapter reviews the various trade-offs and offers policy suggestions for policymakers in Latin America and the Caribbean on how to consolidate such markets and reduce the risks linked to funded pension systems after they reach maturity.

The chapter provides an overview of annuity products, including some basic concepts and the way that their markets operate. It briefly reviews the literature on annuities and discusses the two main uncertainties in annuity markets: longevity risk and investment risk. The chapter then analyzes annuity markets in Latin America and the Caribbean and the challenges facing small countries that are considering introducing annuity products in their economies.

---

[1] For the advantages and disadvantages of these two systems, see World Bank (1994) and Gillion and others (2000).

[2] Other annuity products designed to cover individuals before they reach retirement age—typically disability annuities—are not fully covered by this chapter. But after the implementation of fully funded pension systems, disability annuities play an important role in the development of annuity markets because they come into play soon after the introduction of the new system, hastening the decumulation process of the new schemes.

Annuities: An Overview

An annuity is an insurance contract that states irrevocable financial obligations between the investor and an insurance company and entitles the annuitant to receive regular income for the rest of his or her life in exchange for a premium. The premium can be paid upfront or over the annuitant's working life. In most cases a well-functioning old age pension system based on accumulation of savings for retirement—that is, a fully funded system that follows the defined contribution principle—cannot be complete without a properly functioning annuity market.

Various economists have underscored the welfare gains that result from annuitization. Annuities permit individuals to have efficient, optimum consumption profiles over their lives. Moreover, an annuity product is superior to self-insurance for protecting against longevity and consumption risks (Yaari 1965; Barr 1998).

However, an efficient annuity market requires that certain conditions be met. These conditions are closely linked to the uncertainties stemming from the long-term nature of annuities. In particular, high-quality data on interest rates and annuitants' longevity are needed to price annuities properly. Interest rate risk originates from the need to incorporate an estimated interest rate in the annuity valuation. The term structure of interest rates is used to discount future annuity payments. Ideally, long-term and low-risk assets (such as long-maturity government bonds) are used to calculate the interest rate on the annuity. When these assets do not exist and the corporate bond market is thin, the rates used tend to be conservative—raising the value of annuity products.

Another important source of information involves assumptions about the life expectancy of the annuitant population. Considerable statistical information on mortality patterns, by age and sex, is required to develop the survival forecasts needed to value annuity products. For this purpose annuitant tables are constructed. These are statistical representations of the annuitant population's expected age structure and remaining lifespan. Reliable annuitant mortality tables, necessary to price annuities, are often unavailable in developing countries. More common, yet still difficult to obtain, are general mortality tables, which observe and project mortality trends for the entire population. These may differ considerably from annuitant tables, given the different characteristics of those who buy annuities and the overall population.

Brief Literature Review

The role of annuities has been receiving growing attention and evaluation, especially on the decumulation phase of pension plans. Given the rapid expansion of self-managed retirement accounts, workers will likely bear a growing share of the burden of managing their wealth after they retire. In the United States, for example, the average retiree balance in the most common employer-sponsored retirement account, 401(k) accounts, will increase tenfold between 2000 and 2030, Poterba, Venti, and Wise (1999) estimate. Self-managed retirement resources will be further encouraged by U.S. corporate pension plans that permit, and in some cases encourage, lump sum distributions when participants retire.

Annuities have an increasingly relevant place in theoretical discussions of asset decumulation in life-cycle models. Economists have been baffled that the market for privately purchased annuities is thin and small, even in the United States, and this factor provides the basis for arguing in favor of market intervention due to market failure. Most elderly U.S. households receive social security benefits that provide a form of inflation-indexed lifetime annuity. Others collect nominal annuities from defined benefit company pension plans. Few elderly U.S. households convert financial assets accumulated outside defined benefit pension plans into annuities providing lifetime retirement income. Instead, lump sum withdrawals are the most common distribution option.

Outside social security and company plans, the U.S. market for annuities is very small. In 1998, there were 1.6 million individual annuity policies in a payout or decumulation phase, the American Council of Life Insurance reports. Figures were similar for policy owners currently receiving benefits, the Life Insurance Marketing Research Association reports (LIMRA 1999). These policies covered about 2.35 million people. Many of these policies are joint and survivor annuities that pay benefits to both members of a married couple.

In an environment of developed capital markets, annuitization of part of the portfolio can help achieve the goal of providing retirement income, Lane (2001) shows. Yermo (2001) spells out the main issues and experiences of OECD countries in the development of annuity instruments. James and Vittas (1999) analyze annuity market and financial sector development in several medium- and high-income countries (Australia, Canada, Chile, Singapore, Switzerland, and the United Kingdom), and find that the market is underdeveloped and that mortality tables are distorted.

In addition, research has increasingly focused on pension reform in developing countries, particularly in Latin America and the Caribbean, and on the decumulation phase, the role of annuity products, and their links with capital market development. Mitchell (2000) identifies the requirements for pension reform in developing countries. Several studies of annuities in developed and developing countries have been undertaken (see James and Vittas 1999; Brown, Mitchell, and Poterba 2000a; Poterba 2001; and Yermo 2001, among others). They provide evidence that the values for annuities are lower than the premium paid: that is the Money Worth Ratio (MWR) of value of annuity over premium paid is lower than 1.

Palacios and Rofman (2001) extensively examine annuities in emerging economies, studying them in the context of the multipillar pension systems of some Latin American countries. The authors emphasize the importance of the design of multipillar systems in making annuity markets effective. They explain the need to start reviewing the benefit stage of defined contribution programs even when it will not start for 10 to 20 years. They point out that from a political point of view, the temptation is to postpone the debate.

Building on the work of Palacios and Rofman, this chapter analyzes annuity products in the Latin American and Caribbean market, expands on their review of the region's countries (including features specific to small economies) identifies policy issues, and offers recommendations.

Annuity Designs and Uncertainties

If a government manages the public pension system on a pay-as-you-go basis, workers receive a social security benefit throughout their retirement. Under a funded plan—which can be an alternative or a complement to a PAYG system—after having contributed during their working lives, new retirees are entitled to claim from their employer or pension fund manager the amount of accumulated savings. In designing these schemes, policymakers have to design—and participants have to choose among—various options for the accumulation and decumulation phases.

The design of the accumulation phase must specify features such as who must contribute to the system and how much, the tax treatment of contributions and account investment earnings, the products in which pension fund managers are allowed to invest, the point at which the accumulation period ends, or whether to permit withdrawals.

In designing the decumulation phase, policymakers must decide whether participants will be allowed to take some or all of their assets in a lump sum, if they will be required to acquire annuities, whether annuities will be nominal or protected against inflation, whether annuities will be guaranteed and if so how, the fiscal treatment of the various payout options, and whether the government will guarantee a minimum pension. This chapter covers some aspects of the design of the decumulation phase: lump sum payments versus annuities, types of annuities, and uncertainties associated with annuities.

Lump sum withdrawals are often carefully regulated because some individuals who choose this option may be unable to manage their assets in a way that ensures sufficient income throughout their retirement years (longevity risk). Most individuals who withdraw the entire amount of their accumulated assets use the money to buy a home, pay off debt, or purchase other consumables. Moral hazard is more likely if the government provides a safety net for those who cannot cover their minimum needs.

Another way to use accumulated savings for retirement is to establish a plan for programmed withdrawals. Such a pension would be based on an estimate of the individual's life expectancy. The obvious risk is that if the pensioner outlives that estimate, he or she will run out of income.

Alternatively, a pensioner can transfer the accumulated funds to a life insurance company in exchange for an old age annuity. The most common type of annuity is a contract between a retiree and an insurance company for a guaranteed interest-bearing policy with guaranteed income options. The insurance company pays interest, and the investor does not pay taxes on the earnings until he or she makes a withdrawal or begins receiving annuity income. In most cases the annuity contract earns a competitive return that is safe relative to other types of investments. The ultimate goal for most participants is to maximize their income stream while eliminating the risk of outliving the principal of the investment.[3]

A first distinction should be made between deferred annuities and immediate annuities. These are differentiated by the way that active participants pay premiums (Box 10.1). Deferred annuities are paid by workers over time, with periodic or occasional payments, until retirement. Upon retirement, the principal and compounded earnings can be converted into a stream of payments. This operation also allows workers to defer tax payments on those earnings. Immediate annuities are pur-

---

[3] An exception occurs when retirees want to leave bequests for their heirs. Unless specified in the annuity contract (in a survivorship clause), a retiree who purchases an annuity chooses not to leave an inheritance.

Box 10.1 The Basic Arithmetic of Annuities

The calculations required to understand the life cycle of a single-premium annuity contract require solving two diverging trends: the compound interest that builds up the account on one side and the depletion of the account (through annuity withdrawals) on the other. The premium is denoted as p. The periodic (generally monthly) withdrawal is w, and r is the discount rate (in this case also monthly, to be consistent with w). While the balance for the first period, B_1, is $p - w$, in the second period the interest rate needs to be incorporated, so the balance for the second period is $[(p - w) r - w]$. In the following period, the balance is given by $\{[(p - w) r - w] r - w\}$. This series of balances can be generalized for period i to produce:

$$B_i = p(1+r)^{i-1} - w \frac{(1+r)^i - 1}{r}.$$

To understand pricing, one needs to obtain the periodic withdrawal that makes the balance run out in the predetermined final period L, which can be interpreted as the life expectancy of the annuitant at contract signup. In other words, one needs to find the w^* so that $B_L(w^*) = 0$. The above relationship can be solved for w to get the annuity (that is, periodic withdrawal) that the annuitant is "entitled to" given the initial disbursement p and the agreed discount rate r. The result is given by:

$$w^* = \frac{p(1+r)^{L-1}r}{(1+r)^L - 1}.$$

The annuity withdrawal is higher for higher levels of p and r and for lower levels of L. The implications for pricing should be clear: for a given premium, higher life expectancy and lower discount rates reduce the amount of the periodic withdrawal and thus the value of the annuity. This formulation ignores risk premiums and operating fees that insurance companies may charge. In reality the uncertainties associated with life expectancy and discount rates lead insurance companies to use more conservative pricing. Life expectancy is assumed to be longer than what it probably is and the discount rate adopted is below the market rate level.

Annuity valuation is typically based on the "money's worth" rule: the ratio of the present discounted value of the expected stream of benefits to the annuity premium paid. In particular, the present value calculation requires interest rate assumptions, while the expected benefit stream requires assumptions about longevity (that is, mortality rates of annuitants). If the money's worth ratio is close to 1 (also taking into account administrative costs), then the annuity contract is fair.

Source: Mitchell and others (1999).

chased through lump sum payments, after which annuitants are entitled to receive payments, generally on a monthly basis.

Annuities can also be voluntary or mandatory. With voluntary annuities, active participants are voluntarily saving after-tax income. With compulsory annuities, active participants are saving pre-tax income under the general framework of a recognized retirement plan. An example is a retirement annuity: its ultimate goal is to allow active participants to invest enough capital over time to ensure a regular income source during retirement.

Many voluntary participants buy immediate annuities. A lump sum of their after-tax money is given to an insurance company, which agrees to pay regular annual amounts, split into monthly payments. Investors who need to conform to certain retirement funding laws buy compulsory annuities. This generally occurs when the investor retires, and uses a portion of the proceeds at retirement to buy a compulsory annuity from a retirement fund (such as a pension fund or retirement annuity fund). By doing so, the income tax applied to the monthly annuity payments is at lower rates.

Another product deserves special attention: nonguaranteed annuities. Their value changes with the value of an established portfolio, allowing active participants to spread investment risk among different assets. For long-term risk-taking investors, variable performance-linked annuities can perform better than indexed products, outpacing inflation. The interest accumulated, together with the dividends and the capital gains, remain invested until withdrawals are made. This flexibility has made variable annuities increasingly popular.

A well-functioning annuity market offers a variety of products that depart from the simplest type of annuity (the single-premium annuity). Each of the different annuity products has advantages and disadvantages, and is more suitable for particular participants in specific markets. Still, these products share a common feature. All are based, to varying degrees, on two sets of considerations and assumptions:

- Participants' demographic profile, depending on their life expectancy, gender, and so on. At the micro level, this profile depends on private information about an individual annuitant's health history. At the macro level, it depends on national mortality tables.
- The financial environment at the time of the contract, as well as financial expectations.

Like any other product, annuities must be priced. Given the contractual nature of annuities, their price must include the "cost of certainty": that is, the cost incurred if assumptions about longevity and investment prove wrong. These issues are analyzed below.

Longevity Risk

Annuities reduce longevity risk—the risk of an individual outliving his or her assets. At its basic level, the decision to annuitize implies a trade-off between longevity risk and the bequest motive. The main advantage of annuitization is its reduction of longevity risk. The main disadvantage is that a life annuity has no value after the death of the beneficiary.

Among other things, annuities are priced on the basis of participants' longevity: the longer the expected lifespan, the higher the premium or the lower the annuity (see Box 10.1). Successful pricing depends on how well insurers assess annuitants' life expectancies. These assessments are made using data about similar individuals (such as those of the same age and gender). Mortality tables, when available, are the main source of such data. These tools allow insurers to better understand the structure of the population and the life expectancies of different parts of the population.

When devising a mortality table, it is necessary to collect a large data set on deaths by age and gender in a population over a given period. These data are then used to calculate the probability qx that a member of a particular cohort age x will die in the next year. The estimation of qx can be done by fitting a hazard rate model to the empirical distribution of deaths in the population or by applying a smoothing algorithm to the raw maximum likelihood estimates of qx. The smoothed estimates of qx are used to construct a complete mortality table (see McCarthy and Mitchell 2000; 2002).

Because mortality tables are only estimates of the actual demographic profile, annuity markets can operate below optimal efficiency levels. Adverse selection, a common bias in both developing and industrial countries, is driven by information asymmetries between life insurance companies and annuitants. Annuitants have better information about their longevity, knowing their health and their families' medical history.

People who buy annuities voluntarily often live longer than the average pensioner—increasing the burden for annuity sellers, who raise prices that end up discouraging new purchases. To hedge this risk, insurers sometimes base annuity rates on a group that they believe is likely to buy annuities. But when mortality tables are unreliable, and the amount of unknown private information for potential annuitants is greater, life insurers may be unable to hedge properly. These distortions hamper the development of the annuity market. Evidence supports the existence of adverse selection: the cost of an annuity calculated using population life tables is 7 to 15 percent less than that observed in the market.[4]

---

[4] Various empirical studies have estimated that the difference between the fair actuarial cost of an annuity calculated on the basis of population mortality tables and the observed market price of annuities is between 7 and 15 percent (see Palacios and Rofman 2001). This is often regarded as the impact of adverse selection on the annuity market. See Friedman and Warshawsky (1990); Finkelstein and Poterba (1999); Mitchell and others (1999); Walliser (1998); and James and Vittas (1999).

Investment Risk

Assumptions made about investments—and thus interest rates paid—are also critical in valuing annuities. Moreover, assumptions about mortality and investments are closely linked. When a person is expected to live only a few years, investment returns matter less. Conversely, interest rates gain enormous weight in the overall return from an annuity when a person's life expectancy is high. The projected interest component typically takes into account the future cash flows generated by current assets and reflects the current economic outlook to determine all future years' rates of return.

Insurance companies are careful when pricing their products using information from domestic and international financial markets. Ideally they hedge interest rate—and inflation rate—risk by purchasing assets with a term similar to that of the annuity (the annuitant's life expectancy). But due to market imperfections, assets with such terms are often not available in developing countries, forcing insurers to offer very conservative interest rates on annuities. Insurance companies typically are forced to take a certain amount of basis points off the assumed yield, making the annuitant lose significant retirement income. Only in this way can the companies guarantee—or at least increase the odds of—future solvency. As a result the interest rates paid on annuities are often below optimal levels, damaging consumers and discouraging market growth. This security margin allows insurers to hedge against risk using an approach similar to that taken by governments when issuing long-term securities.

Similarly, potential annuitants evaluate an annuity's price by comparing its returns with those from alternative financial assets. If a market offers secure and long-maturity bonds, life insurance companies are pressed to offer better annuity rates to make this option more competitive and attract investors. When investment alternatives are lacking, annuitants may be penalized by overly conservative assumptions in the valuation of annuities. This distortion is illustrated in more detail in the case studies below.

When designing a fully funded pension system that mandates the purchase of an annuity upon retirement, policymakers should take into account the instability of the interest rates paid on annuities and the overpricing of annuities in the absence of long-term securities (Box 10.2). As noted, when long-term securities are available, annuity rates are intimately connected with the yields on (mainly government) bonds with similar long-term maturities. Those who retire when interest rates are

Box 10.2 Mandatory Annuities

A variety of countries have introduced mandatory defined contribution pension plans, including Argentina, Australia, Chile, Colombia, El Salvador, Mexico, Nicaragua, Peru, Poland, Sweden, and Switzerland. These new retirement systems are increasingly structured around a benefit plan that mandates—among other options—the purchase of an annuity upon retirement. Given their nonvoluntary nature, transactions and regulation of mandatory annuities require careful analysis.

Upon retirement, some participants in defined contribution pension plans have accumulated large sums of money that should enable them to support themselves in old age. But a significant portion of that money can be willfully or accidentally spent or lost—forcing the participants to rely on public assistance for their survival. This type of moral hazard is common because individuals tend to underestimate their life expectancies, avoid the purchase of annuities, and spend down their assets completely before they die. As a result, mandatory life annuities are often deemed necessary because such behavior would overburden public support programs. See the debate between Palacios and Rofman (2001) and James and Vittas (1999).

The design of the payout system is controversial and politically sensitive. Not only must it be consistent with the new defined contribution system, but it also must reflect the socially accepted features of previous retirement arrangements. (For a comprehensive analysis of mandatory annuities, see Doyle and Piggott 2001.) In particular, since a defined contribution system aims to establish a close relationship between contributions and benefits, strict rules for system sustainability and risk coverage need to be taken into account in the payout design.

Defined contribution retirement plans often allow retirees to pick from two or more benefit structures. For example, in Chile's private defined contribution pillar, retiring workers can choose between a programmed withdrawal and a life annuity. Only retirees who have accumulated significant assets—with a total that provides a replacement rate of 70 percent and is worth at least 120 percent of the minimum pension guarantee—can withdraw the remainder as a lump sum. Furthermore, retirees must opt for the programmed withdrawal if the annuity does not provide an income larger than the minimum pension. The annuity is the most common option, taken by 44 percent of beneficiaries in the region.

low end up penalized because their stream of benefits is calculated using that interest rate level.[5] But if long-term maturities are not available, the overpricing of annuities might penalize pensioners.

Thus compulsory annuities are acceptable only when the rates paid on them are relatively stable and their prices are competitive. Otherwise, retirees should be entitled to choose other forms of repayment, including lump sum payments. Another policy implication is that, when introducing a fully funded pension system, access to long-term financial assets should be increased to mitigate some of the problems mentioned above.

---

[5] Obviously only fixed rate annuities are affected by this.

Life Expectancies, Interest Rates, and Annuity Premiums

The discussion above indicates the crucial relationship between life expectancies, interest rates, and annuity premiums. Using work developed in the context of the "money's worth" approach, it is possible to construct a basic formula that determines the expected present value of a nominal annuity with an annual payout of An purchased by an individual of age b, assuming that the individual will not live beyond 115 years:

$$PV\ (An) = An * P_j / II\ (1 + ik),$$

where P_j indicates the probability that an individual of a given age at the time of the annuity purchase will live at least j years after buying the annuity. (This information comes from mortality tables.) The variable ik denotes the annual interest rate k years after the annuity purchase. The II variable denotes the use of a term structure for the interest rate rather than a flat rate.

In equilibrium, the present value calculated in this formula (taking into consideration administrative costs) should constitute the premium charged for an annuity contract. That is, the premium observed in the market should not be significantly different from the present value calculations of the formula. But considerations related to "money's worth" show that the present value calculated in the formula and the premium in the market are not aligned, and that the "money's worth" of an annuity is less than the premium paid—which shows the imperfections of annuity markets, particularly the role of adverse selection.

But in interpreting the present value of an annuity as the premium to be paid for an annuity contract, the critical point that the formula highlights is the inverse relationship between interest rates and premiums and between mortality rates and premiums (Figure 10.1). The basic formula for the present value of a nominal annuity provided above shows that the lower the interest rate, the higher the premium charged. Thus the selection of an interest rate[6] not aligned with the market—a distinct possibility in emerging economies—would lead to an overly high premium, which could discourage the development of an efficient annuity market that responds to demand.

---

[6] Interest rates are in the denominator of the formula for the calculation of the value of annuities and therefore if lower interest rates are used, the present value (B/I) is greater and the premium requested is greater.

Figure 10.1. The Inverse Relationship between Interest Rates, Mortality Ratios, and Annuity Premiums

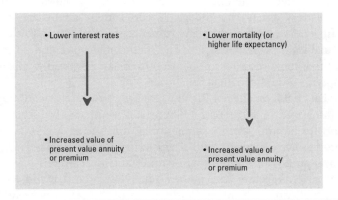

The basic formula also illustrates the inverse relationship between mortality rates (or life expectancies) and premiums. The lower the mortality rate (and the higher the life expectancy), the higher will be the premium charged for an annuity contract. That is, the insurance company will pay a lower annual income the longer it expects to pay benefits. The use of mortality rates lower than those prevailing leads to higher premiums and discourages potential annuity buyers and annuity market development.

Annuity Markets in Latin America and the Caribbean

This section focuses on the main features of annuity markets in countries that have adopted mandatory private defined contribution pension plans: Argentina, Chile, Colombia, and Peru.[7] It then briefly examines markets and products in Bolivia, Trinidad and Tobago, and Barbados, and the main issues facing small emerging economies.

In all countries of the region except one, those who have contributed to the private defined contribution pension plan have the option either of scheduled withdrawals or of buying an annuity at the time of retire-

---

[7] These four countries have the longest experience with reformed pension systems in the region.

ment.[8] Only those investors who have accumulated an amount of funds that guarantee a minimum pension can purchase annuities. Yet as Table 10.1 shows, the annuity market in Latin America is extremely thin, and suffers from weaknesses related to levels of interest rates and mortality rates. In general, fixed annuity instruments prevail, but variable annuities are available in some countries. The inefficiencies are compounded by the fact that most resources of pension funds are invested in government bonds, with little diversification.

Critical characteristics of the countries with mandatory annuity plans are summarized in Table 10.2.[9] Figure 10.2 compares projections of the demand for annuities in these countries from the early 1990s to 2020. The progressive expansion of the pension systems generates a nearly exponential profile for the number of annuitants over time.[10]

The patterns clearly indicate the relatively large demand for annuities in Chile. This is a direct consequence of the maturity of its funded pension system, as well as a legal and regulatory framework including disclosure that makes the annuity the most popular option at retirement. In the other countries many participants in the private systems are still in their working years, accumulating resources toward retirement to then purchase annuities.

In the countries analyzed, the two sources of uncertainty linked to annuity products (demographic and financial) are clearly targeted by public policy instruments. In particular, governments dictate which mortality table and interest rate are to be used in calculating annuities. These preset levels are major factors in the pricing decisions by insurance companies. Lower mortality rates are synonymous with higher life expectancy. By applying lower mortality rates, the premiums that annuitants will be charged will be higher than with higher mortality rates. The same is true for interest rates. If the interest rates used to calculate the premium are lower than those in the market, the premium will go up. Therefore, using misaligned mortality tables and inaccurate interest rates will misprice annuities (leading to higher premiums), discouraging the growth of the annuity market. More details are provided in the sections below.

---

[8] The exception is Uruguay, where the purchase of an annuity is mandatory at the end of the accumulation phase.

[9] While only Bolivia and Uruguay have pure mandatory annuity systems, here the definition of "mandatory" is extended to systems where annuities are optional, based on the observation that they are largely the preferred choice.

[10] Beyond 2020, as coverage reaches an "optimal" level, this pattern is expected to flatten.

Table 10.1 Features of Annuity Markets in Various Latin American Countries

Country	Origin of mortality tables		Period when generated	Interest rate levels	Market for annuities	
	Generated in the country	Free or generated by other countries			Retirees receiving annuities, as of Dec. 2001	Amount paid for annuities, 2001
Bolivia	X	Based on European tables	1990s	Free	About 1,000	Less than $20 million (2002)
Brazil	X	X		Free		More than $1 billion
Chile	X		1980s	Free	100,000–500,000	More than $500 million
Colombia	X		1980s	Free	Less than 100,000	Less than $500 million
Honduras		X		Free		
El Salvador	X		1990s	Mandatory (6%)	Less than 100,000	
Mexico	X		1990s	Free	500,000–1,000000	
Nicaragua					Less than 100,000	Less than $500 million
Peru		X	1980s	Free		
Uruguay	X		1990s	Mandatory (1.75%)		
Venezuela	X		2001		500,000–1,000,000	

Source: Federación Interamericana de Empresas de Seguros.

Table 10.2	Features of Annuity Plans in Selected Latin American Countries			
Feature	Argentina	Chile	Colombia	Peru
Additional life expectancy of 65 year-old males (years)				
From mortality table	15.11	16.65	15.94	16.65
From national table (1995–2000)	13.98	14.79	14.70	13.56
Indexation mechanism	Wage index adjustment	Explicit, using "UF," a basic inflation unit	Indexed with consumer price index	Indexed with Lima's consumer price index

Source: Palacios and Rofman (2001).

Figure 10.2. Projected Number of Annuitants in Various Latin American Countries, 1995–2020

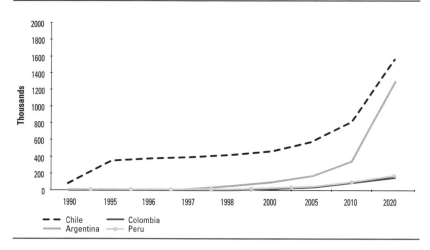

Source: Palacios and Rofman (2001).

Argentina

Before reforming its social security system in 1994, Argentina was the only country among those examined here to have pension plans managed by private companies.[11] In 1994 Argentina introduced a system,

---

[11] Many details in this section come from Callund (1999), Palacios and Rofman (2001), and Rofman (2001).

with a publicly managed pay-as-you-go pillar and a second mandatory pillar with two options: a defined benefit system managed by ANSES (Administración Nacional de Seguro Social) and a defined contribution system, which is fully funded and managed by private pension funds, or AFJPs (Administradoras de Fondos de Jubilaciones y Pensiones). As a result, there are two types of retirement annuities: those deriving from the Seguros de Retiro (which existed before the 1994 reform), made up of individual and group pension plans; and those associated with the AFJPs.

Worsening economic conditions took their toll on the financial sector in the late 1980s and early 1990s. By 1992, because of mergers and acquisitions, there were 26 private pension companies in the market. By December 1998 the leading provider, La Estrella, controlled about half the market, and the second largest, Siembra Retiro, controlled another third. For a regular payment (usually monthly), participants have a right to a portion of a future pension, as of a date determined when the contract is drawn up. Both parties freely determine the conditions of the contract. Despite an initial slowdown in this market upon introduction of the AFJP, the system has continued to grow. But the numbers are still small. In 1998 the total number of policies was 5,639, of which only 83 were individual policies.

The AFJP system was introduced in 1994. In 1995 pension reform annuities represented less than 0.2 percent of the Argentine insurance market. By the end of 1998 this number had grown to 11 percent. Survivor and disability annuities are the leading sources of growth of the country's annuity market. Rapid growth is expected to continue over the next 20 years. As in Chile, Argentine law limits the choice of annuities to the joint and survivor annuity. The survivor benefit for spouses is set at 70 percent of the retiree's benefit, higher than in Chile and Peru but lower than in Colombia. In addition, Argentine workers have the option of taking a lump sum if the remainder of their balance is sufficient to purchase an annuity that provides a replacement rate of 70 percent.

The Argentine government specifies the mortality table to be used to calculate annuity costs. It is GAM71 (Group Annuity Mortality), a table prepared by North American actuaries in 1971, based on the mortality structure of annuitants in the United States during the 1950s and 1960s. The mortality rate of this table is 7.5 percent, lower than Argentina's national mortality level. The reasons for using this table are not fully understood. The overall benefits from preferring a higher-quality database like GAM71 to poor-quality national tables do not seem to outweigh the considerable distortions generated by the conservative life expectancy estimates of GAM71. What is clear is that the costs are ultimately transmitted to annuitants through higher prices that reduce consumer income.

A government decree approved in 2000 introduced various changes in the AFJP pension regulation. Until 2001 contributors to the AFJP system had three main options for receiving benefits at retirement: a life annuity; a standard programmed withdrawal; or a programmed withdrawal under which the member draws down periodically a fixed amount of about AR$115 until the balance is used up—ideal for those with little savings. The latter was by far the most common method for drawing an old age pension, with about 8,000 participants in March 1999.[12]

Until 2001 the required interest rate for annuity returns was fixed at 4 percent. But Argentina also provided a unique feature allowing annuitants to participate in investment returns. If investments yielded a higher return, the gain from the spread was usually shared with customers. Some companies gave lump sum benefits; some increased monthly payments. Indeed, the method and extent of profit sharing was one of the sources of competition among providers. The 2000 decree eliminated the 4 percent ceiling on returns to encourage fund managers to seek out higher returns, but they are still required to provide a minimum return of 4 percent. This change is also expected to increase competition among retirement insurance companies, encouraging them to compete on the basis of investment returns rather than on differences in their method of profit sharing. Another step in this direction is a mandate that all annuities be defined in similar terms, making it easier for customers to choose a provider.

These measures should lead to lower marketing costs, reducing costs for pensioners. However, allowing insurers to compete on the basis of investment returns can be very risky because higher returns are associated with higher solvency risk for insurers—in a way that consumers generally are not aware of because of information asymmetries. This risk might be a sufficient argument to regulate returns and portfolios because in cases of insurer insolvency, the government is likely to be forced to assume insurers' obligations to their clients.

---

[12]The 2000 decree limited programmed withdrawals to a maximum of five years after retirement. Thereafter all pensioners are required to purchase annuities. This limitation is expected to dramatically increase the size of the annuity market in Argentina. As recently as March 1999, only 50 of the 8,000 or so pensioners had purchased an annuity, with the rest choosing programmed withdrawals (although approximately half of survivor pensioners were drawing annuities). See Callund (1999).

The 2000 decree also addressed market concentration. Unlike its neighbors, Argentina requires specialized annuity providers that have separate balance sheets from pension managers. In mid-1998 there were 20 specialized companies selling pension annuities. But there was substantial market concentration, with almost 70 percent of beneficiaries belonging to just five companies. More than 80 percent of beneficiaries opted to buy an annuity from an insurance company affiliated with their AFJP, which explains the market concentration. AFJPs are legally required to inform their retiring members of the existence of different annuity providers. But AFJPs usually inform their related retirement insurance company of the existence of a new customer immediately, increasing the probability that the company will immediately market to and snap up the pensioner. The 2000 decree established a concentration limit of 27.5 percent of market share. This provision, however, risks implicitly subsidizing inefficient firms by constraining customer choices.

Argentina has also made a major change in how customers are assigned to AFJPs. Previously workers who did not choose were randomly assigned to AFJPs in equal proportions. Now they are allocated to the lowest-cost provider. This move is expected to increase cost efficiency and competition among providers. In addition, AFJPs must now declare their fees as a percentage of contributors' income, as opposed to some doing this and some simply having a flat fee. This change is expected to make it easier for consumers to compare AFJPs. Finally, until 2001 annuity providers were supervised by the existing insurance supervision agency, separate from the supervisor of pension funds. Today, however, the Superintendency of AFJPs assumes partial responsibility, which should improve monitoring of the annuities industry.

One factor affecting the size and development of the annuity market is the coverage of the population by the pension system. In Argentina certain groups, such as the military, are exempt from joining the pension system. A bigger problem is the large informal labor force, because workers who are not formally employed are not covered by the system. High unemployment and underemployment also reduce coverage, and evasion has historically been a major issue. Less than half of required contributions are paid each month in Argentina, Palacios and Rofman (2001) estimate.

Another factor that hindered the development of Argentina's annuity market was the decision not to use recognition bonds—unlike Chile, where all workers received a recognition bond at the time of the country's pension reform (1981). The face value of each bond approximated the value of contributions if the worker had contributed to a fully funded scheme in the years before the reform. The bonds were fully paid upon retirement or when survivor or disability benefits were granted, making available to beneficiaries a large balance with which to buy an annuity. Argentina used transitional benefits rather than recognition bonds, reducing the assets in the annuity market.

There is an ongoing debate about the link between the size of annuity markets and the level of capital market development (see Mitchell 2000). While in Chile the accumulation of assets from pension funds has been a major force driving the deepening of capital markets, in Argentina a concomitant expansion of the capital market has not been evident. Furthermore, concerns have been raised about the availability of long-term instruments for the investment of funds, especially in light of the country's recent economic crisis.[13]

The annuity market in Argentina was expected to grow rapidly over the next two decades, with more than 1 million annuitants projected by 2020 (see Figure 10.3). The 2000 decree was a step toward a stronger annuity market, particularly in targeting market concentration and fostering competition between providers. But the expected growth must be reassessed given the current fragile state of the Argentine economy, particularly the financial sector, and the critical situation of the pension system. In late 2001, as its debt obligations increased, the government of Argentina converted debt instruments held by the private pension funds at terms that seriously undermined the values of the assets. Coupled with the poor performance of the government, the public has become disillusioned with the system's functioning and is reluctant to provide pension contributions for investment.

Argentina's experience is a good example of how pension reform cannot occur in isolation, and shows that problems facing capital and annuity markets cannot be solved without a proper reworking of the economy.

---

[13]Unlike in other Latin American countries, annuity providers in Argentina are allowed to invest up to 100 percent of their reserves in federal government bonds. There are limits on all other investment instruments: 60 percent for domestic corporate bonds, certificates of deposit, and mortgage-guaranteed bonds; 29 percent for local corporate bonds and mutual funds; 9 percent for three categories of foreign assets; and 2 percent for derivatives. In Chile annuity providers can invest up to 50 percent of their reserves in government bonds; 40 percent in domestic corporate bonds, stocks, or equity shares; and 10 percent in two categories of foreign assets. In Peru annuity providers can invest up to 30 percent in government bonds, foreign government and multilateral bonds, stocks or equity shares, real estate, mutual funds, or mortgage-guaranteed bonds; 20 percent in certificates of deposit; and 10 percent in corporate bonds (domestic or foreign).

Chile

Chile introduced a fully funded privately managed pension system in 1981, abandoning its defined benefit system. Its long reform period makes Chile a useful case for examining the development of an annuity market. Many observers have pointed out that while the market for annuities was virtually nonexistent before the country's pension reform, it started soaring a few years later. In fact, some attribute much of the growth in the Chilean insurance sector to the expansion of the annuity market.[14]

Between 1991 and 1998 the number of Chilean life insurance companies increased by two-thirds to 28, with increasingly active participation by international firms such as Aetna, AIG, and ING. Rapid market expansion reduced the concentration of sales of policies and caused a 20 percent increase in premium income from life insurance. The rising number of annuitants has also been driven by the growing pool of early retirees, for whom the annuity is the only benefit option upon retirement (Devesa-Carpio and Vidal-Meliá 2001).

Although the annuity market has grown rapidly, two factors may have slowed its pace. First, affiliation to the Chilean pension system is mandatory only for employees. Self-employed workers can join voluntarily, but most have decided not to—and the percentage of self-employed workers is high. Second, about 40 percent of retiring contributors decide to opt for a programmed pension withdrawal, limiting the number of annuitants (see Acuña and Iglesias 2001). (Retiring Chileans can buy annuities only if their saved assets can pay for an annuity above the minimum pension. Otherwise they must contract with a pension fund manager, or AFP, for a programmed withdrawal that produces benefits equal to or above the minimum pension until their funds are extinguished. After that, if they have contributed to the system for at least 20 years, they can receive a minimum pension. See Palacios and Rofman 2001.)

There is a division of labor in Chile's private pension system. Companies that sell annuities are separate from AFPs (Administradoras de Fondos de Pensiones), which collect contributions and manage pension assets. This distinction is intended to limit the market power of AFPs. Thus retirement assets are locked into annuities from the beginning. But insurance companies can segment the market into different risk classes depending on life expectancy. For example, companies may price annuities differ-

---

[14]While in 1988 annuities represented less than 7 percent of the insurance market, in 1998 they accounted for 50 percent of it (Palacios and Rofman 2001).

ently for men and women or for people with different health status. In addition, workers can freely choose from annuities offered by different companies. The government guarantees 75 percent of pension payments, which is an "annuity," above the minimum pension if an annuity insurer defaults at any time. To reduce this risk on the government, annuity reserves are strictly regulated.

Upon retirement, participants are notified about their benefit options. They must choose between a programmed pension withdrawal or (if eligible) an immediate or deferred annuity. Insurance companies use extensive marketing campaigns to convince participants to join their plans, consulting a publicly available list of participants three months from retirement. Once payments start, the government guarantees life annuity payments up to 100 percent of the minimum pension, within certain limits.

Chilean retirees who opt for the annuity also receive coverage for survivorship. Upon the retiree's death, the surviving spouse will receive benefits from the insurance company. Depending on the contract between the insurance company and the annuitant, the spouse will receive the same benefit or a fraction of it, and will be covered indefinitely or for a limited period. Chilean pension benefits maintain their value over time because they are calculated using an accounting unit linked to the cost of living, the Unidad de Fomento (UF).

Chile's pension system uses the RV85 mortality table (Renta Vitalicia), constructed using Chilean data from the 1970s. As in the other countries examined, the RV85 presents substantially higher life expectancy levels than those observed at the national level (see Table 10.2). This distortion greatly penalizes annuitants in terms of higher premiums, lower benefits, or both.

In contrast to the notion that the development of annuity markets requires a sound financial environment, evidence particularly from Chile suggests that this is not a necessary precondition. Despite the widespread initial immaturity of the capital market and the financial and the insurance sectors, the market for annuities has evolved and deepened gradually yet steadily. In particular, the segments that have grown most in the initial years after the reform have been disability and survivorship products.

In Chile, policymakers had a comprehensive vision of the various links among crucial sectors and subsectors: pension systems, privatizations, capital market development, fiscal discipline, and rules of law including corporate governance and supervision. The reform of the pension system and of the annuity markets were regarded as part of a strategy that required the various elements to work in a synergistic form. The actions that the legislative branch, the executive, and the monetary authorities in Chile have undertaken over an extended period of time following the initial pension reform of the early 1980s are described in Bustamante (2004). In particular, the Chilean Parliament passed legislation in 1985, 1989, 1990, 1994, and 1998 to modify and improve the functioning of pension fund investments. Over the same period of time, the central bank updated the limits on investment in the various instruments to make sure that diversification would be achieved. Certainly, inefficiencies remain, particularly in the cost of administrations and also in the annuity market. Nonetheless, the main lesson of annuity and capital markets development in Chile is that political determination and a comprehensive view are essential in the design of policies and strategies and for their success, even when there is a political cost (see Chapter 7).

It is certainly advisable to deepen the financial environment where annuity products are offered, even though annuity products have been able to grow even when capital and financial markets are underdeveloped. However, the absence of long-term government or corporate bonds in the region may pose a threat to the efficiency and the development of the market, slashing rates paid to annuitants for their investment and depressing the potential of the annuity market.

Colombia

Although Colombia's annuity market is growing rapidly, it remains relatively small—representing less than 3 percent of the insurance sector. Low coverage and low per capita incomes imply that the market will remain small in both absolute and relative terms, at least for the next few years. Pension coverage of the Colombian population is far from universal. Reasons include the large informal labor market, high unemployment, and the exemption of certain groups (such as the self-employed) from the mandatory system. Evasion rates are also high; estimates surpass even those of Argentina. All these factors hinder the expansion and efficiency of a market for annuities.

As in Argentina, most of the annuity business is related to survivor and disability benefits. Colombia's current market for annuities shares similarities with Chile's system in its early stages, after that country's 1981 pension reform. At the time of the reform in 1994 all Colombian workers received a recognition bond with a value roughly equivalent to what they would have accumulated had they been in a fully funded system rather than a pay-as-you-go scheme. These bonds are a potential source of assets for annuitants. But only a limited number of new retirees are covered by the fully funded scheme because of the age segmentation between the old and the new systems (73 percent of the members of the new system are 35 and younger). Until these workers retire, the decumulation of assets toward annuitants will be relatively small. This is largely a consequence of the large number of workers under the old PAYG scheme, who at retirement will receive their benefits from the government under the old rules.

Compounding the problem is that workers in the new scheme are allowed to switch back to the PAYG system at any time. Another problem hindering the development of Colombia's annuity market is the option given to members of the new scheme to choose a programmed withdrawal rather than an annuity.[15] The survivor benefit for spouses in Colombia is 100 percent—the highest among the countries examined in this chapter. This benefit is biased in favor of the surviving spouse, usually female. Annuity payments are indexed to inflation.

The Colombian government requires annuity market operators to use the ISS90 mortality table when calculating annuity costs. This table was produced by Colombia's Institute of Social Security based on data from public pension scheme participants. The mortality rate from this table for men age 65 is almost 8 percent lower than the corresponding figure from the national table for 1995–2000. The interest rate used for calculations of reserves is fixed at 4 percent, while the rate for quotations is free, recently hovering around 4 percent as well. Anecdotal evidence throughout Latin America suggests that differences in quotation rates are due not so much to differences in asset yields across countries as to differences in annuity market conditions, as well as the lobbying power of the insurance industry (see Palacios and Rofman 2001).

Like in Chile and Peru but unlike in Argentina, Colombian life insurance companies can participate in the annuity market. Participation tends to be concentrated among the largest life insurance companies, which in turn are often part of financial conglomerates that include pension fund mangers (AFPs). The largest annuity provider, Suramericana, provides 35 percent of annuity products, and the second largest, Alfa, has a 17 percent market share. Among the nine issuers of annuities, the bottom five are very small.

---

[15] Colombia requires workers who have chosen programmed withdrawals to buy annuities if the balances in their accounts fall to the level required to buy a minimum pension. Furthermore, those who have chosen programmed withdrawals are permitted to switch to annuities at any time. The problem is that these switches might exacerbate the adverse selection problem.

Colombia's banking supervisory agency is responsible for supervising not only the financial sector but also pension funds, insurance companies, and annuity providers. While Uruguay shares this approach, it stands in sharp contrast to that taken by other Latin American countries (such as Chile and Peru), where pension funds have independent supervisory agencies and separate insurance supervisory agencies in charge of monitoring annuity providers. Colombia's approach may lead to more relaxed supervision. At the same time, given the links between pension management, insurance provision, and the financial sector, having a single supervisor may generate economies of scale.[16]

The Colombian government guarantees both annuities and the solvency of AFPs that offer scheduled withdrawals. Annuities are guaranteed by a government agency, which guarantees that the social security obligations of insurance companies receive priority in cases of bankruptcy. This mechanism is important for encouraging pensioners to opt for annuities. Studies of capital market development around the world suggest that a major contributing factor is the availability of large reserves of long-term savings for investment (such as pension savings). Colombia is not exempt from this trend, making the growth of annuity reserves an important factor for the development and deepening of its capital markets.[17]

Although Colombia's emerging annuity market is growing, it will probably never be as large as that of Argentina or Chile due to lower levels of coverage and income, as well as smaller population. At present the market suffers from concentration and lack of a competitive environment for providers. While there are government guarantees, these will not be fully tested until the system matures—and overall supervision of the system appears weak. There is a possibility that these problems will not be easily alleviated if the market remains small.

Peru

In 1993 the Peruvian government reformed the national pension system, introducing a privately managed defined contribution scheme to complement the publicly managed pay-as-you-go scheme. New employees had to join the system but could choose between the two schemes.

The pension reform law allows insurance companies to offer two types of annuities: personal and family. Personal annuities are less common and

---

[16]See Dowers, Fassina, and Pettinato (2001), who cite Demaestri and Guerrero (2002).

[17]Although this number is small in comparison to Argentina and Chile, the projected number of potential annuitants is expected to grow to 200,000 by 2020.

are issued in the name of workers by AFPs. Family annuities are in effect joint and survivor annuities issued by insurance companies. Many contract options are available to annuitants, including the type of currency of contributions and benefits, the mix between a scheduled (programmed) withdrawal and an annuity; and the number of years after retirement for which the pension is guaranteed. Accordingly, a wide array of products is available in the market (see Palacios and Rofman 2001).

The Superintendent of Pension Funds, a new independent institution, regulates and monitors the operations of AFPs. It also authorizes them to issue annuities to their participants. Meanwhile, the annuity market is monitored by the existing insurance supervisory agency.[18] Insurance companies are the main annuity providers in Peru, and work closely with AFPs —and are sometimes integrated with them, as is common in Argentina. In 1998 there were 16 insurance companies and AFPs in the Peru.

As in Chile, Peruvian insurance companies must use the RV85 mortality table. But given the higher mortality rate (and thus the lower life expectancy) among Peruvians, this table is even less appropriate for evaluating annuities in Peru than it is in Chile. The resulting upward pressure on annuity prices may be one of the reasons for the small current and projected number of annuitants in Peru (see Figure 10.2), along with the country's large informal workforce and low average income.

Bolivia

Beginning in 2002, life insurers began to offer annuities to employers who have reached retirement. Under the new system, a retiree may either buy an annuity from an authorized insurer using the contributions made over their career, which have accumulated in his individual account in the FCI, or leave the contributions and receive a variable annuity from the AFP. Two life insurers have fulfilled the requirements to offer annuities. The life insurance market, which has played a dynamic role in capital markets in Chile and elsewhere, will not have as great an impact in Bolivia because it is expected to grow slowly for a relatively long period. There are two reasons for this expectation. First, the amount that can be dedicated to buy an annuity is based on the individual accumula-

---

[18]This separation of supervision between pension managers (assigned to the SPF) and annuity issuers (old insurance supervisory agencies) can cause confusion in the responsibilities, given the frequent integration of AFPs and insurance companies. Furthermore, the regulation of the annuity market is obsolete and more suitable for small voluntary annuity markets. Chile and Argentina have changed and reviewed such rules transferring regulatory powers over annuities to the SPF.

tions in the FCI, or the employee contributions, and these have only just begun. Contributions made under the old pension system, the *compensación de cotizaciones* (CC) will be capitalized at the time of retirement and the Treasury will endorse the CC.

Second, the retiree may elect to leave his or her contributions in the FCI and receive a variable annuity. Although the variable annuity provides no guarantee on the value of the benefit of each year, the unused portion remains in the FCI in the retiree's name. This feature may be more attractive than withdrawing all funds in the FCI to purchase an annuity managed by an insurance company.

Barbados and Trinidad and Tobago

Like other English-speaking Caribbean countries, Barbados and Trinidad and Tobago share features in their social security systems and annuity markets.[19] This is despite major differences in income levels and population sizes; Trinidad and Tobago's population is five times the size of that of Barbados. Unlike in many Latin American countries, in both countries pension coverage is publicly managed and based on the defined benefit principle. Pension systems were designed in the late 1960s and early 1970s as comprehensive Beveridgian programs, managed by the state.[20] Another idiosyncrasy common is these countries' rapidly changing demographic structures. The aging of their populations coexists with relatively shallow capital markets, small financial systems, and virtually nonexistent long-term government bonds. (For more details on both countries' social security systems, see Inter-American Conference on Social Security 1995.)

The dominant structures for retirement income are publicly managed PAYG systems. Since these countries' official pension systems are not based on defined contribution or privately managed funds, annuity contracts are purchased voluntarily. But in part because of the low State pension benefits that these plans pay out, parallel schemes have

---

[19]Most of the information on annuity markets in Barbados and Trinidad and Tobago came from interviews and conversations with local experts, actuaries, and market operators— in particular, Reginald Antrobus, Marcus Bosland, St. Auban Callander, Wesley Carter, Charles Herbert, Sharon Howell Clarke, Tim Kimpton, André Lafond, Purcell Lewis, Catherine Mitchell, Richard Nuñez, Kyle Rudden, Terrence Thornhill, and Almroth Williams.

[20]Designed to provide health care, old age, survivor, and disability coverage to the entire population, Beveridgian systems are aimed at protecting against adversities across generations. By contrast, Bismarckian systems focus on linking employee contributions with retirement benefits, generating sustainability within generations.

become common, with the main purpose of complementing public pensions. Typically these are defined benefit schemes, where employers or occupational category associations manage the compensatory plans. At retirement, workers who have contributed to these plans during their working years receive a lump sum—generally proportional to their final salary—that they can use to buy an annuity.

Consequently, demand for retirement annuities is largely dominated by employer-based programs, dwarfing the number of voluntary individual purchases of annuities. An exception are deferred annuity plans, where the employer contributes to an employee's individual retirement account established through a contract between the employee and an insurance company or bank. Occupational insurance policies or, more generally, group ones, pool longevity risk across the members of a plan, reducing mortality-driven uncertainties in annuity products. These products are becoming increasingly common, especially in Trinidad and Tobago.

As discussed above, insurance companies require access to mortality data to assess and price annuities. Given the lack of quality data in both countries, insurers refer to both corporate information—produced within the company and based on past operations—and publicly available mortality tables, like the one used in Latin American countries. These are generally lagged to capture current domestic annuitants' profiles by using past foreign ones. A company's actuaries decide which source to use and how to adapt it to the local pool of annuitants.

At the level of the Caribbean as a whole there are precedents for regional efforts to produce mortality tables and adapt them to better fit the demographic profiles of individual countries. This represents an example of cooperation at the financial and actuarial level among corporations.

Some companies in Barbados and in Trinidad and Tobago manage mortality risk by comparing their own results (actual death claims) with published mortality tables (expected), which are used in the calculation of reserves—generally GAM71 is used and adapted to local conditions. Even when expenditures for death claims are higher than forecast, in general the final ratio of actual to expected claims is in the region of the 99 percent of the forecasted figures. The reference tables should continue to improve as further adjustments are made.

In addition to uncertainties at the demographic level, market operators and experts in both countries have described investment risk as the main source of uncertainty in the provision of annuities. The longest maturity for domestic bonds rarely reaches 10 years, and when it does, it lacks credibility because the securities include clauses that allow the government to redeem them before the term. The natural solution is to offer annuities using conservative discount rates while, at the same time, building up considerable security reserves. The interest risk due to potential rate reductions is the most important margin affecting the reserve calculation, according to the 1999 annual report from Life of Barbados. Furthermore, this margin is established in relation to the current economic and political environment. An additional interest margin is often added to allow for the impact of future dividend expectations of policyholders. The interest margin is also determined to allow for potential asset default.

Large insurance companies have an advantage in generating annuitant data from within, and in carrying out such precautionary measures. A few companies have considerable experience in these markets—sometimes through international operations in similar markets. Given their large scale of operations, they can gather mortality data and cover their risk using large reserves reinvested in local real estate. They are still able to profit from an increasingly lucrative industry.[21] The drawback is the difficulty for smaller and younger companies to enter or survive such markets. Given the expansion of annuity markets in recent years, most operators have declared that regulation of the institutions that invest and annuitize the retirement savings accumulated by workers is lax and incomplete, requiring major updates and additional clauses.

In Barbados major actors in the most common type of market, the deferred annuity market, are commercial banks, credit unions, and trust companies (along with insurance companies). These institutions are growing in number and in customers, and manage registered retirement savings plans. These plans are the other main component of the third level of the retirement income system. Like occupational pension plans, registered retirement savings plans are intended to help people build up retirement income to replace a portion of their preretirement earnings. These plans encourage regular saving for retirement through tax breaks. People deduct the amount of their contributions from their taxable income each year, reducing their income taxes. The money that accrues from year to year on plan investments is also free from income tax until the plan is wound up. Furthermore, people can cash in registered retirement savings plans when they retire and use the proceeds to buy annuities that pay fixed amounts every month. The income from annuities is taxable, but since many people are in lower tax brackets after they retire, they pay less in taxes than they would have during their working lives.

---

[21] In Barbados and Trinidad and Tobago, the main companies providing annuities are Mutual, Life of Barbados, and Clico.

Both Trinidad and Tobago and Barbados will have to make some policy decisions in the near future on pension reform. When making choices, legislators, regulators, and policymakers will have to take into account the weaknesses of domestic annuity, financial, and capital markets. The problems that reforming countries have faced in the past (and are remedying today) may provide lessons for small countries planning to reform their pensions in the same direction.

Conclusion

The ultimate aim of pension arrangements is to alleviate the threat of sharp reductions in income during old age by transferring resources from workers to the elderly. In other words, the arrangements provide workers with the expectation (and, in some cases, the certainty) of a secure stream of income after retirement. The prospect of an old age crisis, however, is an increasingly debated topic among policymakers, driven largely by increasing pressure from unfavorable demographic and structural trends. The simultaneous increase in the size of the group of elderly individuals relative to workers, and the frequently poor management of existing PAYG public pension systems—as well the shortcomings of the private system that the recent financial scandals have brought to light—points to a reform of the principles on which the current systems operate, and the structures that manage them.

As such, it is becoming increasingly important for workers to have access to financial instruments, such as annuities, that help them insure against the risk of outliving or over consuming their assets after they retire. This chapter has examined how life annuity products operate in Latin America and the Caribbean, concentrating on constraints on the expansion of such products.

References

Acuña, Rodrigo and Augusto Iglesias. 2001. *Chile's Pension Reform after 20 Years*. Presentation at a seminar on pension reform, May, The World Bank, Washington, D.C.

Asociación Boliviana de Aseguradores. 2003. *Quincuagésima Cuarta Memoria*. Gestión Julio 2002–Junio 2003. La Paz.

Barr, Nicholas. 1998. *The Economics of the Welfare State*. Stanford, CA.: Stanford University Press.

Blake, David. 1999. *Annuities in Pension Plans.* Commentary at World Bank Annuities Workshop, 7–8 June, Washington, D.C.

Brown, Jeffrey. 2000a. *Differential Mortality and the Value of Individual Account Retirement Annuities.* National Bureau of Economic Research Working Paper No. 7560. Cambridge, MA.

———. 2000b. *How Should We Insure Longevity Risk in Pensions and Social Security?* An Issue Brief for the Center for Retirement Research, Boston College, Number 4 (August), Boston, MA.

Brown, Jeffrey, Olivia Mitchell, and James J. Poterba, eds. 2000a. Mortality Risk, Inflation Risk, and Annuity Products. Pension Research Council Working Paper 2000–10.The Wharton School, University of Pennsylvania, Philadelphia.

———. 2000b. The Role of Real Annuities and Indexed Bonds in an Individual Accounts Retirement Program. In *Risk Aspects of Investment-Based Social Security Reform,* eds. John Y. Campbell and Martin Feldstein. Chicago: University of Chicago Press.

Brown, Jeffrey, Olivia Mitchell, James J. Poterba, and Mark Warshawsky. 1999. Taxing Retirement Income: Nonqualified Annuities and Distribution from Qualified Accounts. *National Tax Journal* LII3 (September): 563–92.

———. 2001. *The Role of Annuity Markets in Financing Retirement.* Cambridge, MA. MIT Press.

Bustamante Jeraldo, Julio. 2004. El sistema de pensiones en Chile. Paper presented at workshop on Pension Reform, Inter-American Development Bank, 8 December, Washington, D.C.

Callund, Jonathan. 1999. *Annuities in Latin America.* Commentary at World Bank Annuities Workshop, 7–8 June, Washington, D.C.

Chiappori, Pierre André and Bernard Salanie. 2000. Testing for Asymmetric Information in Insurance Markets. *Journal of Political Economy* 108 (February): 56–78.

Cutler, David. 2001. Health Care and the Public Sector. In *Handbook of Public Economics,* eds. Alan Auerbach and Martin Feldstein. Amsterdam: Elsevier Science.

Davis, E. Philip. 2002. Issues in the Regulation of Annuities Markets. Working Paper 26/02. Center for Research on Pensions and Welfare Policies, Moncalieri, Italy.

Demaestri, Edgardo and Federico Guerrero. 2002. The Rationale for Integrating Financial Regulation and Supervision in Latin America and the Caribbean. Sustainable Development Department Technical Papers Series (IFM-135), Inter-American Development Bank, Washington, D.C. (November).

Devesa-Carpio, José E., and Carlos Vidal-Meliá. 2001. The Reformed Pension Systems in Latin America. Pension Reform Primer. The World Bank, Washington, D.C. (November).

Dowers, Kenroy, Stefano Fassina, and Stefano Pettinato. 2001. Pension Reform in Small Emerging Economies: Issues and Challenges. Sustainable Development Department Technical Papers Series (IFM-130). Inter-American Development Bank, Washington, D.C. (December).

Doyle, Suzanne and John Piggott. 2001. Mandatory Annuity Design in Developing Economies. Pension Reform Primer. The World Bank, Washington, D.C. (January).

_____. 2002. Integrating Payouts: Annuity Design and Public Pension Benefits in Mandatory Defined Contribution Plans. http://rider. wharton.upenn.edu/~prc/wp2002.html.

Doyle, Suzanne, Olivia Mitchell, and John Piggott. 2001. Annuity Values in Defined Contribution Retirement Systems: The Case of Singapore and Australia. Pension Research Council Working Paper 2001-4, Federación Interamericana de Empresas de Seguros (Fides). Available at http://www.fideseguros.com

Finkelstein, Amy and James Poterba. 1999. Selection Effects in the Market for Individual Annuities: New Evidence from the United Kingdom. National Bureau of Economic Research Working Paper No. 7168. Cambridge, MA.

Friedman, F. and Mark Warshawsky. 1990. The Cost of Annuities: Implications for Savings, Behavior and Bequests. *Quarterly Journal of Economics* (February): 133–54.

Gillion, Colin, John Turner, Clive Bailey, and Dennis Latulippe. 2000. *Social Security Pensions: Development and Reform.* Geneva: International Labour Organization.

James, Estelle and Dimitri Vittas. 1999. Annuities Markets in Comparative Perspective. Working paper presented at the World Bank Conference on New Ideas About Old Age Security, Washington, D.C. Available at www.worldbank.org/pensions

Karacadag, Cem, V. Sudararajan, and Jennifer Elliot. 2003. Managing Risk in Financial Market Development: The Role of Sequencing. In *The Future of Domestic Capital Markets in Developing Countries,* eds. Robert Litan, Michael Pomerleano, and V. Sundararajan. Washington, D.C.: Brookings Institution Press.

Lane, Michael F. 2001. Annuitization: An Eye Opening Analysis. *Journal of Retirement Planning* May–June.

Life of Barbados. 1999. *Annual Report.* Bridgetown, Barbados.

LIMRA (Life Insurance Marketing Research Association). 1999. Report.

McCarthy, David and Olivia S. Mitchell. 2000. Assessing the Impact of Mortality Assumptions on Annuity Valuation: Cross-Country Evidence. Pension Research Council Working Paper 2001-3, The Wharton School, University of Pennsylvania, Philadelphia.

———. 2002. Estimating International Adverse Selection in Annuities. *North American Actuarial Journal* (October).

Mitchell, Olivia S. 2000. Building an Environment for Pension Reform in Developing Countries. In *Foundations of Pension Finance,* eds. Zvi Bodie and E Phillip Davis. Cheltenham, U.K.: Edward Elgar.

———. 2001. Developments in Decumulation: The Role of Annuity Products in Financing Retirement. Pension Research Council Working Paper 2001-9, The Wharton School, University of Pennsylvania, Philadelphia.

Mitchell, Olivia S. and David McCarthy. 2001. Estimating International Adverse Selection in Annuities. Unpublished paper (May). Available at http://rider.wharton.upenn.edu/~mitchelo/OSMsf1401.pdf

Mitchell, Olivia S., James M. Poterba, Mark Warshawsky, and Jeffrey R. Brown. 1999. New Evidence on the Money's Worth of Individual Annuities. *American Economic Review* (December): 1299–1318.

Mitchell, Olivia S., Bodie Zvi, Hammond P. Brett, and Stephen Zeldes, eds. 2002. *Innovation in Retirement Financing.* Philadelphia: Pension Research Council Publication. Wharton School.

Murthi, Mamta J., Michael Orszag, and Peter R. Orszag. 2000. Annuity Margins in the UK. Unpublished paper, Center for Pensions and Social Insurance, Birkbeck College, University of London.

Musalem, Alberto and Thierry Tressel. 2003. Institutional Savings and Financial Markets: The Role of Contractual Savings Institutions. In *The Future of Domestic Capital Markets in Developing Countries,* eds. Robert Litan, Michael Pomerleano, and V. Sundararajan. Washington, D.C.: Brookings Institution Press.

Organisation for Economic Co-operation and Development (OECD). 2000. *Private Pension Systems and Policy Issues.* Paris: OECD.

Orszag, Michael. 2000. Annuity: The Problems. Working paper, Birkbeck College, University of London.

Palacios, Robert and Rafael P. Rofman. 2001. Annuity Markets and Benefit Design in Multipillar Pension Schemes: Experience and Lessons from Four Latin American Countries. World Bank Pension Reform Primer. Available at www.worldbank.org/pensions.

Poterba, James M. 2001. Annuity Markets and Retirement Security. Center for Retirement Research, Boston College (June). Available at http://www.bc.edu/crr.

Poterba, James M., Steven F. Venti, and David A. Wise, 1999. *Implications of Rising Personal Retirement Saving, NBER Reprints* 2209 (also Working Paper 6295), National Bureau of Economic Research, Cambridge, MA.

Rofman, Rafael P. 2001. Annuitization in Pension Schemes. The Case of Argentina. Seminar for Actuaries and Statisticians, International Social Security Administration, 21–22 November, Montevideo.

Rothschild, Michael and Joseph Stiglitz.1976. An Essay on the Economics of Imperfect Information. *Quarterly Journal of Economics* 90: 629–49.

Society of Actuaries (SOA). 1999. Exposure Draft, The RP-2000 Mortality Tables. Working paper. Society of Actuaries, Schaumberg, Illinois (October).

Superintendencia de Administradoras de Fondos de Pensiones. 2002. *Series Estadísticas*. Gobierno de Chile. Available at http:///www.safp.cl/

Tuljapurkar, Shripad and Carl Boe. 1998. Mortality Change and Forecasting: How Much and How Little Do We Know? *North American Actuarial Journal* 2(4): 13–47.

United Nations. 2001. *World Population Prospects* (2000 Revision). Population Division, Department of Economic and Social Affairs, New York.

Walker, Eduardo and Fernando Lefort. 2000. Pension Reform and Capital Markets: Are There Any (Hard) Links? National Bureau of Economic Research, Cambridge, MA.

Walliser, J. 1998. The Effect of Privatization of Social Security on Private Annuity Markets. Congressional Budget Office Working Paper, Washington, D.C. (February).

Weaver, R. Kent.2003. The Politics of Public Pension Reform. Center for Retirement Research, Boston College. Available at http://www.bc.edu-crr.

The World Bank. 1994. *Averting the Old Age Crisis*. Oxford University Press.

————. 2001. Annuities: Regulating Withdrawals from Individual Pension Accounts. Pension Reform Primer. Washington, D.C.

Yaari, M. 1965. Uncertain Lifetime, Life Insurance and the Theory of Consumer. *Review of Economic Studies* 32: 137–50.

Yermo, Juan. 2001. *Private Annuity in OECD Countries*. Paris: OECD.

Zipt, Robert. 2003. *Fixed Income Economics*. San Diego, Calif.: Academic Press.

SECTION FIVE

The Pension Industry
Point of View

CHAPTER 11

Agenda for the Reform of Pension Systems in Latin America

*Agustín Vidal-Aragón de Olives and David Taguas Coejo**

The private sector must participate actively in developing the reforms needed in the social security systems of Latin America. Indeed, financial institutions are the "technology partners" of the Latin American countries in which they operate. They can import the management practices and technology platforms that have been most successful in other regions.

This chapter takes a "chain of production" view toward pension reform, looking comprehensively at the interrelated institutions and processes that make up the pension system.

The analysis and recommendations are based on the joint research of the American Pension and Insurance Division and the Economic Research Department of the Banco Bilbao Vizcaya Argentaria (BBVA Group) which assesses the outlook for pension systems in the region. The BBVA Group has more than 20 years' experience as a major pension fund manager in Latin America and the Caribbean. This experience has enabled the authors to consider the effects of reforms in a broader context and conclude that the results obtained by the reformed systems have been positive in the region, even if lower than expected. Nonetheless, the need to reform the distribution systems is increasing, given the forecasts of demographic aging.

---

* Agustín Vidal-Aragón de Olives is the Managing Director of Pensions and Insurance, Banco Bilbao Vizcaya Argentaria (BBVA Group). David Taguas Coejo is Deputy Chief Economist of the BBVA Group. The views expressed herein are those of the authors and do not necessarily reflect those of the BBVA Group.

Against this backdrop, this chapter presents an analysis and proposals aimed at maintaining the balance of the pension cycle process and ensuring its efficiency.

BBVA's proposal seeks to identify the areas that can make the systems more efficient, thus making it possible to meet the objectives of both economic policy and social security. In short, social security systems must be one more tool contributing to economic development, in a broad sense. The discussion that follows identifies the areas that should be added to the work agendas of the countries with reformed systems to improve the operation and efficiency of their social security systems. The discussion begins with an overview of the chain of production of pension systems.

The Chain of Production of Pension Systems

The main objective of social security systems is to generate savings to finance old age expeditures. They have other goals, including providing financial assistance to surviving spouses and/or children and providing disability income. The latter require specific financial mechanisms. Moreover, because social security systems also contain a social welfare component, disbursements are regulated and must follow guidelines that ensure the availability of capital.

How to cover and finance the contingencies insured by social security systems has not been well analyzed. Yet contingency coverage can have the greatest impact on costs, and are likely to rise in the future.

Pension system reform will require the creation of specialized institutions to administer pensions. Pension administration is currently carried out by pension funds (Administradores de Fondos de Pensiones, or AFPs), which rely on management commissions to set up the operational, financial, and contractual infrastructure to fulfill their duties. To provide reliable life and disability insurance policies, the AFPs will require the support of insurance companies specialized in the coverage of these contingencies.

Moreover, the process of paying out benefits is not risk-free. The payment of a pension from an individual's capitalized account in an optimal situation demands the use of specific financial and actuarial techniques. This process is regulated by law, giving individuals an option as to the form of distribution (whether social security payments, scheduled withdrawals, or some mix), but always ensuring that sufficient capital is available. Thus income adjustments, risks, and administration of surpluses are regulated. Toward that end, AFPs have the obligation to act as custodians of the process, informing participants of the advantages and disadvantages of each option available to them. They must also facilitate fund transfers. If the participant wishes to transfer the risk to an annuity, the AFP makes arrangements with an annuity insurance company.

Thus defined, the pension cycle process entails addressing the overall operation of these interrelated institutions and processes. The amount of contributions, their use, the determination of commissions, the economic value of the benefits guaranteed under the system, and the defined benefits guaranteed must be economically related in such a way that the pension cycle process remains in balance, ensuring its efficiency.

Moreover, these processes take place over a very long time. They are subject to changes in demographic and macroeconomic scenarios, as well as changes in the biometric variables of the population. All these aspects must also be taken into consideration.

Given this "chain of production" view of the pension cycle, pension funds (AFPs) must implicitly or explicitly manage the process as a whole within the defined regulatory framework. They must determine to what extent and through which legal means they can ensure the best performance of the system and reduce risks.

The Management of Demographic and Biometric Risks

The source used to determine the average cost of life insurance and disability insurance are mortality tables. They are also the basis for determining the premium for social security income and the reference for adjusting a pension in a scheduled withdrawal. Thus mortality tables constitute the theoretical basis for determining the price of risk coverage, for social security payments as well as for life and disability insurance.

The sustainability of the operations of the social security system requires identifying, measuring, controlling, and managing both current and future risks. Legal requirements and regulation can provide technical standards for dealing with these risks. As these risks are associated with a process of demographic transition that is especially intense in Latin America, these standards are dynamic in nature and valid only on a temporary basis. Therefore, the process of adjustment must be gradual and based on empirical experience and generally accepted forecasting procedures.

The Management of Underlying Financial and Market Risks

Another significant factor in defining the costs of contingency coverage are trends in interest rates. The average cost of life and disability insurance is the present value of the future return. Thus long-term interest rates are the determining factor of the present value.

Consequently, biometric risks as well as financial risks are transferred to and incorporated into the costs of the system and covered by the commissions charged by AFPs. They constitute the cost of operations—which significantly exceed the operations normally covered by a management commission.

Moreover, most countries administer their pension system through single funds. Some countries offer the option of participating in more than one fund, or multiple funds. (For a discussion of fund options in one of the pioneers in the region, Chile, see Chapters 3 and 7.) In addition to the risks involved for pension participants with private accounts, the use of single funds creates a serious problem for the administration of scheduled withdrawals. Fund management in the drawdown period should adhere to policies and strategies for final investments, in order to ensure that accumulated capital matches the present value of future pensions.

Recall that the option for withdrawal from the individual account is the choice of the participant, with the AFP's advice. The risks and benefits associated with the use of scheduled withdrawals or social security payments are not particularly comparable and need to be carefully considered on an individual basis. Since it is difficult for the AFPs to rely on general policies in all cases, individual policies are needed and the AFPs must support them.

From a structural point of view, it is important to maintain symmetry between contributions to the system and management commissions on the one hand, and benefits covered by the system on the other, in the form of capital and pensions promised. Maintaining such symmetry demands an appropriate economic evaluation that is adjusted over time, as the demography of society, the macroeconomic scenario, and sociocultural values develop. This type of evaluation by the regulator is essential to ensuring the system's sustainability.

Moreover, the AFPs are an integral part of the production chain and thus they must be taken into account in conducting this evaluation. Only by integrating the know-how of the AFPs that provide the services of the pension system into the information system is it be possible to evaluate the entire coverage from an economic point of view.

The Agenda for Reforms

The reforms implemented in the social security systems of a majority of Latin American countries have not been as successful as expected, either from the macroeconomic viewpoint or from that of social security (Gill, Packard, and Yermo 2005; World Bank 1994). Thus a review process is underway in the countries that have undertaken reforms, including those whose social security insurance is still based on more traditional systems.

For each country, it would be advisable to analyze whether the expectations were too high or did not consider the possibility that the reforms would be made in unfavorable macroeconomic scenarios; whether the reforms have failed and thus it would be advisable to go back to the traditional schemes; or whether the reforms have been occurring in the right direction, even if it is necessary to adjust expectations, complete the changes introduced, make others, and reinforce the results achieved in stronger social security systems.

The analysis must address the social security system as a whole. It must consider the public and private subsystems together, bearing in mind that the combination of both must reach the defined objectives. How complementary they are depends on ideological, economic, and technical issues, and may change according to the circumstances at any given time. Therefore, it is important to conclude that the concurrence of the public and private sectors is necessary to identify issues and make the improvements that those systems will need now or in the future. It is not possible to travel separate roads while trying to optimize the funds allocated to those systems, which are, by definition, scarce (see Figure 11.1).

The pension value of any private social security system (in terms of its coverage and sufficiency) can be defined as a function of contribution patterns (in terms of rate and density), the rate of return of accumulated funds (in terms of yield and volatility), and the system's costs (Figure 11.2).

Contributions are a function of the institutionally defined rate considered as a whole (since one portion of the contributions is allocated to the public system and another to the private system), the density of the contributions, and the economy's wage pattern at a given time. The contribution rate distorts the decisions of the companies and families. Those distortions affect leisure and work, consumption and savings, employment and investment. They also affect the level of pensions (in the long term), and the development of an economy and its resulting level of wealth. Thus the contribution rate defines the level of an economy's funds siphoned off for purposes of social security and returned to the economy

Figure 11.1. The Virtuous Circle of Social Welfare

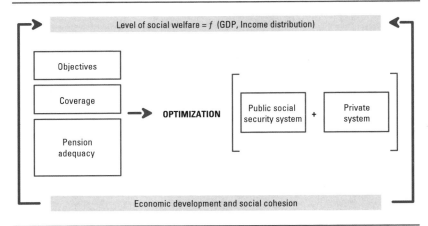

Source: Authors.

Figure 11.2. Basic Equation of Individual Account Portion of Social Security Systems (Second Pillar)

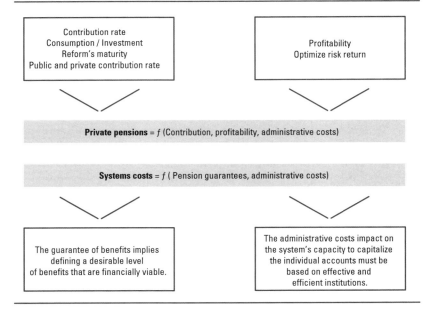

Source: Authors.

through public transfers or private investments. The contribution rate is also an important variable connecting the social security system and the countries' economic and financial systems. As such, it needs to move in tandem with any decision made in terms of financing the benefits to be covered by each of the subsystems of the social security system.

The transition period that most systems are undergoing suggests that the contributions to each of the subsystems could be changed. In any event, an analysis of the scope must be made jointly, including both public and private pensions. Lastly, when analyzing the quality and sufficiency of pensions, both public and private pensions should be considered as well, because in certain countries they are complementary.

The main indicator of the quality of pensions in terms of coverage and sufficiency is contribution density. This is applicable whether related to the frequency of contributions or to the fact that only part of the employed population contributes, even if they contribute on a regular basis. Both situations reflect different deficiencies in the system, which require different solutions.

A basic determinant of the quality of pensions is the rate of return. However, no measure of rate of return is valid from the viewpoint of the contributor. This is because contributors are interested only in maximizing profits on their horizon of accumulating capital, and that means minimizing the volatility of their capital value on that horizon. Nevertheless, once contributors become beneficiaries of the system, they are interested in having their pensions guaranteed in real terms over their lifetime biological horizon and in terms of the basic family obligations that are covered by the system. Thus an analysis should be made of the extent to which the AFPs achieve the profitability objective, as defined.

Another basic determinant of the quality of pensions are administrative costs: that is, commissions. Contributions to a private system are capitalized only after subtracting administrative costs. These costs may be divided into two fundamental areas. The first entails the cost of financing supplementary capital to pay the pensions of participants who do not complete the capitalization period because they die or become disabled during their working lives, as well as the pension of their beneficiaries (surviving spouses and children). Accordingly, improving pension quality requires making pensions that cover both these contingencies and retirement more adequate.

Secondly, administrative costs include remuneration of capital invested and risks taken by the private pension sector. Minimizing those costs by making the processes involved more efficient would certainly improve pension quality.

Having thus defined the main issues, the discussion continues by classifying each of the critical objectives of the social security system and identifying the institutions that need to be reformed to better serve each objective.

Contribution Rates

Contribution rates to the system must be sufficient to meet the level of benefits the society wishes to finance. Society determines the level of benefits, in turn, according to criteria of efficiency and equity. Efficiency is an important factor affecting consumption and investment decisions. Equity must be maintained between generations, as well as among groups within the same generation. Thus the basic requirement is the sufficiency of contributions to meet these criteria. Although this issue is obvious, it is generally avoided in the debate and is obfuscated by making discussions more general.

The contribution rates established by law in the region are about 10 percent of wages. This rate will not lead to very generous benefits in the future, forecasts indicate. This would be true even under a relatively optimistic macroeconomic scenario, in terms of the trend of actual wages and returns on investments. Moreover, in some countries, such as Argentina, rates required by law, which were already low, were decreased even further as an exceptional measure during the economic crisis to encourage employers to retain their employees and to better enable participants to continue making contributions.

As an illustration, the discussion below presents the results of a internal study on the outlook for the Argentine pension system done by the BBVA Group (Taguas Coejo and Vidal-Aragón de Olives 2005). The study's conclusions are generally true for the rest of the region. Interpreting the results of this type of exercise requires extreme caution because of the complexity involved. However, simulations have shown that if the contribution level in Argentina remains at 7 percent, replacement rates in terms of final wages could drop from the current rate of 60 percent (pertaining to the recipients of public and private benefits) to 22 percent by 2050.

An increase in personal contribution rates to 11 percent, as required by the Pension Reform Law 24,241 of 1994, brings them to a level similar to the rates in effect for countries with reformed pension systems. This would slightly improve the scenario for Argentina. Focusing on the beneficiaries of both subsystems (public and private) simultaneously, the average monthly benefit would go from about 500 pesos in 2003 to 640 pesos in 2050 (in constant 2003 pesos). Although the replacement rate would also fall, it would do so to a lesser degree than in the prior scenario, reaching 30 percent in 2050, 21 percent higher than the current rate (Figure 11.3).

An even more crucial variable is formal employment, approximated by contribution density: that is, the number of months a year that a worker is employed and contributes to the system. A simulation was done of the replacement rates for young workers, classified by the regularity of their contributions. Workers making ten contributions per year had a replacement rate of 51 percent; those contributing six times per year, about 21 percent; and those contributing twice a year, 8 percent.

The second determining factor is the distribution of revenues from contributions to the public and private subsystems. During the transition phase, all systems show a deficit, as a portion of the contributions is allocated to new private accounts, while obligations do not decrease until several fiscal years later. In most countries the deficit is temporary. It takes two decades for the public subsystem to start showing a surplus. An empirical analysis of Argentina's situation shows that in actuarial terms, a surplus accumulated through 2050 could exceed 25 percent of GDP.

Thus one measure for increasing the replacement rate of private pensions could consist of lowering the employer's contribution rate—totally allocated to the public subsystem in Argentina—and increasing the personal contribution rate to the private account system. According to BBVA's calculations, the employer's contribution rate could be decreased by 2.5 percent for system participants, while the personal contribution rate to private accounts could be increased in the same proportion, up to 13.5 percent, and an actuarial equilibrium could be maintained. As shown in Figure 11.4, that would permit a significantly higher accumulation of funds in the AFPs. The average monthly benefit would exceed 750 pesos (in constant 2003 pesos): some 43 percent higher than the current benefit, with a 35 percent replacement rate in terms of the final salary.

The results for Argentina, which also apply to the majority of Latin American economies, confirm the importance of contribution rates. That includes their pension component, which is a determinant of the benefit level, as well as their macroeconomic impact on the budget. Given the transition costs associated with any reform, it is crucial that such an analysis be done in each country using actuarial techniques, and not exclusively based on annual revenues and expenditures.

In short, contribution rates should be thought of as a dynamic parameter of the social protection system, defined in each period under technical actuarial, financial, and social criteria.

Figure 11.3 Simulation of Replacement Wages and Replacement Pension Rates, Argentina
(11% Contribution)

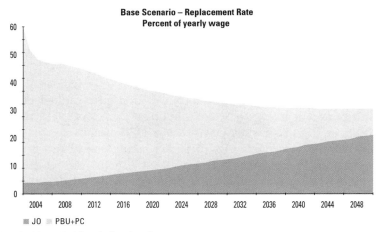

Base Scenario – Replacement Rate
Percent of yearly wage

■ JO ■ PBU+PC

Note: Recipients of public and private benefits
Wage in 2004 = 900 pesos (2003 prices); in 2050 = 2152 pesos (2003 pesos)

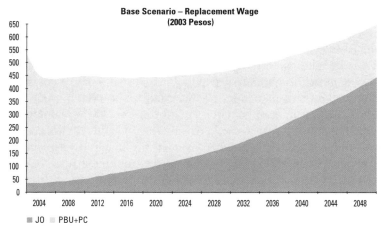

Base Scenario – Replacement Wage
(2003 Pesos)

■ JO ■ PBU+PC

Note: Recipients of public and private benefits

JO = private pension system benefits.
PBU = Prestación Básica Universal, the minimum pension.
PC = Prestación Complemetaria a benefit recognizing contributions under old social security system.
Source: BBVA and authors' estimates.

Figure 11.4. Funds Accumulated in the AFPs, Argentina
(percentage of each year GDP)

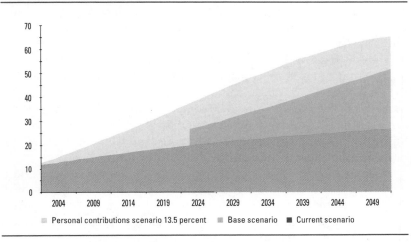

Personal contributions scenario 13.5 percent   Base scenario   Current scenario

Note: GDP in 2050 estimated at 1.98 billion pesos (in 2003 pesos).
Source: BBVA and authors' estimates.

Rate of Return on Investments

The institutional framework within which investments are developed is designed under the assumption that what optimizes their yield is the market competition between the AFPs, as if these were investment funds within certain risk parameters. In other words, inspired by investment fund regulation in the countries that developed this system, regulators decided to apply it to social security savings. That approach was perfectly compatible with the role assigned to market rules and the possibility that participants could switch to another manager at any time, in hope of getting a better comparative return.

However, this approach minimized the importance of the final nature of the funds used to finance social security benefits. Consequently, in their definition of asset management policies and strategies for active participants as well as pensioners (scheduled withdrawals), the AFPs inevitably must pay attention to a predetermined time horizon. This means that optimization of the invested capital is valid only insofar as it occurs at the appropriate time. Otherwise, serious harm could come to the system's participants and beneficiaries as a result of market volatility.

Furthermore, competition based on the rate of return obtained by the system as a whole as a *benchmark* has created a herd effect that has invalidated competition as a generator of efficiency. This is because the risks for the private pension industry—which result from defining a guaranteed minimum rate of return based on that *benchmark*—are disproportionate, relative to the advantages of being competitive by differentiating themselves in terms of their rates of return.

Thus the sector as well as regulators must face the challenge of reviewing the array of institutions and standards that affect the management of the funds' assets. The purpose of this review is to define an institutional framework that assigns to market competition the added value that it can actually add. Furthermore, it must allow the implementation of final investment strategies and policies, within risk guidelines deemed appropriate in each country and market.

An investment process reform of this magnitude is not possible unless marketing procedures and accounting standards are similarly reformed. The key elements of the current institutional design must be reviewed.

The best management strategy in terms of return/risk is one focused on maximizing the accumulated capital for each participant to the date that he or she retires and starts receiving benefits. The management focus should be personalized and oriented to the ultimate stream of benefits.

It is unrealistic to think that such detailed management could be carried out at a reasonable cost. However, considerable progress can be made toward optimizing capital accumulation up to the retirement date. A first approximation would be to separate the single mandatory pension fund into several funds designed to manage contributions accumulated by participants in different age segments. Next, the capital accumulated in one fund could be transferred to the appropriate fund when the age limit set by the previous fund is reached. These steps represent a formula for adjusting management strategies and policies to meet the ultimate objective. Lastly, a different fund should be set up for retiree groups, with a management style close to that of Asset Liability Management (ALM). A fund of that nature should be based on long life expectancies and bring benefits to an adequate level. In this way, the accumulated capital will be sufficient for the entire life of participants, as well as the period required to cover the benefits promised to their beneficiaries.

The allocation of contributions to a specific fund would be done in accordance with a participant's yield/risk preferences—or, as a default option, to the fund corresponding to a participant's age segment. That freedom of choice would be limited when the general interest of the system's operations must take priority over an individual's choice. For example, choice would be limited for participants who are very close to their retirement age or who are already receiving a retirement pension.

Chile has been pursuing such an approach since launching the multiple funds, or *multifondos* program, that enable participants to participate in more than one fund (see Chapter 7). Mexico and Peru have recently taken steps in that direction as well. There is still room to improve the separation of the funds to adjust management to the priority of maximizing the accumulated capital at the time of retirement. Meeting that objective would provide a high degree of certainty in terms of the amount to be received as the date of retirement approaches.

This matter must be considered carefully because of the impact a given valuation system may have on a participant's accumulated capital at the time he/she either retires or becomes disabled, and could affect his/her beneficiaries, should the participant die.

Correct valuation under strict market guidelines facilitates transparency and prevents arbitrage between the actual value and the book value. Such arbitrage could lead to asymmetries between those who remain in one fund and those that transfer from one fund to another at a given time.

On the other hand, strict valuation at market prices creates significant differences between a participant's accumulated capital at the time of retirement and the capital a participant would have accumulated if he/she had retired at another time. Such differences are the result of the volatility of the market value of financial assets. This situation is magnified if the pension fund is a single fund and management must consider the final average horizon of all participants. Figure 11.5 shows the annual return of a Type-C Fund in the Chilean pension system, since inception.

Returns were highly volatile in the period analyzed. In some years, the accumulated capital increased by double digits, reaching almost 30 percent in one of those years; in other years, rates of return were negative. Under these circumstances, the loss of profits for retired participants in certain periods compared with profits for retirees in other periods has introduced marked differences in the level of benefits obtained.

Should the funds become volatile assets, as can happen to equities, the risk of loss in the value of the accumulated capital in the short term could be very high. This would give rise to a high degree of uncertainty as retirement age approaches, in terms of the benefit to be obtained at the time of disinvestment.

As a participant gets older, the progressive allocation of the accumulated capital to funds whose management focuses on guaranteeing less volatility allows greater certainty as to the amount a participant will receive at the time of retirement.

Figure 11.5. Real Return of Pension Funds, Chile
(annual percentage)

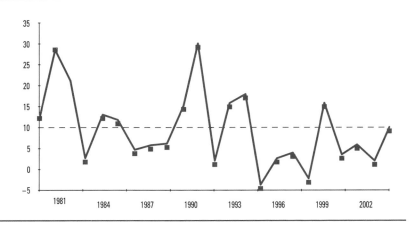

Note: The standard deviation of the returns is 8.6.
Source: SAFP, Chile.

Using the proposed multiple fund scheme to reach the defined objectives, it would be possible to propose valuations based on market prices for all funds, except the funds backing the benefits of the group in the age segment close to retirement and the group of participants that had already retired. In these two cases, funds would be valued considering financial assets at acquisition price. Returns generated by the assets would then be added over time until maturity, accrued at the investment's internal rate of return.

To apply this valuation method, it would be necessary to establish mandatory restrictions regarding three issues. The first is the correlation—in time and amount—of the flows generated by the assets with those forecast for the group of participants in each fund. This aspect is especially important in the management of funds that back scheduled withdrawals. The second is the relationship between the assets' present value and the flows forecast for participants. This aspect is also especially important in the management of funds that back scheduled withdrawals. Lastly, it makes no sense to allow participants to switch from these funds to another valued at market prices.

Obtaining a minimum rate of return relative to the system's average rate of return is a regulatory guarantee in all Latin American countries except Mexico and Bolivia. This guarantee works against the efficient management of the funds. This objective is unrelated to the time horizon to which assets must be managed. That horizon may be very different for different funds. Moreover, it triggers the herd effect, forcing all the funds to position themselves in the same manner as the majority of the system, and it does not guarantee competitive management.

The need to establish a formula that guarantees efficient management could be defined through regulations as well as by activating market forces—to the extent that participants may choose a manager and a fund. The following guarantee mechanism could be used as an alternative:

- A VaR (value at risk) limit for the fund according to a basket used as the benchmark for each category or type of fund, and
- An absolute VaR limit supplemented by regulatory limits by instrument and term, for each type of fund.

This proposal is not simple to implement, as it requires identifying the benchmark or portfolio distribution for each type of fund, the horizon where the value at risk[1] is determined, and the hypotheses supporting the determination of that VaR.

The introduction of this type of solution would make it less necessary for AFPs to provide cash reserves as collateral for the guaranteed minimum rate of return, and to guarantee the managers' solvency, since that guaranteed minimum would disappear and be replaced by the proposed formulas.

Standards on Transfer of Funds

There are currently no restrictions on voluntary fund transfers, except in very rare cases. Historical experience shows that under normal circumstances, transfers have not served the purpose of maximizing profits for the participant. By way of illustration, note the differential between the average rate of return earned throughout the life of the individual capitalization system in Chile for the system as a whole, and that earned by the most profitable fund each year (Figure 11.6).

A participant who chose in advance the most profitable fund for the entire period (not year by year, as shown in the figure above) would have had an average yearly rate of return that is 3 percent higher than the system's average rate of return.

---

[1] In every instance, the value at risk would be related to the time horizon of benefits to be paid and could be different for each fund.

Figure 11.6. Profitability Differentials between Type C Funds in Chile
(annual percentage)

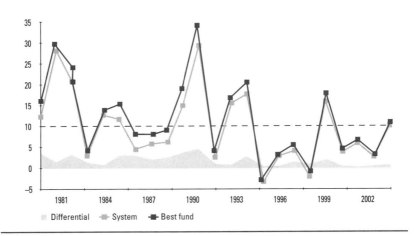

Source: Chile's Superintendence of Pensions Funds and BBVA.

This analysis raises the question of whether the transfer costs associated with protecting payments are justified and whether a limit on the number of transfers per year between funds is justified. Does it make sense to have an operation in which only new contributions can be transferred? A contributor would receive capital accumulated in different pension funds, upon retirement.

Another aspect worth contemplating is whether transfers to funds in the same category with different managers should be made in cash or in kind. This will undoubtedly be related to the valuation procedure chosen for each type of fund.

A final matter is the latitude for transferring amounts accumulated in one fund to the appropriate fund, when the age limit is reached for a participant managed in the first fund. If the time at which they must make their transfer coincides with a cyclical downturn as transfers, within reason, must be made in cash, there should be some leeway available to the participants to prevent their accumulated capital from being penalized.

The regulations governing pension funds include a wide range of risk limits, basically dealing with credit risk, and concern such matters as the maximum concentration authorized per instrument, the issuer, and the sector. In addition, in the case of the Mexican retirement investment funds (Sociedad de Inversión Especializada de Fondos para el Retiro, or

Siefores), there are market risk limits that are measured in terms of VaR (see Chapter 8).

The formula of specialized funds for the different age groups may require a standard as to the portfolio's allocation by type of instrument and term, together with a maximum VaR. Alternatively, it could provide for a maximum relative VaR against a selected benchmark, based on the type of guidelines selected.

Regulatory restrictions and the state of development in the local capital markets have given rise to excessive portfolio concentration in domestic public debt instruments. The limited depth of local capital markets has led to a search for alternatives, as managers seek to diversify portfolios through foreign investment. Many participants in this industry defend the objective of maximizing the capital accumulated for participants when they retire, disregarding other considerations such as the fact that pension funds contribute to internal savings and the growth of the local economy.

The BBVA Group places a high priority on both objectives. BBVA deems it critical to earmark a portion of these funds for financing investment projects using the guarantee of financial soundness offered by sophisticated structured financial instruments today. Fortunately, projects and structured notes for financing infrastructure have started to show up in most of the countries where pension funds participate actively. However, these investments are still small relative to the total amount being managed. To illustrate this, some of these projects are presented in Table 11.1.

Another issue to consider related to investment management efficiency is the need to update fiduciary management regulations to optimize the accumulated capital of the participants. Excessive regulation may end up limiting management efficiency. Moreover, regardless of any regulations in effect, the manager, as the fund's legal representative, must meet its fiduciary responsibilities and despite the regulatory restrictions, must be guided by best practices. Such practices must translate into rigorous procedures to select and manage all types of risks. These procedures must be at least as rigorous as those used by a trader in trades for his/her own account. The interests of the managed fund must take priority whenever there is a conflict with the manager's own interest. These procedures must be expressly formalized and approved by the governing bodies of the respective institutions, so they may be subject to the supervision of the oversight authorities in each of the systems.

Publication of investment policies and the reasonable potential value at risk associated with those policies is highly recommended in the sphere of fiduciary responsibility.

Table 11.1	AFP Participation in Productive Projects		
Country	Project	Total amount of the issue (US$ million)	% Financing provided by pension funds
Chile	* Financing of concessions for 8 projects	2,286	41
	* Participation in the capital of concessions 10 projects	645	4
	* Direct investment in infrastructure	961	41
Argentina	* Agriculture projects (2 projects)	14	25
	Forestry investment	21	86
	Investment in buildings	45	52
	Others	116	15
Peru	* Financing of direct/project/concessionaries (14 Projects)	650	14
Bolivia	* Financing titling or collection rights for two infrastructure projects	23	43

In addition, within the proposed operating scheme, the pension fund manager's advice and recommendations acquire special importance. This would include the proper time for switching among the different funds assigned to the various age segments and the most appropriate solution at the time of retirement.

Administrative Expenses: Commissions

Although the commissions charged by the AFPs in the various countries differ in amount and structure, in general, they must all be sufficient to cover the following activities:

- Benefit payments for contingencies: that is, for benefits not financed by the participant's contributions because of an interruption in the capitalization process due to death, disability, or other reasons defined in the system itself.
- The operating costs of processes delegated for management by the private sector.
- Return on capital promised by the AFPs in their typical business activities for the exposures they assume.

Given that the covered contingencies and guaranteed benefits in each system are different, Figure 11.7 presents a breakdown of the cost of

Figure 11.7. The Contingency-Cost Component of Commissions over Contributions

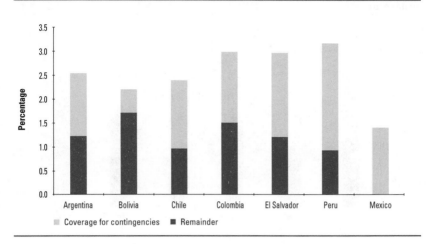

Source: Chile's Superintendence of Pensions Funds and BBVA.

covering contingencies by country, based on the current membership structure. The figure allows a comprehensive comparison with the other two components for which commissions are earmarked.

The comparison of commissions paid by participants in the countries included in Figure 11.7 is not trivial because of the different kinds of contingency coverage that must be considered and the special operating features of each system.[2]

Setting the cost of contingencies aside, commissions are about 1.5 percent of base contribution wages in the majority of countries. The exceptions are Peru, where commissions are considerably higher, and Bolivia, where commissions are much lower. These variations may be justified by the implicit differences in the processes managed by the AFPs, as discussed below.

However, a figure showing commissions in relation to contribution wages does not allow a comparison of these commissions with international standards in similar industries, such as fiduciary asset management. It is also not possible to present commissions graphically on a long-term

---

[2] Furthermore, Figure 11.7 includes only commissions defined as a percentage of wages. This formula is not the only one used. Some systems define commissions based on the total funds under administration or the profits made.

Figure 11.8. The Contingency-Cost Component of Commissions over Balance under Administration

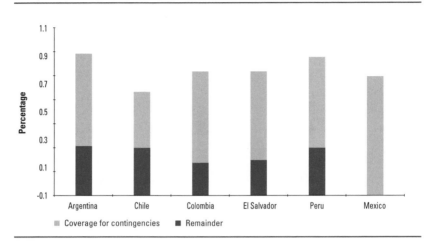

Coverage for contingencies   Remainder

Source: Chile's Superintendence of Pensions Funds and BBVA.

horizon because administration commissions are invoiced up front, at the time of the contribution, for management throughout the capitalization period. This is why, for purposes of analysis and valuation, it seems advisable to establish financial equivalency between commissions over base contribution and equivalent commissions over funds under administration (Figure 11.8).

The possibility of billing commissions based on the balance under administration has been suggested. Some of the AFPs' processing costs, such as marketing costs, are tied to new contributions. However, others are clearly tied to the assets under management, such as investment management. Finally, by its nature, the cost of covering contingency benefits is more closely related to the age profile of the participant universe, along with the contingencies covered and guaranteed benefits.

Generally speaking, commissions are now charged based on new contributions. For this reason, a change to a system based on balance under administration would require a progressive process, to avoid duplicating commissions already charged on contributions. The discussion that follows presents a breakdown of the components that must be earmarked for administrative commissions: the cost of financing coverage, management costs, and remuneration of capital.

The Cost of Financing Coverage of Contingency Benefits

The financing of contingency benefits is of a different nature than administrative costs. It is based on political decisions, rather than the efficiency of the institutions created to administer the social security system or the effectiveness of private industry.

From a conceptual point of view, an individual account system pays for benefits that are financed by individual contributions. However, society has deemed that benefits must also be paid that are only partially financed by individuals. This applies to cases in which the individual's accumulation process has been interrupted by death, disability, or certain causes set forth in the system, and the individual incurs needs that are deemed worthy of social protection. To complete the financing required, contributions are withdrawn from the system as a whole in the form of commissions or other means. This affects the adequacy of the retirement pensions of the participants as a group, to the extent that a lower proportion of their contributions is being capitalized.

Survivor's and disability pensions are a highly significant cost component in the reformed social security systems. In fact, only about 70 percent participants in the private account system will eventually collect a retirement benefit. The remaining 30 percent will collect a disability benefit, or their beneficiaries will receive a pension for surviving spouses or children. Figure 11.9 illustrates the probability that a participant in the system from the age of 20 will collect a retirement pension, in accordance with the mortality tables required by regulations in each country.

The importance of this factor was shown in Figures 11.8 and 11.9, given the high percentage of the commission that must be earmarked for covering contingency benefits. Figure 11.10 shows the significance of the monthly cost of insurance to cover contingencies, measured in constant terms for the entire working life of an participant. This is compared with the monthly contribution to the fund needed to accumulate the capital required for a monthly income of 1,000 monetary units as of the retirement date.

The cost is spread over the working life of the participant. However, this cost grows throughout each participant's life, as can be seen in Figure 11.11 for Argentina.

Thus at the aggregate level, this is a growing cost for the entire portfolio of participants, inasmuch as the total participant group is aging.

The Transfer Certificate or recognition bond finances some of the shortfall in this contribution rate. It is worth noting that the pensions

Figure 11.9 Probability of Receiving a Retirement Pension

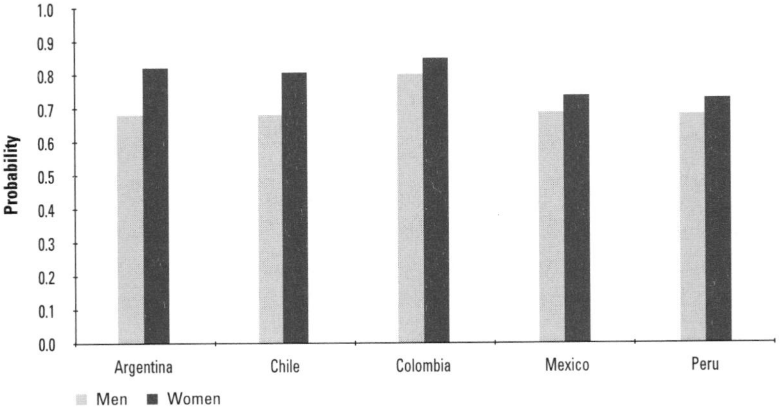

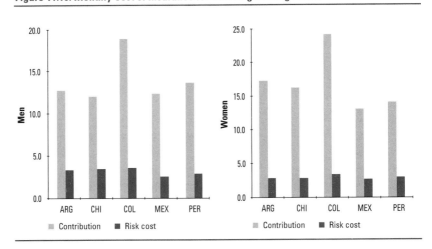

Source: BBVA.

Figure 11.10. Monthly Cost of Insurance for Covering Contingencies

Note: Contributions and monthly cost per 1,000 units of yearly retirement income.
Source: BBVA.

of the participant in the reformed system who have no history in the prior social security system will be smaller in real terms, unless the contribution rate of the private system is raised and the cost of covering contingencies increases more than proportionally. Thus the new partici-

Figure 11.11. Cost of Social Security Exposure: Death and Disability in Argentina

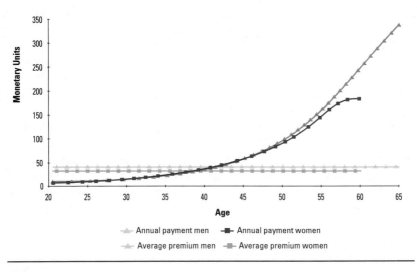

Source: Authors' calculations.

pants will have to sustain a higher commission to finance the coverage of contingencies, and they will have a smaller fund accumulated, at the same contribution rate.

In sum, the increasing costs of covering contingencies represent one of the aspects of the social security system that needs the most in-depth review. This must be done from both the conceptual and practical points of view. Not only are costs rising for individuals, but increases are also inevitable for the group as a whole, even if not a single participant were added: that is, for a closed group system.

This rise will be significant. It will affect the ability of pension fund managers to carry on their activities with the current commission levels. It will also have a systemic effect, in terms of the portion of the contributions earmarked for investment. To the extent that higher costs have repercussions on commission levels, there will be less capital invested in the individual accounts.

The cost to the social security system of benefits for disability and surviving spouses and children basically depends on policy definition and conventional determination of certain generally accepted technical standards. Policy definition refers to the way in which the system wishes to address these needs.

These benefits are generally defined based on the last salary received and collected by the originator of the benefit. However, this cost, as discussed above, would have an impact on the entire system based on the implementation of the mechanisms for financing it.

Moreover, from a technical point of view, the determination of costs in terms of the present value of life insurance and disability benefits will be a function of technical standards (biometric and actuarial) and the financial standards used to calculate them.

Currently all the social security systems under study define a set of technical and financial standards used to determine the present value of their defined benefits. These are determinants of the cost of covering contingencies in every one of the systems. In short, they are systemic costs that affect the proportion of the contributions that are capitalized in individual accounts and the portion of the contributions earmarked for financing system-wide costs. These standards also determine the solvency of the private entities with commitments to manage these systems. The standards in the major countries of Latin America under analysis are presented in Table 11.2.

Table 11.2	Technical Standards Used to Determine the Costs of Life and Disability Benefits	
Country	**Mortality Tables for Retirees**	**Type of Interest**
Argentina	GAM-71 (M/F)	4 percent annual The reference rate for lifetime rents for pensioners for the investments was 3.54 percent in Dec. 2003
Chile	RV-85 (M/F)	The interest rate for actuarial reserves is 3 percent. It allows for up to 80 percent coverage of the commitments. The interest rate applied to the pensioners for lifetime annuities are on average 5.28 percent annual during the years 1991–2002
Colombia	ISS80-89 (M/F)	It should not be higher than the average yield of the investments described in the Financial System Statutes. It is around 4 percent, similar to the reference rate for banks reserves.
Mexico	EMSS-97 (M/F)	To determine the net premium of the pension reserves, the rate of interest is 3.5 percent real.
Peru	RV-85 (M/F)	3 percent in the interest rate for the commutation of the mortality tables. The scheme permits the use as discount rate the one that comes out of the methodology

Source: BBVA.

A Proposed Procedure for
Evaluation of the Costs of Contingencies

As discussed, the private pension systems consist of two subsystems that operate simultaneously. The first subsystem provides retirement pensions, is the second mandatory pillar and is a scheme of individual capitalization and defined contributions. The first subsystem is supported by the first public pillar, which guarantees minimum pensions and assistance pensions.

The second subsystem forms the basis for covering contingencies arising from the death or disability of the participants in the private account system. Because both are financed jointly by the participants' individual contributions, only a joint analysis of both subsystems will allow an adequate evaluation of the performance and prospects of reformed systems as such.

Four aspects are most important to conducting such an analysis:

- Define the contingencies to be covered and the beneficiaries with rights to a benefit (including spouses, parents/grandparents, and legitimate and illegitimate descendants).
- Define the quantitative limits of benefits to be covered by the social security system, in both overall and individual terms for beneficiaries. Compare the current configuration of survivor and disability pensions with retirement pensions in each system. This comparison could identify asymmetries that are not justified by conscious, considered decisions in the social security systems.
- Analyze duplication of benefits for the same reason and the same event in different social security systems (pension systems, workers compensation coverage for accidents, and so on). Define maximum pensions and the system for handling concurrent benefits in the pensions of various social security systems. Covered contingencies vary among countries, and there are asymmetries among the different kinds of benefits. Many cases of duplication of benefits exist among different subsystems within the social security systems.
- Analyze the technical standards upon which determination of benefits and guaranteed principal is based, in order to adapt to the actual demographic, biometric, and financial variables the systems attempt to represent and anticipate.

Correcting these situations by standardizing reforms may help cut the costs of covering contingencies. This would leave more savings contributions for increasing the capital accumulated as of retirement.

Finally, other solutions should not be ruled out. For example, the contingency cost could be separated from the administrative costs and commissions to pension fund managers. These solutions would make the efficiency of the AFPs vis-à-vis the management of the processes assigned to them in the reformed social security systems much more apparent.

Cost of Managing Processes Assigned to AFPs

A basic business analysis could be conducted of the processes assumed by the AFPs, including marketing, collection, investment management, and general administration of the system (see Figure 11.12 for a breakdown). The analysis could focus on the costs and contributions each of these processes makes to the priority objectives of the social security systems: increased coverage by the systems and pension adequacy.

Some aspects of these processes that could be improved are discussed below. The discussion focuses on reducing costs that do not add value to the pursuit of objectives defined as high priority for the social security systems. The possibility of reducing commissions is not ruled out.

Marketing Costs

As Figure 11.12 shows, the marketing cost is significant in the majority of the systems. Table 11.3 identifies the ratio of the sales cost to the volume of the fund under administration on the date of the measurement (June 2004). The purpose is to compare the cost associated with sales representatives with the improvement in rate of return that could potentially be achieved through transfers.

This measurement of costs on a specific date and time introduces distortions, to the extent that it does not consider the dynamic trend of this variable as the system matures. Thus it compares different systems at various stages of maturity as if they were homogeneous. A better approximation would be to consider the ratio of an equivalent commission and marketing cost as a percent of the fund value over the working life of the participant, as shown in Table 11.4.

As noted above, a participant in the private account system in Chile from the inception of that system would have improved his/her rate of return by an average of 0.3 percent per year compared with the fund's average rate of return. This assumes that the participant remained in the fund with the best return for that period. Currently, the differences in rates of return among the various funds are much less that they were.

Figure 11.12. Breakdown of AFPs' Operating Costs
(per 100 units of commissions)

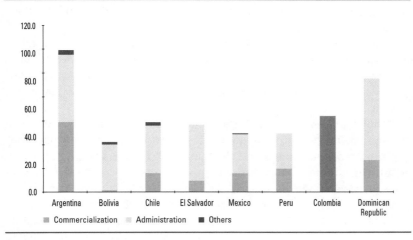

Note: In the case of Colombia, represents total expenditures.
Source: AIOS and authors estimates.

Table 11.3	Commissions and Marketing Costs as a Percent of Fund Value	
Country	Fees as a percent of fund value	Marketing cost as a percent of fund value
Argentina	1.4	0.80
Chile	0.7	0.11
El Salvador	2.5	0.23
Mexico	2.9	0.44
Peru	2.5	0.48
Dominican Republic	1.7	0.44

Source: International Association of Pension Fund Supervisors (AIOS).

Table 11.4	Commissions and Marketing Costs as a Percent of Fund Value over Working Life	
Country	Fees as a percent of fund value over working life	Marketing cost as a life percent of fund value over working life
Argentina	0.95	0.54
Chile	0.69	0.10
Colombia	0.82	n.a.
El Salvador	0.82	0.07
Mexico	0.80	0.12
Peru	0.92	0.18

Source: Authors' calculations.
n.a. Not applicable.

Thus it is questionable whether anyone could achieve a 30-basis-point difference in rate of return today. Given these modest gains, the transfer cost in Chile currently represents about ten basis points on an annual basis calculated on the balance under administration.

In Argentina, the cost of the sales representatives is huge. It currently represents 0.54 percent per year over the fund under administration. It could be difficult for a participant to recover this amount consistently by selecting a fund with a rate of return higher than the average for the system.

All this suggests that the marketing war to obtain transfers is a sterile effort in terms of the interests of the participant. To cut marketing costs and reduce commissions, the number of transfers could be restricted to a maximum for each participant per time period. Alternatively, transfer costs could be applied only to new contributions. Under this arrangement, upon retirement, a participant would collect the capital accumulated in the various funds to which he/she contributed throughout his/her working life.

Collection Process

The process of collecting the participants' contributions is carried out differently by the AFPs in every system, based on the institutional framework defined in each country. The tasks assigned to the AFPs determine the costs they incur for this activity, and thus the costs inherent in this process for the system as a whole.

Each company makes independent efforts within the competitive framework to minimize its administrative costs. Nevertheless, it is the regulator's responsibility to establish the most efficient arrangements to reduce the costs for private companies in the system, along with the commissions, and thus reduce the costs to the system.

Table 11.5 illustrates the ratio of AFPs' administrative costs to total amounts collected.

From this first approximation, one cannot conclude that there is a cause/effect relationship between the type of collection system (centralized or decentralized) and cost levels. It stands to reason that there are various approaches for reaching more precise conclusions. Thus a better breakdown must be done of the administrative costs to determine whether the costs are in fact linked to the collection process. Moreover, collection is a process in which costs are affected by economies of scale, information technology, and collection/payment procedures, among other factors. However, these matters are highly regulated in each system.

Table 11.5	Administrative Costs and Collection System	
Country	Administrative costs over amounts collected (percentage)	Collection system
Argentina	12.10	Centralized
Bolivia	1.90	Decentralized
Chile	5.40	Decentralized
Dominican Republic	3.90	Centralized
El Salvador	7.10	Decentralized
Mexico	6.60	Centralized
Peru	8.00	Decentralized

Source: Authors' calculations and compilations.

Thus to improve processes, the initial focus must be on the system and its regulations more than on its operations.

Fewer regulatory restrictions, to the extent that they are not needed to guarantee optimal long-term returns for the participants, could result in a reduction in labor, processing systems, and operations. This would lead to cost reduction, and by the same token, a reduction in commissions.

Pension Funds' Profits

Inasmuch as the AFPs represent a key element in the structure of the privately managed pension systems, a return on their business activities is one way to guarantee the stability of the social security system as a whole. A clear distinction must be made between the capital required for operations and the business risks involved. In other words, equity capital must be distinguished from the regulatory requirements for cash reserves or minimum capital.

Most reformed systems require that the pension fund manager acquire 1 percent of the total funds or maintain minimum capital equal to that amount. This means that capital contributions must be growing. Thus at the margin, these contributions must be disproportionate in terms of the capital required from a business management perspective. Figure 11.13 illustrates the percentage of their own equity earmarked by the AFPs as a group, by country, to meet the cash reserve requirement.

The importance of cash reserves in countries such as Chile and Mexico is evident, given the significant volume under management. This is the result of the longer time the system has been in effect and the size of the market.

Figure 11.13. Cash Reserves Held by the AFPs
(percent of equity)

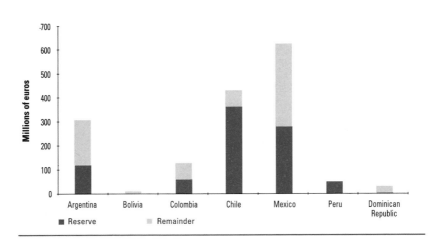

Source: BBVA.

From a strictly business point of view, it would be possible to finance the capital requirement with the company's own equity and finance the surplus regulatory capital with outside financing. However, such an operating proposal is neither economically efficient nor possible under the regulations of the majority of the countries.

From the point of view of revenues, the AFPs' returns are tied to collections. In other words, they are tied to the business cycle, job creation, the trend toward a formal economy, and the trend of real wages. Their returns are a function of economic phenomena that are completely different from those that determine investment requirements in terms of capital held by shareholders in order to carry out business activities.

Costs basically depend on the cost of covering life insurance and disability contingencies. They also depend on implementing the tasks of marketing, collection, investment management, and administration linked to the administration of social security systems.

The costs of contingencies as defined above are a function of the institutions in the system. Their future trend depends on the natural trend of the group subject to risk. To a certain degree, this dynamic development of the demographic and biometric variables can be forecast. It depends on variables completely different from those that make up the fund managers' revenues and capital requirements.

In terms of covering contingencies, to a large extent, optimization of processing costs depends on the institutional system that defines the rules of the game. The AFPs' marketing activities are related to a highly regulated product, as is appropriate for mandatory, purposeful savings. Thus private initiative and management efficiency based on optimizing operating criteria are less important than the requirements of the system.

An adequate return, defined as one that is capable of creating value, is currently unsatisfactory for the shareholders of the AFPs. This is because the three factors that define shareholder satisfaction—capital linked to business activity, revenues, and operating costs—have dynamic trends that are inevitably cut off from pure business operations. Investors require much higher growth rates (mandated by the logic of savings that blends contributions and profitability) than growth of operating revenues (linked only to economic growth). This has an impact on the forecasted trend of returns. Moreover, revenues are growing at a rate substantially below that of costs, especially the costs related to covering contingencies, as discussed above. As a result, the trend of profits is inevitably downward, which will be the trend of returns for the time being.

This means that operating results, whether deemed high or low today, will not be sustainable over time. Thus the pension fund management sector is headed for a reduction in value that is incompatible with economic activities in the sphere of the market economy.

Given this situation, the most reasonable solution would be to eliminate the obligation to invest in cash reserves and to limit regulatory capital to that deemed economically related to the operating risks of pension fund management. Financing of contingency coverage should also be separated from administrative commissions. All these proposals could be adopted to the extent that a profitability guarantee fades away, replaced by other alternatives.

Conclusions: Toward a New Agenda

As emphasized in the Barcelona Development Agenda signed by a group of economists in September 2004 to supersede the Washington Consensus, the time has come to embark upon a new reform agenda for pension systems. A good point of departure is to adopt the third of its seven lessons: "There is no single economic policy that can guarantee sustained growth. The priority is to identify the most binding constraints to growth and to address them through adequate microeconomic and macroeconomic policies."[3]

The low national savings rates that characterize the region, the insufficient development of capital markets, and the need to increase the State's financial margins are factors that support extending and improving the reforms already carried out.

There is a direct and reciprocal relationship between the development of social security systems and the development of capital markets. Thus reforms that set up or stimulate the development of private pension funds require a certain degree of development of the capital markets. But capitalization systems also invariably stimulate national savings and boost the development of capital markets in the local currency.

Strengthening the first pillar is a necessity in Latin America. It is not advisable to reduce the second pillar—much less to propose that it be managed by the public sector. This second pillar, based on individual accounts, must be privately administered.

As to the third pillar, which is voluntary, experience in many developed countries has shown that it must be based on tax incentives that defer taxes on income contributed until the time of retirement.

It will be possible to reduce costs and thus lower management commissions only through regulations that address and limit the administrative scope of the social security system. To achieve greater efficiency, regulators and the pension fund management sector must jointly undertake an exhaustive analysis of the processes involved in the social security system: such processes as collecting contributions, administering individual accounts, investing the funds' assets, covering and financing contingencies, paying and managing benefits, and marketing.

A set of proposals that could become a working agenda for the reform of social security systems is summarized below.

1. Better define and adjust contribution rates.
   - Define contribution rates as the sum necessary to finance a benefit that will amount to an adequate percentage of the final wage.
   - Progressively adjust those rates in both the public and private pillars, once the transition period has elapsed.

2. Manage a fund's investments so as to maximize the capital at the time of each participant's retirement.

---

[3] "From the Washington Consensus toward a New Global Governance Forum," Barcelona, September 2004.

- Create specialized life cycle funds and a fund for managing scheduled withdrawals.
- Value funds at market prices, except for the fund for scheduled withdrawal for the age group near retirement.
- Eliminate a guaranteed minimum rate of return tied to the system's rate of return. This would eliminate or substantially reduce the need for the mandatory cash reserves.
- Introduce risk limits for the funds in terms of absolute value at risk or relative value at risk, tied to a reference benchmark.
- Provide investment regulations and alternatives that allow funds' portfolios to be diversified, reducing the exposure to local country risk.
- Reduce regulatory restrictions and delegate the introduction of fiduciary responsibility best practices to the pension fund managers.

3. Define a competitive framework that limits marketing costs by restricting transfers to those that make sense for reasons of service or for reaching the basic objectives defined.

4. Redefine system arrangements for financing contingency coverage.
   - Unlink administrative commissions from the cost of covering contingencies in order to establish the contingencies as a separate system benefit.
   - Review the following elements of the management and control of the costs tied to this capital:
     a) Amount of benefits promised
     b) Nature of the beneficiaries as a group
     c) Structuring of concurrent benefits and payment of pensions
     d) Technical calculation standards that can be adjusted to the empirical experience in each country, taking into consideration mortality tables and technical interest rates.

5. Review commissions to lead to potential reductions.
   - Review basic definitions, such as the basis for distributing death and disability benefits, to ensure they are in line with final objectives.
   - Review the commission structure, setting a "base" to cover system costs and a "variable" that is competitive, tied to achievement of objectives.

Finally, it must be pointed out that the reform of social security systems constitutes an important tool of economic development. To be most effective, the adjustments to and improvements in the systems discussed above are needed. Complementary reforms in other spheres of the economic, financial, and fiscal systems are also needed.

BBVA's experience demonstrates that the reforms are unquestionably going in the right direction. However, it is necessary to adjust expectations, complete these reforms, and carry out related institutional changes that reinforce the effects of the social security system reforms. This position is based on the fact that the results achieved, while below expectations, are positive and that they provide many lessons for systems that have yet to be reformed.

Bibliography

Gill, Indermit, Truman Packard, and Juan Yermo. 2005. *Keeping the Promise of Social Security in Latin America.* Stanford, CA: Stanford University Press.

Gill, Indermit, Truman Packard, Todd Pugatch, and Juan Yermo. 2005. Rethinking Social Security in Latin America. In *Keeping the Promise of Social Security in Latin America,* eds. Indermit Gill, Truman Packard, and Juan Yermo. Stanford, CA: Stanford University Press.

Packard, Truman. 2001. Is there a Positive Incentive Effect from Privatising Social Security? Evidence from Latin America. Unpublished paper, The World Bank, Washington, D.C.

Packard, Truman, Naoko Shinkai, and Ricardo Fuentes. 2002. The Reach of Social Security in Latin America and the Caribbean. Background paper for regional study on social security. The World Bank, Washington, D.C.

Taguas Coejo, David, and Agustín Vidal-Aragón de Olives. 2005. Hoja de ruta para la reforma de los sistemas de pensiones en América Latina. Working Paper 01/05. Study Services BBVA, Madrid.

The World Bank. 1994. *Averting the Old Age Crisis. Policies to Protect the Old and to Promote Growth.* New York: Oxford University Press.

U.S. Social Security Administration (SSA). 1999. *The Future of Social Security.* Washington, D.C.: U.S. Social Security Administration.

The Global Financial Well-being Study

Principal Financial Group*

Introduction and Methodology

This chapter presents the results of a report conducted by The Principal Financial Group for the third year to evaluate the attitudes and perceptions held by workers in twelve countries (Brazil, Chile, Mexico, and the United States, in the Americas; China, India, Hong Kong SAR, and Japan, in Asia; and France, Germany, Great Britain, and Italy, in Europe) about their current financial situation and expectations for retirement. The survey firm, NOP World, conducted the field work for the study through telephone interviews in Chile, China, France, Germany, Great Britain, Hong Kong, Italy, and Japan, and through door-to-door interviews in Brazil, India, and Mexico (http://www.nopworld.com). Interviewing was conducted in February and March 2004 in all countries. A market research firm with expertise in financial services research, Mathew Greenwald & Associates, Inc., provided input for the questionnaire and analyzed the results of the study.[1]

---

* This chapter presents the findings of an annual survey conducted by The Principal Financial Group®. The Principal®, a member of the Fortune 500, offers businesses, individuals, and institutional clients financial products and services, including retirement and investment services, life and health insurance, and banking, through its diverse family of financial services companies.

[1] Founded in 1985, Greenwald & Associates has conducted public opinion and customer-oriented research for more than 100 organizations, including many of the nation's largest companies and foremost associations (www.greenwaldresearch.com).

All respondents in the survey are age 25 or over, employed or self-employed, and do not consider themselves retired. Respondents who qualified to participate in the study were asked their household income or socioeconomic status to ensure that respondents from different countries would have comparable purchasing power. Respondents in Japan are from the top 80 percent of households, with annual income equivalent to US$27,500 or more. In Hong Kong, respondents represent the top 70 percent of households, with annual household income equivalent to US$20,500 (or more). Respondents in China are from the top 50 percent of households, with annual income equivalent to at least US$2,800. In Chile and Brazil, respondents from the top 50 percent and 40 percent of households, respectively, by socioeconomic status are included in the survey, representing households with annual income equivalent to US$11,500 or more (Chile) and US$3,500 or more (Brazil). Respondents in Mexico are from the top 30 percent of households by socioeconomic status, representing households with annual income equivalent to at least US$11,500. Finally, Indian respondents are from the top 25 percent of households by socioeconomic status and have annual household income equivalent to at least US$1,550. Respondents from France, Germany, Great Britain, and Italy were not qualified by household income or socioeconomic status.

The margin of error for each country in this study (at the 95 percent confidence level) is plus or minus approximately four percentage points. Where data are available, results of the global study are compared to the domestic second quarter 2004 results of The Principal Financial Well-being Index. Harris Interactive conducted this index for The Principal Financial Group in May 2004 among employees (ages 18 years or older) of small and mid-sized U.S. businesses, using an online methodology. Results are also compared to U.S. data obtained from the 2004 Retirement Confidence Survey sponsored by the Employee Benefit Research Institute (EBRI), American Savings Education Council (ASEC), and Mathew Greenwald & Associates (Greenwald) (http://www.ebri.com/pdf/surveys/rcs/2004/0404ib.pdf).[2] The percentages presented in the tables and charts contained in this report may not total to 100 percent due to rounding and/or missing categories.

---

[2] U.S. data from EBRI/ASEC/Greenwald 2004 Retirement Confidence Surveys, Washington, D.C.

Retirement Pillage

Against a backdrop of global economic recovery and improving capital markets, one might have expected the third annual Principal Global Financial Well-being Study to reveal increased confidence and optimism about the future. Surprisingly, that is not the case. The study demonstrates that the world's population is so discouraged about achieving a financially secure retirement that only a minority (22 percent) is very confident that they will have enough money to pay for basic expenses—food, shelter, clothing—during retirement. Moreover, the percentage of respondents who foresee a worsening standard of living in retirement has actually increased between 2003 and 2004 in eight out of the twelve countries surveyed. In particular, nearly half the people in the United States (49 percent, up from 29 percent in 2003) are more likely to say their standard of living in retirement will be worse than it is now. To make matters worse, in every country, there is a disturbing lack of financial preparation for retirement. If there are any positives emerging from this year's study, it is that participants' view of their current financial well-being is often positive, in sharp contrast to their view of the future.

The Global Financial Well-being Study

The Principal Global Financial Well-being Study is a comprehensive survey of international financial well-being and retirement security, covering more than 5,000 people in 12 countries (Brazil, Chile, China, France, Germany, Great Britain, Hong Kong SAR, India, Italy, Japan, Mexico, and the United States).

This is the third consecutive year that The Principal has conducted its annual Global Financial Well-being Study. Over that time period, the world has experienced bear markets and rallies, economic recessions and recoveries. Through these economic ups and downs, the study has reported one constant, affecting households all around the world: a profound and deep-seated pessimism about living out a financially secure retirement. In most countries, the study found a moderate to healthy level of satisfaction with participants' current financial well-being. Yet looking out into the future, to when participants will be relying on retirement savings provided by government, employer, or themselves, the study's three-year cumulative findings reveal concern and outright hopelessness about the prospects of maintaining a decent standard of living.

The 2004 study discovered one notable paradox—a false confidence in planning for retirement. People worldwide recognize that putting money aside for retirement is important and overwhelmingly feel that they are doing a great job as individuals of planning for a financially secure retirement. However, the study effectively demonstrates that their confidence in planning for retirement is not backed up by their behavior. Most people, in fact, have done nothing about putting money aside for retirement. Many have not even begun planning for retirement, and those that have admit they are way behind schedule. The apathy towards individual retirement planning is surprising because a majority in every country do not believe they can trust the government to help them save for retirement, and are also not convinced they will receive the benefits they are entitled to from their employers' retirement or pension funds.

Summary of Latin American Findings

Chile's defined contribution system is clearly a success, both in its ability to help workers save adequately for retirement and its ability to engender confidence in the system. Mexico has modeled its defined contribution system after the Chilean model, and Mexican survey participants are more likely than others to feel that they are doing very well in providing for their retirement security and that they are ahead of schedule in saving for retirement. Despite a ready-built system for delivery of financial and retirement planning information, however, these countries do not do an adequate job of delivering advice. Half of Mexican participants and more than one-third of Chilean participants say they receive no advice. Four in ten Brazilians also receive no advice, though the delivery mechanism is more complicated in that country, as the pension system is still in transition.

Brazil

Recent efforts to reform Brazil's pension system have not reassured most Brazilians about their retirement security. Brazilians are most apt to feel that several entities each share a great deal of responsibility to ensure they have a financially comfortable retirement: themselves (82 percent), the government (68 percent), and employers (68 percent). Yet confidence in receiving full benefits from the government and employers is not high, and almost seven in ten Brazilians (67 percent) have yet to start planning for their retirement. When asked how satisfied they were with recent pension reforms, 73 percent of Brazilians say they are not very or not completely satisfied. More than half (53 percent) feel they are behind schedule in saving for retirement. This may be an underestimation, since only 12 percent have actually tried to calculate how much they need to save for retirement. One-third of Brazilians name experts such as banks and insurance or pension companies when asked where they receive financial or retirement planning advice, but others name less reliable sources, and four in ten say they do not receive any advice. Finally, a majority of Brazilians (62 percent) are also very concerned about the effect of inflation on their retirement savings. It is not surprising that 45 percent expect their standard of living during retirement to be worse than now (up from 38 percent in 2003).

Chile

With a mandatory defined contribution pension system, encouragingly, half of Chileans are looking forward to a standard of living in retirement that will be about the same as it is now. One-fourth say they expect their standard of living to be better; one-fourth say they expect it to be worse in retirement. The large majority (85 percent) believe they are doing well in performing their role to ensure that they have a financially secure retirement, and two-thirds think they are ahead of schedule (32 percent) or on track (36 percent) when it comes to retirement planning and saving. However, most do not know how well they are really doing. Almost six in ten (57 percent) completely or somewhat agree that they have not yet planned for retirement savings/security, and more than one-third (36 percent) receive no retirement planning advice. Less than three in ten (28 percent) have tried to calculate how much they need to save for a comfortable retirement.

Mexico

Seven years into a mandatory defined contribution retirement system, Mexicans are comparatively optimistic about retirement. However, a lack of financial preparation, perhaps exacerbated by a lack of financial advice, may have left them overly confident about their future well-being. Eight in ten participants believe that their standard of living will be better than (32 percent) or the same as (49 percent) it is now, yet eight in ten are also very concerned about their long-term financial future. While more than seven in ten are convinced they are ahead of schedule (38 percent) or on track (34 percent) in their retirement planning and saving, just two in ten know how much they need to save in order to achieve a comfortable lifestyle in retirement. Only 53 percent are confident they will be able to save their estimated amount needed for retirement, the second lowest percentage of all countries surveyed. Of equal concern is the fact that Mexicans, on average, tend to underestimate the number of years they will need to fund for retirement by 11 years.[3] Some of this poor retirement planning behavior may be the result of a lack of financial and retirement planning advice; more than half (52 percent) report they currently receive no advice of this type.

Detailed Report of Findings

The Beholden Years

Retirement often has been described as "the golden years," suggesting walks on the beach, afternoons of golf, and plenty of time (and resources) to travel, take classes, or enjoy other leisurely activities. That is not a view shared by most participants in the study. In fact, many study participants think their standard of living in retirement will be worse than it is now. At least four in 10 survey participants in Brazil, France, Germany, Italy, Japan, and the United States, and smaller proportions elsewhere, foresee a worsening standard of living. Moreover, the percentage of respondents giving this response has increased between 2003 and 2004 in eight out of the 12 countries surveyed. In particular, people are more likely to say their standard of living in retirement will be worse than now in Germany (44 percent, up from 34 percent), Italy (40 percent, up from 28 percent), Hong Kong SAR (29 percent in 2004, up from 17 percent in 2003), and most notably, the United States (49 percent, up from 29 percent).

Perhaps the most distressing finding in the three-year history of the study came this year. An especially disturbing view has emerged of participants' outlook on their future financial well-being. A minority of participants in each of the countries surveyed are very confident that they will have enough money to take care of their basic needs during their retirement. Only 13 percent of participants in France, 8 percent in Italy, and 3 percent in Japan responded that they thought they could cover their basics.

---

[3] Unfunded years in retirement calculated from life expectancy at retirement age, World Health Organization, *World Mortality 2000 Study.* Geneva, Switzerland.

Concern About Financial Well-being

While the majority of Indian (74 percent, down from 80 percent in 2003), British (63 percent), and French (53 percent) respondents are extremely happy with their current financial situation, only minorities from most other countries have similar feelings. Less than half of Germans (47 percent) and Italians (45 percent, down from 58 percent) are content with their current financial well-being. Roughly four in ten in Brazil (40 percent), China (39 percent), Chile (38 percent, up from 30 percent), and Hong Kong (37 percent) indicate feeling this way, while respondents in Japan (33 percent), Mexico (32 percent), and the United States (28 percent) are least likely to be extremely happy with their current financial situation (Figures 12.1 and 12.2).

People become much more concerned about their financial situation as they look toward the future. The large majority of respondents in most countries show concern about their long-term financial future. Even Indian (76 percent) and British (64 percent) respondents who tend to be upbeat about their current financial situation are likely to say they are very concerned about their long-term financial well-being. The least likely to indicate concern about the future are respondents in Germany (52 percent) and Hong Kong (48 percent), but about half in these coun-

Figure 12.1. I Am Extremely Happy About my Current Financial Well-being
(percentage agree)

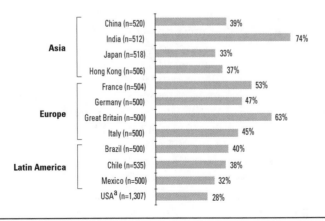

a. U.S. data from Principal 2nd Quarter 2004 Financial Well-being Index.
Source: Principal Global Financial Well-being Study, 2004.

Figure 12.2. I am very concerned about my (and my family's) long-term financial future (percentage agree)

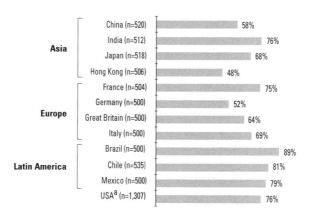

a. U.S. data from Principal 2nd Quarter 2004 Financial Well-being Index.
Source: Principal Global Financial Well-being Study, 2004.

tries still show concern. Compared with 2003, Germans (52 percent, up from 34 percent) and Italians (69 percent, up from 57 percent) are more likely to say they are very concerned about their financial future.

Expected Standard of Living in Retirement

Many respondents are looking toward a standard of living in retirement that they believe will be less prosperous than what they now have (Table 12.1). Significant proportions of respondents in France, the United States, Japan, Brazil, Germany, and Italy say they expect their standard of living in retirement to be worse than it is now. One-third of British respondents (34 percent) and at least one-quarter of those in Hong Kong (29 percent) and Chile (26 percent) expect their standard of living to get worse once they retire. Respondents in India, China, and Mexico are far more optimistic. One-third or more in these countries believe their standard of living in retirement will be better than it is now.

Around the globe, people are increasingly likely to expect their standard of living to decline once they retire. Respondents in France (62 percent in 2004, up from 56 percent in 2003), the United States (49 percent, up from 29 percent), Brazil (45 percent, up from 38 percent), Germany (44 percent, up from 34 percent), Italy (40 percent, up from 28 percent),

Table 12.1 Do you think your standard of living in retirement will be better than it is now, worse than it is now, or about the same as it is now? (percent)

	United States[a] (n=1,307)	Asia				Europe				Latin America		
		China (n=520)	India (n=512)	Japan (n=518)	Hong Kong (n=506)	France (n=504)	Germany (n=500)	Great Britain (n=500)	Italy (n=500)	Brazil (n=500)	Chile (n=535)	Mexico (n=500)
Better	13	36	45	8	18	8	13	12	11	22	24	32
About the same	34	43	32	36	52	29	41	53	44	32	48	49
Worse	49	16	16	53	29	62	44	34	40	45	26	18

[a] U.S. data from Principal 2nd Quarter 2004 Financial Well-being Index.
Source: Principal Global Financial Well-being Study, 2004.

Great Britain (34 percent, up from 25 percent), Hong Kong (29 percent, up from 17 percent), and India (16 percent, up from 11 percent) are more likely than last year to expect their standard of living to be worse in retirement than it is currently. At the same time, a smaller share of Chinese respondents than in 2003 expect their standard of living in retirement will be better than it is now (36 percent, down from 44 percent).

Retirement Confidence

Confidence about being able to maintain an adequate standard of living in retirement is not high (Figures 12.3 and 12.4). Only a minority in each country is highly confident that they will have a retirement that is at least as affluent as their parents'. Four in ten in China and roughly one in three in Great Britain and India believe they will be at least as well off in retirement as their parents. Much smaller proportions in Italy, France, and Japan expect their retirement to be as affluent as their parents'. Moreover, at best, approximately one-third of respondents are very confident about having enough money to take care of their basic expenses during retirement. Only two in ten in Hong Kong and Mexico, and very few in France, Italy, and Japan are very confident about being able to afford basic expenses once they retire.

Figure 12.3. You will have a retirement that is at least as affluent as your parents (percentage very confident)

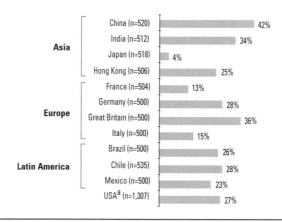

a. U.S. data from Principal 2nd Quarter 2004 Financial Well-being Index.
Source: Principal Global Financial Well-being Study, 2004.

Figure 12.4. You will have enough money to take care of your basic expenses during your retirement. (percentage very confident)

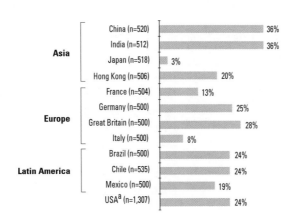

a. U.S. data from Principal 2nd Quarter 2004 Financial Well-being Index.
Source: Principal Global Financial Well-being Study, 2004.

Compared with 2003, smaller proportions of Indians (34 percent in 2004, down from 51 percent in 2003) and Germans (28 percent, down from 40 percent) are very confident about having a retirement as affluent as their parents' retirement. Indians (36 percent, down from 57 percent) and Germans (25 percent, down from 43 percent) are also less likely to be very confident about having enough money for basic expenses in retirement, as are the British (28 percent, down from 36 percent). On the other hand, Chinese respondents are more likely to say they are very confident that their retirement will be as affluent as their parents' (42 percent, up from 24 percent) and that they will have enough money for basic expenses (36 percent, up from 19 percent).

Although Indian (36 percent) and Chinese (31 percent) respondents are more likely to be very confident, at best, two in ten respondents in the other countries surveyed are very confident that they will not have to worry about financial matters once they retire (Figure 12.5). Among the least confident are the Italians, French, and Japanese. Likewise, roughly two in ten or fewer respondents in most countries feel very confident about maintaining their pre-retirement standard of living after they retire. Again, those in India (38 percent) and China (27 percent) tend to be more optimistic (Figure 12.6).

While Chinese respondents are more likely in 2004 to say they are very confident about not having to worry about financial matters after

Figure 12.5. You will not have to worry about financial matters after you retire (percentage very confident)

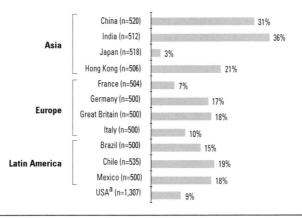

a. U.S. data from EBRI/ASEC/Greenwald 2004 Retirement Confidence Surveys.
Source: Principal Global Financial Well-being Study, 2004.

Figure 12.6. You will be able to maintain your pre-retirement standard of living after you retire (percentage very confident)

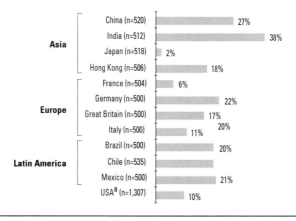

a. U.S. data from EBRI/ASEC/Greenwald 2004 Retirement Confidence Surveys.
Source: Principal Global Financial Well-being Study, 2004.

Figure 12.7. Index of Future Financial Well-being

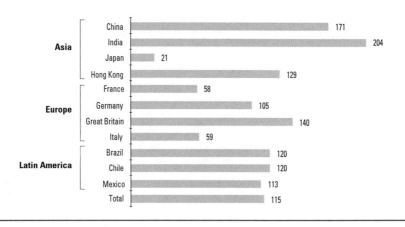

Source: Principal Global Financial Well-being Study, 2004.

they retire (31 percent, up from 11 percent in 2003), Indians are less likely to be highly confident (36 percent, down from 43 percent).

Index of Future Financial Well-Being

The various measures of retirement confidence have been combined to form an index of future financial well-being, or the extent to which respondents of each country are confident about their financial well-being in retirement (Figure 12.7).[4] Consistent with their high confidence, Indians are the most optimistic about their financial well-being during retirement with a score of 204, followed by the Chinese with a score of 171. British respondents trail a distant third with an index score of 140. Italians (59) and the French (58) tend to have significantly lower scores, while the Japanese are the most pessimistic about their well-being in retirement, with a score of 21.

---

[4] This index is calculated by adding the percentage saying they expect their standard of living to be a lot better in retirement than it is now and the percentages saying they are very confident about each of the following: having enough money for basic expenses, having a retirement that is at least as affluent as their parents, not having to worry about financial matters after retirement, able to maintain their pre-retirement standard of living after retirement, and receiving full benefits entitled to from pension (or from government-mandated defined contribution plan for Chile and Mexico).

Retirement Planning

Personal Responsibility for Retirement

While many respondents believe they should take on a great deal of responsibility for providing themselves a financially comfortable retirement, they tend to think they fall short in actually performing their role (Figure 12.8). In particular, two-thirds or more in Great Britain, Brazil, India, Chile, Hong Kong, Mexico, and Germany indicate that they have a great deal of responsibility for ensuring they have a financially secure retirement. However, less than four in ten in every country except India (69 percent) feel they are doing very well in following through and performing this job (Figure 12.9).

Compared with 2003, fewer Indians (77 percent in 2004, down from 90 percent), Chileans (74 percent, down from 82 percent), Germans (66 percent, down from 78 percent), Japanese (59 percent, down from 70 percent), and Italians (54 percent, down from 61 percent) say they have a great deal of responsibility for ensuring themselves a financially comfortable retirement. Respondents in India (69 percent, down from 78 percent) and Japan (5 percent, down from 17 percent) are also less likely to feel they are doing very well in their role to ensure that they have a financially secure retirement.

Figure 12.8. How much responsibility do you think you (and your spouse) should have for ensuring that you have a financially comfortable retirement? (percentage great deal of responsibility)

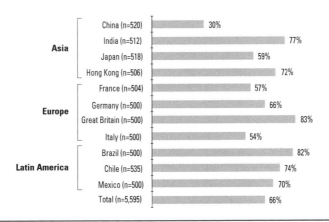

Source: Principal Global Financial Well-being Study, 2004.

Figure 12.9. How well do you think you (or your spouse) are doing in performing your role to ensure that you have a financially secure retirement?
(percentage very well)

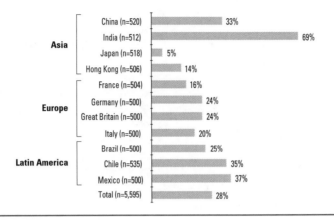

Source: Principal Global Financial Well-being Study, 2004.

Index of Personal Responsibility

An index of personal responsibility was calculated for each country to understand the extent to which respondents' feelings of personal responsibility are offset by the sense that someone else will provide for them in retirement (Figure 12.10).[5] The index gives Great Britain, Chile, and Hong Kong the highest ratings, with scores of 54, 46, and 46, respectively. (Chile and Great Britain also earned the highest scores last year.) China, followed by Italy, receive the lowest ratings, with negative scores of 18 and 15, respectively. This is due to a much greater reliance on government support in these countries.

---

[5] This index was calculated using the following formula:

[(% you yourself have great deal of responsibility + $1/2$ % employer has great deal of responsibility) – (% government has great deal of responsibility + % family has great deal of responsibility)].

The theory behind the construction of this index is to the extent others have responsibility for an individual's financial security in retirement, the individual does not have to take action or responsibility. Thus the perceived responsibility of government and family was subtracted from the individual's responsibility. Because the employer's responsibility is, to an extent, earned by an individual, half of the level of the employer's responsibility was added to the total.

Figure 12.10. Index of Personal Responsibility

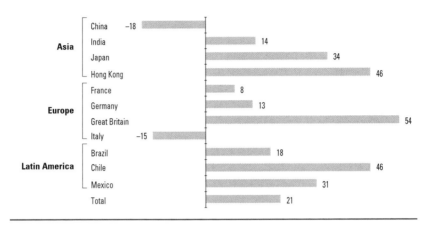

Source: Principal Global Financial Well-being Study, 2004.

Formal Retirement Planning

People may believe they have personal responsibility to ensure their financial security in retirement, but many have yet to begin planning for it (Figure 12.11). Despite scoring highly on the index of personal responsibility and rating saving for retirement very important, more than one-third of respondents in Great Britain and Hong Kong, and similar proportions in Japan and Germany, agree they have not yet planned for their retirement savings or security. Roughly half in Italy, France, Mexico, China, and India say they have yet to plan for retirement, while those in Brazil (67 percent) and Chile (57 percent) are most likely to agree. By comparison, just one-quarter of respondents in the United States agree they have yet to begin retirement planning.

Indians (47 percent in 2004, down from 54 percent in 2003) and Chileans (57 percent, down from 64 percent) are not as likely as last year to say they have yet to start planning for retirement. On the other hand, respondents in Germany (34 percent, up from 24 percent) and Great Britain (40 percent, up from 34 percent) are more likely to agree with this statement.

Progress in Retirement Planning and Saving

Despite the fact that few rate their performance in ensuring their financial security in retirement highly, a plurality in most countries think they

Figure 12.11. I have not yet planned for retirement savings/security
(percentage agree)

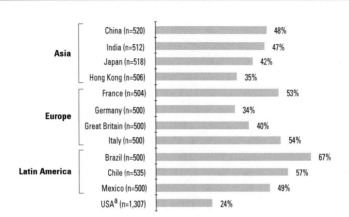

a. U.S. data from EBRI/ASEC/Greenwald 2004 Retirement Confidence Surveys.
Source: Principal Global Financial Well-being Study, 2004.

are on track when it comes to planning and saving for retirement (Table 12.2). Nevertheless, significant proportions in each country admit to being behind schedule. Respondents in the United States, Japan, and Brazil are among the most likely to say they are behind schedule in their planning for retirement, followed by those in Hong Kong, France, Great Britain, and Italy. Approximately one-third of Chinese and Germans, and one-quarter of Chileans, Indians, and Mexicans, feel that they are behind schedule. Mexicans (38 percent) and Chileans (32 percent) are especially likely to respond that they are ahead of schedule, perhaps due to their governments' defined contribution systems.

Calculation of Retirement Savings Needs

Many people may not really know whether they are on track in saving for retirement, however, because only a minority of respondents have tried to calculate the amount of savings they will need to ensure they have a comfortable retirement (Figure 12.12). Roughly one-third of respondents in India, Germany, and Great Britain report they have tried to figure out the amount of money they will need, and more than one-quarter in Hong Kong, Chile, and Japan say the same. Respondents in Italy (17 percent), China (15 percent), Brazil (12 percent), and France (12 percent) are the

Table 12.2 And when it comes to planning and saving for retirement, would you say that you are on track, ahead of schedule or behind schedu (percent)

	United States[a] (n=1,307)	Asia				Europe				Latin America		
		China (n=520)	India (n=512)	Japan (n=518)	Hong Kong (n=506)	France (n=504)	Germany (n=500)	Great Britain (n=500)	Italy (n=500)	Brazil (n=500)	Chile (n=535)	Mexico (n=500)
Ahead of schedule	5	6	21	13	10	6	12	6	6	12	32	38
On track	23	47	47	16	40	48	57	49	52	34	36	34
Behind schedule	72	35	26	61	47	45	30	44	39	53	27	24

a U.S. data from EBRI/ASEC/Greenwald 2004 Retirement Confidence Surveys.
Source: Principal Global Financial Well-being Study, 2004.

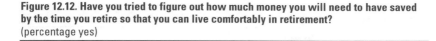

Figure 12.12. Have you tried to figure out how much money you will need to have saved by the time you retire so that you can live comfortably in retirement?
(percentage yes)

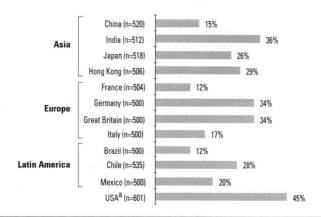

a. U.S. data from EBRI/ASEC/Greenwald 2004 Retirement Confidence Surveys.
Source: Principal Global Financial Well-being Study, 2004.

least likely to indicate they have tried to calculate the amount needed for retirement. Those in the United States (45 percent) are more likely than others to report calculating how much they need to save.

The Chinese (15 percent, down from 21 percent) and Japanese (26 percent, down from 32 percent) are less likely than in 2003 to say they have tried to figure out how much money they will need to save for retirement. However, Indians (36 percent, up from 27 percent) are more likely to mention having tried to calculate this amount.

Close to half of Indian and Chinese respondents who have calculated the amount needed for retirement are very confident that they will be able to save the amount needed, but fewer are confident in the other countries surveyed (Figure 12.13). Roughly one-third of Germans, British, Chileans, and Mexicans are very confident about their ability to save this amount. Residents of Italy (17 percent), France (17 percent), and Japan (13 percent) are the least likely to be highly confident in their ability to save their estimated amount needed for retirement.

The proportion of Indian respondents who are very confident has dropped since 2003 (49 percent, down from 68 percent), while the share of Chinese who are highly confident has increased during this period (47 percent, up from 17 percent).

Figure 12.13. How confident are you that you will be able to save this amount?
(percentage very confident)

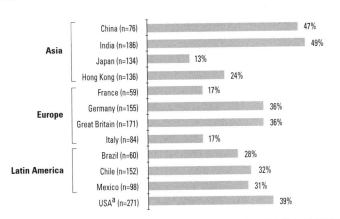

a. U.S. data from EBRI/ASEC/Greenwald 2004 Retirement Confidence Surveys.
Source: Principal Global Financial Well-being Study, 2004.

Retirement Age and Expected Duration

On average, respondents plan to retire at about the normal retirement age for their country. Chinese and Hong Kong respondents expect to retire the earliest (at a median age of 55), while Japanese and German respondents think they will retire latest (at median ages of 62 and 63, respectively). Those in the other surveyed countries say they will retire at about age 60.

Most think their savings will need to last 10 to 20 years in retirement, with the Chinese and Mexicans planning the shortest retirements (a median of 10 years) and Europeans, Hong Kong, and Chilean respondents planning the longest (a median of 20 years). Combining the number of years in retirement with expected retirement age suggests that respondents in three countries—China, Mexico, and Japan—may be significantly underestimating their life expectancy at retirement: by 12 years, 11 years, and 7 years, respectively (see Table 12.3).

Table 12.3 Retirement Age and Years Savings Will Need to Last
(median years)

	Total	Asia				Europe				Latin America		
		China	India	Japan	Hong Kong	France	Germany	Great Britain	Italy	Brazil	Chile	Mexico
Average retirement age	60	55	60	62	55	60	63	60	60	60	60	60
Years retirement savings will need to last	20	10	15	16	20	20	20	20	20	15	20	10
Unfunded years in retirement	n.a.	12	0	7	2	3	1	1	2	3	0	11

n.a.=Not applicable.
Source: Principal Global Financial Well-being Study, 2004. Des Moines, Iowa, except for unfunded years in retirement calculated from life expectancy at retirement age, World Health Organization, *World Mortality 2000 Study.*

Financial Advice

Sources of Financial and Retirement Planning Advice

Given the large proportions of respondents in most of the countries surveyed who say they receive no financial or retirement planning advice, perhaps it is not surprising they appear so poorly prepared for retirement and are concerned about burdening their children once they retire (Table 12.4). The overwhelming majority of Japanese respondents (81 percent) and more than half of Italian (55 percent) and Mexican (52 percent) respondents say they do not currently receive any advice, as do four in ten in Brazil, Great Britain, and India, and one-third in Chile and France. At least one-quarter in the remaining countries surveyed also report receiving no advice.

When respondents receive advice, they do so from a wide variety of sources, some of which may not deal well with the complexities of retirement planning. Banks tend to be a popular source of advice, particularly among the French (47 percent) and Brazilians (29 percent). Banks and insurance or pension companies are equally likely to provide residents of Hong Kong (31 percent and 30 percent, respectively) and Germany (27 percent each) with financial or retirement planning advice. Books, magazines, and newspapers, as well as television and radio, are more common tools used by the Chinese (33 percent and 28 percent, respectively), followed by Brazilians (20 percent and 22 percent, respectively). Indians (23 percent) most often receive financial and retirement planning advice from friends or relatives, while British respondents (27 percent) are most likely to use personal financial advisors. Some Chinese (18 percent) and British (14 percent) report receiving some advice through their employers, but other nationalities are less likely to receive information from this source. Finally, three in ten Chileans (29 percent) receive financial or retirement planning advice from their AFP (Pension Fund Administrator).

Several countries have posted increases in the past year in the percentage of residents reporting they do not receive any financial advice. These include Italy (55 percent, up from 42 percent), Mexico (52 percent, up from 23 percent), Brazil (41 percent, up from 29 percent), India (38 percent, up from 29 percent), China (28 percent, up from 13 percent), and Hong Kong (28 percent, up from 14 percent).

Table 12.4 From whom do you currently receive any financial or retirement planning advice? *(percent)*

	Total (n=5,595)	Asia				Europe				Latin America		
		China (n=520)	India (n=512)	Japan (n=518)	Hong Kong (n=506)	France (n=504)	Germany (n=500)	Great Britain (n=500)	Italy (n=500)	Brazil (n=500)	Chile (n=535)	Mexico (n=500)
Banks	19	3	19	2	31	47	27	12	15	29	9	18
Insurance or pension companies	12	2	14	2	30	15	27	8	6	3	15	9
Books, magazines, or newspapers	12	33	11	7	19	6	13	5	8	20	7	1
Friends or relatives	12	17	23	2	10	10	18	5	8	6	18	9
Television or radio	9	28	8	5	12	1	12	3	6	22	4	1
Employer	7	18	3	3	2	9	8	14	2	2	5	7
Personal financial advisors	6	—	4	1	1	3	12	27	8	—	3	2
Internet	5	8	2	3	6	1	9	2	3	8	7	1
Accountants	3	*	5	1	*	1	13	3	2	1	5	3
AFP (Chile only)	3	—	—	—	—	—	—	—	—	—	29	—
Lawyers	2	—	2	*	*	1	3	1	*	2	4	3
Stockbrokers	1	*	2	1	1	1	3	1	1	1	2	*
Do not receive advice	42	28	38	81	28	35	24	40	55	41	36	52
Don't know/Refused	3	4	8	1	4	1	3	4	3	*	1	*

*Less than 0.5 percent
— Not available.
Source: Principal Global Financial Well-being Study, 2004.

The Employer Component

Employer Responsibility

Most respondents do not hold their employer highly responsible for ensuring that they have a financially comfortable retirement (Figure 12.14), yet only a few believe their employer is doing very well in performing their role (Figure 12.15). Brazilians (68 percent) are, by far, the most likely to say their employer has a great deal of responsibility for their financial security in retirement. Roughly four in ten in Italy and Mexico feel this way, but only about one-quarter in France, Germany, India, China, and Chile, and fewer elsewhere, say their employer has a great deal of responsibility for ensuring that they have a financially comfortable retirement. However, only about one in ten in most countries think their employer is doing very well in performing its role to ensure them a secure retirement. Indian (20 percent), British (17 percent), and Brazilian (17 percent) respondents are somewhat more likely to think their employer is performing very well, while Japanese respondents (1 percent) are less likely to do so.

Compared with 2003, smaller proportions of respondents in several countries say their employer should have a great deal of responsibility for

Figure 12.14. How much responsibility do you think your employer should have for ensuring that you have a financially comfortable retirement?
(percentage great deal of responsibility)

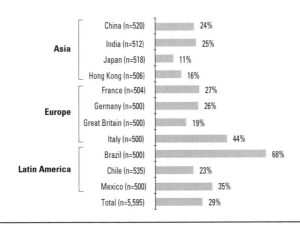

Source: Principal Global Financial Well-being Study, 2004.

Figure 12.15. How well do you think your employer is doing in performing their role to ensure that you have a financially secure retirement?
(percentage very well)

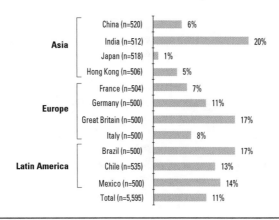

Source: Principal Global Financial Well-being Study, 2004.

ensuring that they have a financially comfortable retirement. Specifically, respondents in Italy (44 percent in 2004, down from 54 percent), Chile (23 percent, down from 33 percent), India (25 percent, down from 31 percent), Japan (11 percent, down from 16 percent), Hong Kong (16 percent, down from 21 percent), and France (27 percent, down from 39 percent) are less likely to think that their employer should have a great deal of responsibility.

The Role of Government

Government Responsibility

In general, most respondents do not think the government should have a great deal of responsibility for ensuring that an individual has a financially comfortable retirement (Figure 12.16). However, half in China and France, and roughly seven in ten in Brazil and Italy say the government should have a great deal of responsibility for this task. Four in ten in Germany, but fewer elsewhere, respond that the government should have this much responsibility.

At the same time, the vast majority do not think the government is doing a very good job at performing their role in ensuring they have a secure

Figure 12.16. How much responsibility do you think the government should have for ensuring that you have a financially comfortable retirement?
(percentage great deal of responsibility)

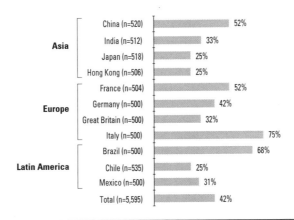

Source: Principal Global Financial Well-being Study, 2004.

retirement (Figure 12.17). Two in ten in India and one in ten in China and Chile say the government is doing a good job. Even smaller proportions in other countries report that the government is doing this well in ensuring them a secure retirement. In particular, respondents in Italy and Brazil, who are among the most likely to indicate that the government has a great deal of responsibility for ensuring a financially comfortable retirement, are among the least likely to indicate the government does this job very well (2 percent and 4 percent, respectively).

Moreover, most respondents have little confidence that the government will either help them maintain a good standard of living in retirement or help them to save for retirement (Figure 12.18). Few in the United States and Japan say the government will help them maintain a good standard of living after they retire, or trust the government to help them save for retirement. However, Chinese and Indian respondents are considerably more likely to have faith in their governments' ability to help them cope with retirement (Figure 12.19). Six in ten Chinese and almost half of Indian respondents think their government will help them maintain a good retirement standard of living, and roughly half of Chinese and Indians report their government helps them to save for retirement.

Figure 12.17. How well do you think the government is doing in performing their role to ensure that you have a financially secure retirement? (percentage very well)

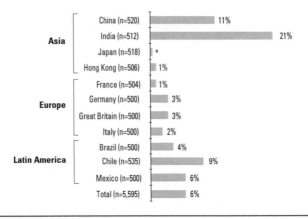

*Less than 0.5 percent.
Source: Principal Global Financial Well-being Study, 2004.

Figure 12.18. The government will make sure that I will be able to maintain a good standard of living after I retire (percentage agree)

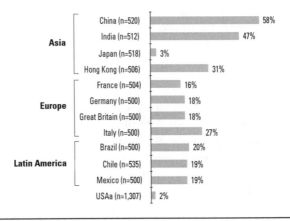

a. U.S. data from Principal 2nd Quarter 2004 Financial Well-being Index.
Source: Principal Global Financial Well-being Study, 2004.

Figure 12.19. I trust the government to help me save for retirement
(percentage agree)

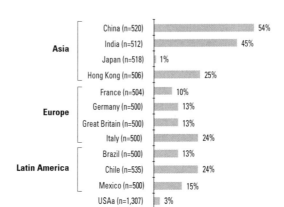

a. U.S. data from Principal 2nd Quarter 2004 Financial Well-being Index.
Source: Principal Global Financial Well-being Study, 2004.

Confidence About Receiving Retirement Benefits

Similarly, only very small minorities are very confident that their pension system will continue to provide benefits equivalent to those received by retirees today (Figure 12.20). Brazilians (13 percent) are most likely to say they are very confident about an equal level of continuing benefits, while less than one in ten are very confident in other countries asked this question.

Respondents in two countries with defined contribution plans—Mexico and Chile—were asked how confident they are about receiving benefits they are entitled to from their plans (Figure 12.21). Only two in ten in Mexico (19 percent) and just 16 percent in Chile say they are very confident about receiving full benefits. Interestingly, while confidence about receiving entitled benefits is higher than among countries with defined benefit plans, it cannot be called high.

Figure 12.20. How confident are you that national old age insurance will continue to provide an equal level of benefits to those received by retirees today? (exact wording varies by country) (percentage very confident)

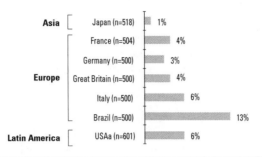

a. U.S. data from EBRI/ASEC/Greenwald 2004 Retirement Confidence Survey.
Source: Principal Global Financial Well-being Study, 2004. Des Moines, Iowa.

Figure 12.21. How confident are you that when you retire, you will receive: (Chile) a retirement pension from the voluntary saving pension plan you engaged individually / (Mexico) the full benefits you are entitled to? (percentage very confident)

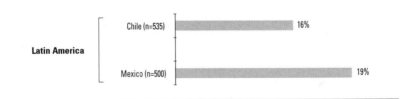

Source: Principal Global Financial Well-being Study, 2004.

A Call to Action

It has been well documented that government-run defined benefit pension systems, particularly in Europe, will be stressed beyond the breaking point with the coming age wave. Participants in the study expressed concern over their ability to adequately retire, not knowing how large their financial resources need to be and whether their employer or government retirement pillars of support will be sufficient. Remedies governments can implement to close the shortfalls are:

- Extend the period until participants can receive full benefits
- Reduce the availability of early retirement benefits
- Provide mechanisms for voluntary contributions (tax incentives, catch-up provisions)
- Develop annuity streams so that retirees do not outlive their lump sum payouts
- Develop alternative investments based on individual abilities and tolerances for risk and stage of life (lifecycle funds).

The Study also indicates a stark need for additional retirement advice and financial education. Governments' support for the delivery of education was a constant message evoked from all countries surveyed. Participants did not indicate they had access to crucial financial information from reputable and knowledgeable sources, and the sources that were most often referenced were less than reliable. Making an expert available in a fiduciary role to assist employees and workers with information and planning in the planning and accumulation phase would better prepare them for a successful payout period.

Another solution evident from the research was the near unanimous support for an employee benefit plan that would allow employees to contribute to their employers' pension fund. With the infrastructure already in place, it would decrease the distribution costs and provide more access to a greater segment of society. In addition, if the earlier suggestion regarding education were implemented, it would be a natural to supply it through the worksite.

ABOUT THE AUTHORS

Alberto Arenas de Mesa is Deputy Director of the Budget, Ministry of Finance, Chile. His research has focused mainly in the issues of social security, social protection and the fiscal effects of pension reform in Latin America. He has published with the International Labour Organization, the Inter-American Development Bank and the Economic Commission for Latin America and the Caribbean. He holds a Ph.D. in economics from the University of Pittsburgh and is a professor at the Universidad de Chile, where he teaches a special course on the economics of social security.

Carolin A. Crabbe is a finance specialist in the Infrastructure and Financial Markets Division of the Inter-American Development Bank. Prior to joining the IDB she was the CEO of the Global Finance Group, LLC, a company providing project finance services to small and mid-size markets. From 1994 to 1997, she was Director of the USAID Private Sector Department in Russia, working closely with Russian reformers to establish the stock exchange, OTC, create the first pilot mutual funds and broker dealer organizations, corporate restructurings and business development centers. Before becoming a senior Foreign Service officer with USAID, she worked for money center banks in corporate and project finance, and at the World Bank where she held a number of staff positions. She did her graduate work in economics at George Washington University and the Economic Development Institute and has been adjunct professor at American University.

Javier Díaz Cassou is an economist specializing in international affairs at the International Economy and International Relations Department of the Bank of Spain. He has worked on the reform of the international financial architecture and the prevention and resolution of financial crises in emerging markets. He teaches at the European University of Madrid and is the Vice President of Fundación CILAE (Centro de Investigación Latinoamérica-Europa, www.cilae.org). He holds an advanced degree in economic and business science from the Universidad Autónoma de

Madrid and a masters degree from the School of Advanced International Studies of the Johns Hopkins University.

Kenroy Dowers is a Senior Financial Specialist at the International Finance Corporation. Prior to joining the IFC, he was a finance specialist at the IDB. He has written on various topics associated with financial matters.

Juan A. Giral is an economist specializing in fiscal, financial and social security matters. He has consulted extensively on these matters for the Inter-American Development Bank and participated in the restructuring of the social security systems in Argentina and Uruguay. From 1976 to 1991, he was a senior economist at the World Bank and was also involved in social security reform (Costa Rica and Uruguay). He has held various positions at the Organization of American States (OAS), and the Banco de Comercio and the Banco Nacional de Cuba. He did his graduate work in economics at Yale University, where he qualified for a Ph.D. degree.

Guillermo Larraín Ríos is the Regulator of the Pension Funds of Chile, Chairman of the Chilean Commission of Risk Classification, Vice-Chairman of the International Association of Pension Funds Supervisors (AIOS) and Professor of Economics. From 2000 to 2003, he was the Chief Economist of BBVA Bank Chile. Previously, he was the Economic Policy Coordinator and Chief Economist of Chile's Ministry of Finance and a research associate at the OECD Development Centre. He holds a Ph.D. and M.A. in Economics from the École des Hautes Etudes en Sciences Sociales, Paris, as well as a Magister in economics and economist (commercial engineering) degrees from the Catholic University of Chile. He is the author of a recent study on the impact of low densities of contributions on social security savings. He has also published several studies on exchange rate policies and trade reform; emerging market risks and sovereign credit ratings; fiscal effects of the massive privatizations of public enterprises in Argentina and Chile; and fiscal policy.

Pietro Masci is Chief of the Infrastructure and Financial Markets Division of the Inter-American Development Bank. Previously, he was Chief of the IDB's Cofinancing and Project Financing Division. He also worked for the Italian Treasury and was responsible for the external borrowing programs, management of public debt and government bonds, export financing and multilateral aid programs. He managed the US portfolio for Italian mutual funds companies. He has also served as Chairman of the

Audit Committee and board member of several Italian banks. Mr. Masci is a graduate of the University of Rome, holds a diploma in international banking from London Polytechnic and an MBA in finance from George Washington University.

Carmelo Mesa-Lago is Distinguished Service Professor Emeritus of Economics and Latin American Studies at the University of Pittsburgh. He is one of the leaders in social security (pensions, health care) research in Latin America and the Caribbean, has worked in 22 countries in the region, and published 35 books and more than 100 articles on these themes. He has been an advisor on social security and development at the Economic Commission for Latin America and the Caribbean, a visiting professor at Florida International University and Berlin's Free University, a researcher at Oxford University, the Max Planck Institute, and institutions in seven other countries, as well as a lecturer in 36 countries. He has law degrees from the Universities of Havana and Madrid, a Masters in economics from the University of Miami and a Ph.D. specializing in social security from Cornell University. He is a member of the National Academy of Social Insurance and has received the Alexander von Humboldt Stiftung Senior Prize and two Senior Fulbrights in the field of social security.

Stefano Pettinato is Program Manager at the United Nations Development Programme. He is co-author of the 2003 and 2004 editions of the United Nations Human Development Report. He has also published several articles and chapters on inequality, poverty and subjective well-being. From 1999 to 2002 he was Senior Policy Advisor at the Brookings Institution and has held positions at the Inter-American Development Bank, the World Bank, the Carnegie Endowment for International Peace and the United Nations Economic Commission for Latin America and the Caribbean. He has completed graduate studies in development and public economics at the University of Florence and the Johns Hopkins School of Advanced International Studies.

Vinícius C. Pinheiro was Brazil's Secretary of Social Security (1999–2002) and the main policymaker responsible for the elaboration and implementation of the country's pension reform. From 2002 to 2004, he worked as a consultant in the Financial Affairs Division of the Organization for Economic Cooperation and Development (OECD). He has carried out studies on private pension regulation and supervision and government workers pension schemes and provided technical assistance to several countries (such as Russia, Mexico and Kenya). He was also in charge of developing economic surveys for Brazil and Chile. He is currently a senior program officer specializing in social protection at the International Labour Organization. He has written several articles and been involved on the development of learning activities on extension of social protection, pension schemes and social security financing, and pension fund management.

Rafael P. Rofman is a senior economist specializing in social protection at the World Bank. He has been Director of Studies at the Superintendency of Pension Fund Managers and Vice President of Nacion AFJP in Argentina. He has also written widely on pension fund systems in Latin America and Eastern Europe, and worked as a consultant for various governments and international organizations. He has also been adjunct professor at the University of Buenos Aires, the University of California at Berkeley, the University Torcuato Di Tella and New York University.

David Taguas Coejo is Assistant Director of Research Services and Deputy Chief Economist of the Banco Bilbao Vizcaya Argentaria (BBVA Group). Prior to joining the BBVA Group, he was an advisor to Spain's Ministry of Finance and to the General Secretariat of Budget and Expenditure. He is a professor at the Universidad de Navarra, and has also taught at Universidad Pompeu Fabra and Universidad de Deusto. He has published works on macroeconomic modeling, fiscal policy, growth and regional policy. He received a Ph.D. in economics from the Universidad de Navarra and holds statistics degrees from the Universidad Autónoma de Madrid and the Instituto Nacional de Estadística.

Lawrence H. Thompson is a senior fellow at the Urban Institute in Washington, D.C. and recently completed a four-year term as President of the National Academy of Social Insurance. He specializes in public pension design and administration and serves as a consultant to the World Bank, the Asian Development Bank and the International Labour Organization. His analysis of the economic issues involved in public pension design, which was undertaken for the International Social Security Association, was published in 1998 (*Older and Wiser: The Economics of Public Pensions*). He has been Principal Deputy Commissioner of the U.S. Social Security Administration, Assistant Comptroller General of the United States at the U.S. General Accounting Office (GAO), and Chief Economist of the GAO. He holds a Bachelor of Science degree from Iowa State University, a Masters of Business Administration from the Wharton

School of the University of Pennsylvania, and a Ph.D. in economics from the University of Michigan.

Agustín Vidal-Aragón de Olives is Managing Director, Pensions and Insurance, Banco Bilbao Vizcaya Argentaria (BBVA). He is a leading expert on the management and investment of pension and insurance funds in Latin America and the Caribbean where BBVA is a market leader. He is on the Board of numerous pension fund administrators controlled by BBVA. Prior to joining BBVA, he was Deputy Director of Hércules Hispano, S.A. de Seguros y Reaseguros (1997), Director General of VIMAR Seguros y Reaseguros (1993), and General Manager of DAPA Compañía de Seguros y Reaseguros (1985). He holds degrees in law, economics and business as well as a Masters in economics, financial and legal business administration from the Instituto Directivo de Empresas, (ICADE E-3) and the Instituto de Estudios Superiores de Seguros (IESE).

Isaac Volin Bolok Portnoy has extensive experience as a regulator serving for nine years as Vice President of the Commission on Pension Savings Regulation (CONSAR) and Director General of the Commission on Banking and Securities (CNBV) of Mexico. He received a degree from the Instituto Tecnológico Autónomo de México and a Masters in Administration from the University of Michigan. In 1988, he received first prize in National Financial Investigation competition.